Java® and Mac OS® X

Java® and Mac OS® X

T. Gene Davis

Wiley Publishing, Inc.

Java® and Mac OS® X

Published by
Wiley Publishing, Inc.
10475 Crosspoint Boulevard
Indianapolis, IN 46256
www.wiley.com

Published by Wiley Publishing, Inc., Indianapolis, Indiana

Published simultaneously in Canada

ISBN: 978-0-470-52511-1

Manufactured in the United States of America

10 9 8 7 6 5 4 3 2 1

For general information on our other products and services or to obtain technical support, please contact our Customer Care Department within the U.S. at (877) 762-2974, outside the U.S. at (317) 572-3993 or fax (317) 572-4002.

Library of Congress Control Number: 2010923561

To my Mom, who always told me to keep writing.

About the Author

T. Gene Davis has programmed computers professionally since the 1990s. He wrote his first computer program on an Apple II in the early 1980s and never stopped programming for Apple's computers. Years later, he switched to Java programming with the release of Java 1.1 on the Mac. He currently works as a senior Web applications programmer at the Institute for Clean and Secure Energy. He also writes and maintains Shogi software (also known as Japanese chess) for his company, Gene Davis Software. Prior publications include *Interview with Chuck* (a book of poetry) and *Learning Java Bindings for OpenGL* (a programming book for hobbyists).

Credits

Acquisitions Editor
Aaron Black

Executive Editor
Jody Lefevere

Project Editor
Martin V. Minner

Technical Editor
Ben Schupak

Copy Editor
Gwenette Gaddis

Editorial Director
Robyn Siesky

Business Manager
Amy Knies

Senior Marketing Manager
Sandy Smith

Vice President and Executive Group Publisher
Richard Swadley

Vice President and Executive Publisher
Barry Pruett

Project Coordinator
Lynsey Stanford

Graphics and Production Specialist
Andrea Hornberger

Quality Control Technician
Laura Albert

Proofreading and Indexing
C. M. Jones
BIM Indexing & Proofreading

Media Development Project Manager
Laura Moss

Media Development Assistant Project Manager
Jenny Swisher

Media Development Associate Producer
Marilyn Hummel

Contents

Part II: Bringing Guidelines, APIs, and Languages Together 183

Chapter 6: Porting and Designing 185

Chapter 7: Integrating Windows, Menus, and Dialog Boxes.............. 213

Introduction

This book is for Java programmers interested in developing OS X applications, but not interested in leaving Java behind. Java applications can look and feel just like other OS X programs. Your Java programs can take advantage of any OS X technology.

In this book, I describe the following:

- Dock usage for Java applications
- Help Viewer integration
- Java application bundle creation
- Adding NSViews to Java windows
- Java screen saver creation
- Java application deployment
- Application menu implementation
- Icon creation for Java applications

Apple welcomes Java development. Java programming is not an afterthought on Apple's computers. OS X was designed with Java development in mind. Java development on OS X has changed a great deal since the first computers shipped with OS X preinstalled, but the ability to create native feeling applications with Java on OS X has only improved.

This book is not an introduction to Java programming for first-time programmers. To read this entire book, you need some programming experience. Basic understanding of Java is required. Some of the more advanced chapters also require a very limited understanding of C. I make every effort to describe in detail any code that is not Java, so you do not need a great deal of knowledge about any languages other than Java.

If you are new to Java, or programming, keep an introductory manual close by as you work your way through the examples in this book. Many of the examples in this book will make sense to new programmers, as well as more experienced programmers. However, some of the advanced topics might be beyond the beginning programmer.

Understanding the Organization of This Book

This book is divided into three parts: Getting Started; Bringing Guidelines, APIs, and Languages Together; and Architecting Alternative Applications. The chapters progress from introductory material to standard integration topics to advanced integration topics.

Getting Started

Part I begins with the history of Java on Apple computers. Java and Apple actually predate the coming of OS X. Chapter 1 explores this fascinating history.

Chapter 2 jumps into a discussion of the Java environment on OS X. This includes setting preferences for preferred Java versions. Also, I explain the JAVA_HOME on OS X and JAR installation.

In Chapter 3, I give an overview of Xcode and other development tools available for free on OS X. Even if you use an IDE other than Xcode as your primary IDE, occasionally, you may want to start a Java project with one of Xcode's project templates. Understanding Xcode makes this task easier.

Code does no good until compiled. Complex projects can be time-consuming to build. Chapter 4 is all about automating builds of Java applications on OS X. I explore using Xcode, Ant, and shell scripts in the build process.

Deploying standard applications is quite different on OS X than other platforms. Chapter 5 explains details of icon creation, application bundling, and distribution unique to OS X. After reading Chapter 5, you can distribute your applications in style—the OS X style, that is.

Bringing Guidelines, APIs, and Languages Together

Part II explains the nuts and bolts of making your Java applications behave and look like real OS X applications. Chapter 6 reviews the architecture of OS X, along with an introduction to Apple's Human Interface Guidelines.

Chapter 7 contains information on implementing the application menu, the Help Viewer, and the Dock into your application. Also, this chapter explains usage of your application bundle to store your Java software's resources.

Did you know that you can add Cocoa widgets and components to your Java windows? Chapter 8 explains all about adding Objective-C NSViews to your Java Windows and JFrames. This chapter also begins the discussion of JNI as an interface to OS X technologies.

Architecting Alternative Applications

JNI is the official Apple-endorsed bridge between Cocoa and Java technologies. Part III begins with a detailed chapter explaining JNI on OS X. Chapter 9 explains using native features from Java. Chapter 9 also explains creating JVMs from inside native code. This is called the Invocation API.

Java applications can control any Objective-C framework. However, getting the JVM is the tricky part. Chapter 10 demonstrates wrapping the Screen Saver Framework with a Java controller. The JVM is invoked from the native framework and then takes over from there. After understanding this chapter, you will realize that Java has no limits on OS X.

In Chapter 11, I explain Terminal application User Interfaces. Many applications run from the Terminal. In fact some programmers prefer not to use GUI applications for controlling their servers. This chapter explains how to make respectable text-based UIs.

Using This Book

A minimum of Java 6 and Snow Leopard (Mac OS X 10.6) are required for making the most of this book. I created the source code in this book on Snow Leopard. Also, the screen captures in this book are from Snow Leopard. Earlier versions of OS X may be used for much of the book with minor alterations to the coded examples. Screenshots of earlier versions of OS X may also differ from Snow Leopard screenshots. Refer to Apple's developer documentation for details of changes to Java and OS X with the release of Snow Leopard.

I wrote this book so that reading it from cover to cover makes sense. Having said that, not everyone has time to read hundreds of pages of documentation. So you can take shortcuts if you are interested in reading only certain chapters.

For those interested in writing traditional applications for OS X, you definitely should read these chapters: Chapter 2 on OS X's Java environment, Chapter 5 on deploying applications, Chapter 6 on Apple's Human Interface Guidelines, and Chapter 7 on integrating OS X features into your Java application.

If you want to automate your complex Java project builds, then read Chapters 2 and 4. Chapter 2 explains the Java environment, and Chapter 4 explains Ant projects and shell scripting. You can completely automate your builds no matter how complex they are.

If your interests are in using JNI to integrate advanced OS X features into your Java applications, then read Chapters 8, 9, and 10. Chapter 8 gives an introduction to JNI in the context of Cocoa Components. Chapter 9 explains details of JNI on OS X, including use of the Invocation API. Chapter 10 gives an example of creating a Java application that wraps a native framework using the Invocation API. In this case, the example application is a Java screen saver.

Writers of servers and server utilities should look at Chapter 11, which describes text-based User Interfaces. Many servers are controlled via ssh or terminals, so Chapter 11 explains how advanced applications should interact with users on the command line.

Using the Companion Web Site

All programming examples in this book are on the book's companion Web site. Find the Web site at the following URL

```
www.wiley.com/go/javamacdevref
```

When reading a chapter, begin by downloading the source code for the projects in that chapter. Follow along with the chapter using the source from the Web site.

Getting Started

Programming Java for OS X

W hat's so different about Java on a Mac? Pure Java applications run on any operating system that supports Java. Popular Java tools run on OS X. From the developer's point of view, Java is Java, no matter where it runs.

Users do not agree. To an OS X user, pure Java applications that ignore the feel and features of OS X are less desirable, meaning the customers will take their money elsewhere. Fewer sales translates into unhappy managers and all the awkwardness that follows.

In this book, I show how to build GUIs that feel and behave like OS X users expect them to behave. I explain development tools and libraries found on the Mac. I explore bundling of Java applications for deployment on OS X. I also discuss interfacing Java with other languages commonly used on the Mac.

This chapter is about the background and basics of Java development on OS X. I explain the history of Java development. I show you around Apple's developer Web site. Finally, I go over the IDEs commonly used for Java development on the Mac.

Reviewing Apple Java History

Apple embraced Java technologies long before the first version of OS X graced a blue and white Mac tower. Refugees from the old tan Macs of the 1990s may vaguely remember using what was called the MRJ when their PC counterparts were busy using JVMs.

MRJ stands for Mac OS Runtime for Java. MRJ was Apple's version of the JVM.

Classic Macs running OS 8 and earlier had a wonderful GUI. Macs were famous for their GUIs. What Macs were not famous for were their shells and command line interfaces. Old versions of the Mac OS were not Unix-based or Unix-friendly.

Those were the wild days before Java-friendly IDEs such as Xcode, Eclipse, and NetBeans ruled the world. Java used (and still uses) command-line tools, such as 'java,' 'javac,' and 'jar.' These tools did not have GUI equivalents. Apple filled the gap with GUI equivalents

 In This Chapter

Exploring the history of Java on Apple computers

Installing developer tools on OS X

Looking at the Apple Developer Connection (ADC)

Introducing Java IDEs available for OS X

of the most useful Java tools named after their command line counterparts. Figure 1.1 shows the MRJ folder with Apples GUI versions of the Java tools.

Figure 1.1

Classic Mac OS folder containing the MRJ GUI versions of the Java command-line tools

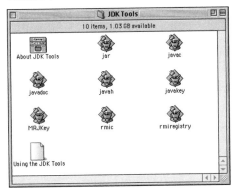

The javac command-line tool found on Windows or Unix had a GUI tool on the Mac, as shown in Figure 1.2. To compile a Java class, you double-clicked the javac application. You were presented with a form to fill out. After adding the source files, destination folder, and classpath desired, you clicked the Do Javac button.

Figure 1.2

Classic Mac OS MRJ javac tool

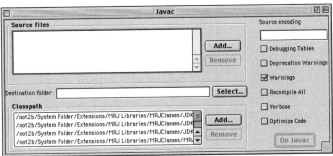

Interfacing Java and native C code was another hurdle. Under Mac OS 8, a technology called JDirect provided access to native C code on the Mac. JManager allowed C-based programs to

invoke Java. JNI was also available, but JDirect and JManager were meant to be easier to use for beginners.

With the new millennium came a new Mac OS: OS X is built on top of Darwin. Darwin provides a shell that Java's command-line tools run from. Apple added the Terminal application to OS X, giving access from its top-notch GUI to Darwin's shell. OS X came with new Java Cocoa APIs that provided easy access to OS X libraries from Java applications. Xcode arrived and turned out to be a Java-friendly IDE. Even OS X's new Interface Builder provided tools for easy creation of OS X-specific Java GUIs.

The classic OS and the MRJ began to disappear. Java programmers had a new arsenal of Java tools and libraries on OS X, and life was wonderful.

After years of real-world use, Apple discovered that Java programmers creating applications for Mac OS X used Swing and AWT for their Graphic User Interfaces instead of the Interface Builder and the Cocoa APIs for GUI development. Also, advanced Java programmers integrated with Apple's Cocoa libraries using JNI instead of Apple's custom bridges.

Because they were not needed, the Java Cocoa libraries were deprecated. Support for building Java UIs from inside of Interface Build was also removed. However, Xcode still supports Java development with several Java project templates built into Xcode. Also, diehard Mac OS X Java programmers can always use JNI to interface with Apple's Cocoa APIs.

CROSS-REF

Java Native Interface programming specific for Mac OS X is discussed in depth in Chapter 10.

NOTE

JNI is not the only technology for interfacing Java with Mac OS X-specific technologies. In this book, I explain Java integration with JNI, AppleScript, JavaScript, and the remaining non-deprecated Cocoa Java libraries. Integrating Java code with most OS X technologies is possible with a small nudge in the proper direction.

Apple continues to update Java for OS X. Many Java applications are distributed and tested specifically for OS X. Java is alive and strong on the Mac.

Installing the OS X Developer Tools

A suite of high-grade developer tools ship with every Mac. These tools include Xcode, GCC, Dashcode, and other useful GUI and command-line tools. Xcode is a top-notch IDE with built-in Java support. Ant and the command-line Java tools are also included. The full suite of development tools is free with every Mac.

NOTE
Ant is used by Xcode to build Java projects.

NOTE
Xcode has several predefined Java project templates. Predefined Xcode Java templates include a basic GUI application template, a JNI template, and a command-line tool template.

The OS X developer tools are not installed by default, because only developers find the tools useful. Install the developer tools using the following instructions:

1. **Insert your Mac OS installation DVD.**

2. **Navigate to your** XcodeTools **installer.**

You should find a folder called `Optional Installs` at the top level. Inside that folder is the `Xcode Tools` folder. Finally, in the `Xcode Tools` folder, you find the `XcodeTools` installer, as shown in Figure 1.3.

Figure 1.3

Install DVD Xcode Tools folder

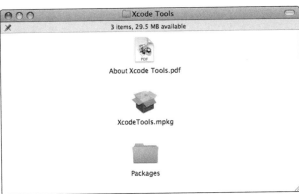

3. **Start up the** XcodeTools **installer.**

4. **Continue through the installer, and choose Custom Install.**

You see five packages on the Custom Install screen: Developer Tools Essentials, System Tools, UNIX Development Support, Mac OS X 10.3.9 Support, and WebObjects.

5. **Select Developer Tools Essentials, System Tools, and UNIX Developer Support.**

6. **Click continue, and finish installing the developer tools.**

   You are now prepared to learn Java development on OS X.

During the OS X tools installation, developer tools Essentials is selected for you, as shown in Figure 1.4. Essentials contains Xcode, Interface Builder, Dashcode, and GCC.

TIP

The default installation location of the OS X developer tools is the `Developer` directory at the root of your primary drive. You have the option of changing the installation location of the developer tools, but I recommend sticking with the default `Developer` directory. Sticking with the `Developer` directory prevents confusion later when documentation says to look there for something that you don't realize you installed elsewhere.

System Tools is a collection of applications that helps you debug and analyze your applications. Unix Development Support installs UNIX tools in the `/usr` directory. Make sure you select these two packages during installation of the developer tools. You need these tools later in the book.

Support for Mac OS X 10.3.9 may be useful to you. Some projects require support for older OS versions. You do not need the Mac OS X 10.3.9 Support package for this book.

WebObjects allow development for Apple's proprietary Java Web server. These applications are typically deployed on Mac OS X Server. WebObjects and Web applications are very large topics and are not covered in this book.

Figure 1.4

Install Xcode Tools screen

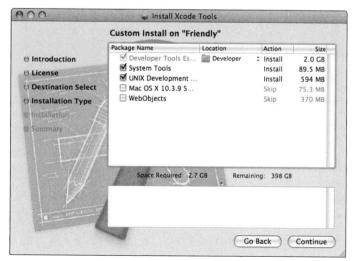

Exploring the Apple Developer Connection

Apple provides a wealth of Developer Articles, software seeds, developer news, and mailing lists for the community of developers making OS X their home. Apple consistently has high approval ratings from its customers. The company is often described as having a cult-like following of customers and developers.

After getting to know your way around Apple's Developer Connection, you may appreciate the support Apple gets from customers and developers a little better. The Developer Connection is typically easy to navigate and user-friendly for anyone trying to create Mac OS X applications. Technologies as diverse as Python, Perl, and even Java find a home on OS X. The Developer Connection does not ignore this diversity.

Exploring Reference Library topics

Apple offers an extensive library for developers on the Developer Connection site. One of the libraries targets Java, but several of the libraries are useful to Java developers. You do not need a membership in the Apple Developer Connection (ADC) to view the Reference Library.

The Reference Library is on Apple's Developer Connection site. The Developer Connection is at `http://developer.apple.com/`. Get to know your way around the Web site. Knowing the ins and outs of the Developer Connection will save you many random searches of the Internet. Follow these steps to find the library:

1. **Open** http://developer.apple.com **with Safari or the Web browser of your choice.**

   You are greeted by the Apple Developer Connection home page.

2. **Look at the top of the Web page for the Dev Centers drop-down menu.**

3. **Select Mac Dev Center from the drop-down menu. This brings you to the Mac Dev Center Web page.**

4. **Select the link to the Mac Reference Library on the Mac Dev Center Web page.**

Looking over the Mac OS X Reference Library Web page, you first notice the list of Reference libraries on the left. More than 50 reference libraries are listed by topic, and alphabetically. Other libraries worth noticing are Compiler Tools, User Experience, System Configuration, Screen Saver, Carbon, Cocoa, and Preference Panes. All these topics and more are covered in this book. These libraries are a great resource for learning additional details after reading this book.

N O T E

Finding a link to the Developer Connection on Apple's main Web site is difficult and maybe even impossible. You probably want to bookmark or memorize the address. The Developer Connection is found at:

`http://developer.apple.com/`

The Mac OS X Reference Library Web page contains a prominent tabbed pane containing Overview, Getting Started, Required Reading, and Featured tabs. Browsing these tabs gives you a quick overview of OS X development.

Under the tabbed view is a searchable list of documents available for OS X development. Enter **java**, and search. The search returns more than 60 Java-related documents on the developer site. The search returns a few JavaScript documents, but most are actual Java development articles and documents.

Hidden at the bottom of the page is a link to the RSS Feeds page. Traditionally, checking for the latest and greatest news and tips required navigating to the page with the news every day or multiple times each day. You can now avoid wasted random trips to the Reference Library just to see if new articles of interest have appeared.

RSS stands for Really Simple Syndication. RSS is simply a custom news feed, in this case, from the Reference Library. Apple's Safari Web browser contains a built-in RSS reader, as shown in Figure 1.5. Even better, bookmarking RSS feeds in Safari works the same as bookmarking Web pages.

Figure 1.5

Built-in RSS reader of the Reference Library

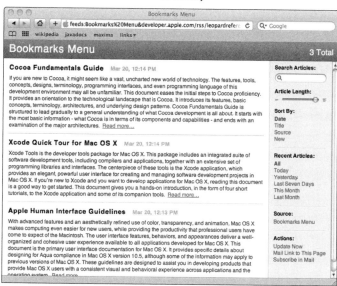

If you browse to the Mac OS X Reference Library site with Safari, you see an RSS at the bottom right of the page, as shown in Figure 1.6. The RSS link is a little obscure, considering the utility it offers. Below are the steps for tracking the Reference Library RSS feed with Safari.

Figure 1.6

RSS link at the bottom right of the Mac OS X Reference Library Web page

1. **Click the RSS link to bring up a selection of RSS feeds offered by the Apple Developer Connection. The link is at the bottom-right corner of many of the Developer Connection pages.**

2. **Select an RSS feed from the list of Developer Connection feeds. ADC Headlines is a good choice for keeping up with the latest Developer Connection news.**

   The feed appears in Safari's built- in RSS reader.

3. **Bookmark the feed by selecting Add Bookmark... from the Bookmarks menu.**

Hidden at the bottom of the Mac OS X Reference Library page is the legacy documents link. Scroll down to the bottom of the left navigation links list and find the link entitled Legacy Mac OS X Reference Library. If you are tasked with fixing an older software project, this section is invaluable. The Legacy Documents page looks very similar to the regular reference library. However, the guides and code found there apply only to legacy development.

Finding developer articles

You are a Java programmer, and you want to see Java programming articles now. The Mac OS X Reference Library is the place to begin your search. The Developer Connection has more articles than you may ever read on Java and related topics. As I mention earlier, searching the Documents in the Mac OS X Reference Library brings up around 60 Java-related documents.

Many useful documents are not listed specifically as Java documents, so you need to browse around a bit. For instance, the Apple Human Interface Guidelines is invaluable for the creation of Java applications that conform to expected OS X application behavior. The Apple Human Interface Guidelines is listed in the Guides documents. To quickly find the link, click Guides in the left navigation of the Mac OS X Reference Library Web page, and then type **human** in the Documents search field. The remaining listed link is for the Apple Human Interface Guidelines.

TIP

The Developer Connection has three Dev Centers. The Dev Centers are targeted for iPhone, Safari, and Macs. Most of the Java information you need is found in the Mac Dev Center.

Obtaining software seeds

To take full advantage of the Apple Developer Connection, you need an ADC Membership. Until you have an ADC membership, you cannot download software seeds or beta releases. Look around the Apple Developer Connection Mac Dev Center page to find a link to register for ADC membership.

Alternately, you may click "Log in" at the top of many of the Developer Connection pages. The login page has a link for "Join now." This allows you to register, too.

TIP

Paid memberships are encouraged, so some pages about membership do not have a big blinking button shouting, "Join here for free!" Just poke around a little, and you will spot the free Online membership link. On the `http://developer.apple.com/products/membership.html` Web page, the link is at the bottom-left corner under the title ADC Online Membership.

Currently you can choose from four levels of membership: Premier, Select, Student, and Online. The Online membership is free, but it has fewer benefits than the other paid memberships. Online (free) memberships have access to Introductory Videos for Coding and beta releases of new JDKs. Premier membership, costing around $3499, provides a World Wide Developer Conference (WWDC) ticket, access to Apple's compatibility labs, discounts on hardware purchases, and more advanced technical support.

To become a member, you must accept a membership agreement. The ADC membership agreement doesn't require you to spend time washing windows at the local Apple Store, but you're wise to read through the agreement anyway to see if you feel comfortable with it. Typically, the agreement prohibits you from talking about seeds and beta releases that you download, other than to technical support. See the agreement for full details.

If you choose the free ADC membership, log in and look around. Often, you have access to previews of future JDKs for OS X. If you are previewing these future Java releases and find bugs in them that affect your programs, be sure to create test cases and submit bug reports with the test cases to Apple. The developers at Apple will do their best to address them, and may even make your job easier by fixing bugs you report before they make it into a full Java release.

Apple distinguishes between the previews available with free ADC membership and the official Software Seeding Program. Much of the time, the online ADC membership is enough for Java developers on OS X. However, if you want to test your software on seeds of the newest OS X beta or try out the newest pre-release of Xcode Tools, a paid membership with ADC monthly mailings is what you need.

Benefiting from membership

As mentioned earlier, you can choose from four types of memberships to the Apple Developer Connection: Online, Student, Select, and Premier. Online is free and gives you access to Apple Development Connection previews of some Java code in development. Having access to some previews is often seen as enough by Java developers on OS X. These previews are not as numerous as the actual Software Seeding Program.

If you download betas of JDKs or Xcode in development by Apple, remember that the non-disclosure agreement required by members usually prohibits you from speaking (or writing) about them to anyone except technical support.

TIP
You don't need an ADC membership to sign up for the Java developer technical discussions list. This is a Mac OS X specific list for Java development. Subscribe at:

```
http://lists.apple.com/mailman/listinfo/java-dev/
```

NOTE
At one time, discussion of beta releases of Java on the Mac was allowed on the Mac Java developer list. Currently, discussion of Java previews is not permitted on the list because of the ADC non-disclosure agreement.

Premier and Select members may get the Software Seeding Program in addition to their membership. Seeds often include pre-release versions of operating systems, betas of company products, development kits, and development tools. Currently, these may be delivered electronically or by snail mail on DVDs.

ADC on iTunes and Coding Headstarts are two more benefits of ADC membership. ADC on iTunes provides videos of training sessions for developers. These videos are (surprise, surprise) viewable on iTunes. Coding Headstarts are videos dedicated to teaching developers techniques for adding features to OS X software. The Online and Student Members have limited access to these benefits. Premier and Select members have full access to both ADC on iTunes and Coding Headstarts.

Student, Select, and Premier members have access to hardware discounts. A special version of the Apple Store is available for these purchases. Of course, the number of times the discounts can be used scales with the level of membership. Currently, Premier can purchase 10 systems per year at the discount, Select one per year, and Student one system (ever, not per year).

All ADC members can purchase extra technical support. Premier and Select members get a limited number of technical support incidents per year but can purchase additional support as needed. The available technical support is one-on-one time with Apple engineers selected to help you with your specific issues. If you are a diehard cutting-edge OS X developer, you may find this included personalized support useful. I have never needed it myself. (I like to think that is because Macs are such a good development platform.)

Avoiding Deprecated Java Cocoa Libraries

Apple provides several Java classes directed at developers seeking to create Java desktop applications that feel and behave like native applications. Apple's Java classes typically inhabit packages labeled `com.apple`. The number of `com.apple` packaged classes has dropped significantly over the last few years due to older classes being deprecated and removed. Also, Apple's native GUI designer, Interface Builder, has dropped direct support for Java programming.

It is tempting to believe the number of deprecated classes and lack of Interface Builder support on OS X for Java is an indication that Java applications with native behavior can no longer be created for OS X. The changes to Java development on OS X are rather the acknowledgement of real-world use by Apple of development tools. These changes have occurred because Apple understands how the majority of Java developers on their OS create native-feeling applications.

This section explains the streamlining process that has resulted in the current state of Java applications development on OS X.

Understanding the history of Java Cocoa libraries

At the turn of the millennium when Apple introduced OS X, Java was still in its infancy. Java was an exciting buzzword in the development world. Apple already supported Java on OS 8 and OS 9. Apple was excited to continue supporting Java in the OS X environment.

Few of the Java GUI design tools commonly used now existed then. The GUI tools that developers used contained little ability to customize Java desktop applications to look and behave like native applications. This especially applied to OS X.

Mac application developers used a new GUI creation utility built for OS X called Interface Builder. Interface Builder allowed for drag-and-drop creation of application interfaces; mouse-driven creation of connections between GUI elements and class place holders; and then either Java or Objective-C class generation, as shown in Figure 1.7, depending on the type of project under development. Creating Java applications with a native look and feel was easy with this tool, because the GUI was actually native.

Figure 1.7

Legacy Interface Builder's Class Inspector with Java option selected

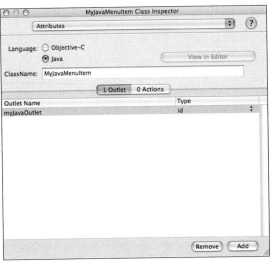

Apple's Java Bridge was still a commonly used tool for interfacing Java with Cocoa libraries. The Java Bridge was easy to use for simpler applications. JNI and the Java Bridge were both used depending on the complexity of the application developers built.

The OS X API, called Cocoa, came in two flavors: Objective-C and Java. The API was further divided into the Application Kit and the Foundation API. The Application Kit contained mostly classes that wrapped Apple's native GUI components. The Foundation API contained classes that supported the Application Kit and classes that contained functionality found in Cocoa, but not in standard Java.

With the release of OS X 10.4, Apple announced that the Java Bridge and the Java Cocoa Frameworks were deprecated. Apple dropped the Bridge in favor of JNI. The 200+ Java Cocoa Framework classes and interfaces were deprecated and replaced by seven Apple Java Extension classes.

Many Java programmers fond of OS X felt this was the end of native-feeling applications written in Java. However, Java is alive and well on OS X. As I show in this book, Java still interfaces with Apple native technologies through Apple Java Extensions, JNI, AppleScript, and JavaScript.

Reviewing deprecated libraries

The deprecated Java Cocoa Framework contained over 200 classes and interfaces. These are deprecated and should not be used. If you inherit a Java project that uses these classes and interfaces, begin refactoring the code to use pure Java with Apple's Java Extensions and other Apple-supported Java Technologies. This section is intended to give you a quick overview of the legacy Java Cocoa Framework, so you have some idea of where to begin the refactoring process. The rest of this book is intended to give you knowledge necessary to write Java code that seamlessly integrates with current Apple-supported technologies.

Apple currently provides support for several Java packages. They include `javax.script`, `com.apple.eawt`, and `com.apple.eio`. If your project contains packages beginning with `com.apple.cocoa`, the packages need to be refactored out of your program. The `com.apple.cocoa` packages are always part of the legacy Java Cocoa Framework. Any classes contained in the `com.apple.cocoa` packages will cease to function on OS X at some point.

N O T E

javax.script is supported by Apple as the natural interface for AppleScript and Java. com.apple.eawt provides classes that make Java GUIs behave like native OS X applications. com.apple.eio contains classes that access OS X features that do not have parallel features in the standard Java APIs.

The Cocoa libraries are split between the Application Kit framework and the Foundation framework. The Foundation framework provides base classes and utility classes that form the "foundation" of Cocoa applications. The Application Kit framework provides GUI related classes.

The Java Foundation package is `com.apple.cocoa.foundation`. The Foundation classes are made up of useful utilities, data types, and classes that support Cocoa design patterns that did not exist in pure Java.

For example, several of the Java Foundation classes come in mutable and immutable varieties. Simply put, mutable mean changeable and immutable means final, in the Java sense of final. Having two like named classes, one optimized for changing and the other optimized for use without changing was uncommon in Java 1.1, back in 2000. Cocoa used this paradigm, so Java Foundation classes were created to match up with their Objective-C counterparts.

The Foundation framework's `NSObject` is worth special notice. `NSObject` is the root object of Cocoa Java classes. Think of it as the Cocoa counterpart to the Java `Object` class. `NSObject` has similar functionality as `Object`, such as cloning, equality comparisons, and hashing.

The Java Application Kit package is `com.apple.cocoa.application`. The Application Kit provides classes that represent Apple's OS X native GUI components and events. Some of the native widgets include `NSAlertPanel`, `NSComboBox`, and `NSMenu`.

N O T E

You may have noticed that the Cocoa Java classes by convention start with NS and not OSX as expected. NS stands for NextStep. NextStep was an OS that had its origins in the 1980s. NextStep evolved into OpenStep which in turn evolved into OS X. The NS naming convention is a reminder that OS X is not a descendent of the classic Mac OS.

The Applications Kit's NSApplication controls the Cocoa application event loop. Whether opening files, terminating the program, or showing help, NSApplication handles the events. NSApplication uses delegates to listen for applications events. Assigning methods in other classes to handle methods as delegates replaces the need to subclass NSApplication or provide an interface implementation as you see in pure Java applications when handling events. NSApplication is not subclassed normally.

NOTE

The current Javadocs for com.apple packages is located at:

```
http://developer.apple.com/documentation/Java/
Reference/1.5.0/appledoc/api/index.html
```

NOTE

The legacy Java Foundation classes and interfaces are documented at:

```
http://developer.apple.com/documentation/
LegacyTechnologies/Cocoa/Reference/Foundation/
Java/index.html
```

NOTE

The legacy Java Application Kit classes and interfaces are documented at:

```
http://developer.apple.com/documentation/
LegacyTechnologies/Cocoa/Reference/ApplicationKit/
Java/index.html#//apple_ref/doc/uid/20001094
```

The Cocoa Java paradigm felt very different from pure Java because it was written to match up with its Objective-C counterpart. With any luck, you will never need to refactor an old Java Cocoa application to be more of a pure Java application. If the application view is simple, you likely are better off creating a Swing view and rewriting the interface to your Java controller from scratch. It will save you lots of time and frustration.

Understanding why Java Cocoa libraries were redundant

The Java-based Cocoa Framework met a need that existed when OS X was first released. Along with the Java Bridge, the Java Cocoa Framework allowed for easy integration of Java code with native OS X frontends. Swing and AWT, at the time, were still a bit clunky and buggy. At the time, it was common for even diehard Java developers to refer to Java GUIs as "write once, debug everywhere." The OS X user interface was solid, groundbreaking, and beautiful. The Java Cocoa libraries allowed Java programmers to take full advantage of this elegant new operating system.

The Java Cocoa Framework, Interface Builder, and the Java Bridge were useful for simple communication between Objective-C and Java code. Soon it became clear that these two languages were too different for easy communication. The Java Bridge could not translate advanced behavior between code written in these two languages. Also, the libraries of GUI components provided with the Cocoa Framework could not be mixed and matched with Swing or AWT components. Unexpected crashes appeared if they were.

As OS X matured, so did Java. Swing and AWT views became easier to create and less buggy. Better tools for generating Java GUIs emerged. Java developers on OS X showed a definite preference toward using Swing, AWT, and third-party libraries over Interface Builder and the Java Cocoa libraries. With the proper subset of Java classes supported by Apple, JNI, and interfaces with JavaScript and AppleScript, no other technologies are needed to make a Java application feel like a fully native application.

Exploring Available IDEs

In the early days of Java development on OS X, the only choice for an OS X Java IDE was Xcode. Now several are available. The three most common are Netbeans, Eclipse, and Xcode. All three are excellent IDEs. All three are free (as in food). Eclipse and Netbeans have the advantage of being Java-centric environments. Xcode has the advantage of being OS X centric.

NOTE

Two common types of free software exist. Software that is referred to as "free as in food" is software that costs nothing. Software that is referred to as "free as in freedom" is software that makes its source code available. The second type of software sometimes costs money. The two types of "free" software are not mutually exclusive. Software may be "free as in food" and also "free as in freedom."

Many arguments have occurred over which of the three free IDEs should be used on OS X. All three are excellent IDEs and have common IDE features, including line numbering, project templates, debuggers, and version control integration. I tend to use a combination of Eclipse and Xcode (and TextEdit) when developing on OS X. NetBeans is also a valid option. In this section, I discuss the benefits of all three.

Developing with Xcode

If you intend to write an application that is heavy in Java code, but also integrates with native OS X libraries or applications, you should consider using Xcode as your development environment. Figure 1.8 shows Xcode. Xcode and related tools allow for easier integration of pure Java with OS X features. In this book, I use Xcode for most examples. Several of the chapters in this book explain the integration of Java with Xcode-specific technologies. Install Xcode to follow along more closely with the example code in this book.

Figure 1.8

Xcode IDE

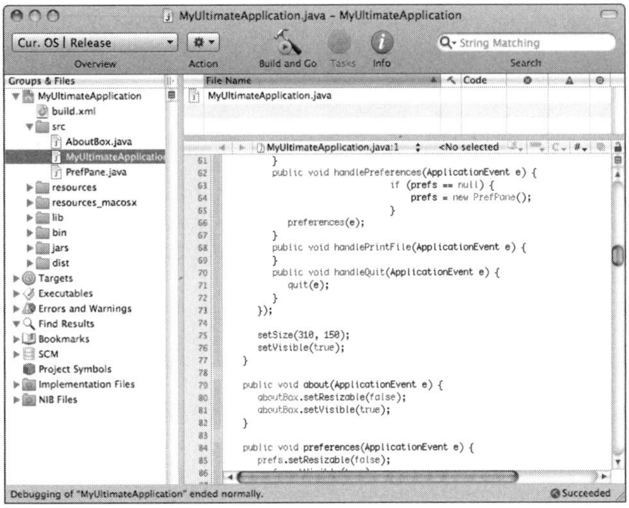

![Xcode IDE screenshot showing the MyUltimateApplication.java file open in the editor]

NOTE

Install Xcode for free from your OS X installation disk.

Xcode ships with six Java-specific templates. These templates are for Java Applets, applications, JNI applications, signed Applets, command-line tools, and Web Start applications. Programmers interested in Java Enterprise Edition development of Web applications with JSP, Servlets, and Enterprise Java Beans often choose NetBeans or Eclipse as their preferred environment. Xcode is used frequently by developers of Java desktop applications and Java client applications.

Xcode has built-in support for Source Code Management (SCM). CVS, Subversion, and Perforce are supported by the default install. Secure SSH connections to code repositories are supported also.

Xcode is highly customizable. As is expected in a modern IDE, many preference settings control editing, builds, and code versioning. As shown in Figure 1.9, the scripting menu supports the reorganizing, addition, and editing of custom and built-in scripts.

My favorite feature of Xcode is the ability to automatically package resources, icons, and libraries into OS X application bundles. Native OS X applications are actually folders with a structured set of files. The folders look and behave like double-clickable executable files to users on OS X. Application bundles are the preferred distribution method for applications on OS X. If you are distributing your applications as double-clickable JAR files, use of the application feels awkward to OS X users.

Figure 1.9

User Scripts dialog box in Xcode

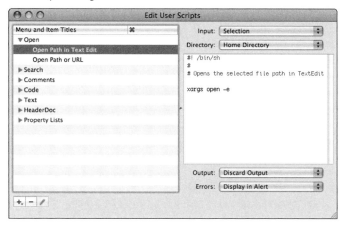

Developing with Eclipse

Eclipse, shown in Figure 1.10, is available on multiple operating systems. A big appeal in using Eclipse is that if you are required to use other operating systems such as Linux, you can still use the IDE you are comfortable with. Eclipse uses SWT instead of Swing for its interface. SWT is a library that is OS specific. Versions of SWT are available for most major operating systems.

Figure 1.10

Eclipse in Java perspective

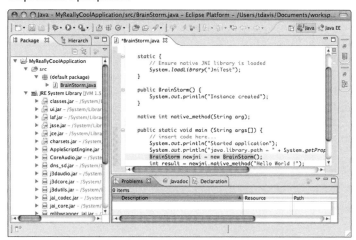

NOTE

Installing the Enterprise Java bundle of Eclipse from `http://www.eclipse.org/` allows you to create client-server applications and traditional desktop applications.

NOTE

Many developers who use Eclipse swear by JFormDesigner for Java GUI development. JFormDesigner is made by FormDev Software found at:

`http://www.formdev.com/`

Eclipse has distributions and modules for many programming languages other than Java, but it shows its real strengths in creating and maintaining Java-based projects. Projects in Eclipse can be created based off Ant build scripts or simply using default project templates.

Eclipse makes heavy use of tabbed perspectives. Eclipse has perspectives for Java, Debugging, Java EE, SVN, Database Development, and many more. Swapping between multiple views during development of one project is common.

Updates and custom add-ons to Eclipse can often be accomplished from the Eclipse Software Updates and Add-ons dialog box, shown in Figure 1.11. Very rarely do modules used by Eclipse require anything more than a URL and a few clicks of the mouse before complete integration into Eclipse is accomplished.

Figure 1.11

Eclipse Software Updates and Add-ons dialog box

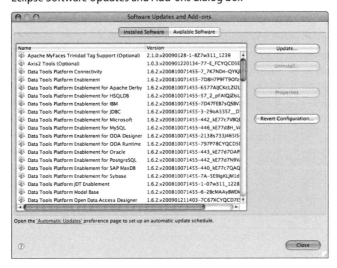

Developing with NetBeans

Years ago, NetBeans was considered the slowest of the three IDEs. These days, NetBeans responds just as you would expect any well-behaved application. NetBeans has a large user base and is sponsored by Sun. NetBeans, shown in Figure 1.12, is a strong contender for Java developers on OS X.

Figure 1.12

Netbeans on OS X

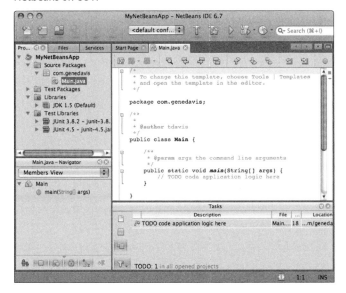

NOTE

NetBeans IDE is available in several flavors from:

```
http://www.netbeans.org/
```

NetBeans supports GUI development with the Swing GUI Builder. Swing GUI Builder provides a drag-and-drop approach to GUI creation. Drag Swing components from the palette to the provided canvas. Swing GUI Builder, shown in Figure 1.13, comes free with NetBeans. Free is great when your budget is tight.

As with Xcode and Eclipse, NetBeans supports C/C++ and quite a few other languages including JavaScript, PHP, Ruby, and Python. NetBeans supports traditional application development and enterprise Web application development. Choose from seven different bundles on the download page at `http://www.netbeans.org/downloads/index.html`.

Figure 1.13

NetBean's Swing GUI Builder

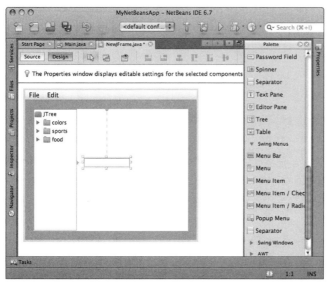

Summary

In this chapter, you read about the long history of Java programming on the Mac. Apple provided Java for its computers before OS X became the OS of choice for Macs. Apple introduced Java Cocoa frameworks to ease the transition of Java programmers from the classic Mac OS to OS X. After Java programmers made the move to OS X, Apple deprecated the Java Cocoa frameworks.

You explored the Apple Developer Connection Web site. ADC membership comes at several levels and with various benefits, depending on your level. Even free members have access to articles, downloads, and tons of Java-related reference material on Apple's developer Web site.

Three free IDEs for developing Java are available on the Mac. They are Xcode, Eclipse, and NetBeans. All three are excellent IDEs. However, I use Xcode for the projects and examples in this book.

Introducing the Environment

No computer matches the support for Java out of the box that you find in a Mac. OS X ships with support for Java applets in Safari, natively packaged Java applications, a Java-friendly IDE, native-interface APIs, and several Java tools and applications. Support for Java upgrades is integrated into the directory structure and system updates. Apple even maintains and builds an optimized version of Java just for the Mac.

Java configuration is different on Macs than on other computer systems. Setting up extensions and version preferences is easy, but it requires some explanation. Knowledge of the Terminal application and the shell environment is useful too.

In this chapter, I cover the nuances of Java configuration on OS X. This includes installing JAR and JNI libraries, setting the default JVM, and properly setting JAVA_HOME. I also introduce the Terminal application, environment properties, dot files, and storage of system configurations.

Configuring the JVMs

Effective Java programming on OS X requires an understanding of the Finder and the Terminal applications. Navigation of directories and running of applications by users (like you and me) is accomplished through either the Finder or the Terminal. The Finder and Terminal applications provided essentially the same service to users. One is GUI based. The other is command-line based.

The Finder application is the GUI directory and file browser for OS X. Many beginning OS X users do not even know they are using an application to browse their desktop or hard drive.

The Finder is always open. Otherwise, you could not browse directories and files. The Finder is a permanent part of the Dock. On the Dock, it is has the square smiley face icon on the far left, as shown in Figure 2.1.

Figure 2.1

Finder icon on the Dock

Finder is an application that can be restarted just like any other application without restarting the whole computer, which is nice and modular, just the way programmers like it. To restart your Finder without restarting your computer, follow these steps:

1. **Press Cmd-Opt-Esc.**

This command brings up the Force Quit Applications dialog box.

2. **Select Finder from the list of applications in the Force Quit Applications dialog box.**

Notice the Force Quit button's label changes to Relaunch.

3. **Click the Relaunch button.**

The Finder closes all the open Finder windows, quits, and restarts.

Knowing how to restart the Finder comes in handy later in the chapter when I discuss environment variables. Also, on the very rare occasion when the Finder stops working properly, relaunching it may fix your problem.

The Terminal application, shown in Figure 2.2, is very similar in purpose to the Finder. The Terminal allows command-line browsing of directories and files. It is analogous to the DOS window in Windows. Applications of all sorts are launched from the command line in the Terminal application.

The Terminal application is a little tricky to find. You will use the Terminal constantly throughout this book, and you'll find it invaluable after you are familiar with its use. To find the Terminal application, open your Applications folder in a Finder window. Look for a folder called Utilities. The Terminal application is in the Utilities folder.

Now that you can open the Terminal application, it is time to find and configure Java on your computer.

Figure 2.2

Terminal application

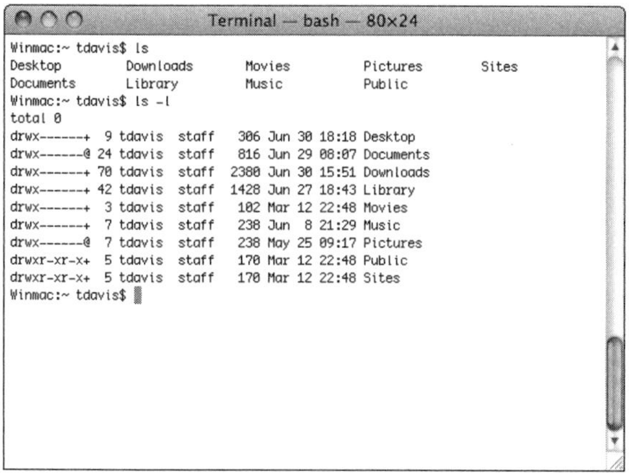

Identifying JVM locations

Finding Java for the first time on OS X is a bit tricky. If you are an experienced Java programmer, you might decide to check the `JAVA_HOME` environment variable first. From the Terminal on my default install of OS X, executing `echo $JAVA_HOME` produces no results. No `JAVA_HOME` variable is set.

If you are an experienced Unix programmer, you might think to check the location of the `java` command-line tool. However, `which java` returns:

```
/usr/bin/java
```

Usually the `java` command is in a `bin` directory under `JAVA_HOME`. If you list the `/usr` directory, it reveals a directory that looks nothing like a typical `JAVA_HOME`, because it isn't. Enter `ls -la /usr/bin/java` to find out if this is actually the `java` command, and you discover that `/usr/bin/java` is actually a link to:

```
/System/Library/Frameworks/JavaVM.framework/Versions/
Current/Commands/java
```

By following links to links to links, eventually anyone persistent enough finds a real JAVA_HOME. In fact, poking around the directory system exposes several versions of Java with several `Home` directories. Explore this directory for an interesting exercise:

```
/System/Library/Frameworks/JavaVM.framework/Versions/
```

In addition, executing `/usr/libexec/java_home` returns the following:

```
/System/Library/Frameworks/JavaVM.framework/Versions/1.6.0/Home
```

Also, there is the `/Library/Java/Home` directory that turns out to be linked to:

```
/System/Library/Frameworks/JavaVM.framework/Home
```

CAUTION

If you are well versed in the art of links with `ln`, you may be tempted to modify the links to java tools, `/Library/Java/Home` or other directories. Using `ln` to modify Java configuration links may cause issues with using Java or Java updates later on.

You are probably wondering which path you should use for `JAVA_HOME` when requested by an installation program. The correct answer is execute:

```
/usr/libexec/java_home
```

This returns the correct version path to your currently set Java home. This little app is handy when you don't want to fire up the JVM to find the path of home. You also can use it to dynamically set `JAVA_HOME` in shell scripts. The returned value changes based on your Java Preferences setting.

CROSS-REF

Terminal creation and use of shell scripts are explained in greater detail in Chapter 4, which is about building Java apps, but the shell scripting information found there can be applied to situations other than setting up Java builds.

This is the perfect excuse to test Xcode for the first time, while verifying that `/usr/libexec/java_home` actually agrees with your JVM about its home directory. The following code example requires Xcode. If you have not yet installed the OS X developer tools, install Xcode now.

NOTE

The `JavaHome` Xcode project is available on the book's Web site. Download the Chapter 2 code from the book's Web site to access the `JavaHome` Xcode project.

CROSS-REF

In Chapter 3, I explain Java tool project creation with Xcode, and an alternative approach with Organizer.

Below, I explain how to start Xcode, and "Build and Run" the Java tool project called `JavaHome`. A Java tool is a simple Java application that normally starts with the `java` command. Typically Java tools are used by scripts or from the command line, though no rules or regulations prevent you from expanding a basic Java tool to be a fully windowed event-driven application.

The `JavaHome` project prints the location of the running JVM's home directory. Because this tool does not have a Window or Dialog to display the information, I describe how to build and run the application in the Xcode Console window. This provides a display for standard output. Follow these steps:

CROSS-REF

Instructions for installing the free OS X developer tools were given in Chapter 1.

1. **Start Xcode.**

   Xcode is located in `/Developer/Applications`. You find the `Developer` folder by double-clicking your default startup disk.

2. **Click File ⇨ Open....**

   You now see the Open dialog box.

3. **Select the JavaHome Xcode projects in the** `JavaHome` **project, as shown in Figure 2.3.**

Figure 2.3

Selecting the JavaHome Xcode project from the Open dialog.

4. **Click the Open button to open the** `JavaHome` **project.**

5. **Select the** JavaHome **class in the Group & Files panel on the left side of the Project window, as shown in Figure 2.4.**

Figure 2.4

JavaHome class file in Project window

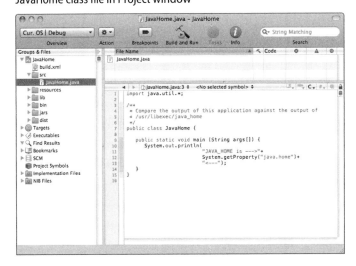

6. **Ensure the** main() **method contains the following code.**

The following code queries the JVM for the `java.home` System property.

```
public static void main (String args[])
{
    System.out.println(
        "JAVA_HOME is --->"+
        System.getProperty("java.home")+
        "<---");
}
```

7. **Open the Xcode Console window found in Run ⇨ Console, and click Build and Run.**

You should see a similar result to that shown in Figure 2.5.

CROSS-REF

Xcode projects are explained in detail in Chapter 3.

Figure 2.5

Xcode Console with correct Java Home path

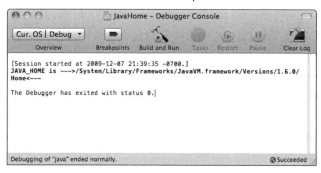

This program verifies that your Java tool executing from Xcode and `java_home` executing from the Terminal agree. In the next section, I explain how to change the Java version pointed to by `java_home` and `java.home`.

As I mention above, the Java home path given by the `java_home` application varies based on your settings in Java Preferences. You may run into a circumstance where you must use a specific version of Java on the OS and want to ignore the directory returned by `java_home`.

A simple solution is to hardcode the path to the `Home` directory of a specific version of Java. In the `/System/Library/Frameworks/JavaVM.framework/Versions/` directory, you see additional directories named after several versions of Java, as shown in Figure 2.6. Some of these have `Home` directories in them. If you need a specific version of Java, hardcode your path to the `Home` directory of the Java version you want to use.

Figure 2.6

`/System/Library/Frameworks/JavaVM.framework/Versions/` in Terminal

```
Winmac:~ tdavis$ ls -l /System/Library/Frameworks/JavaVM.framework/Versions/
total 56
lrwxr-xr-x  1 root  wheel    5 Jun 15 21:44 1.3 -> 1.3.1
drwxr-xr-x  3 root  wheel  102 Jul 18  2008 1.3.1
lrwxr-xr-x  1 root  wheel    5 Jun 15 21:44 1.4 -> 1.4.2
lrwxr-xr-x  1 root  wheel    3 Jan 14 05:40 1.4.1 -> 1.4
drwxr-xr-x  8 root  wheel  272 Jan 14 05:40 1.4.2
lrwxr-xr-x  1 root  wheel    5 Jun 15 21:44 1.5 -> 1.5.0
drwxr-xr-x  8 root  wheel  272 Jan 14 05:40 1.5.0
lrwxr-xr-x  1 root  wheel    5 Jun 15 21:44 1.6 -> 1.6.0
drwxr-xr-x  8 root  wheel  272 Mar 13 14:20 1.6.0
drwxr-xr-x  8 root  wheel  272 Jun 15 21:44 A
lrwxr-xr-x  1 root  wheel    1 Jun 15 21:44 Current -> A
lrwxr-xr-x  1 root  wheel    3 Jun 15 21:44 CurrentJDK -> 1.5
Winmac:~ tdavis$
```

Using the version option of the `java_home` command-line tool is a better solution than hard-coding the path of a specific `Home` directory. For example:

```
/usr/libexec/java_home -v1.5
```

produces the path to the 1.5 `Home` directory:

```
/System/Library/Frameworks/JavaVM.framework/Versions/1.5.0/Home
```

To see the manual for `java_home`, enter `man java_home` in a Terminal window. `man` is a command-line tool for viewing command-line tool manuals. Use the up and down arrows to browse up and down in `man` manuals. Type `q` to quit the `man` application.

CAUTION

Hardcoding paths to specific versions of JVMs is discouraged. The path may change later with a system update. However, in some cases this still may be the solution you prefer. The preferred method to find a path to a specific Java version is to pass a JVM version to `java_home` command-line tool.

CROSS-REF

Application bundles provide an `Info.plist` you can configure to require or suggest a version of Java that the Java application uses. Chapter 5 provides information on `Info.plist` configuration.

Setting Java Preferences with "Java Preferences"

Java Preferences is found in the `Applications/Utilities` directory. Starting the application, you see a window with four tabs: General, Security, Network, and Advanced. The General preferences tab, shown in Figure 2.7, contains the option to specify the version of Java that you want to use with either applets or Java applications.

To specify your preferred version of Java to use, drag the Java version up or down the list. The top entry is the most preferred version of Java to use. If an application cannot be run with the preferred version, then the next most preferred version is used.

The Java Applet Plugin section of the General preferences tab has the additional ability to specify options to use when starting applets. Click the Options... button, and the Applet Options dialog box becomes visible, as shown in Figure 2.8. From here, you can set applet runtime parameters in a text box. Also, you can select to smooth text in Java applets.

Figure 2.7

Java general preferences in Java Preferences application

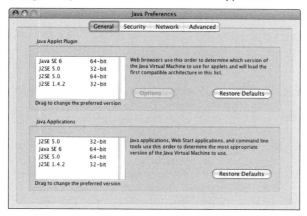

Figure 2.8

Applet options dialog box

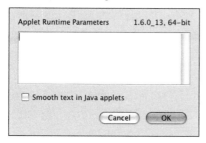

Click the Advanced tab at the top of the Java Preferences window. This tab contains a host of useful configuration settings, as shown in Figure 2.9. The advanced options include enabling tracing, logging, and showing applet lifecycle exceptions. You can configure whether to show or even start the Java console. You can configure many security settings as well.

Figure 2.9

Advanced tab of Java Preferences

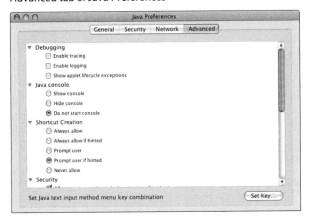

NOTE

If you are using a 32-bit version of Safari, then applets running inside of Safari must use a 32-bit version of Java. This means that you are reverted to J2SE 5.0, instead of using Java SE 6, which is available only in 64-bit on OS X. However, Web Start applications started from a 32-bit Safari still run in Java SE 6 if desired.

TIP

If you set Java Applications to the latest version of Java in the Java Preferences, but a Java application is ignoring this setting, check the `Info.plist` setting for the application. If the application has an `Info.plist` setting specifying the use of an older version of Java, the `Info.plist` overrides the preferred setting in Java Preferences.

Adding Libraries

Java programmers speak of *the classpath,* clumping all classpaths into one category. Java actually has three categories of classpaths. Each of the three classpath types has a distinct purpose and should be used properly. The purpose of this section is to review the categories of classpaths in Java and explain their locations and uses.

The three classpath categories are user, extension, and bootstrap. These also are called the application classpath, the optional classpath, and the core classpath, respectively. Most Java developers mean all three when they say classpath. However, developers often only manipulate the user classpath, avoiding the other two as much as possible.

Exploring library locations

The core classpath is reserved for the JVM's JAR files. Only the actual implementer of the Java Virtual Machine should be populating this classpath. The system property for the core path is `sun.boot.class.path`, and it can be retrieved at runtime by the following command:

```
System.getProperty("sun.boot.class.path");
```

The core path is located in the same directory as the Home directory. It is in the `Classes` directory.

I mentioned earlier in this chapter that the location of the active `Home` directory varies based on the setting in Java Preferences. As mentioned earlier, you can find the location of the active `Home` directory by calling the command-line tool `/usr/libexec/java_home`. Modify the resulting directory path by replacing `Home` with `Classes`, and you have created the active core classpath's path. On my system the active core path is as follows:

```
/System/Library/Frameworks/JavaVM.framework/Versions/
1.6.0/Classes
```

On your system, it may be different.

The optional classpath (or extension classpath) stores JARs that extend Java. These are JARs that are intended for use by applications running on the computer that do not actually install the libraries. For instance, if you create the newest and sleekest widget that everyone assumes is available for their applications, you install the JAR'ed widget in the proper optional classpath, and every application and applet running on the computer has instant access to it.

On OS X, three optional classpaths are active at any given time. You may be familiar with the traditional `lib/ext` directory located in the active Java home. This directory exists on OS X, but should not be used.

CAUTION

Do not use the Java Home directory's `lib/ext` directory for Java optional packages. System Update tends to change the location of this directory or even delete this directory without warning.

These are the two other optional classpaths:

```
/Library/Java/Extensions
```

```
/System/Library/Java/Extensions
```

The second path, starting with System, is for Apple's exclusive use. That leaves `/Library/Java/Extensions` for developer and application to use. `/Library/Java/Extensions` has a huge benefit: If the user changes the preferred version of Java on the Mac, this optional classpath stays active. Dependent applications keep on working. (Thanks Apple!)

The system property for the extension classpath is `java.ext.dirs`. Access the `java.ext.dirs` property at runtime with this command:

```
System.getProperty("java.ext.dirs");
```

User (or application) classpaths are defined by default as the directory the application is started from or the current JAR from which the application is running. If the classpath option of the `java` command is redefined, then the current directory or JAR's path must be included in the new path.

The application classpath provides the application with the locations of additional libraries specific to it.

CAUTION

If the application classpath contains classes that already exist in one of the other classpaths, then the JVM ignores the duplicates in the application classpath.

The system property for the user classpath is `java.class.path`. To access the application classpath at runtime, use this command:

```
System.getProperty("java.class.path");
```

Including JARs and native libraries

You will need to include JARs or native libraries in your Java applications, eventually. Two common methods for including JARs are available. The first is to modify the `java` classpath option to include the JARs. When modifying the `java` classpath option on OS X, path separators are colons (`:`) and directory separators are forward slashes (`/`). The second method of loading needed libraries is to place your JARs in the appropriate directory, so the JRE loads them when needed.

To make your JARs or native libraries available to all Java applications, place them in `/Library/Java/Extensions`. Java class files are not recognized in this directory unless they are in JARs. Native libraries used in Java Native Interface (JNI)-based applications can be placed in `/Library/Java/Extensions` loose. Shared native libraries do not require packaging of any sort load from the `Extensions` directory.

TIP

On OS X, Java Native Interface libraries follow the naming convention `lib<lib name>.jnilib`. This naming convention differs slightly from Linux or Windows.

Creating custom libraries

Any JAR file works as a library. To create a custom library using Xcode, use the `JavaHome` project from earlier in this chapter and remove the `main()` method. Creating native libraries is not much more difficult. Use the JniTest project from the book's Web site to create native libraries. Later in this book, I explain details of Ant project creation for JNI. For now, use the Xcode project that I provide.

Creating custom libraries sounds easy because it is. Still, the following demonstration clears up potential confusion. This simple example uses an Xcode-generated JNI project. JNI scares many developers, but there isn't much to it. I will go easy on you for our first JNI example.

CROSS-REF

Chapter 9 covers JNI on OS X in depth.

CROSS-REF

In Chapter 3 I explain creating Java tool projects with Xcode and Organizer.

As a reminder, JNI applications use Java code to call a natively compiled (usually C) library. This comes in very handy when you need to interface your application with prebuilt libraries to save the time and expense of rewriting the libraries in pure Java. Also, if you have small chunks of code that need optimizing in C, JNI works for that too.

In this sample, I use a default JNI Xcode project called JniTest. Xcode 3.2 does not currently have a simple JNI project template, but I had one hanging around from Xcode 3.1. It works fine with Xcode 3.2 and with a little tweaking makes a great base template for JNI development in Xcode 3.2.

After compiling and testing the JniText project, I move the native library to the `Extensions` folder and the Java class to the `Desktop`. At this point, running the class from the command line works because the `jnilib` is in the optional classpath. Follow these steps:

1. **Open Xcode and choose File ⇨ Open...**

2. **Choose the JniTest project file from the JniTest project, as shown in Figure 2.10.**

3. **Open the projectby clicking the Open button.**

4. **Open the Xcode Console by selecting Run ⇨ Console.**

5. **Click Build and Run at the top of the console, as shown in Figure 2.11.**

This creates the native library and class we need for our test.

Figure 2.10

Selecting the JniTest project in the Open dialog

Figure 2.11

Successful Build and Run

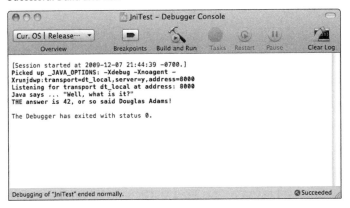

6. **Navigate in the Finder to the** bin **directory in your project.**

   The `bin` directory should contain the `JniTest.class` and the `libJniTest.jnilib` files.

7. **Copy the** JniTest.class **to the Desktop and the** libJNITest.jnilib **to** /Library/Java/Extensions.

8. **Open a Terminal window and navigate to the desktop by typing** cd Desktop **after opening the Terminal window.**

9. **Enter** java JniTest **in the Terminal.**

   The output should read:

   ```
   Java says ... "Well, what is it?"
   THE answer is 42, or so said Douglas Adams!
   ```

TIP

JNI builds with Xcode on OS X 10.5 seem to require a 32-bit JVM. If Xcode fails to build the built-in JNI template on your Mac, just change the preferred JVM to a 32-bit JRE in the Java Preferences application.

Finding Environment Variables

Every program you write has variables contained in it. You are already familiar with the creation of variables in Java. In addition, Java gives programs access to JVM-specific system variables called properties. Earlier in this chapter, I discussed the `sun.boot.class.path`, `java.ext.dirs`, and `java.class.path` properties.

The environment that starts a Java program (or any other program) also has variables associated with it. These OS X variables are called environment variables. Earlier, I described both the Terminal and the Finder. Both applications have environment variables. These variables are inherited by applications opened through them.

Setting JAVA_HOME

When you type any command into the Terminal, the command is executed by a shell program. Bash is the shell that runs by default in the Terminal window. These instructions assume bash is your shell and running any scripts you execute. If you discover you are using a different shell, consult the documentation for that shell. Documentation for all the common shells is just an Internet search away.

Bash contains two types of variables: environment variables and shell variables. Environment variables are inherited by applications opened from a Terminal window. Shell variables are not inherited by programs opened from the Terminal window.

TIP

Application bundles you normally open with a double-click in the Finder can be opened from the Terminal by using the `open` command. For example, use `open /Developer/Applications/Xcode.app`.

By running applications from the Terminal, you change the set of inherited environment variables to match the parent Terminal window instead of the Finder. Opening from the Terminal allows you to modify applications' environment variables from the shell.

Check the Terminal's environment variables by entering `env` in the shell. Check the shell variables by typing `set` in the Terminal window. Notice that the shell variables include the list of environment variables.

When set or displayed in bash, variables start with a name followed by an equal sign followed by a value. Do not place spaces directly before or directly after the equal sign. By convention, the names of environment variables are always completely uppercase. (Sysadmins shout a lot.) Words in variable names are typically separated by underscores.

TIP

Type `env` in the Terminal, and you see the full list of environment variables. Look at the variable names and values. One variable is named `SHELL`. Notice `SHELL`'s value. If you have a default installation, it is probably `bash`. This is a handy way to check which shell is running.

Create a new environment variable in a Terminal window for practice. Use this form:

```
export MY_VARIABLE="some value"
```

The export command makes variables available to the environment. Quotes are only needed if the value contains spaces. The variable does not appear in other Terminal windows.

CROSS-REF

Shells and shell scripts are discussed in detail in Chapter 4.

As mentioned earlier, a common environment variable often available in Terminal windows is JAVA_HOME. JAVA_HOME is discouraged on OS X in favor of other options mentioned earlier. OS X does not come with the environment variable JAVA_HOME set by default.

Many Java-based servers and complex Java applications look for a JAVA_HOME variable when running installation shell scripts or startup scripts. Ideally, set these applications to point to the correct home via the `java_home` command-line application discussed earlier.

If you cannot get around the requirement for a JAVA_HOME environment variable, set JAVA_HOME locally in a startup script for the application that needs it. Most applications that need JAVA_HOME are using a script to start. The script begins with a line similar to this:

```
#!/bin/bash
```

Place the exported variable somewhere after this declaration line.

Setting JAVA_HOME locally in a startup script allows other applications that require JAVA_HOME to have the variable set to a different value without accidentally having an application use the wrong value.

Of course, you can hardcode the JAVA_HOME value; however, dynamically setting it to match Java Preferences is better. Setting JAVA_HOME locally in a shell script or from the command line to equal java_home is accomplished with this command:

```
export JAVA_HOME=`/usr/libexec/java_home`
```

Notice the backticks. The backticks execute java_home and provide the return value as the value of JAVA_HOME.

Exploring dot files and dot folders

I explained setting environment variables for the Terminal in the preceding section. These variables affect only the Terminal or applications that start from the Terminal. If you double-click an application in the Finder, the Terminal environment variables are ignored in favor of Finder's environment variables.

There is an easy fix for this situation. You can set environment variables for both the Terminal and the Finder. First, you need some background information.

On OS X, and other Unix systems, users have a home directory. When you log in via telnet or ssh or open a Terminal window, you are located in your home directory. To return to your home directory after changing your current directory, simply enter one of the following:

```
cd
```

```
cd ~
```

The tilde at the beginning of a directory path represents your home directory.

Browsing directories in the Finder hides many files and folders from your view. This is especially true of your home directory and the root directory. For example, open a Finder window and navigate to the root of your default hard drive and then open a Terminal window and go to the same location and list the root directory using these commands:

```
cd /
ls
```

You find that the directories beginning with lowercase names are visible to the Terminal, but not immediately visible or navigable by the Finder. To get to these hidden directories in the Finder use the Go ⇨ Go to Folder.... menu command.

Complex applications store user state, serial numbers, preferences, file paths, URLs, and a great deal of other information in property files that are changed constantly. By convention on OS X and other Unix platforms, user-specific information and application state is often stored in dot files or dot folders in the user's home directory.

Dot files (or folders) are hidden from casual users even in the Terminal. If a file or folder has a name that begins with a dot, such as `.my-folder`, the Finder does not display it. Also, the `ls` command entered in a Terminal window does not display dot files and dot folders.

To display dot files in the Terminal, use this command:

```
ls -a
```

To display dot files in the Finder, you need to issue the following command in a Terminal window:

```
defaults write com.apple.finder AppleShowAllFiles -bool true
```

Then relaunch the Finder either through the Force Quit Applications window (explained earlier in this chapter) or by restarting your computer. To hide dot files in the Finder (because you will get tired of the clutter quickly), use the following command in the Terminal, followed by a relaunch of the Finder:

```
defaults write com.apple.finder AppleShowAllFiles -bool false
```

Notice that the only difference between the two commands is the Boolean value at the end of the command. You cannot create dot files or folders from the Finder, as shown in Figure 2.12. Instead, use the Terminal. Follow these steps to see a demonstration:

Figure 2.12

Dialog box stating no dots allowed in folder or filenames

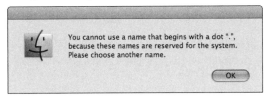

1. **Open a Terminal window.**

   By default, you begin in your home directory.

2. **Enter** mkdir .dirtest2toss, **and press Return.**

3. **Enter** touch .filetest2toss.properties, **and press Return.**

4. **Enter** ls -a**, and press Return.**

You now see the .dirtest2toss directory and the .filetest2toss. properties file.

The three commands mentioned above are: mkdir, touch, and ls. mkdir means make directory. touch (in this case) means create a new file by this name. ls means list. These commands are common on my Unix operating systems.

N O T E

The touch command line utility modifies access and modification times of files. Creating files is not its purpose. However, creating non-existent files is a useful side effect of touch.

Using system-wide properties

I've given you some basic background on hidden files on OS X and a brief explanation of the home directory, so you are now ready to understand global environment properties.

Earlier, I mentioned that setting environment variables in Terminal windows affects only that Terminal where the change is made and the applications launched from that Terminal window. The Finder remains unaffected by changes made to Terminal environment variables.

Apple understood the need for setting environment variables in both Terminal and Finder spawned applications. Their solution is a hidden property file that does not exist by default on OS X. The file is:

```
~/.MacOSX/environment.plist
```

From my earlier discussion of the home directory and hidden folders, you probably recognize that the tilde represents your home directory and the directory beginning with a dot is a hidden directory.

Check to see if the ~/.MacOSX directory exists by typing ls ~/.MacOSX in the Terminal. If the directory exists, and you have an environment.plist file in the directory already, then you may navigate to it by using the Go to Folder... menu item under the Go menu in the Finder application. Once there, double-click the environment.plist file to open the Property List Editor.

If the file or folder does not exist, you can create it from the Property List Editor. The Property List Editor is one of the developer tools installed with Xcode. The path to Property List Editor is as follows:

```
/Developer/Applications/Utilities/Property\ List\ Editor.app
```

The Utilities directory, shown in Figure 2.13, contains the Property List Editor application and several other useful utilities.

TIP

When giving a path from the root directory / in the Terminal, remember the Finder equivalent is found by opening your startup drive and browsing from there.

Figure 2.13

Utilities directory containing Property List Editor.app

You can edit many types of Mac property files with Property List Editor. In this case, the property file is `environment.plist`. You will learn other types of property files that the Property List Editor manipulates throughout this book.

CAUTION

Don't forget to restart your computer after saving changes to `environment.plist`.

As shown in Figure 2.14, the `environment.plist` is an XML file with a `Root` node of type `Dictionary`. Add children to the `Root` by clicking the Add Child icon at the top of the window. When you restart the computer, all the children of Root load into your global user environment.

Save your changes to the `environment.plist` to the path `~/.MacOSX/`. This seems fairly straight forward, but remember that you cannot see `.MacOSX`, because it is hidden! Three methods seem easiest for getting around this problem.

Figure 2.14

Property List Editor with a Root element

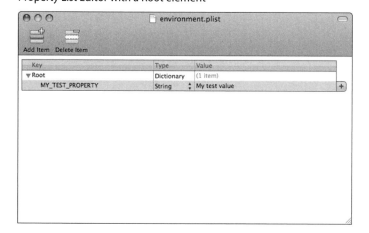

 CAUTION

Remember to save `environment.plist` in XML Property List format. That is the default format.

First, if `.MacOSX` does not exist, you can create it from inside Property List Editor's Save dialog box. Ignore the warning about dot folders shown in Figure 2.15, and create the directory. You will automatically be placed in that directory and can save your file there.

Figure 2.15

Warning in Save dialog box about dot folders

Second, if the `.MacOSX` folder exists and the `environment.plist` exists, navigate to the directory using Go ➪ Go to Folder... in the Finder. Next, open the file by double-clicking it. Now you simply click Save, and the plist saves to the proper location.

Third, if the `.MacOSX` folder exists, but the `environment.plist` does not, modify Finder temporarily to display dot folders as described earlier in this chapter. Then you may navigate to `.MacOSX` to save your new `environment.plist` at will.

NOTE
Restarting is required to reload the current values of `environment.plist`. If you are setting variables globally for both the Finder and the Terminal, you probably won't do it often enough for restarting to become a problem.

TIP
When debugging environment settings for the Finder, I suggest using the `open` command from the Terminal to simulate opening from Finder. Changing environment variables in the Terminal is quick and easy between application launches.

Accessing OS X environment

Now that you can modify environment variables for a given user account using `environment.plist`, it is time to look at using these variables in your Java programs.

Earlier, I explained that several Java-specific properties are accessible through the `System.getProperty()` method. It might seem obvious to look for some standard property that changes based off the environment variable name.

It turns out that accessing environment variables is much simpler than that. The method is `System.getenv()`, and it takes a `String` for its only argument. If you have an environment variable named `MY_PROJECT_HOME`, accessing it at runtime is simply a matter of calling `System.getenv()` as follows.

```
String path = System.getenv("MY_PROJECT_HOME");
```

Summary

In this chapter, I explained configuring Java and Java applications. Java ships with multiple versions of Java. New versions of Java are installed from the system updates, on occasion. Finding a correct path to a desired Java `Home` directory is as simple as using the `/usr/libexec/java_home` tool. Set your preferred version of Java through the Java Preferences application.

Add optional Java libraries to all Java applications by adding them to the `/Library/Java/Extensions` directory. Class files must be in JARs in this directory. Native libraries for JNI do not need JAR'ing.

Access system environment variables in Java by way of the `System.getenv()` method. Set environment variables locally for a specific Terminal window and applications started from that window, or set them globally for all applications started by the user.

Understanding Xcode

E ven if you use Eclipse or NetBeans as your primary IDE on OS X, Xcode contains many useful templates for native OS X integration. Integrating your Java application with Objective-C, com.apple.eawt packages, Cocoa Frameworks, or screensavers starts with Xcode.

I use Xcode for many programming examples in this book. Understanding Xcode simplifies learning native OS X application integration. Xcode provides programmer resources including a quick-start welcome screen, means for modifying the view of the IDE, macro editing, and many other features that increase your productivity.

In this chapter, I provide an overview of creating Java projects in Xcode. I explain Xcode features that improve your development experience. Also, I explore the Organizer, a tool for managing and running projects.

Exploring Project Templates

As of version 3.2, Xcode supplies one Java template. It is called the JNI Library. The name "JNI Library" is deceiving. This library is actually a fully integrated Java/Cocoa application template. If you want to see how a fully integrated Java OS X application looks in Xcode, you want to start with the JNI Library.

The JNI Library is overwhelming, if all you want is a basic Java project for pure or mostly pure Java development. For instance, you may plan on doing some Objective-C work and you want to stick to one IDE rather than switching between a Java-specific IDE and Xcode constantly.

For this reason, I start this chapter by explaining Java project creation in Xcode. This section explores Java console project creation, Java Swing project creation, and Java applet project creation from within Xcode. These projects allow Xcode to build, clean, and run the projects.

Finally, I give an overview of the JNI Library project. I explain the project creation and the overall set up of this powerful template.

In This Chapter

Creating Java projects in Xcode

Configuring Xcode

Creating class diagrams with Xcode

Managing projects with Organizer

Creating Java Console Application Projects

Console-based applications and tools are extremely popular among Unix developers. Many users choose Mac OS X because it has a wonderful Terminal to complement its wonderful GUI. This was the feature that pulled me back from the Linux world to a Mac OS X prerelease version in 1999, and I have heard similar stories from other OS X developers.

A great example of a popular console application is `grep`. The `grep` tool is used to match patterns and is combined with other command-line tools to perform searches in files, such as logs, or directories. It is probably the favorite tool of die-hard Unix users and sysadmins.

I start with an explanation of creating an Xcode Java console application project. Typically, Java-based console applications require a longer Java command to start than their C-based counterparts. This is easily fixed with a wrapper shell script.

CROSS-REF

I explain how to wrap Java console applications with shell scripts at the end of Chapter 4.

To create a Java console application project with Xcode 3.2, follow these instructions:

1. **Select File ⇨ New Project from the Xcode menu bar.**

2. **Select Empty Project from the Other templates group on the left, as shown in Figure 3.1.**

3. **Name the new project** ConsoleApp.

4. **Open your new project folder in the Finder.**

5. **Create** src, resources, **and** lib **folders in your project folder.**

Adding the new folders to your project is a little tricky.

6. **Select your** ConsoleApp **project in the Groups & Files tree, control-click Add ⇨ Existing Files... from the context menu, select the new folders, and add them. When the dialog box appears asking for information on how to add the folders, add them using Create Folder References for any added folders, as shown in Figure 3.2.**

Figure 3.1

Empty Project selected in New Project window

Figure 3.2

How to add folders in Xcode

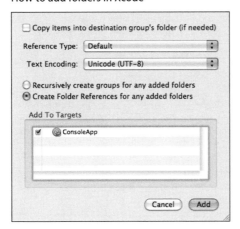

7. **Create a file called** build.xml **at the root of your project in the ConsoleApp directory. Create the XML file from within Xcode by selecting** ConsoleApp **and Control-clicking. Select Add ➪ New File... from the context-sensitive menu. Choose Empty File from the Other template catalog, and create the** build.xml **file as part of the** ConsoleApp **project.**

This is your Ant build file. With this setup, Xcode uses Ant when building your project.

8. **Fill** build.xml **with the following code.**

This Ant build is based loosely on the Xcode 3.1 Java tool template, but should work with the latest version Xcode.

TIP

If you create a custom `build.xml`, include the `install`, `run`, and `clean` targets.

CROSS-REF

I explain Ant builds in Chapter 4.

```xml
<?xml version="1.0" encoding="UTF-8"?>
<project name="ConsoleApp"
        default="install"
        basedir=".">
  <!-- setting up classpath for install -->
  <fileset id="lib.jars" dir="lib">
     <include name="**/*.jar"/>
  </fileset>
  <path id="lib.path">
     <fileset refid="lib.jars"/>
  </path>
  <target name="install"
         description="Exactly what the man says.">

     <mkdir dir="bin"/>
     <javac deprecation="on"
            srcdir="src"
            destdir="bin"
            source="1.6"
            target="1.6"
            includeAntRuntime="no"
            classpathref="lib.path"
            debug="true">
     </javac>
```

```
            <!-- Assembling final JAR file -->
            <mkdir dir="jars"/>

            <jar jarfile="jars/${ant.project.name}.jar"
                basedir="bin"
                manifest="resources/Manifest">

                <fileset dir="resources/"
                        excludes="resources/Manifest" />
                <zipgroupfileset refid="lib.jars"/>
            </jar>
            <!--
                Create the 'dist/' directory, and
                assemble in the 'dist/' directory
            -->
            <mkdir dir="dist"/>
            <copy toDir="dist">
                <fileset dir="jars">
                    <include name="*.jar"/>
                </fileset>
            </copy>
        </target>
        <target name="run"
                depends="install"
                description="Run the console application">
            <!-- Run the assembled application -->
            <java classname="${ant.project.name}"
                classpath="bin"
                fork="true">
            </java>

        </target>
        <target name="clean"
                description="Delete all compile directories">
            <delete dir="bin"/>
            <delete dir="jars"/>
            <delete dir="dist"/>
        </target>
    </project>
```

9. **Create** ConsoleApp.java **in your** src **directory. Create the Java file from within Xcode by selecting** src **and Control-clicking. Select Add⇨New File… from the context-sensitive menu. Choose Empty File from the Other template catalog as shown in Figure 3.3, and create it in the** src **directory. If there is an extra reference to the file in the Groups & Files tree, remove the reference.**

Figure 3.3

Empty File selection

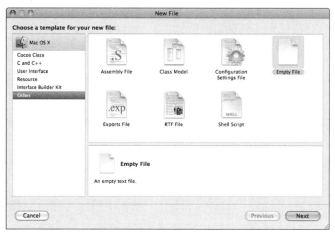

10. **Add the following source to the** ConsoleApp.java **file.**

```java
import java.util.Scanner;
/**
 * Java based console application.
 *
 * @author T. Gene Davis
 */
public class ConsoleApp
{
   public static void main (String[] args)
   {
      System.out.print( "What is your name? " );

      Scanner scn = new Scanner( System.in );
      String name = scn.nextLine();
      System.out.println( "Hello " + name + "!" );
   }
}
```

11. **Add a** Manifest **file to the** resources **directory. Create the** Manifest **file from within Xcode by selecting** resources **directory and Control-clicking. Select Add ⇨ New File... from the context-sensitive menu. Choose Empty File from the Other template catalog and create the** Manifest **file as part of the** ConsoleApp **project in**

the resources **directory. If there is an extra reference to the file in the Groups & Files tree, remove the reference.**

The source for the Manifest is simply this:

```
Main-Class: ConsoleApp
```

Your project is ready to use. In fact, if you prefer building from the command line, `cd` to your project root in Terminal and type `ant` to build your project, `ant run` to run your project, and `ant clean` to clean your project.

If you prefer to build, run, and clean your project from inside of Xcode, you use a few more steps to polish off your project setup. You need an Executable and a Target.

These steps give you a properly configured Target:

1. **Control-click the Targets node of the Groups & Files tree.**

2. **Select Add ⇨ New Target...**

3. **Select External Target from the Other group, as shown in Figure 3.4. Name your new target** ConsoleApp**, and add it to your** ConsoleApp **project.**

Figure 3.4

External Target selected

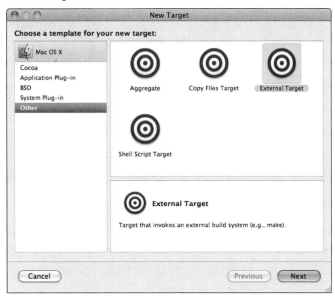

4. **Double-click your new ConsoleApp Target.**

This brings up the Target: ConsoleApp dialog box.

5. **Set the Build Tool to** /usr/bin/ant.

6. **Set the Arguments to** -emacs $(ACTION), **as shown in Figure 3.5.**

Figure 3.5

Configured target dialog box

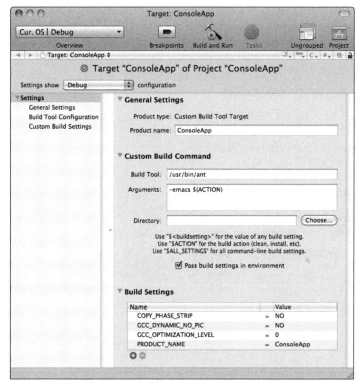

Your Target is ready to use. This allows building and cleaning of the project. Before the next step, click Build ➪ Build. This builds an executable JAR for setting up your Executable to run. Next, from inside Xcode, create the Executable by taking these steps:

1. **From the Executables context menu, select Add ⇨ New Custom Executable...**

2. **Name your executable** java.

3. **Select the path to your** java **command.**

   That is /usr/bin/java.

4. **Add the new Executable to your project.**

5. **Open your new** java **executable by double-clicking it.**

6. **Select the General tab, shown in Figure 3.6, and set Custom directory to your project's** dist **directory.**

Figure 3.6

General tab in Executable configuration

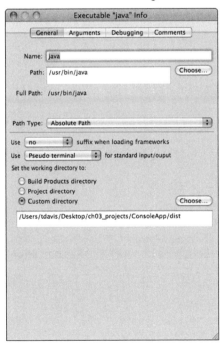

7. Select the Arguments tab shown in Figure 3.7, and add the argument -cp
ConsoleApp.jar ConsoleApp.

Figure 3.7

Arguments tab in Executable configuration

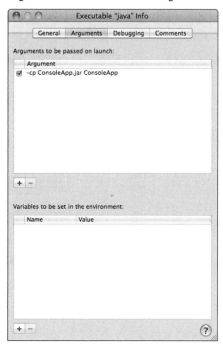

8. Select the Debugging tab shown in Figure 3.8. Set the Java Debugger to the
default debugger. Select Wait for next launch/push notification. Deselect all
other check boxes.

Figure 3.8

Debugging tab in Executable configuration

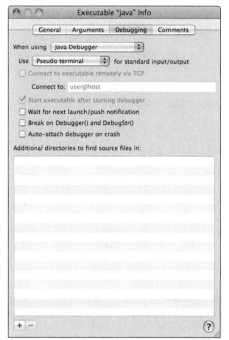

Your project is now set to run from Xcode. Open the Console by selecting Run ⇨ Console. Click the Build and Run button at the top of the console window. You interact with the console application directly in the Debugger Console window.

Creating Java application projects

Console applications have their uses, but typical end-users prefer nice point-and-click interfaces. The current version of Xcode is missing a pure Swing project template. Still, setting up a pure Swing project in Xcode is fairly easy. In fact, the console application project I explained in the preceding section easily morphs into a GUI application by replacing all console input and output with a Swing or AWT interface.

In this section, I explain setting up a Swing Xcode project in detail.

Begin creating a Java Swing application project for Xcode 3.2 by following these instructions:

1. **Select File ⇨ New Project from the Xcode menu bar.**

2. **Select Empty Project from Other templates, as shown in Figure 3.1.**

3. **Name the new project** GuiApp**.**

4. **Open your new project folder in the Finder.**

5. **Create** src, resources, **and** lib **folders in your project folder.**

6. **Copy the** resources_macosx **from the book's Web site Chapter 3** GuiApp **source code.**

The resources_macosx folder contains a default icon file named after the project and an info.plist with the properties displayed in Figure 3.9. You also can create these two items from scratch instead of downloading the files from the book's Web site.

Figure 3.9

The file info.plist contains the properties for this project.

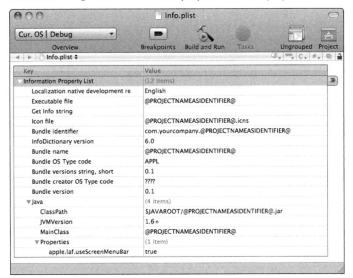

NOTE

The resources_macosx folder for this project is on the book's Web site.

CROSS-REF

Icon creation is detailed in Chapter 5.

CROSS-REF

`info.plist` files are detailed in Chapter 5.

7. **Add the new folders, including** resources_macosx, **to your project. This is a little tricky. Select your** GuiApp **project in the Groups & Files tree. Control-click and select Add ⇨ Existing Files... from the context menu. Then select the new project folders and add them. A dialog box comes up asking for how to add the folders. Add the folders using Create Folder References for any added folders, as shown in Figure 3.2.**

8. **Create a file called** build.xml **at the root of your project.**

This is your Ant build file. With this setup, Xcode uses Ant when building your project.

9. **Fill** build.xml **with the following code.**

This Ant build is based off the Xcode 3.1 Java application template, but it should work with the latest version Xcode. If you create a custom `build.xml`, include the `install`, `run` and `clean` targets. I explain Ant builds in Chapter 4.

```xml
<?xml version="1.0" encoding="UTF-8"?>
<!-- Based on Xcode 3.1 Java application template -->
<project name="GuiApp"
         default="install"
         basedir=".">
  <property name="jvm.framework"
  location="/System/Library/Frameworks/JavaVM.framework"/>
  <property name="apple.appstub"
  location="${jvm.framework}/Resources/MacOS/¬
JavaApplicationStub"/>
  <property name="application.macos"
            location="dist/${ant.project.name}.app/Contents/¬
   MacOS"/>
  <property name="application.macos.stub"
            location="${application.macos}/${ant.project.¬
   name}"/>
  <property name="application.resources"
            location="dist/${ant.project.name}.app/Contents/¬
Resources"/>
  <property name="application.resources.java"
            location="dist/${ant.project.name}.app/Contents/¬
Resources/Java"/>
```

```xml
<fileset id="lib.jars" dir="lib">
  <include name="**/*.jar"/>
</fileset>
<path id="lib.path">
  <fileset refid="lib.jars"/>
</path>
<!-- Call mkdir and javac -->
<target name="compile"
        description="Run javac">
  <mkdir dir="src"/>
  <mkdir dir="lib"/>
  <mkdir dir="bin"/>
  <javac deprecation="on"
         srcdir="src"
         destdir="bin"
         source="1.6"
         target="1.6"
         includeAntRuntime="no"
         classpathref="lib.path"
         debug="true">
  </javac>
</target>
<!-- Create application JAR -->
<target name="jar"
        depends="compile"
        description="Jar everything">
  <mkdir dir="jars"/>
  <jar jarfile="jars/${ant.project.name}.jar"
       basedir="bin"
       manifest="resources/Manifest">
    <!-- Inject resources -->
    <fileset dir="resources/"
             excludes="resources/Manifest" />
    <!-- Merge library jars into final jar file -->
    <zipgroupfileset refid="lib.jars"/>
  </jar>
</target>
 <!-- Create the '*.app' package and copy resources  -->
 <target name="install"
         depends="jar"
         description="Make application bundle">
  <mkdir dir="dist"/>
  <mkdir dir="${application.resources.java}"/>
  <mkdir dir="${application.macos}"/>
  <copy toDir="${application.resources.java}">
    <fileset dir="jars">
```

```
        <include name="*.jar"/>
      </fileset>
    </copy>
    <copy file="${apple.appstub}"
          toFile="${application.macos}/${ant.project.name}"/>
    <!-- file permissions set -->
    <exec executable="/bin/chmod">
      <arg line="755 '${application.macos.stub}'"/>
    </exec>
    <copy file="resources_macosx/Info.plist"
          toFile="dist/${ant.project.name}.app/Contents/¬
Info.plist">
      <filterset>
        <filter token="PROJECTNAMEASIDENTIFIER"
                value="${ant.project.name}"/>
      </filterset>
    </copy>
    <copy file="resources_macosx/${ant.project.name}.icns"
          toDir="${application.resources}"/>
  </target>

  <!-- The 'open' tool runs the application -->
  <target name="run"
          depends="install"
          description="Run application bundle">
    <exec dir="dist"
          executable="/usr/bin/open"
          os="Mac OS X">
      <arg line="${ant.project.name}.app"/>
    </exec>
  </target>
  <target name="clean"
          description="Clean by deleting all compile¬
 directories">
    <delete dir="bin"/>
    <delete dir="jars"/>
    <delete dir="dist"/>
  </target>

</project>
```

10. **Create** GuiApp.java **in your** src **directory. Create the Java file from within Xcode by selecting** src **and Control-clicking. Select Add ⇨ New File... from the context-sensitive menu. Choose Empty File from the Other template catalog, as shown in Figure 3.3, and create it in the** src **directory. If there is an extra reference to the file in the Groups & Files tree, remove the reference.**

11. **Add the following source to the** GuiApp.java **file.**

```java
import java.awt.Color;
import java.awt.Container;
import java.awt.Graphics;
import javax.swing.JFrame;
import javax.swing.JPanel;
/**
 * Java based GUI application.
 *
 * @author T. Gene Davis
 */
public class GuiApp
{
    public static void main(String[] args)
    {
        JFrame appWindow = new JFrame("GuiApp");
        appWindow.setSize(600, 400);
        Container content = appWindow.getContentPane();
        content.add(new MyPanel());
        appWindow.setVisible(true);
    }
    private static class MyPanel extends JPanel
    {
        public void paint(Graphics g)
        {
            g.setColor(Color.BLUE);
            g.drawString("Put your app here", 10, 100);
        }
    }
}
```

12. **Add a** Manifest **file to the** resources **directory. Create the** Manifest **file from within Xcode by selecting** resources **directory and Control-clicking. Select Add ⇨ New File… from the context-sensitive menu. Choose Empty File from the Other template catalog and create the** Manifest **file as part of the** GuiApp **project in the** resources **directory. If there is an extra reference to the file in the Groups & Files tree, remove the reference.**

The source for Manifest is simply this:

```
Main-Class: GuiApp
```

Your project is ready to use. If you prefer building from the command line, cd to your project root in the Terminal and type ant to build your project, ant run to run your project, and ant clean to clean your project.

If you prefer to build, run, and clean your project from inside of Xcode, you need to do a few more steps to polish off your project setup. You need an Executable and a Target. The following steps give you a properly configured Target:

1. **Control-click the Targets node of the Groups & Files tree.**

2. **Select Add ➪ New Target...**

3. **Select External Target from the Other group, as shown in Figure 3.4. Name your new target GuiApp, and add it to your GuiApp project.**

4. **Double-click your new GuiApp Target.**

   This brings up the Target dialog box titled Target: GuiApp.

5. **Set the Build tool to** /usr/bin/ant, **as shown in Figure 3.10.**

Figure 3.10

Configured GuiApp Target dialog box

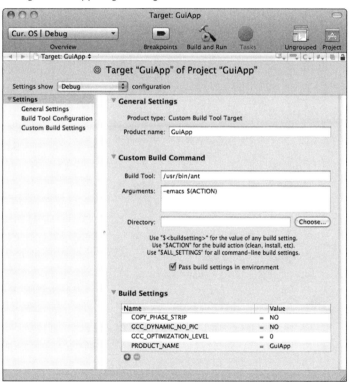

6. **Set the Arguments to** -emacs $(ACTION).

Your Target is ready to use. This allows building and cleaning of the project. Before the next step, select Build ➪ Build. This creates an application bundle for setting up your Executable to open. From inside Xcode, you create the Executable by taking the following steps:

NOTE
Build your GuiApp project before attempting to create your Executable.

1. **Control-click on Executables to see the context menu, and select Add ⇨ New Custom Executable...**

2. **Name your executable** GuiApp**.**

3. **Select the path to your** dist/GuiApp.app **command.**

   That is your newly built application bundle.

4. **Add the new Executable to your project.**

5. **Open your new** java **executable by double-clicking it.**

6. **Select the General tab.**

   The default settings should work, but if not, compare your settings to Figure 3.11.

Figure 3.11

General tab in GuiApp Executable configuration

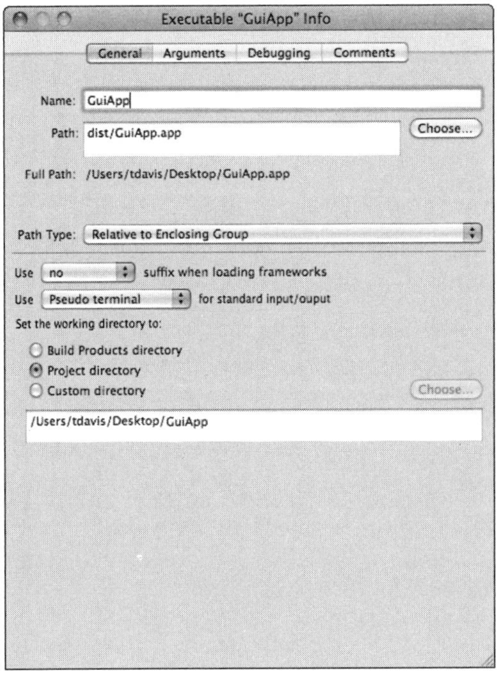

No customization of the Arguments tab or the Debugging tab is necessary. Your project is now set to run from Xcode. Click the Build and Run button at the top of the project window. You also can open your new Swing application from inside of the Finder by double-clicking the application bundle your project's `dist` folder.

NOTE

If the `GuiApp` project fails to build and run properly, double-check the project against the version of the project from the book's Web site. Check the directory names, source code, and package contents for differences that may prevent proper building or running of the project.

Creating Java Applet projects

Applets are a staple of Java development for the Web. Commonly, Applets supply a client tier to multi-tier Web applications. Some Applets provide useful graphing and scientific utilities to researchers. Applets provide simple Web-based distribution of a variety of Java applications.

As with Swing applications and Terminal applications, Applet development is easy to set up in Xcode. As of Xcode 3.2, no built-in template for Applet project creation is available, but with a few pointers, building and running Applets from inside Xcode is relatively painless.

To create a Java Applet application project with Xcode 3.2, follow these instructions:

1. **Select File⇨New Project from the Xcode menu bar.**

2. **Select Empty Project from Other templates, as shown in Figure 3.1.**

3. **Name the new project** BasicApplet**.**

4. **Open your new project folder in the Finder.**

5. **Create** src, resources**, and** lib **folders in your project folder.**

6. **Add the new folders to your project. Select your** BasicApplet **project in the Groups & Files tree, and Control-click Add⇨Existing Files... from the context menu. Then select the new folders and add them. A dialog box comes up asking for how to add the folders. Add the folders using Create Folder References for any added folders, as shown in Figure 3.2.**

7. **Create a file called** build.xml **at the root of your project.**

   This is your Ant build file. With this setup, Xcode uses Ant when building your project.

8. **Fill** build.xml **with the following code.**

   This Ant build is based loosely on the Xcode 3.1 Java Applet template, but it should work with the latest version Xcode.

   ```
   <?xml version="1.0" encoding="UTF-8"?>
   <!-- Based off Xcode 3.1 Applet template build.xml -->
   <project name="BasicApplet"
   ```

```xml
                    default="install"
                    basedir=".">
<property name="jarfile"
        location="jars/${ant.project.name}.jar"/>
<property name="html.file"
        location="resources/basic_applet.html"/>
<fileset id="lib.jars" dir="lib">
   <include name="**/*.jar"/>
</fileset>
<path id="lib.path">
   <fileset refid="lib.jars"/>
</path>
<!-- Call mkdir, javac and jar -->
<target name="compile"
        description="mkdir, javac and jar">
   <mkdir dir="lib"/>
   <mkdir dir="bin"/>
   <mkdir dir="jars"/>

   <javac srcdir="src"
          destdir="bin"
          source="1.6"
          target="1.6"
          includeAntRuntime="no"
          classpathref="lib.path"
          debug="true">
   </javac>
   <jar jarfile="${jarfile}"
        basedir="bin">
           <!-- Merge final JAR -->
        <zipgroupfileset refid="lib.jars"/>
   </jar>
</target>
<!-- Create and fill dist directory -->
<target name="install"
        depends="compile"
        description="Create and fill dist directory">
   <mkdir dir="dist"/>
   <copy toDir="dist">
      <fileset dir="jars">
         <include name="*.jar"/>
      </fileset>
   </copy>
   <copy file="${html.file}" todir="dist"/>
</target>
<!--
```

```
     The project Executable actually opens the
     appletviewer. This target is here for Ant purists.
     -->
<target name="run"
        depends="install"
        description="Run the JApplet in Applet Viewer.">
   <exec dir="dist"
         executable="/usr/bin/appletviewer"
         os="Mac OS X">
      <arg value="basic_applet.html"/>
   </exec>
</target>
<target name="clean"
        description="Delete build directories.">
   <delete dir="bin"/>
   <delete dir="jars"/>
   <delete dir="dist"/>
</target>
</project>
```

9. **Create** BasicApplet.java **in your** src **directory. Create the Java file from within Xcode by selecting** src **and Control-clicking. Select Add ➪ New File... from the context-sensitive menu. Choose Empty File from the Other template catalog, as shown in Figure 3.3, and create it in the** src **directory. If there is an extra reference to the file in the Groups & Files tree, remove the reference.**

10. **Add the following source to the BasicApplet.java file:**

```java
import java.awt.Color;
import java.awt.Graphics;
import javax.swing.JApplet;
/**
 * Xcode Applet project template.
 *
 * @author T. Gene Davis
 */
public class BasicApplet extends JApplet
{
   public void paint(Graphics g)
   {
      g.setColor(Color.GREEN);
      g.drawString(
         "Put your JApplet here",
         10,
         100);
   }
}
```

11. **Add an HTML file called** basic_applet.html **to the** resources **directory. Use the same process as Step 9.**

The source for the HTML file is as follows:

```
<html>
<head>
   <title>Basic Applet</title>
</head>
<body>
   <applet archive="BasicApplet.jar"
           code="BasicApplet"
           width=600
           height=400>
      <a href="http://java.com">Java</a> required.
   </applet>
</body>
</html>
```

Your Applet project is ready to use. If you prefer building from the command line, cd to your project root with the Terminal and type ant to build your project, ant run to run your project, and ant clean to clean your project.

If you prefer to build, run, and clean your project from inside of Xcode, you need to follow a few more steps to polish off your project setup. You need an Executable and a Target. The following steps give you a properly configured Target:

1. **Control-click the Targets node of the Groups & Files tree.**

2. **Select Add ⇨ New Target...**

3. **Select External Target from the Other group, as shown in Figure 3.4. Name your new target** BasicApplet, **and add it to your** BasicApplet **project.**

4. **Double-click your new** BasicApplet **Target.**

This brings up the Target dialog box titled Target: BasicApplet.

5. **Set the Build tool to** /usr/bin/ant.

6. **Set the Arguments to** -emacs $(ACTION), **as shown in Figure 3.12.**

Figure 3.12

BasicApplet Target settings

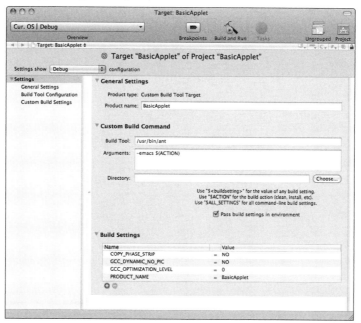

Your Target is ready to use. This allows building and cleaning of the project. Before the next step, click Build ⇨ Build to make sure your Applet JAR builds properly. Next, from inside Xcode, create the Executable by taking the following steps:

1. **From the Executables context menu, select Add ⇨ New Custom Executable...**

2. **Name your executable** appletviewer**.**

3. **Select the path to your** appletviewer **command.**

That is /usr/bin/appletviewer.

4. **Add the new Executable to your project.**

5. **Open your new** appletviewer **executable by double-clicking it.**

6. **Select the General tab, and set Custom directory to your project's** dist **directory as shown in Figure 3.13.**

Figure 3.13

General tab for appletviewer Executable configuration dialog box

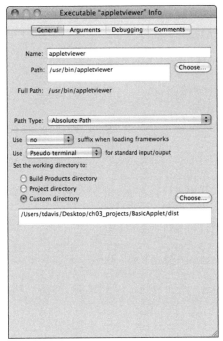

7. Select the Arguments tab, and add the argument 'basic_applet.html' by clicking the "+" button below the Arguments table as shown in Figure 3.14.

Figure 3.14

Arguments tab in appletviewer Executable configuration

8. **Select the Debugging tab. Set the Java Debugger to the default debugger. Use the default setting for this tab as shown in Figure 3.15.**

Figure 3.15

Applet Debugging tab in Executable configuration

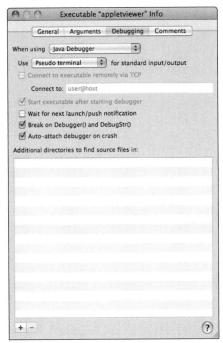

Your project is now set to run from Xcode. Click the Build and Run button at the top of the project window. The Applet Viewer opens your HTML file and displays your Applet based on the HTML file's applet tag.

Using JNI Library projects

Xcode provides one type of Java template: the JNI Library project. The name *JNI Library* is misleading. This project gives developers a fully Cocoa Framework integrated template showing Address Book integration by way of JNI.

Looking at the JNI Library project, you quickly realize it is far more complex than the three example projects that I explained earlier in this chapter. In fact, you may need to read Chapters 4, 7, 8, and 10 before taking full advantage of the JNI Library project. It is not a project for beginners.

CROSS-REF

Chapter 9 contains a thorough explanation of JNI and tips for use of JNI with Objective-C.

However, despite the JNI Library's complexity, you need to start somewhere. In this section, I explain how to set up the JNI Library project. I also give you a brief overview of the parts of the JNI Library.

To create a default JNI Library project follow these instructions:

1. **Select File ⇨ New Project... in Xcode.**

2. **Select the Java project named JNI Library from the New Project dialog box, as shown in Figure 3.16.**

Figure 3.16

New Project dialog box with JNI Library template selected

3. **Click the Choose... button.**

4. **Select a location, and name your new project an appropriate name such as** MyJNIApplication.

5. **Click the Save button.**

The result is a spiffy new JNI Library project. Click the Build and Run icon at the top of the Xcode window to make sure your new project runs properly. You should see an application window that looks something like Figure 3.17.

Figure 3.17

The JNI Library running the Example Java App

The Example Java App that Apple integrated with the JNI Library is a common Model View Controller (MVC). If you followed the instructions in this section for creating the JNI Library project, then your `main()` method is in `com.example.MyJNIApplication`. Your `main()` method sets up the controller. The main controller is the `ApplicationController` class. After constructing the `ApplicationController`, the `main()` method initializes the view and model using `ApplicationController`'s `init()` method.

Your initial view is a typical `JFrame` constructed by the `MainWindowController` class. The object name is, not too surprisingly, `mainWindow`. Nothing too inspiring.

The model is where the cool factor of this project comes to play. The model for the JNI Application project is the local Address Book. Access to the local model is handled in the `NativeAddressBook` class. The `NativeAddressBook` class loads the `AddressBook` library and contains the `native` methods `getMyUID()` and `getNativeAddressBook-Contacts()`.

NOTE
The file extension * . m indicates an Objective-C file. The file extension of * . mm indicates an Objective-C++ file. Objective-C files have header files with an * . h extension, just as their C counterparts do.

The Objective-C implementations of the `getMyUID()` and `getNativeAddressBookCon-tacts()` methods are in the `NativeAddressBook.m` file. Look for the two `JNIEXPORT` method implementations near lines 47 and 68. The implementation names are very long and contain the Java package name, class name, and the method names. The local Cocoa AddressBook.framework is accessed in these two functions.

If you look at the targets for this project, you see three targets: the Compile Java target, the Compile Native target, and the Assemble Application. If you are already familiar with Ant builds, you may wonder why three targets were used instead of a single Ant build. You certainly can arrange the entire build and clean from an Ant script. The three targets in the JNI Library project allow for closer integration with Xcode.

Setting the Xcode Java Compiler

Whether you inherit an older Xcode Java project or create a brand new JNI Library project, you may find that generics, annotations, Java's foreach loops, or even newer Java syntax additions may prevent you from compiling a Java project. Never fear. Here is a quick project fix to get you compiling and running.

To get your project compiling with new Java syntax, make two changes. Change the `build.xml` compile target to use your desired source and target Java version. Also, add your desired `JAVA_HOME` to the project target Build Settings.

Open your project's `build.xml` file. The `build.xml` file specifies the source version and target versions of Java to compile against. Skim down the list of targets until you see the `compile` target. It looks something like this:

```
<target name="compile"
    depends="init"
    description="Compile code">
    <mkdir dir="${bin}"/>
    <javac deprecation="on"
    srcdir="${src}"
    destdir="${bin}"
        source="1.3" target="1.2"
        includeAntRuntime="no"
        classpathref="lib.path"
    debug="${compile.debug}">
    </javac>
</target>
```

Notice that the source and target are set to `1.3` and `1.2` respectively. (If you are using the default `build.xml` found in the Xcode 3.2 JNI Library, they both are set to 1.5.) For a Java 6 project, I change these settings to `1.6`. After the change, the `compile` target looks like this:

```
<target name="compile"
    depends="init"
    description="Compile code">
    <mkdir dir="${bin}"/>
    <javac deprecation="on"
    srcdir="${src}"
    destdir="${bin}"
        source="1.6" target="1.6"
        includeAntRuntime="no"
        classpathref="lib.path"
    debug="${compile.debug}">
    </javac>
</target>
```

The second change is necessary for Java projects created with versions of Xcode before 3.2 or if you intend for Xcode to use a different version of the JVM than your system uses. The change is adding a `JAVA_HOME` property to the Debug and Release versions of your Java project's target. Follow these steps:

1. Open your project's target by double-clicking the target bull's eye on the left side of your project window.

2. Navigate to Custom Build Settings.

   This dialog box displays the properties that pass to Ant when executing tasks such as `compile`.

3. Add a new property by clicking the plus icon below the Build Settings table.

4. Set the name of your new property to `JAVA_HOME`.

5. Set the value of your new property to your desired Java home.

continued

continued

Use a static rather than dynamic value here. If you are unsure of the correct location of your desired Java home, use the `java_home` tool to discover the correct directory. For instance,

```
/usr/libexec/java_home 1.6
```

displays

```
/System/Library/Frameworks/
    JavaVM.framework/
    Versions/1.6.0/Home
```

on OS X 10.5.7. Your Custom Build Settings should now contain `JAVA_HOME` as shown in the figure.

JAVA_HOME in Custom Build Settings

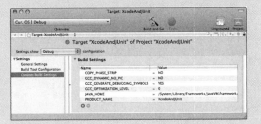

Remember to add the `JAVA_HOME` property to Debug and Release settings for your target!

Highlighting Xcode Features

Sometimes IDEs are forced on us by a project requirement or an employer requirement. Most experienced computer programmers have an IDE preference. Several Java IDEs are available for OS X, but only Xcode completely embraces the OS X experience. The native OS X features and feel of Xcode draw many developers to use Xcode exclusively for their work.

In this section, I explore Xcode's features above and beyond providing Java projects and Java syntax coloring. I introduce the Welcome to Xcode screen, view customization, creating class models, and shortcuts for common tasks. This section introduces the heart of the Xcode experience.

Browsing the welcome screen

The first time you open Xcode, you see the Welcome to Xcode window, as shown in Figure 3.18. The window provides quick links to recent projects, as well as quick links to common tasks performed when launching Xcode.

The link most interesting to new OS X developers is probably "Getting started with Xcode". You may use a different IDE than Xcode for your Java development, but the preconfigured projects in Xcode provide a wonderful starting point for applications that integrate with OS X. I suggest learning the basics of Xcode even if you use Eclipse or NetBeans for most of your Java development.

Clicking the link labeled Getting started with Xcode on the Welcome to Xcode window brings up the Xcode Quick Start window, shown in Figure 3.19. Glancing at this window reveals it is more about general OS X development resources than Xcode.

Figure 3.18

Welcome to Xcode window

Figure 3.19

Xcode Quick Start window

The Welcome to Xcode window provides three quick starts for coding. The link labeled Create a new Xcode project is a shortcut to the File ⇨ New Project... menu item. The right navigation shows a list of recently opened projects and also the last date the project was modified. Also, if you are looking to open a project not in the Recent Projects list, click the Open Other... button on the bottom-left side of the welcome window.

TIP

If you uncheck the box for Show this window when Xcode launches in the Welcome To Xcode window and later want to see the window at launch again, select Help ⇨ Welcome To Xcode from the Xcode menu. This opens the Welcome to Xcode window. From there, you can reselect the box for Show this window when Xcode launches.

Setting up a source code repository

I am not sure whether any standard software development tool has more names and multiple interpretations of its acronyms than source version control does. A Source Configuration Management (SCM), or Software Control Management (SCM), or Software Configuration Management (SCM), also known as a Version Control System (VCS), or simply as a *repository*, provides Time-Machine-like features to software developers. It seems fitting that versioning software has so many versions of its own identity.

SCMs have been around for many years longer than Time Machine and do not require an extra hard drive to set up. Source Code Management focuses on source files, such as `*.java` files and `*.xml` files, though any type of file can be versioned in a source code repository.

Version control is useful for teams of developers or individuals working solo. If you are working alone on a project, you may get to a point in development where you realize you should not have made certain changes to your source code. You wish you could go back to an earlier version that worked better, or you simply don't want to start completely over to get rid of some changes you made.

With version control, this situation is no big deal. You look up your code history, pick a version you committed sometime in the past, and revert to your earlier version of the code that you actually like.

Version Control Systems work locally on your local hard drive or remotely served by another computer. Remote setups work nicely as a backup of your source. If you catch a virus, or your hard drive flakes out on you, you simply install a new hard drive and check out your project to the new hard drive. You are up and running with minimal hassles.

If you are working on multiple computers, say a home computer and an office computer, you commit your code to the version control server before shutting down your computer. When you start working on your alternate computer, check out the code you last committed to the current computer. At this point, you have the newest version and continue developing as though you are using the same computer.

All these benefits apply to team development. Also, if all code for a project is committed regularly to the same repository, integrate frequent automated builds and tests to keep code conflicts from slowing development.

The best part about Version Control Systems is that developers working on the same file (such as a java file) can work completely independent of each other, and when they check in their code, the merging of the code often happens without any verbal or written communication. This is not always the case, but often automatic merges do work smoothly.

Xcode supports three Version Control Systems. They are Subversion (also known as SVN), CVS, and Perforce. Perforce is a commercial SCM with per user licensing, educational licensing, and free open-source licensing. CVS is open-source software, licensed under a GNU General Public License. SVN is also open-source software, using an Apache style license.

TIP

Subversion, CVS, and Perforce all support remote versioning of code. This means that developers at different sites working on different operating systems can all develop against the same code base.

Perforce competes against two widely supported, top-notch, free version control systems. That's some tough competition. Perforce holds its own by producing an excellent product with better features than its free competitors. Perforce excels at branching and merging branches. Automated merging is a strong feature. Perforce also supports several cross-platform development environments.

NOTE

The Perforce Web site is `http://www.perforce.com/`.

CVS is likely the most widely used version control system. It was released in 1990 and is free (as in food and speech.) Age and price have both contributed to its popularity. However, CVS is a powerful and stable piece of technology. All other version control system developers compare their products to CVS.

NOTE

The CVS Web site is `http://www.nongnu.org/cvs/`.

CollabNet Inc created Subversion (SVN) to replace CVS. Early adopters of Subversion felt CVS was buggy and lacked features. The creators of SVN wanted to create a better CVS. Personally, I was an early adopter of SVN because I liked the SVN rename feature.

N O T E
The Subversion Web site is `http://subversion.tigris.org/`.

N O T E
SVN saw rapid initial development. SVN developed so fast that about one year after development began, it was used to version its own code. The pace of development allowed for a large user base in a short time.

As mentioned earlier, Xcode supports SCM but does not come pre-configured with a repository for your projects. After you install the OS X developer tools, you have access to both SVN and CVS. For the following example, I use SVN.

If you are working with a team, you probably already have a repository. Ask for the connection information. For the following example, I use the HSQLDB Java project hosted on `source-forge.com`. This example retrieves the current Java source of HSQLDB and adds it to the newly created `MyDB` project. Follow these steps:

1. **Create a Java Tool project as described earlier in this chapter.**

2. **Name the project** MyDB.

3. **Select SCM ➪ Configure SCM Repositories... from the SCM menu.**

This opens the Xcode Preferences with the SCM tab selected.

4. **Click the plus button under the Repositories list on the left side of the window.**

The Repositories list is empty until you click the Add button.

5. **Select a name for the repository.**

I selected `db_repository`.

6. **Fill in the URL. For HSQLDB, the repository is at** https://hsqldb.svn.sourceforge.net/svnroot/hsqldb.

Entering this URL causes the scheme, host, and path to automatically fill, as shown in Figure 3.20.

7. **Select SCM ➪ Repositories from the Xcode menu.**

The Repositories window opens. The directories found in the repository may take a short while to become visible depending on the speed of the SVN server. Be patient.

8. **Select** src **under the** base/trunk **directory, as shown in Figure 3.21.**

Figure 3.20

Repositories list and window

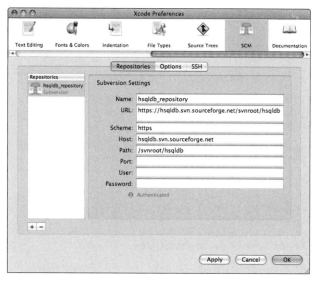

Figure 3.21

Repositories window with base/trunk/src selected

9. Select the Export icon at the top of the Repositories window.

10. Navigate to the MyDB **project directory, and select it; click the Export button, and replace the current** src **directory in the** MyDB **project.**

If you open the `src` folder from Xcode, you see the source for HSQLDB in addition to the original source file created by Xcode's Java Tool template. You cannot commit any changes back to the HSQLDB project. This example only lets you retrieve the code anonymously.

The following example assumes that you have already created a project to import and added a repository for importing into. Adding and configuring a repository are described in the preceding example. To import a new project into a repository, follow these steps:

1. Select SCM ⇨ Repositories from the Xcode menu.

   This opens the Repositories window.

2. Select the repository for your import, and navigate to the directory you will import your project into.

3. Click the Import icon at the top left of the window.

4. Navigate to the Project directory, and click the Import button.

If you have commit permissions to the repository, then your project is added to the repository.

Modifying the View

Like other modern IDEs, Xcode's view is customizable. You can tune it to suit your tastes or your current project. Besides splitting and resizing panes, you can quickly change syntax coloring, code folding, and the toolbar buttons.

Various layout and shortcut options are available from the menu at View ⇨ Layout. Whether these options are available depends on which window or panel within a window has focus. For instance, the Show/Hide Navigation Bar is not available from the Groups tree in the project window. However, it is available from source-code editors in the same window, as shown in Figure 3.22.

Figure 3.22

Status bar, favorites bar, and page control menu

Show Navigation Bar
Hide Status Bar
Show Favorites Bar
Show Page Control

TIP

To remember the behavior of the status bar and favorites bar in Xcode, think of their Safari counterparts the Safari status bar and the Safari bookmarks bar.

View ⇨ Layout ⇨ Hide/Show Navigation Bar toggles the navigation bar. A navigation bar is the thin bar above an editor window, as shown in Figure 3.23. It contains, not too surprisingly, navigation elements. These elements include back and forward arrows, a file history drop-down, class hierarchy navigation, and a drop-down for selecting methods in your class to focus.

Figure 3.23

Editor window with navigation bar

```
import java.util.*;

// This is the default Java Tool template provided by Xcode.

public class MyJavaTool {

    public static void main (String args[]) {
        // insert code here...
        System.out.println("Hello World!");
    }
}
```

View ⇨ Layout ⇨ Hide/Show Status Bar toggles the status bar at the bottom of project and editor windows. If you are familiar with Web programming, you probably are familiar with status bars in Web browsers. The status bar in Xcode is similar. It displays the current activities of Xcode. For instance, if Xcode is building the project, watch the status bar and you see when it completes the build.

Toggle the favorites bar in the Xcode window by selecting View ⇨ Layout ⇨ Hide/Show Favorites Bar. The favorites bar works like the bookmarks bar in Safari. It is a very handy feature, if you have a few configuration files or Java classes that you constantly modify or refer back to.

Creating a favorite on your favorites bar is not hard. Here's how:

1. **Toggle on your favorites bar while the Project window is in focus by selecting View ⇨ Layout ⇨ Show Favorites Bar from the menu.**

2. **Browse to a configuration file or source-code file in the Groups & Files tree.**

3. **Drag the file to the bar.**

Xcode's project window can display the source-code editor, or double-clicking a Java file opens a detached source-code editor. If you prefer editing in a detached window instead of the Xcode project window, you can reduce the project window to display just the Group & Files tree.

1. **Toggle on the Page Control buttons while the Project window is in focus by selecting View ⇨ Layout ⇨ Show Page Control from the menu.**

2. **Click the Morph button in the Page Control at the top of Xcode's project window.**

3. **Optionally, hide the Page Control by selecting View ⇨ Layout ⇨ Hide Page Control from the menu.**

Now you see the Groups & Files tree and optionally the favorites bar and your customized toolbar, as shown in Figure 3.24.

Figure 3.24

Project window morphed via page control

TIP

When using two monitors, reserve one for tools and the primary monitor for coding. To do this, morph the Project window so that only the toolbars and Group & Files tree are visible, and then place the resulting window on a second monitor. Then open your source editor by double-clicking the file in the morphed Projects window, and maximize the source editor on your primary monitor.

The display and formatting of source in editor windows is configurable, too. Selecting View⇨Text reveals a menu, as shown in Figure 3.25, for changing tab settings, line wrapping, line endings, file encodings, showing control characters, and showing spaces.

Figure 3.25

View⇨Text menu

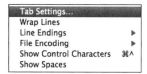

TIP

If the text in a source file looks wrong because of an extra line between every line of code or certain characters don't appear to display properly until retyped, try messing around with the settings in View⇨Text⇨Line Endings and View⇨Text⇨File Encoding. Changing these setting may fix the editor window's view of the source.

Showing control characters and spaces are exceptionally useful for debugging Java property and configuration files. Sometimes, unseen control characters or extra spaces in a configuration files are a real hassle to track down. Toggling Show Control Characters and Show Spaces reduces debug time in these cases. The result is similar to Figure 3.26.

Figure 3.26

Show/hide control character and show/hide spaces

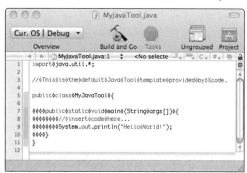

Customizing the Xcode Project window's toolbar is another great view change that makes development with Xcode pleasant. To quickly get to the Customize Toolbar dialog box, follow these steps:

1. **Control-click to the left of the Build and Run icon or to the right of the Info icon on the Project window's toolbar.**

   In other words, Control-click the toolbar, but not on an icon it contains.

2. **Select the Customize Toolbar menu item in the context menu that pops up.**

3. **Drag icons to the toolbar from the Customize Toolbar dialog box.**

The Customize Toolbar dialog box, shown in Figure 3.27, and the toolbar are intuitive to use. Remove icons the same way you remove them from the Dock. Just drag them off, and watch for the satisfying puff of smoke. The icons and text available for adding to the toolbar include drop-down menus, spaces, and a default toolbar to replace your custom setup. Drag them on to the Project window's toolbar as desired. Rearrange the icons on the toolbar by dragging them to their new positions.

Figure 3.27

Customize toolbar dialog box

Watching tasks with the Activity window

The status bar at the bottom of the Xcode Project window is great for seeing the state of builds in Xcode. The status bar does not detail all of Xcode's activities, though. For instance, when you create a new project, Xcode proceeds to index it. Indexing allows quick refactoring of the code.

The indexing activities of Xcode are not mentioned on the status bar. To see the state of indexing, you need to open the Activity window, shown in Figure 3.28.

To open Activity Viewer, select Window ⇨ Activity from the menu. Activity is an unimposing window that sits empty most of the time. It is handy to leave open on a second monitor or an unused corner of your main monitor.

Figure 3.28

Project indexer in the Activity window

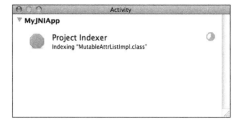

Architecting with Xcode

Apple includes class modeling tools in Xcode. Class models help software designers and architects to visualize code. Class models turn code into pictures. You quickly understand relationships between classes with a well-organized model.

You can approach creating class models with Xcode in two ways. One is Quick Model, and the other is Project Class Model. The end result is the same.

To create a Quick Model, follow these steps:

1. **Expand your** src **(or** Source/java**) folder in the Groups & Files tree.**

2. **Select the Java class(es) you desire to model.**

⌘-click to select individual files, or select the src folder if you want to model the entire project source.

3. **Select Design ⇨ Class Model ⇨ Quick Model from the Xcode menu.**

The result should be a model that looks something like Figure 3.29. You can save a Quick Model as a permanent part of your project at any time by selecting File ⇨ Save from the Xcode menu bar.

NOTE

The class model figures in this section are based on the source for HSQLDB located at `http://hsqldb.org/`. HSQLDB is release under a BSD style license.

Figure 3.29

Quick Model of HSQLDB

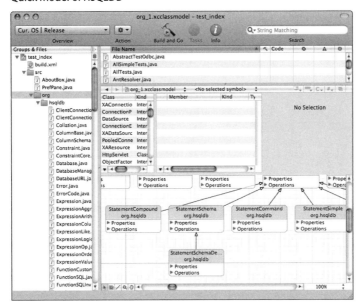

NOTE

Both Quick Models and Project Models save as `*.xcclassmodel` files.

TIP

Save and commit your `*.xcclassmodel` files to your version control system to give other developers a quick understanding of how your code is put together.

A detail-oriented alternative to Quick Model is the Project Model approach. Project Models create a model file as part of your chosen project. Project Models also provide a nice selection list of classes to add to your model.

To create a Project Model, follow these steps:

1. **Select File ⇨ New File ... from the Xcode menu bar.**

In some versions of Xcode, you must open the New File dialog box from a Group & Files folder's context-sensitive menu. The contents of the New File dialog box may vary based on how it is opened.

2. Select Class Model from the Other category of file template types, as shown in Figure 3.30.

Figure 3.30

Selecting class model

3. Click next.

4. Choose a model name, location, and project to add your model into, as shown in Figure 3.31.

5. Click the Next button.

6. Add *.java files to your initial Class Model. Browse the given project tree. Select *.java **files, and click the Add button, as shown in Figure 3.32.**

Figure 3.31

New Class Model File dialog box

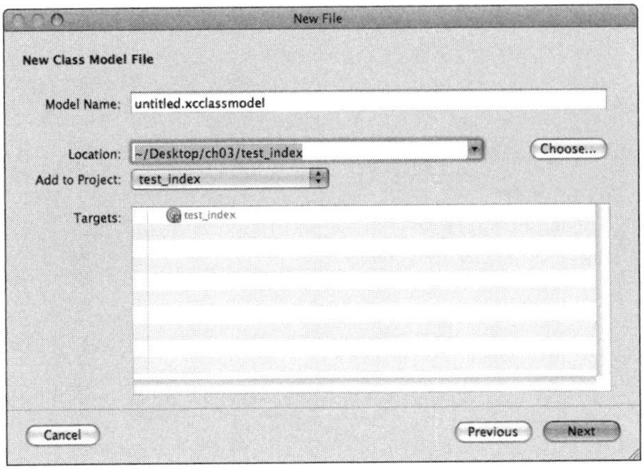

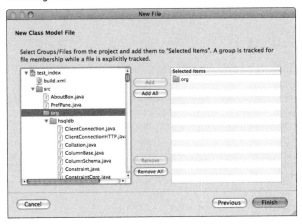

Figure 3.32

Selecting classes for a new class model

7. Click the Finish button.

You now have a customized class model in your project directory. You see it in the Group & Files section of your Xcode Project window.

Project Models are saved to a file during creation. Quick Models are not saved to a file unless you explicitly chose to save them from the File ➪ Save menu item. Use Quick Models when you do not want to save your model but just want to understand an aspect of your code.

CAUTION

Models created with Xcode are actually packages. Packages are folders that behave like a single file. For all practical purposes, they are a file. However, if you try e-mailing the package or placing it in on a Web site, zipping it first. Otherwise, you may not see your class model shared the way you intend.

Changing Xcode preferences

I discuss SCMs in Xcode earlier in this chapter. During the SCM discussion, I introduced the Xcode Preferences window. Now let's explore the Xcode Preferences window in more depth.

To open the Xcode Preferences, select Xcode ➪ Preferences... from the Xcode menu bar. The Xcode Preferences window behaves like a tabbed pane. Instead of the tabs, the top portion of the windows has icons in a scroll pane. Select the icon corresponding to the preference panel you want to modify.

TIP

To include a preferences window like Xcode does in your own Java applications, start from the Java JNI Library template I discussed earlier in this chapter. The `ApplicationController` class is responsible for handling Preference `MenuItem` events. See the `showPreferences()` method in `ApplicationController`. It lacks an actual window when set up from the template, but that is just a matter of adding code to the `showPreferences()` method.

Key bindings in Xcode are all customizable. Select the Key Bindings icon in the Xcode Preferences to see the Menu Key Bindings and Text Key Bindings options, as shown in Figure 3.33. Xcode comes with four sets of predefined key bindings available from the Key Bindings Sets drop-down list. The predefined sets of key bindings are Xcode Default, BBEdit Compatible, Metrowerks Compatible, and MPW Compatible.

BBEdit, Metrowerks, and MPW are well known to longtime developers of OS X applications. If none of these presets are of interest to you, create a new key binding set and customize it to your heart's content.

NOTE

You cannot modify any of the four initial key sets provided by Xcode. Instead, duplicate a desired key set by selecting it and clicking the duplicate button. Then make your changes to the duplicate key set.

Figure 3.33

Key Bindings preferences

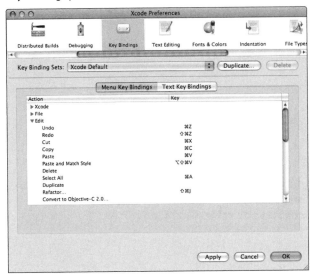

Here is an example of creating a custom key binding set with Control+C set to copy instead of ⌘+C. No, this is not a very Mac-like key binding, but if it makes your OS X experience more pleasant, so be it. Follow these steps:

1. **Open the Xcode Preferences window by selecting Xcode ⇨ Preferences....**

2. **Select the Key Bindings icon To open the Key Bindings panel.**

3. **Click the Duplicate button to create a duplicate of the current key binding set.**

4. **Name your new set** My Key Bindings, **as shown in Figure 3.34.**

Figure 3.34

Naming a new key binding set

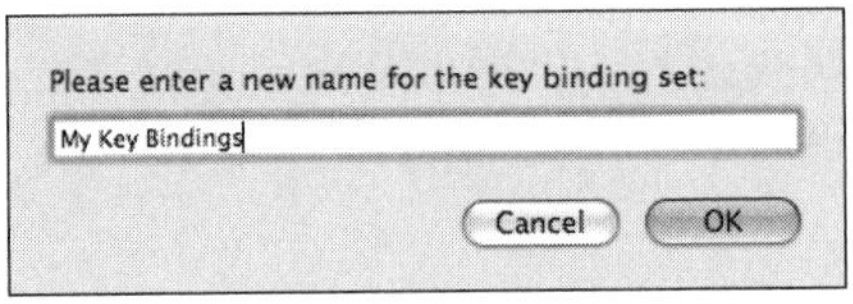

5. **Double-click the key column next to the Copy Action in the Menu Key Bindings tab.**

This selects the old key binding, if any exists.

6. **Press Control+c.**

You have set your new key binding for the Copy command.

7. **Click the OK button to apply the changes and close the Xcode Preferences window.**

Now you can copy text in the Xcode's editor window using Control+c. Somewhere an Apple developer is rolling over in his grave.

You may revert to the original key bindings by opening the Key Bindings preference panel and selecting Xcode Default from the Key Binding Sets drop-down list. Apply the changes by clicking the OK button.

TIP

Remove custom Key Binding Sets by selecting the set from the Key Binding Sets drop-down list and clicking the Delete button. You can delete only custom Key Binding Sets. The Delete button deactivates when you select one of the four default Key Binding Sets

Click the Text Editing icon of the Xcode Preferences window to see options for display, editing, and saving. If you want to toggle line numbers, this is your panel. I can't live without line numbers, so this is my favorite preference.

The Text Editing panel, shown in Figure 3.35, has options for setting the new line character(s) and the default file encoding. Between these settings you can probably match any file encoding you ever run into. You also have the option of preserving or changing the new line character for existing files you open.

Figure 3.35

Text Editing preferences

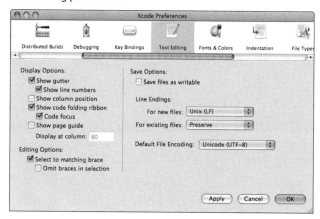

The Indentation preference panel, shown in Figure 3.36, is available by clicking the icon of the same name. The Indentation preferences include tab settings, line wrap settings, and syntax-aware indenting preferences. Setting tabs to spaces or literal tabs is available from this pane. Also, you can set lines to wrap with a set indent from this pane.

Figure 3.36

Indentation preferences

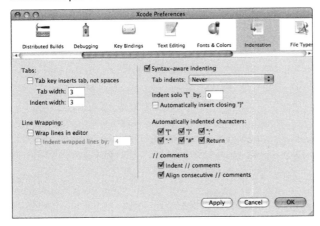

You may not find File Type preferences, shown in Figure 3.37, immediately obvious. This preference pane lists all the file extensions that Xcode is aware of with the accompanying application with which Xcode opens the file type. If you want to open a certain file extension with a custom application instead of editing it from within Xcode, make that change here.

Figure 3.37

File Type preferences

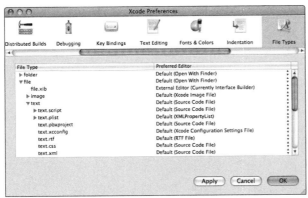

Inserting Java Code using macros

Xcode comes with several built-in macros and shortcuts for entering common Java code. In the Xcode menu, select Edit ➪ Insert Text Macro ➪ Java, as shown in Figure 3.38, to see five basic macros. They include Catch Block, Finally Block, Println() Call, Synchronized Block, and Try / Catch Block. If you program Java, you already know what these look like.

Figure 3.38

Java macros menu

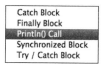

Do not limit yourself to the Java text macros. Java is a C-based language. Several of the C macros, shown in Figure 3.39, also conform to Java syntax. For instance, selecting Edit ➪ Insert Text Macro ➪ C ➪ If Block, gives you a perfectly valid Java `if` block.

Figure 3.39

C macros menu

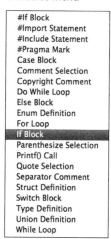

Now, you may wonder what good it does you to have to navigate through multiple menus when you could just type the code quicker. Remember my description of key binding sets earlier in this chapter? You guessed it. All these macros are available in the Xcode Preferences Key Bindings preferences panel, as shown in Figure 3.40. Make them accessible at your fingertips with a convenient key binding of your choosing.

Figure 3.40

Key bindings for macros in preferences pane

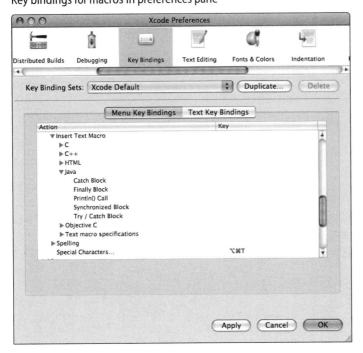

TIP

When typing a class name or object name followed by a period, use Control+. (period) to find known method or attribute completions of the code you are typing. Cycle through known completions by repeatedly typing Control+. (period).

TIP

Type ⌘+/ (slash) to quickly comment or uncomment selected code.

Using Organizer

Most IDEs allow developers to manage multiple projects. Xcode goes a step beyond managing multiple projects. Xcode provides the Organizer.

With Organizer, add projects, folders, and files to the convenient Projects & Source tree. In Organizer, you can create new Java templates based on the Xcode Java Templates. You can build, clean, and run any projects managed by Xcode in Organizer. Also, the toolbar at the top of the Organizer window is customizable in the same way as the Project window.

TIP

Control-click the Organizer toolbar to bring up the associated context menu. Select Customize Toolbar... to view the Customize Toolbar dialog box for Organizer.

Managing projects

Open the Organizer window from the Xcode menu by selecting Window ⇨ Organizer. The first time you open Organizer, it is blank, as shown in Figure 3.41. Not even your current project is contained by Organizer. Any changes you make to the Projects & Sources list appear when Organizer is opened later.

Figure 3.41

Empty Organizer view

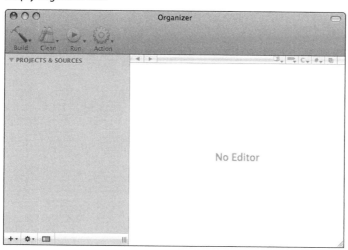

Adding projects, templates, and files to the Projects & Sources list is effortless. This example shows you how to add a project to Organizer:

1. **Open the Organizer window by selecting Window ⇨ Organizer in Xcode.**

You do not need to have an Xcode project open in order to open Organizer.

2. **Select the plus icon at the bottom left of the Organizer window, as shown in Figure 3.42.**

Selecting the plus icon opens a drop-down list containing New File, New Folder, New From Template, and Add Existing Folder....

Figure 3.42

Drop-down list at bottom left of Organizer

3. **Select Add Existing Folder.... to bring up a standard file dialog box.**

4. **Choose a project folder, and click the Open button.**

The selected project becomes available in Organizer.

Running projects

With Organizer, you not only have access to the source files for multiple projects, but you also can run any of the projects you add to Organizer. Select the root folder of the project you want to execute, and click the Run button on Organizer's toolbar.

If you select a project to run in Organizer and click Run, make sure you have already built the project first. You may be in the habit of using the Build and Run button from in the Project window. The Organizer does not have a Build and Run button. Nothing too terrible happens if you have not built your project before you click Run. Typically, you get an Xcode Console window with an error saying "Task not found at path."

Creating Java projects from Organizer templates

Organizer has another trick up its sleeve. You can create Java projects with Organizer. The projects that Organizer creates are all Ant-based projects, but from inside Organizer you can build, run, and clean those Ant projects just as you do normal Xcode projects in the Xcode project window.

Earlier in this chapter I explained the creation of Java projects in Xcode. Most of those examples involved creating a empty Xcode project and adapting the empty project to work with an Ant-based Java project. If you choose, you can do the same for each of these Organizer Java project templates.

Organizer comes with five built-in Java project templates. The Java project templates, shown in Figure 3.43, are:

- Java Applet
- Java Application
- Java Signed Applet
- Java Tool
- Java Web Start Application

Figure 3.43

Organizer Java project template choices

Java Applet
Java Application
Java Signed Applet
Java Tool
Java Web Start Application

Create the Java project of your choice in Organizer by following these steps:

1. **Select the "+" menu at the bottom-left corner of the Organizer window.**

2. **Select New From Template, as shown in Figure 3.44.**

Figure 3.44

New From Template menu.

New File
New Folder
New From Template   ▶
Add Existing Folder...

3. **Select Java Templates.** This is the only menu to choose. You can't miss it.

4. **Select a Java template, such as Java Application.**

5. **Choose a name and location for your new Ant-based Java project, as shown in Figure 3.45.**

After you create your new Java project, it appears in the Organizer window. You can now run, build, and clean your application from the Organizer window.

TIP

The Java projects created from the Organizer templates are standard Ant-based projects. This means that other IDEs besides Xcode can use these projects, too.

Figure 3.45

Creating a new folder from the "Java Application" template in Organizer

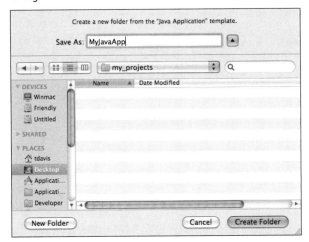

CROSS-REF

I explain Ant projects in depth in Chapter 4.

Summary

In this chapter, I described pure Java template projects and the hybrid JNI Library project. Creation of pure Java application, Applet, and command-line applications from scratch is simple and clearly documented with sample projects on this book's Web site. The JNI Library project is a great place to start for more advanced users who need full OS X native framework support.

I also discuss preferences, shortcuts, and view customizations available in Xcode. Xcode includes support for three common version control systems. Xcode also contains built-in class diagramming tools for program architecting and design.

Finally, I discuss managing and running projects with Organizer. With Organizer, you manage multiple projects and source files. Organizer also allows you to build and run the projects you manage with it.

Building Basic Projects

Writing code is important, but any code you write is irrelevant until it is built. During initial research phases of projects, you may have only five or ten classes to worry about building. Early on, you may even build one class at a time. In the beginning, you easily manage your build process.

As your project progresses, you accumulate more classes and libraries. You start giving your manager or testers packaged builds. You integrate your code with that of other developers. In short, your build becomes complex. With time, the building and packaging of your code can take an hour or even several hours. Spending more time building and packaging code rather than writing it becomes a reality.

You do not want to spend hours of your day building and packaging code for your manager or testers. You are busy and don't have time for that. The more automation you put into your build process, the less time you spend away from your code. This chapter explores automating Java builds on OS X so you can focus on coding.

Building Xcode Projects

Automated Java builds on OS X fall into three categories: IDE project builds, build tool scripts, and shell scripts. Xcode is an excellent IDE, freely available to OS X developers. You can use Xcode's default JNI Library template to set up your initial Java project build. Default builds are used mostly in simple projects that do not involve complex packaging for delivery to your manager, testers, or clients.

Ant is a common build utility for OS X. Using Ant provides quick builds and delivery of code to your end user. Xcode uses Ant in building Java projects. This means that any Ant builds you write may also integrate into your Xcode project for use with just a click of a button in the Xcode IDE.

Shell scripts provide a third method for automating your build. OS X contains all the common UNIX tools necessary for creating complex scripted builds. Integrating your shell scripts into an existing Ant or Xcode project is simple and provides more options for your build process.

In This Chapter

Building Java projects with Xcode

Understanding Ant and build.xml files

Creating shell scripts for building Java projects

You also may use shell scripts and Ant builds standalone or integrated into a cron job that results in a nightly or weekly build. Shell scripts and Ant projects both integrate with other common Java IDEs besides Xcode. In this section, however, I focus on building, running, and debugging projects from Xcode. Later in this chapter, I give much more detail on scripting builds.

Understanding the Xcode Build Process

To fully master Xcode builds on OS X, you need to understand the Xcode build cycle, customizing builds with Ant, and getting down and dirty with shell scripting. With these three skills, you will not encounter a Java build that cannot be fully automated.

In this section, I explain basic builds with Xcode. I also discuss Xcode's tools for running and debugging projects. Testing builds by running and debugging is essential to successful development cycles.

Begin with a simple project. Create a new Xcode JNI Library project with the assistant. For this project, follow these steps:

1. **Click the File menu.**

2. **Select New Project ...**

3. **Browse the Framework & Library templates.**

4. **Choose the JNI Library.**

5. **Name your project MyApp.**

CROSS-REF

The JNI project that the Xcode assistant can create is detailed in Chapter 3. Chapter 3 also details creation of Java Swing applications, JApplets, and Java Console applications with Xcode.

Look at the Groups & Files tree, as shown in Figure 4.1, on the left of your main Xcode window. Folders and files are red, especially in the Products folder. Red indicates empty or non-existent. If you look in all your project folders, you will find files, except in the folders with red names.

Click the Build and Run button in the Xcode window to see what the template gives you. After clicking Build and Run, notice the red named files in the Products folder turn black as they are created.

As Figure 4.2 shows, you now see a fully functional, though limited, Java JNI and Swing application execute. Build and Run is the quickest way to run your applications or find newly coded bugs. The keyboard shortcut is ⌘+Return for Build and Run.

Figure 4.1

Initial Xcode project window

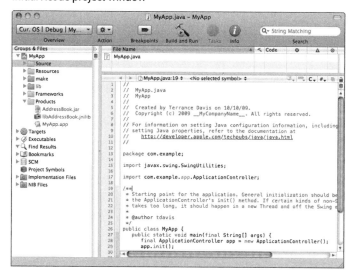

Figure 4.2

Swing Address Book application run from default JNI template

In the Groups & Files table again, look for the red circles icon that looks like a bull's eye. Next to it is the name Targets. Expand Targets, and you will see the MyApp target, named after your project. Double-click the MyApp target, and the Target window opens, as shown in Figure 4.3.

Click the General tab in the MyApp target window. Notice that it contains three direct dependencies: Compile Java, Compile Native, and Assemble Application. These three dependencies are listed as targets in the Target folder of the Groups & Files tree. Each of these targets does what its name implies. Compile Java and Compile Native take care of the Java and Objective-C compilation for your JNI application. Assemble Application integrates the rest of the application, but it does not assemble the application bundle.

Figure 4.3

Target window for MyApp target

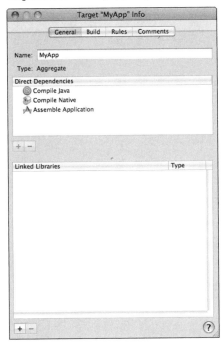

Close the MyApp target, and open the Compile Java target, as shown in Figure 4.4. This Target window details how the Java portion of your application builds. Normally, you do not want to change any of these settings, but you need to understand the basics in case you do need to customize your build.

Notice that under the Custom Build Command, the build tool selected is /usr/bin/ant. Ant is used to build all the Java projects in Xcode. If you chose to use Maven or shell scripts instead of Ant, this is where you make that change.

TIP

Look in your project's `build.xml` file. It is in the `make` folder. The Ant targets you find include `clean` and `compile`. These are the bare minimum targets to implement in a custom build script if you integrate a custom Ant build into Xcode.

The instructions for the actual Ant build are found in the `build.xml` file. Find this file under your project's `make` folder. Click the `build.xml` file to see its source. You may recognize the source as XML. If you want to customize what your Java target results are, make customizations in the `build.xml` file. I discuss how to understand and create build files in great detail later in this chapter. All that XML in the build file will make sense soon.

Figure 4.4

Target window for Compile Java target

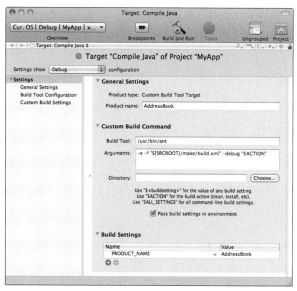

So far I have shown the build from inside the Project window. Another useful view of the build is the Build Results window. To get to the Build Results window, select Build Results under the Build menu. The Build Results window opens, as shown in Figure 4.5, with an overview of the build in the top half of the window.

TIP

The default organization of Xcode behaves much like a Web browser without tabs. Clicking icons and buttons often opens new windows. If you lose track of your main project window, press zero while holding down the ⌘ key. Your main project window's view returns to the front.

Click Build at the top of the Build window. You see an overview of the steps used to build your project. The steps are presented as a collapsible tree. The root nodes are the targets I just described. These expand to give detailed transcripts of your build. The transcripts and the overview are great resources for keeping track of what each of your targets is actually doing during a build. All this information is useful when you need to find obscure bugs during a bad build.

Each successful step of the build is marked with a green check mark in the overview. If the build fails, there are red exclamation points next to the steps that failed to complete.

Figure 4.5

Build Results window

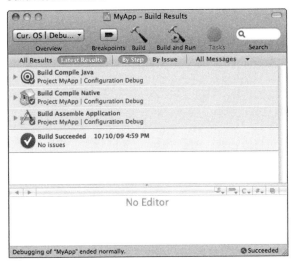

Deliberately introduce a broken line of code into your `MyApp.java` file by removing a semi-colon. Now, build your application by clicking the Build tool at the top of the Build Results window. The build fails with a satisfying red exclamation point next to the node "Run external build tool." Expand that node, and scroll down to see the actual error. In my case, it was this:

```
/Users/tdavis/Desktop/MyApp/src/java/com/example/
app/Actions.java:16: ';' expected
import javax.swing.*
```

Running Xcode projects

As you know, after you have your project building, you are ready to run. If there are any obvious flaws in your program, running the code is the first method of finding them. Running in Xcode is similar to other IDEs.

At this point you have built your application, which is called MyApp. Building your application created a double-clickable Mac OS X application to run your Java code. You don't need to search the file system for the double-clickable application, though. There is an easier approach to quickly jump into the project folders.

To see your application in a Finder window:

1. **Navigate to the** Products **folder in the Groups & Files tree on the left in your Project window.**

2. **Open the** Products **folder to reveal the** MyApp.app **application.**

3. **Control-click** MyApp.app**, or right-click if you have a two button mouse.**

A context menu opens, as shown in Figure 4.6.

4. **Select Reveal in Finder from the context menu.**

Figure 4.6

Selecting Reveal in Finder
from the MyApp.app
context menu

You should now have a Finder window open showing your fully functional OS X Java application. Having access to the build is nice, but it's not as useful as running and debugging inside of
your IDE. There are several different ways to run your application from inside Xcode.

Returning to the project window, take a look at the menu items under the Run menu shown in
Figure 4.7. Running with and without debugging are the two obvious choices. However, do not
miss the Run with Performance Tool submenu. Xcode is integrated with several advanced performance tools. For instance, select CPU Sampler from the Run with Performance Tool submenu, and you receive real-time feedback about what your JNI application is doing with your
computer.

Optimize the application you run against quickly for release or for debugging. Locate the Build
Configuration drop-down menu at the top of either the project window or the top of the Build
Results window. Use this menu to select your Active Configuration. Your two default choices are
Debug and Release.

Figure 4.7

Run menu contains several options for executing your application.

As you may guess, if Debug is selected, your `MyApp.app` application builds with more debug information embedded. While the resulting application may be suitable for limited testing by select users, typically you don't want a debug build to get out to your general user base. The Release selection optimizes your application and removes much of the debugging information from the application, speeding up your application in the process. Ship Release builds, and test with Debug builds. It can't get much easier than that.

Debugging Xcode projects

After you have found the easily spotted problems in your program by running it, it is time to examine the workings of the code in detail. Like most modern IDEs, Xcode contains great support for debugging. Using the debugger, you can examine any section of code at runtime to determine if the actual behavior matches the desired behavior of your program.

Debugging in Xcode is not too different from other IDEs common in the Java world. You start with a breakpoint and create a breakpoint by clicking to the left of code, the same way you would in other IDEs such as Eclipse. As shown in Figure 4.8, you see an arrow pointing to the code that pauses the Debugger. For this discussion, I have placed my breakpoint at the left side of the `new ApplicationController()` constructor in the main method of `MyApp.java`.

NOTE

Clicking a breakpoint deactivates the breakpoint but does not remove it. To remove a breakpoint, right-click (or Control-click) the breakpoint and select Remove Breakpoint.

TIP

By default, Xcode has line numbers turned off. To turn line numbers on, select Xcode ⇨ Preferences…, and navigate to the Text Editing preferences. The line numbers checkbox is on the left side of the Text Editing preference panel.

Figure 4.8

Breakpoint to the left of the `MyApp` constructor in `MyApp.java`

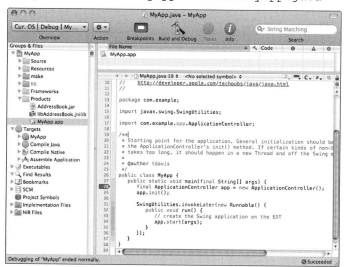

Open the Debugger window by clicking Debugger in the Run menu. If you click Build and Debug at this point, you will be disappointed. Your breakpoint is ignored. You must first select the Java Debugger for your executable, as shown in Figure 4.9.

Figure 4.9

Debugger window with Activate button

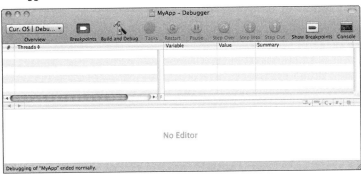

1. **Navigate to your Xcode project window.**

2. **Double-click the MyApp executable.**

3. **Select the Debugging tab in the Executable configuration.**

4. **Select Java Debugger from the "When using" drop-down list.**

Now you are ready to debug. Click Build and Debug in the Debugger window. Your application stops at your breakpoint.

TIP
Click the Breakpoints button at the top of the Debugger window to open the Breakpoints window. The Breakpoints window contains information about specific breakpoints you have selected.

TIP
For direct access to the Java Debugger, click the Console button at the top right of the Debugger window.

Writing Ant Build Files

In the realm of Java programming Ant and Maven are the two most common cross-platform build tools. Ant is installed along with Xcode and the other OS X developer tools. Java builds in Xcode use Ant. Because of Ant's availability and integration into Xcode, I focus on Ant builds in this section instead of other build tools such as Maven.

In this section, I discuss enough about Ant to enable you to put together highly complex and full-featured professional quality builds. After reading this section, you will be able to create Ant builds that satisfy your employer's need to automate builds and to deploy your code.

This section contains a review of XML. I discuss Ant projects, targets, properties, attributes, and values. I discuss the depends attribute and the creation of multi-targeted builds. This section also covers numerous task elements needed for building, cleaning, and deploying projects. Also, I cover the `exec` task for integrating Ant with shell scripts and other tools.

The contents of this section do not cover all advanced Ant topics. This section does not cover conditionals, error handling, interactive user input, and creating custom Ant modules. These topics were left out due to space considerations and because many users have no desire to explore these topics.

NOTE
Maven can use Ant tasks for added flexibility, so learning Ant is a good first step to learning Maven also.

Understanding Ant

Ant is a tool for compiling, cleaning, and deploying Java builds. Customizing Java builds in Xcode requires a firm grasp of Ant. Ant builds created for OS X usually work on other operating systems that support Java. This section introduces Ant.

Ant was created by James Duncan Davidson. Ant stands for Another Neat Tool. Think of actual ants and how they do simple repetitive tasks over and over to produce complex results. That was the inspiration for Ant. Ant is excellent at automating repetitive tasks that waste your time as a developer.

When you create a bunch of code, many steps must happen before your customers use the code. You first must compile the classes. You need to create JARs, WARs, or EARs. You must copy images, XML, and property files to your deployment folder or folders. Often, you need to run JUnit to test the finished version of the application before customers see it. You may even have to copy the results to a remote server for distribution.

NOTE
JARs, WARs, and EARs are all essentially zip files. JARs package Java libraries and resources for any type of Java application. WARs and EARs provide packaging for Web-based applications.

If you have ever had to deploy or partially deploy a program over and over and over while trying to debug one line of code, you know that you can spend far more time with the list of tasks that need to happen during compiling and deploying than you actually do coding. Worse yet, you may find out later that your bug was really just an error in your deployment process, caused by repeating the same brainless tasks over and over at 2 A.M.

Wouldn't it be nice to have an intern or junior coder take care of these brainless tasks that are drawing your attention away from solving bugs and writing code? Wouldn't it be nice to make a trip to the vending machines while the tasks unrelated to fixing code were done for you?

That is what Ant is all about. Consider Ant your friendly helper. Using Ant, you can automate builds, copying resources, run tests, and deploy finished code. You set it up once and literally type three letters...ant. That's all.

In the Java community, Ant has gained lots of popularity, which is not surprising. Ant frees up time for programmers so they can attend to more important tasks, such as chatting at the water cooler. Ant is used mainly to script build processes. Ant is a Java application, so it is available on any system with Java. Of course, that includes OS X.

NOTE

Ant is an Apache project. The project home is at `http://ant.apache.org`.

NOTE

Ant is a build tool. If you are more interested in a full project management tool, look into Ant combined with Ivy, or Maven standalone. Ivy and Maven are popular Java-based project management tools maintained by the Apache Software Foundation. Maven is similar in functionality to Ant plus Ivy.

I do not discuss Maven or Ivy in this book, but you may want to explore their features on the Web. The project home for Ivy is at `http://ant.apache.org/ivy`. The project home for Maven is at `http://maven.apache.org`.

As mentioned earlier, Xcode uses Ant to build Java applications, so an understanding of Ant opens up the full power of Xcode's build process to the developer. Every Java project created from an Xcode template comes with an Ant build.xml file that you can open and modify. Also, double-clicking your Java target in the project window of Xcode opens the Target window with configuration information for how Ant is set up in the project.

CROSS-REF

In Chapter 3, I give three examples of integrating custom Ant builds with new Java projects.

Check to see if you have Ant on your system. Open a Terminal window. Type `ant -version`. If the result is a line telling the version and compile date of the version on your system, you have Ant. Ant should be installed, if you have Xcode on you computer. You can check for new versions of Ant at the Apache Ant project home (`http://ant.apache.org`). However, Apple does a great job of keeping the Xcode tools up to date with recent versions of Ant, so you won't need to make checking for new versions of Ant a priority.

Creating a basic Ant build file

In this section, I discuss the basics of Ant build files. The Ant tool parses a build file to determine how to proceed with building, cleaning, or deploying code. Understanding build files is the first step to understanding how to use Ant.

The default build file for Ant is named `build.xml` and is placed in the directory that the Ant command is issued. The default build file is `build.xml`, but don't feel constrained by this. You can change the file that is executed by specifying the `-buildfile` option at the command line. With your build file named `my_project.xml`, your command line looks like this:

```
ant -buildfile my_project.xml
```

TIP

The arguments `-f` and `-file` have the same function as `-buildfile`. Using the command ant `-f my_project.xml` causes Ant to execute using `my_project.xml` instead of `build.xml`.

Build files for Ant are XML files. XML consists of a prolog, elements, attributes, comments, and text. Nest elements between other elements in a similar fashion to HTML to form more complex XML documents.

NOTE

XML is a standard for defining markup languages. The XML standard defines tag construction and how to define tag elements and attributes. The tags used in different implementations of XML differ, but the way tags are defined, constructed, and interoperate remains the same from version to version.

Looking at an Xcode generated `build.xml` file, you will note that the first line is as follows:

```
<?xml version="1.0" encoding="UTF-8"?>
```

This is the prologue. Every XML file should start with a prologue similar to it. Notice, it contains the version of XML used and the encoding. The encoding in this case is UTF-8, representing the character set used. You don't need to memorize this prologue; you can just write it once and copy and paste it everywhere else you use it. It isn't likely to change.

XML element tags follow the prologue. Figure 4.10 shows the relationship among elements in Ant. Elements take two forms: paired opening and closing tags such as `<project></project>` or single tags such as `<property />`. Look for the placement of the forward slash to determine paired or single XML tags. In paired tags, the first tag doesn't have a forward slash, but the second tag starts with a forward slash. The first tag in a paired element is called the opening tag. The second tag in a paired element is called the closing tag. In single tags, the tag ends with a forward slash.

Figure 4.10

Relationship among projects, targets, properties, tasks, attributes, and values

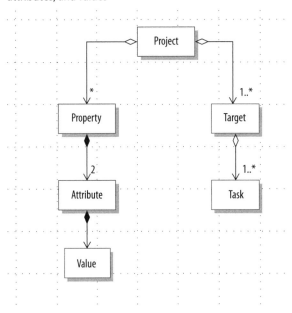

Elements may be nested between opening and closing tags. The outer elements are called parents and the inner elements are called children. Single element tags may not hold other elements. In the case of paired tags, the opening and closing tags must both be enclosed by the same element tags. For instance, the following is valid:

```
<target>
   <echo>
   </echo>
</target>
```

However, the following is NOT valid XML, because the enclosed echo element does not have a closing tag nested between the opening and closing target elements:

```
<target>
   <echo>
</target>
   </echo>
```

Also, the following is NOT valid XML, because you don't place an element inside of another element:

```
<property <echo />    />
```

TIP
XML elements follow almost exactly the same rules as traditional HTML. The two main differences are that elements such as `<p>` in HTML can get away without a closing tag (`</p>`) and non-paired elements like `<br>` in HTML often don't need a trailing slash (`<br />`).

You may have already guessed that XML supports elements being presented as paired elements or as single elements. For instance, the following are equivalent, and you can use them interchangeably:

```
<echo></echo>

<echo />
```

Attributes are always associated with an element's opening tag. Attributes are never in a closing tag. Attributes consist of a name and a value. The value is surrounded by double or single quotes. Attributes take the following form:

```
name="the_actual_name"
```

When the name attribute is used in a project element tag, it looks like this:

```
<project name="some_cool_name">
</project>
```

I have discussed prologues, elements, and attributes. They are all pretty simple to understand and use. None of them is as simple as the last part of XML: text.

Text is just what it says. Text is nested in a paired element tag. Text is never outside of enclosing element tags.

Let's use the `echo` element as an example again. If you use `echo` with an element tag and an attribute, it looks like this:

```
<echo message="I'm a an echoed message">
```

However, you may use text instead of an attribute. In the case of echo, it replaces the message attribute, thus the following is a valid use of text in XML:

```
<echo>I'm a an echoed message</echo>
```

Comments are another form of tag. Instead of housing an element type, they have comments. Comments begin with `<!--` and end with `-->`. Comments may be nested at any level in your XML. Anything appearing in a comment tag is ignored by Ant during the build, just as you would expect. Be careful not to place a comment inside another comment, or Ant will not know how to interpret it. Even a double dash (`--`) without the closing angle bracket will foul up the comment, so don't do it.

CAUTION

Programmers commonly use the XML comments to disable chunks of XML during debugging of a script. Just be careful that the XML you comment out does not already have a comment in it, or surrounding the XML in a comment tag will result in illegal XML that will not parse properly.

As I have discussed, the default build file for Ant is `build.xml`. The build files are XML. They follow all the rules mentioned above about XML and additional Ant-specific rules. The Ant-specific rules apply to what are and are not valid names for elements and attributes. The Ant-specific rules also cover the description of valid placements of different types of XML elements that it uses to determine the build process it executes.

Create a simple Java file to manipulate with Ant:

1. **Create the file** AntExample.java.

2. **Populate** AntExample.java **with the following code:**
```
public class AntExample
{
   public static void main (String args[])
   {
      System.out.println("Ant done!");
   }
}
```
3. **Place this shiny new Java file in a directory by itself.**

You want it by itself so other files do not inadvertently interfere with your example Ant build.

You can easily build and run this file from either Xcode or from the command line using the `javac` and `java` commands. Instead, use the `ant` command. If you `cd` to the directory that contains `AntExample.java`, type `ant`, and press enter, you wait a second or so and get the following message.
```
build.xml does not exist!
Build failed
```
No harm done. Your next step is to make the requested `build.xml` file:

1. **Create a file named** build.xml.

2. **Place it in the same directory as the** AntExample.java **file.**

3. **Fill the build file with the following text:**
```
<?xml version="1.0" encoding="UTF-8"?>
<project default="compile">
   <target name="compile">
      <javac srcdir="." />
   </target>
         </project>
```

Now when you issue the Ant command from that directory, you get the following:

```
Buildfile: build.xml
compile:
    [javac] Compiling 1 source file
BUILD SUCCESSFUL
Total time: 0 seconds
```

You have written your first Ant build script. Issuing the `ls` command confirms that the `AntExample.class` file exists. Now do the following:

1. **Take a deep breath.**

2. **Stretch your legs.**

3. **Stop by the water cooler.**

4. **Brag to all your co-workers.**

   It's okay. They already know you are a geek.

Looking at the build file, you will see three XML tags: `project, target,` and `javac`. Project is the root element. Project defines the default command to execute. In the case of your build file, that is the compile command.

NOTE

XML documents are set up like trees. The root element is like a trunk with nested elements representing branches. Terminal data and attributes represent leaves.

The target element is a collection of actions collected in one command. In your file, the command is compile. It is no accident that the project default value and the target name are the same. The `ant` command checks the build file for a project root element, and checks project for a default target name to run. After finding what target name it should run, Ant makes all the requested actions in the named target happen.

In your build file, the target contains only one action: `javac. javac` is the same as the Java `javac` command. The `javac` element requires at minimum a source directory specified by the name `srcdir. AntExample.java` is in the same directory as `build.xml`, so use a period for your source directory. You also could use a fully qualified path to the directory.

Think of the build file in terms of Java programs. The project element is like a Java class. The target is like a method. The contents of the target are similar to the commands in a method.

Placing all your project files into one directory gets confusing. You can separate your source and destination directories. The shell command for creating a new directory is `mkdir`. Conveniently, the command for creating a directory in Ant is the same. The following line creates a new directory called build in the directory that the Ant build runs:

```
<mkdir dir="build/">
```

Next, you need to let your Ant `javac` element know to place your compiled classes there. Add the `destdir` attribute to the `javac` element. The entire build file looks like this:

```
<?xml version="1.0" encoding="UTF-8"?>
<project default="compile">
    <target name="compile">
        <mkdir dir="build/" />
        <javac srcdir="." destdir="build/" />
    </target>
</project>
```

Execute this build with the Ant command from the directory that contains your Java file and `build.xml`. You should see, among other comments, the comment BUILD SUCCESSFUL. The build directory is now created, and the `AntExample` class is in it.

TIP
The `mkdir` task in Ant does not error if the directory already exists. In this case, the `mkdir` command is quietly ignored.

Defining multiple targets

Ant supports multiple targets in one project. Each target is enclosed by an opening and closing target tag. Below you see an example of a project with two targets. Your options for running the following build script are `ant` and `ant test`, which both do the same thing because `test` is specified as the project's default target. Also, `ant init` is a valid command to run the `init` target below. You can always specify which target you want to use, even if you want to override the project's default target.

```
<project default="test">
    <target name="init"
            description="Normally would do important things">
        <echo message="Initializing..."/>
    </target>
    <target name="test"
            depends="init"
            description="Testing multiple targets">
        <echo message="other elements go here"/>
    </target>
</project>
```

Notice that the test target element contains the `depends` attribute. Using the `depends` attribute tells Ant that the specified target or targets must execute first. When the test target executes, first the `depends` attribute is checked. Any targets that test relies on are executed before the test target runs. The `depends` effect cascades, so that if the `init` target depended on other targets, those targets would execute before `init`.

TIP

Think of `depends` as you would a Java method call. `depends` essentially calls another target, which may in turn call yet other targets with its own `depends` attribute.

Avoid circular dependencies when setting up `depends` attributes. If two targets depend on each other, then the Ant command outright fails with a message signaling that the offending targets have circular dependencies. For instance, if the above project were changed to specify the `init` target depending on the `test` target, you would see the error shown in Figure 4.11 when attempting to execute Ant.

CAUTION

Multiple targets should never depend on each other. This is called a circular dependency. Creating a loop of target calls will cause Ant builds to fail.

Figure 4.11

Terminal display of Ant build indicating a circular dependency

To specify multiple targets in the depends attribute, just separate the targets with commas, like this:

```
depends="init, compile"
```

If you did not have the `depends` attribute in the targets above, you could still execute `init` and then `test` targets in that order from the command line. You may specify multiple targets with Ant from the command line. Execute the targets `init` and `test` from the command line like this:

```
ant init test
```

Running Ant executes any given target only once. For instance, suppose you have three targets: `init`, `clean`, and `build`, defined like this:

```
<target name="init"></target>
<target name="clean" depends="init"></target>
<target name="build" depends="init, clean"></target>
```

If the target clean depended on init and the target build depended on init and clean, you would not need to worry about the init target being executed multiple times when ant build is executed. The target init is specified in two different depends attributes but executes only once.

TIP

If a target is called by multiple depends attributes during a build, it is executed the first time only. In this way, depends is different from a Java method call.

At times, you want to discourage command-line use or misuse of a target, for instance, if a target generally runs from within a target instead of using a depends attribute. Or perhaps the target should conditionally execute after some tasks have first executed.

In these cases, include a dash at the beginning of the target name. For example, if you have two targets, -init and compile, you can set compile's depends attribute to the following:

```
depends="-init"
```

This allows -init tasks to execute when ant compile executes, but not directly from the command line.

When discouraging use of targets, avoid using the description attribute in the target. In this way, the target is left out of the description of the project created by the command, ant -projecthelp.

TIP

Use both a dash to start a target name and leave the description attribute out of a target when you want to discourage the target's public use.

Notice the description attribute in the targets above. Remember when your professors told you to always comment your code? In Ant build files, you can comment your code in the regular XML fashion:

```
<!-- some comment here -->
```

For targets, you also can include a one line description attribute. It functions like the XML comment, except it is an attribute. The description attribute has the added benefit of appearing in the list of targets provided by the -projecthelp option of Ant. You can quickly list all targets of a build file along with its default target by typing either of the following:

```
ant -projecthelp

ant -p
```

An added benefit of using the description attribute is that XML tools recognize the description attribute and associate it with the proper target element. A typical XML comment does not have this benefit. So use descriptions in any important build file.

Now I introduce a build file that matches a little more closely with the real world. In the real world, you use packages. In the real world, you don't know the package or class names when you write the Ant script. In the real world, at the very least, you want a double-clickable JAR file for quick testing. At the very minimum, you want a build file that performs clean builds.

Use a basic Java class such as the following. This time it is in a package.

```java
package com.genedavis;
import javax.swing.*;
public class AntExample
{
    public static void main (String args[])
    {
        JOptionPane.showMessageDialog(null, "You clicked?");
    }
}
```

I place this Java file in a directory representing the package: com/genedavis.

Here is the build script. Do not worry if you don't understand it yet. I go over it in detail.

```xml
<project default="build">
    <target name="clean"
            description="Removes previous build">
        <echo message="Cleaning up old build..." />
        <delete file="AllOfIt.jar" />
        <delete verbose="true">
            <fileset dir="build">
                <include name="**/*.class" />
            </fileset>
        </delete>
        <delete dir="build" />
    </target>
    <target name="build"
            depends="clean"
            description="Build the project">
        <mkdir dir="build" />
        <javac srcdir="." destdir="./build" />
        <jar jarfile="AllOfIt.jar"
            basedir="build">
            <manifest>
                <attribute name="Main-Class"
                        value="com.genedavis.AntExample" />
            </manifest>
        </jar>
    </target>
</project>
```

Two targets exist in this build: `clean` and `build`. The default target is `build`. The target `build` does depend on `clean`, so `clean` is executed before the build tasks are executed. I describe the clean target first.

TIP

Remember, double-clickable JARs are JAR files that specify a `Main-Class` in their manifest file. For example, the JAR's manifest file may contain the single line `Main-Class: com.genedavis.AntExample` if the main method is found in that package and class.

You have seen the `project`, `target`, and `echo` elements before. `delete`, `fileset`, and `include` are all new. `delete` is used three different ways in this target. `delete` is used to remove a single file, to remove multiple files, and to remove a directory with all its contents.

Deleting the class files in this case was not strictly necessary, because I turn around and delete the directory which contains them. Deleting the directory would have deleted the class files and all other files, too. Deleting the build directory also recursively deletes all its subdirectories as well. The extra `delete` task was used, just to give an example of how it is set up.

Deleting a single file is straightforward. In this case, it was a JAR file. All you need is the `delete` tag and a `file` attribute. Here is the task:

```
<delete file="AllOfIt.jar" />
```

Deleting a single directory is also straightforward. Use the `delete` tag with a `dir` attribute, like this:

```
<delete dir="build" />
```

TIP

Use a combination of the `<delete dir="some_directory">` and `<mkdir dir="some_directory">` to quickly clean recursively all files from a build directory.

Deleting all the class files in the build directory, recursing through all the subdirectories in the process, is a little more complex. First, notice that I have set the verbose attribute of `delete` to `true`. So the opening `delete` tag is this:

```
<delete verbose="true">
```

If you do not have `verbose` set to `true`, then the files deleted are not enumerated. After the script is working the way you want, that is no problem, but while writing and debugging a build file, you want to know what is happening.

Nested in the paired `delete` tags, I have a set of `fileset` elements. The attribute is just a `dir`. Use the `fileset` tag only for specifying the directory from which you want files deleted.

Nested in the `fileset` tags is your include tag. Include specifies a pattern of the files that you want to remove. In this case, include looks like this:

```
<include name="**/*.class" />
```

The double asterisk matches zero or more directories and subdirectories. The single asterisk matches zero or more characters in a filename.

NOTE
For the complete list of directory and file patterns supported by Ant, check the official Ant Manual at `http://ant.apache.org/manual/dirtasks.html#patterns`.

Above, I store source and class files in separate directory trees, but many projects keep the source and builds in the same tree for convenience. It is common, though obviously undesirable, in legacy code to have files that are compiled for which the source is lost. Obviously, removing all compiled files is disastrous in such cases.

In projects where some (but not all) files of a given type should be removed, use the `exclude` tag. In your sample project, the `exclude` tag is placed on the line immediately after the `include` tag, so they are both nested in between the `fileset` tags. The `exclude` tag would look something like this, if you wanted to `exclude` all classes named `MySpecial` from being deleted:

```
<exclude name="**/MySpecial.class" />
```

To summarize, the sample clean target does the following:

- It echoes "Cleaning up old build…".
- It deletes a JAR.
- It deletes all classes in the build directory.
- It deletes the build directory.

Consider the `build` target. After the `clean` target is finished, the `mkdir` task is executed. The `dir` attribute specifies the name of the directory to create. In this case, the directory is `build`. The element looks like this:

```
<mkdir dir="build" />
```

Next, compile the Java code using the `ant` command for the Java tool `javac`. Not too surprisingly, the Ant element name is also `javac`. The attributes are `srcdir` and `destdir`, meaning source directory and destination directory, respectively. If you pay close attention to what the script is doing, you notice that `<javac/>` recurses through subdirectories and compiles everything it finds. In an actual project, you may get more files compiled than you anticipated unless you are careful not to have any Java files in subdirectories of the specified source directory.

Here is the `javac` element I used:

```
<javac srcdir="." destdir="build" verbose="true" />
```

The `javac` task above has only the attributes `srcdir` and `destdir`. Other useful attributes include `debug`, `deprecation`, and `optimize`. If you build for a code release, you might want your `javac` task to look more like this:

```
<javac srcdir="."
       destdir="build"
       verbose="true"
       debug="false"
       deprecation="true"
       optimize="true"
/>
```

`debug="false"` prevents extra debug information from being placed in the compiled code. `optimize="true"` tells the compiler to optimize the code. `deprecation="true"` and `verbose="true"` add extra information to the output of the `ant` command. You may want `verbose` and `deprecation` set to `false`, if you already know this is a fully working release build.

For fun, swap out `true` with `on` or `yes` and `false` with `off` or `no` in the above `javac` task. You will see that those additional values work just as well.

Finally, use the Ant `jar` task to create a double-clickable JAR. The JAR name is specified by the `jarfile` element. The `basedir` attribute specifies which directory to recursively place into the JAR file.

The manifest is created with the nested manifest element, which in turn holds the attribute element. The name and value attributes of the attribute element are used to specify name/value pairs you want to appear in the final manifest file of the JAR file. I use it to specify the `Main-Class: com.genedavis.AntExample` name value pair that specifies which class to use when the JAR is double-clicked or run with the `java -jar AllOfIt.jar`. The full `jar` task looks like this:

```
<jar jarfile="AllOfIt.jar"
    basedir="build">
  <manifest>
     <attribute name="Main-Class"
                value="com.genedavis.AntExample" />
  </manifest>
</jar>
```

The resulting manifest is named `MANIFEST.MF` and placed in the `META-INF` directory inside the JAR. If you extract the manifest, it will contain the following:

```
Manifest-Version: 1.0
Ant-Version: Apache Ant 1.7.0
Created-By: 1.5.0_16-133 (Apple Inc.)
Main-Class: com.genedavis.AntExample
```

Remember, if you double-click this JAR file, it has output to standard output only. To see the output when double-clicking it, instead of running it from the command line, open the Console application. The date and time of the application's output appears on a line with the resulting output. The Console application is located in the `Utilities` subdirectory of your `Applications` directory.

Learning properties and advanced elements

In this section, I discuss how Ant uses variables. I cover common variables accessible to Ant. I discuss various advanced tasks, such as the `exec` task. Also, I have a table of all the Ant tasks I have covered, for easy reference.

Variables in Ant are called properties. Properties can be defined inside and outside of project files. Properties are case sensitive.

Properties are defined with a name and a value in an XML element, like this.

```
<property name="some_name" value="some_value" />
```

A very common use for property elements is to define the path to a directory. This type of property has a location attribute instead of a value attribute and would look more like this:

```
<property name="some_place" location="actual_path" />
```

Properties are accessed with the notation `${some_property}`. For instance, to create a build directory with a predefined property, the XML would look like this:

```
<property name="build_path" location="build" />
<mkdir dir="${build_path}" />
```

Properties can be defined outside of targets. If you change a property element's value inside of a target, the new value applies to the property even when accessed inside of other targets.

To demonstrate property use, here is another complete `build.xml` file:

```xml
<?xml version="1.0" encoding="UTF-8"?>
<project name="property_test"
         default="compile"
         basedir=".">
    <property name="build_message"
              value="building..."/>
    <property name="build_directory"
              location="build"/>
    <property name="source_directory"
              location="src"/>
    <target name="clean"
            description="Removes previous build">
```

```
        <!-- remove the build directory -->
        <delete dir="${build_directory}" />
    </target>
    <target name="compile"
            depends="clean"
            description="Compile code in new directory">
        <mkdir dir="${build_directory}"/>
        <echo message="${build_message}"/>
        <javac srcdir="${source_directory}"
               destdir="${build_directory}" />
    </target>
</project>
```

Notice that three properties are defined at the top of the project and all are outside of targets. This is the most common place to find properties defined. Two of the properties have location attributes, while a token third has a value attribute. The `build_directory` property is used in both the `clean` and the `compile` targets. The properties are all accessed inside of quotes as though they were the actual text that they are replacing. No special extra syntax is needed to access the properties other than the standard $ { } syntax.

N O T E
All System properties available inside of Java are available to Ant when an Ant build is running.

Quite a few properties are predefined and can be accessed from within Ant. Some are from Java's system properties, and some are from Ant itself. Table 4.1 lists the more useful properties that you can access in Ant builds.

Table 4.1 Ant Accessible Properties

Property	Description
ant.file	Full path of this build file
ant.home	Location of ant (same as which ant)
ant.java.version	Version of Java being used
ant.project.name	Value of project name attribute
ant.version	Version and compile date of Ant
Basdir	Directory that Ant executes from unless redefined
file.separator	/ on the Mac
java.class.path	All paths in the Java class path
java.ext.dirs	All paths of Java extensions
java.home	Actual path to Java Home

Property	Description
java.version	Version and build of Java being used
line.separator	\n on OS X
os.arch	Hardware used by Java (probably i386)
os.name	Name of OS (Mac OS X)
os.version	Version of the OS
path.separator	: on Mac or Linux and ; on Windows
user.dir	Directory user ran ant from
user.home	/Users/your_home_directory
user.name	Abbreviated version of login name

After creating a JAR, you may want to copy it and additional resources, such as properties files, to a deployment folder. Perhaps you just want to place the JAR into an OS X application package. Ant provides the `copy` task for this.

The syntax for copy is simple. Provide a file to copy and then the directory to copy the file to. Also, specify whether you want to overwrite existing files in the destination directory.

In the following example task, the `copy` task copies the file `our.jar` from the current directory to the `/Users/myhome/Desktop/release` directory and overwrites any existing `our.jar` file.

```
<copy file="./our.jar"
      todir="/Users/myhome/Desktop/release"
      overwrite="true" />
```

If you test the `copy` task, you will notice that the task copies files but leaves the original behind. So it is copying in the true sense of the word. If you want to copy the file without leaving the file behind, use the `move` task. The `move` task has the file, `todir`, and `overwrite` attributes like `copy`.

If you write complex Ant builds, eventually you will want to run a Java application or execute a shell script or command-line tool from within the build. Never fear, Ant can do this too. The tasks for using Java and for executing a shell command look like this:

```
<java classname="com.genedavis.AntTest"
      classpath="build">
   <arg value="some_argument_for_java" />
</java>
<exec dir="/execute/command/from/here"
      executable="some_tool_to_execute">
   <arg line="-args -for -tool"/>
</exec>
```

The `java` task is probably obvious to you as a Java programmer. However, the `exec` task is a little trickier. The `dir` attribute is the directory that you want the command executed in. Imagine using the `cd` command in the Terminal to change your directory and then executing a command from the new directory. The `executable` attribute is the actual tool or shell script to execute. The `arg` element is used to pass command-line arguments to the shell script or tool.

TIP

The **exec** task is great for integrating Ant with shell scripts and command-line tools.

TIP

If you want to use **exec** to run a command-line tool and you don't know the path to that tool, use the **which** command. Type **which** followed by the name of the tool. For example, **which ls** reveals the location of the **ls** command in the directory structure.

TIP

Many developer tools that you normally think of as purely GUI tools also have a command-line interface built especially for scripting. Check your documentation, and you may be surprised to find your favorite GUI development tools can be integrated into Ant using the **exec** task or even their own custom Ant modules!

Here is an example of using the basic `ls` command from your current directory with the arguments `-la`.

```
<exec dir="."
      executable="ls">
   <arg line="-la"/>
</exec>
```

Later in this chapter, I present writing shell scripts in greater detail. Executing tools from inside Ant opens the full power of OS X to your build. If your computer can do it, your build can do it.

TIP

If you are using Ant from inside Xcode, you can access command-line tools and shell scripts from your Xcode Ant build, too.

Ant tasks fall into two large categories: core tasks and optional tasks. Core tasks are tasks like `javac` and `copy` that are available in Ant for build scripts to use. Optional tasks require at the very least an extra JAR to be included to become available for Ant to use. Optional tasks have additional library dependencies that core tasks do not have.

The `scp` task is an example of an optional task. `scp` cannot be used without including the `jsch.jar`. The `jsch.jar` can be obtained from here:

```
http://www.jcraft.com/jsch/index.html
```

You must include this JAR in the classpath available to Ant for the `scp` task to work. You can check the JARs in use by Ant by typing `ant -diagnostics` in the Terminal window. The actual use of the `scp` task is then something like this:

```
<scp file="mydeployment.jar"
     todir="username@remotehost:/my/webapps"
     password="scp_password"/>
```

Other optional tasks include such tasks as `sound`, `splash`, `junit`, and `ftp`. A good place to check for optional and core tasks not discussed in this section is on Ant's official project page at `http://ant.apache.org`.

N O T E

You may find the complete reference to core Ant tasks and optional Ant tasks in the official Ant manual on Apache's Ant page at `http://ant.apache.org/manual/index.html`. For quick reference, in Table 4.2 I list the tasks I have gone over while discussing Ant.

Table 4.2 Ant Tasks Quick Reference

task	attributes
copy	file, todir, overwrite
delete	dir, file, verbose
echo	message
exec	executable
jar	jarfile, basedir
java	classname, classpath
javac	srcdir, destdir, verbose, debug, deprecation, optimize
mkdir	dir
move	file, todir, overwrite
scp	file, todir, password

Other features of Ant that I cannot address here include conditionals, error handling, interactive user input, and creating custom Ant modules. Remember that Ant is used by Xcode to build Java projects, so all the power of Ant is available to you in creating Java builds for OS X Xcode projects. Ant builds also integrate with other Java IDEs such as Eclipse and NetBeans. Ant can take care of any build that you need on OS X.

Configuring Ant options

Ant comes with several command-line options to customize the behavior of the tool. The command-line options vary from setting the verbosity of build output to specifying the name of the build file to something other than `build.xml`. Place Ant options before the names of the targets you execute. For example, if you run a target called `clean` in a build file called `other_build.xml`, issue the following command:

```
ant -f other_build.xml clean
```

Several of the options are not used with executed targets. For instance, use `ant -h` or `ant -v` without a target name.

`ant -h` displays the list of options shown in Table 4.3.

Table 4.3 Ant Options

Options	Use
-help, -h	Displays the option list
-version	Displays Ant's version
-projecthelp, -p	Displays project information
-buildfile, -file, -f <file>	Overrides build.xml with custom build file
-find, -s <file>	Finds build file looking up directory tree
-quiet, -q	Displays no debug information
-verbose, -v	Displays some debug information
-debug, -d	Displays lots of debug information
-main <class>	Specifies a custom main for Ant
-nice <number>	Main thread priority (5 is default)
-emacs, -e	Produces unadorned logging information
-lib <path>	The search path for jars and classes
-logfile, -l <log_file>	Specifies the log file
-logger <classname>	Specifies a custom logger
-listener <classname>	Adds a project listener
-keep-going, -k	Prevents failure of whole build on individual target failures
-D<property>=<value>	Specifies name/value pair for property
-propertyfile <name>	Loads properties from a file properties specified with ant's -D option take precedence
-inputhandler <class>	Chooses class to handle requested input
-noinput	Prevents interactive input
-nouserlib	Ignores user JARs in ${user.home}/.ant/lib
-noclasspath	Ignores CLASSPATH
-autoproxy	Uses the proxy settings for your OS
-diagnostics	Displays diagnostic information for Ant

Another way to view the options and some additional help is to type man ant in the Terminal. Use the up and down arrow keys to see the full document. The q key is used to quit man. The man tool is used to display the manual for command-line tools on OS X.

TIP

The man tool displays manuals for command-line tool usage. Type man man (yes two mans) in the Terminal for a details manual of man's usage.

Compiling from the Terminal

In this section, I explain the differences between shells, the Terminal, and command-line tools. I review Java's command-line tools, specifically javac, in detail. Ultimately, I steer this discussion to shell scripts and supply some details about the construction of shell scripts.

Shell scripts script command-line tools. Many complex projects rely solely on shell scripts to perform all compiling, configuring, and deploying of code. You can use shell scripts with cron jobs to create nightly or weekly builds of your project.

Shell scripting via the Terminal is a powerful and respected approach to compiling and deploying Java projects. If you chose to rely on shell scripting in your project, some programmers may disagree with your choice. However, no experienced programmer denies that shell scripting is a powerful and versatile tool that can supply any needs your project demands.

NOTE

While command-line tools are usually written in C and shell scripts are not, telling the difference based on their behavior is often difficult. No stigma in the OS X world is associated with using scripts instead of pre-compiled tools.

Reviewing the Java command-line tools

Many programmers who fall in love with OS X do it because of the Terminal application. The Terminal is easy to use, is highly configurable, supports standard cut and paste, and opens access to the shell and to a host of command-line tools that programmers find useful. Command-line tools are applications that are accessed via a keyboard instead of a GUI interface driven by a mouse.

NOTE

The terms *Terminal, command-line tools,* and *shells* can get a bit confusing. The Terminal is an application for accessing shell environments. Shell environments provide a way for you to navigate and use your OS from the keyboard. Command-line tools run inside a shell. Command-line tools are applications written specifically for shell environments.

Many diehard shell users actually get angry if an application requires them to use a mouse, because it slows down their typing. The intention of shells is to give users more powerful and precise tools than are accessible from GUIs. GUI applications are harder to script and configure than command-line tools in the opinion of most diehard shell users.

Be careful when using command-line tools in the shell. Command-line tools are less forgiving than their GUI cousins. If you tell your command-line tool to wipe out everything on your computer, it probably will, and it will do so cheerfully without asking if you're nuts. Shell users are expected to be careful and not depend on their environment to hold their hand asking if they are sure they want to do what they just chose to do.

Several shell environments exist, but the default on OS X is called Bash. Bash tends to be the most popular shell on most Unix systems. Most programs written for one shell will work in other shells, with the exception of some scripts. (I discuss shell scripts later in this chapter.)

NOTE

Programs and tools of all types are specifically written for shell environments. This includes word processors, programming tools, and even multiplayer networked games.

Java comes with a large set of command-line tools, and many more are available on the Internet. Table 4.4 shows the Java tools that are shipped with OS X. For additional tools, check out the MacPorts Project at `http://www.macports.org/`, and the Fink project at `http://www.finkproject.org/`.

Table 4.4 Java Tools Shipped with OS X

Tool	Description
Appletviewer	Views applets without a Web browser
extcheck	JAR versioning and conflict checker
idlj	Java to CORBA interface generator
java	Runs java applications
javac	The Java compiler
javadoc	Generates Java documentation
javah	Generates C headers and stubs (JNI)
javap	Disassembler for Java classes
jar	Zips Java applications with the "jar" extension
jarsigner	Signs JAR files
jdb	A powerful Java Debugger
keytool	Keystore and certificate tool
native2ascii	Converts native languages to compilable Unicode Latin-1

Tool	Description
policytool	Policy file manager
rmic	RMI stub and skeleton generator
rmiregistry	RMI registry service
rmid	RMI daemon
serialver	RMI tool for serialVersionUIDs
tnameserv	Naming service access

All these tools have man pages. In the Terminal, you can type man followed by the name of the tool and see a short text-based manual explaining its use. Use the up and down arrow keys to navigate the man pages, and type q to quit reading the man page.

You will never use all these tools. However, javac is of particular interest in this discussion of building Java projects on OS X. In the next section, I introduce more details of the javac tool.

Configuring Javac

The four basic Java command-line tools that you should know when programming Java on OS X are java, javac, javadoc, and jar. I focus here on javac. The location of javac is found by typing, which followed by javac. You will see that which javac returns /usr/bin/javac.

Case closed? No.

Execute the command ls -la /usr/bin/javac in the Terminal and you see something like this:

```
lrwxr-xr-x  1 root  wheel  74 Mar 13 14:20 /usr/bin/java -> /System/Library/
    Frameworks/JavaVM.framework/Versions/Current /Commands/javac
```

Notice that the javac location, /usr/bin/javac, is followed by -> and then a much longer and unpleasant-looking address:

```
/System/Library/Frameworks/JavaVM.framework/Versions/Current/Commands /javac
```

This longer address looks like it is the actual location of the javac command. In fact, if you list the directory that contains the various versions, you discover that the actual directory is this:

```
/System/Library/Frameworks/JavaVM.framework/Versions/A/Commands/
```

The redirection is all done by links. Check the man page for link by typing man link in the Terminal window. Links are like aliases, except that links are tailored to work transparently with command-line tools and shells scripts.

NOTE

Links are to Terminal applications what aliases are to Finder applications.

Scripts and command-line tools are written to work with other tools and directories that are in predetermined locations. For instance, Ant can be written to assume that the `javac` command is in `/usr/bin/`. If the guys over at Apple changed `javac`'s location with an automatic OS X update, Ant and a whole bunch of other applications would need to be reconfigured, or worse yet...rebuilt.

Links come to the rescue. If you link `/usr/bin/javac` to the actual location of `javac` (or in this case, a link to a link to the actual location), then no command-line tools or other applications break when the actual location is changed. The links just need to be kept up to date.

CAUTION

In extreme cases of debugging, you may need to change where the links in **/usr/bin/** point. I don't recommend this, however. If you forget to change the links back, later you may see problems related to your version of the JVM that are hard to debug.

Several versions of the Java tools are on your OS. Apple rarely removes old versions (though sometimes they overwrite old versions) when a new one is installed. See the complete list of versions with this command:

```
ls -la /System/Library/Frameworks/JavaVM.framework/Versions
```

Your output will look something like this:

```
drwxr-xr-x  11 root  wheel  374 Aug 28 14:05 .
drwxr-xr-x  12 root  wheel  408 Aug 28 14:41 ..
lrwxr-xr-x   1 root  wheel    5 Aug 28 14:05 1.3 -> 1.3.1
drwxr-xr-x   3 root  wheel  102 Jul 20 17:35 1.3.1
lrwxr-xr-x   1 root  wheel   10 Aug 28 14:05 1.5 -> CurrentJDK
lrwxr-xr-x   1 root  wheel   10 Aug 28 14:05 1.5.0 -> CurrentJDK
lrwxr-xr-x   1 root  wheel    5 Aug 28 14:05 1.6 -> 1.6.0
drwxr-xr-x   8 root  wheel  272 Aug 28 14:41 1.6.0
drwxr-xr-x   9 root  wheel  306 Aug 28 14:41 A
lrwxr-xr-x   1 root  wheel    1 Aug 28 14:05 Current -> A
lrwxr-xr-x   1 root  wheel    3 Aug 28 14:05 CurrentJDK -> 1.6
```

Notice the many link (->) symbols in this list. If you explore these directories, you discover all the common Java tools and libraries for each version of Java listed. Having all these complete historical versions of Java allows older Java applications to run on user- or programmer-specified JVMs.

Using `javac` directly from the command line is useful when you need to modify only one or few classes. Using the `javac` tool directly speeds up some quick modifications and deadline-related hacks. It also helps debug your code in cases where you do not trust your build tools are working properly.

Table 4.5 displays the common `javac` options.

Table 4.5 Common Javac Options

Option	Description
-Akey[=value]	Annotation processor options
-bootclasspath <path>	Overrides bootstrap classes
-classpath <path>	Locates classes and annotation processors
-cp <path>	Same as -classpath
-d <directory>	Build location
-deprecation	Displays deprecation warnings
-endorseddirs <dirs>	Overrides endorsed standards
-extdirs <dirs>	Overrides extensions
-g	Generates all debug information (more than default)
-g:{lines,vars,source}	Generates specified debug information
-g:none	Generates no debug information
-help	Displays options with short descriptions
-implicit:class	Classes generated for implicit references
-implicit:none	No classes generated for implicit references
-J<flag>	Runtime flags
-nowarn	No warnings
-proc:none	No annotation processing
-proc:only	Only annotation processing
-processor <class>[,<class>,...]	Annotation processors
-processorpath <path>	Annotation processor path
-s <directory>	Generated source file path
-sourcepath <path>	Locates source files
-verbose	Displays compiler actions
-encoding <encoding>	Source file character encoding
-source <release>	Accepted source version (1.3, 1.4, 1.5, 5, 1.6, or 6)
-target <release>	Class compatible with this release
-version	Displays Javac version
-X	Displays nonstandard options

The most common options that you will use are `-cp` (classpaths), `-d` (build path), and `-sourcepath` (only the paths, not the source files). All these options require a path or multiple paths. Providing these paths on OS X may be a bit different than you are use to.

On OS X relative paths start with a `./` or just a dot if you are referring to the current working directory. Indicate the path to a directory in the current working directory with a dot followed by a forward slash, followed by the directory name and another forward slash, such as `./some_directory/`.

Specifying your build path is not exactly as you would think. If you want your class to build in the current directory, you need to use the option `-d .`, that is a dash "d" followed by a space and a period. However, if your class is in a package, the directories under the current directory are created and the class is placed in that directory rather than the current directory. This is annoying if you keep your classes and Java source in the same directory. Instead, compile the source without using the `-d` option. This places the source file in the current directory regardless of whether it is part of a package.

Explicit file paths on OS X always start with a forward slash (`/`). Fully qualified file paths do not begin with a drive name or letter. If you type `ls /` into the Terminal, you are listing what is referred to as the root directory. The root directory always represents the drive that the operating system started from.

The logical question is where are all the other drives located? There is a directory called `Volumes` in the root directory. Its path is `/Volumes`. (Note the capital V.) `Volumes` contains all the drives connected to your computer. If you `ls -la /Volumes` you even see a link to the root path with the name of your boot drive for the link name.

CAUTION

One warning about using the drives in the `Volumes` directory: If you have a raid attached to your computer, you may see the names of each of the raid drives listed in addition to the name of the raid. If the directory you want to access is on the raid, use the name of the raid, not the name of one of the drives in the raid, for your path.

You have already seen that the path to the root directory is a forward slash. The forward slash is also the default directory separator on OS X. The only time you see a backslash used in directory paths on OS X is preceding a space. Backslashes escape spaces in OS X paths. Forward slashes are used to separate directory and filenames in paths used in all Java commands, such as `javac`. If you are listing multiple paths, use a colon (`:`) for the separator between paths.

TIP

If you have a hard time remembering the difference between forward slashes and backslashes, you are not alone. Most programmers start out having a hard time remembering the difference. Always judge the direction of the slash based on the direction you draw them when writing English. Forward slashes lean forward toward the next word in a sentence, and backslashes lean backward toward words you already read. In other words, if gravity took over, forward slashes would tip forward and backslashes would fall over backward.

A sample `javac` command using the directory information I have just discussed might look like this:

```
javac -cp .:/my\ classes:/my\ other\ classes -d /build MyApp.java
```

A source file for the class `MyApp` is compiled using two class paths inside directories called `my classes` and `my other classes` at the root. The resulting class is placed into a directory called `build`, also at the root.

You do not really want to place a build, class libraries, and sources files in the root directory. However, placing this build in the root directory shows how to use paths on OS X with Java command-line tools' options.

Scripting builds

Many Java developers on OS X prefer to script builds directly in the shell. Recall that the shell is used to execute commands, such as `javac` or `ant`, and then see the results of executing those commands.

You may run these same shell scripts from inside of Xcode by setting the Java target build tool from `/usr/bin/ant` to the path and name of the shell script as the new build tool.

You also may use shell scripts from inside of Ant by using the `exec` tag as described earlier in this chapter.

The default shell used by the Terminal is called Bash. If you issue the command `which bash` in the Terminal, you see that `bash` is located in the `/bin` directory. Bash is not the only shell offered in a default install of OS X and OS X tools. Other popular shells are TENEX C shell (`tcsh`), KornShell (`ksh`), and Z shell (`zsh`). You can learn details about each of these shells by typing the command `man` followed by the shell, for instance `man tcsh`. Here, I use `bash` because it is the default for OS X, even though I am somewhat partial to `tcsh`.

N O T E

An advantage of scripting over writing a C application for the command line is the ease of interacting with existing tools. Scripts incorporate other tools and scripts as easily as a C program includes C libraries.

Scripting directly in the shell, gives direct access to all the shell tools without using special commands, such as `exec` in Ant. Because `javac` and other Java tools are directly available to shells, scripting is a powerful and quick way to set up Java builds. Browsing the Internet, you can find many open-source Java projects that use shell scripts to build their projects on OS X.

Shell scripts are just text files. They do not need an extension (such as `.txt`) though. By convention, shell scripts either have no extension or preferably a `.sh` extension.

Create a text file called `test.sh`, and add the following lines to it.

```
#!/bin/bash
# my comment
clear
echo building the test file
javac -d . Test1.java
echo build complete
```

Save this file as `test.sh`.

Immediately, you recognize the `javac` command. It is entered exactly the same as it is entered from the command line. This true of most of the commands entered into shell scripts.

The first line of the shell script, `#!/bin/bash`, just declares which of the shell environments you want to execute your script. The default is `bash` anyway, so this line can be left out when you know the script will always be executed in the shell it is written for. Simple scripts run on all the common shells, so you may not need to specify which shell to use while executing simple scripts.

The pound symbol (#) indicates a comment follows. Comments last until the newline. The # behaves similar to a `//` in Java. If you wanted to put the comment after a command like `clear`, just end the command with a semicolon and then proceed with your comment. It looks like this:

```
clear;#clearing now
```

The `echo` command works like `System.out.println("")` in Java. It is best to surround your output with double quotes, although for pure text, going without quotes usually does not change the output.

Other common commands used in shell scripts are `cp` (copy), `mv` (move), `mkdir` (make directory), and `rm` (remove).

BE CAREFUL with `rm`. System Admins are often making jokes involving `rm` because of its power. A slip of the fingers while using `rm` can wipe out your entire hard drive. No joke.

Now that you have been cautioned about `rm`, you can use it...carefully. Using `rm` followed by a filename removes the file from your computer. It won't come back, and it is not in the Trash folder. You do not get a chance to say you did not want to do that.

If you try using `rm` on a folder, it fails unless you use the proper options. If you wanted to remove a folder called `my_trash_2_toss` and all of the files and folders in that folder, then this would be the command:

```
rm -rf my_trash_2_toss
```

CAUTION
The most common joke about misusing `rm` is to use this command on the root directory. Be careful. This is an easy mistake to make while typing. If you start typing `rm /something/something`, but you finger slips on the Return key just after typing `rm /`, you will accidentally destroy most everything on your hard drive (and maybe lose your job in the process.) I advise always typing in the file or folder name and path before typing `rm` so that a stray pinky hitting the Return key does not cause such dire results.

Done. The `mkdir` command is used to create directories. Follow the `mkdir` command with the new folder's name.

The `cp` and `mv` command work much the same. Type the command followed by the source and then the destination. A nice trick is to make the destination name different from the source name. (Try that with drag and drop!)

The extension of the shell script does not make it executable. Instead, you need to use the command `chmod` to make the file executable. If you are in the same folder as a shell script called `test.sh`, type either of the following commands:

```
chmod 755 test.sh

chmod +x script.sh
```

The version with 755 tends to be more "old school" than the version with +x. So if you want to prove yourself young and edgy, use the second version. I am neither young nor edgy, so I use 755.

Executing the new script is now just a matter of typing it in. Entering `./test.sh` executes the script. If you don't like using the `./` before the script, you can place the script in a directory defined by the `PATH` environment variable or add the script's directory to the `PATH` variable. Typically, that behavior is not wanted, because too many executables in the path can lead to command name collisions, and then all kinds of confusion ensues.

Shell scripting provides command-line arguments, variables, functions, user input, and conditionals as you would expect in any programming language.

Variables are defined without being strongly typed as you would see in Java. If the variable is a string, use quotes to surround the value. If the value is a number, no quotes are necessary.

For instance, the following defines a string and a number:

```
my_special_var="This is a string value."
YOU_ARE_NUMERO=1
```

Typically, variable names are all caps with underscores separating words. Lowercase letters are also acceptable, though.

To recover the value of a variable, precede the name with a dollar sign. Using the `YOU_ARE_NUMERO` variable from above would echo the value `1` :

```
echo $YOU_ARE_NUMERO
```

Special variables are used for retrieving command-line arguments passed to the script. `$#` retrieves the number of arguments passed to the script. Each variable passed in is stored in a variable of the number of argument it is. If you typed `./test.sh I have 4 arguments`, then `echo $#` would echo `4`, meaning there were four command-line arguments. `echo $2` would output the value `have`, the second command-line argument. Also, `echo $4` would print the value `arguments`, which is the fourth command-line argument. Notice these variables are not zero based as the `main()` method's array is in Java. The value of `$0` is the actual name and path of the shell script that is being executed.

TIP

One way to remember `$0` as the name and path of the shell script is to think of the command to execute the shell script as the first argument in a zero-based array of arguments and `$#` as returning the highest valid argument index.

Functions in Bash are defined in multiple ways, but the easiest for Java programmers to remember is the name of the function followed by parentheses and the code surrounded by curly braces.

```
my_function() {
    echo hi
}
```

To call this function, simply add this line to your script:

```
my_function
```

The function must be defined prior to use, in a similar way to C functions. (Not very Java-like, really.)

To pass arguments to functions, just tack on the arguments like you do to any command-line tool. As mentioned earlier, access the number of the arguments passed to the function by using `$#` and access each argument from its number. So the third argument is echoed by a line, `echo "The third argument is $3"`.

NOTE

Because arguments and total argument count are retrieved the same way for functions and the script itself, you might expect `$0` to retrieve the name of the function as `$0` retrieves the name of the script.

It doesn't. It just returns the name of the script.

You must return values from Bash functions as numeric values. The command `return` followed by a number terminates a function. To retrieve the return value of a function, use `$?` immediately after the function call. The `return` command immediately exits the function.

The command exit works the same way as `return` except that it exits the whole script. The exit command takes a numeric value to `return` also.

TIP

The `exit` command is a great way to get out of a function when the purpose of the function is complete.

Getting user input and placing it into a variable is easy. Simply use the `read` command followed by a variable name. The variable does not need to be previously defined to be used by `read`. Here is a complete example:

```
#!/bin/bash
echo -n "Build the Test1 class? "
read my_answer
echo "Your answer was, $my_answer"
javac -d . Test1.java
echo build complete
```

Notice the option `-n` in the first `echo`. The `-n` option suppresses the newline after the echoed print.

The above code really needs some sort of check for "yes" versus "no." You need conditionals. Bash scripts provide for conditionals. The `if` and `else` are present in Bash scripts but different from Java. Here is a short example:

```
MY_VAR1=1
MY_VAR2=2
if [ $MY_VAR1 == $MY_VAR2 ]; then
echo "equal"
else
echo "not equal"
fi
```

The space after the `if` and before the first square bracket is not optional. No space after the `if` means you have a broken script.

CAUTION

Remember to place the closing `fi` and the space between `if` and the square brace in Bash `if` statements.

Other differences from Java exist. There are no curly braces. Square brackets are used to contain the actual condition. The condition is followed by `; then`. This takes the place of the opening curly brace you would see in Java. To close the `else`, I have the strange-looking backward `if`, `fi`. The `fi` takes the place of a closing curly brace that you see in Java. Other than being totally different, it is just like Java.

The arithmetic comparisons are like Java. They are <, >, <=, >=, ==, and ! =. Bash scripts have a set of logical operators specifically for strings. The script comparisons are = (equals), ! = (not equals), < (less than), > (greater than), –n (not empty), and –z (empty string).

Using what I have now discussed about Bash scripting conditionals, you can rewrite the example above that asks if you really want to compile `Test1`:

```
#!/bin/bash
echo -n "Build the Test1 class? "
read my_answer
if [ -z $my_answer ]; then
    echo -n "Your answer must be yes or no: "
    read my_answer
fi
if [ $my_answer = "no" ]; then
    exit 0;
fi
javac -d . Test1.java
echo build complete
```

Now, if you type *no* for your response to the question, the build is not performed and the script exits. Also, notice the check for an empty string. The –z $my_answer check is equivalent to Java's my_answer.isEmpty().

Quick Manifest from the Command Line

Here is a nice trick for whipping up a quick manifest file without using an editor. From the Terminal window, type these two lines:

```
echo Created-By: T. Gene
    Davis>manifest
echo Main-Class:
    MyTest>>manifest
```

The echo command means just that. Whatever comes after echo is written to standard output. This is a common shell and DOS command, so you have probably seen it before.

Why didn't you see the text echo though? The > and >> are to blame. The single angle bracket redirects standard output to a file and overwrites the contents. The double angle brackets redirect the standard output to a file appending the contents. You may recognize this convention from some programming languages you know.

Check the results by typing this command:

```
less manifest
```

You should see the following:

```
Created-By: T. Gene Davis
Main-Class: MyTest
```

Exit less by typing q for quit. You now have a new manifest file for use in building a double-clickable JAR.

Summary

In this chapter, you learned to use Xcode, Ant, and shell scripts to fully automate your builds. Xcode comes with a JNI template that already has a useful Ant build created. Custom Ant builds allow you to expand the types of Java projects that Xcode can handle. For simple projects, Xcode's default build script is enough.

Xcode uses Ant to build your project. With Ant, you can make extensive modifications to default Xcode Ant builds. You can even create your own standalone Ant builds from scratch, if you do not wish to use Xcode to perform your builds.

You also may choose to use shell scripts to perform your build. Shell scripts allow you to take full advantage of all the UNIX command-line tools that OS X contains. You may integrate shell scripts with an Ant build or stick with a pure shell script solution for your project's build.

Deploying Applications

I n this chapter, I explore the creation of OS X application bundles from Java applications. JAR files do not have icons associated with them and are treated as documents by OS X until you bundle them as application bundles. OS X application bundles contain everything applications need to run. This includes libraries, images, icons, and property files.

Part of creating a desirable application on OS X is icon creation. Icons on OS X are works of art. As such, I explain the roles of vector drawing programs and raster art creation in implementing beautiful application icons.

Finally, I explain the installation options available for your Java applications on OS X. Installations vary from simple drag-and-drops, to creating more complex installers with programs like izPack. I explain the Apple's recommended installation method (using DMGs) in detail.

A demo application with icon art is available from this book's Web site for use in producing the packages, installations, and icons described in this chapter. The application is Checkbook Demo. It includes two JAR libraries, command-line interface integration, an image for an icon label, an embedded database, several source files, and a basic application icon. I intend Checkbook Demo to demonstrate deployment of a feature-rich application, not to work as functional checkbook software.

Learning Application Bundle Basics

Apple's user base loves refinement. Since the first Mac rolled of an assembly line, Apple has focused on improving the user experience. OS X currently spearheads the drive to impress users. In addition to being a rock-solid twenty-first century operating system, OS X is the most luxurious of operating systems.

Double-clickable JAR files are functional, but they fail to impress OS X users. JAR files do not have an OS X feel to them. To impress your OS X savvy users, you need to package your Java applications with them in mind.

Contrasting bundles and packages

Before I explain bundling of Java applications as OS X applications, I need to explain some terms. The terms *package* and *bundle* are used almost interchangeably. In an elementary math class some years ago, you probably learned that all squares are rectangles, but not all rectangles are squares. A similar relationship exists between bundles and packages. Packages are always bundles, but bundles are not always packages.

Bundles are folders with suffixes, like `.app` or `.framework`, as shown in Figure 5.1. Some bundles, such as applications (`*.app`), behave to OS X users as though they are only one file. Bundles that behave as though they are only one file are called packages. Some bundles are browsable just like regular folders. Examples of bundles that behave similar to regular folders are frameworks (`*.framework`). These are bundles, but not packages.

Figure 5.1

Directory filled with different types of OS X bundles

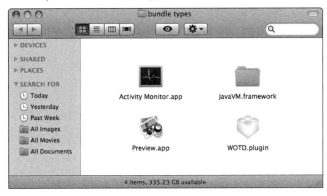

Types of bundles include libraries, plug-ins, and document bundles. This chapter explains Java application packaging and distribution. In the next section, I give a quick tour of a basic application bundle before examining the JAR Bundler application.

All the applications in your `/Applications` folder are bundles. For your first look at the interiors of application bundles, we should avoid inadvertently damaging an application you care about. Also, you probably don't know which of those applications are Java based, Objective-C based, or developed with another language.

Exploring application packages

Pulling apart Java-based application packages is a good way to start learning about creating your own application packages. Obviously, you are better off potentially destroying application bundles that you don't care about. Avoid destroying application bundles containing applications you actually paid for.

Prior to Snow Leopard, Xcode had a handy Java application template project that built Java application packages. Xcode version 3.2 does not have a simple built-in Java application project, but that is only a minor hurdle. In chapter 3, I explain multiple ways to create Java based Xcode projects. Also, later in this chapter, I explain JAR bundle creation.

This chapter isn't about making Java based Xcode projects, so I provide a pre-constructed Java project on the book's Web site. The Xcode project on the Web site is called `BasicAppBundle`. `BasicAppBundle` is a Java based application project created from the Xcode 3.1 Java Application template. `BasicAppBundle` works fine in Xcode 3.2, though. Use the `BasicAppBundle` project to an unlimited number of Java application bundles to experiment with.

CROSS-REF
Chapter 3 explains Java application creation with Xcode.

After downloading the `BasicAppBundle` project from the book's Web site, build the application. Building the application creates an application package in the `dist` directory. The `dist` directory is at the root level of the `BasicAppBundle` project. The `dist` directory contains a Java application bundle named `BasicAppBundle.app`. You may or may not see the `.app` extension, depending on whether you have set up your system to see extensions by default.

TIP
To view file extensions by default, navigate to the Finder preferences. Select Advanced preferences and toggle the "Show all files extensions" checkbox.

Double-clicking a normal folder opens the folder for browsing. Double-clicking the `Basic AppBundle.app` runs the Java program contained in the `BasicAppBundle` package. To see the contents of the `BasicAppBundle.app`, control-click the `BasicAppBundle.app` package and select Show Package Contents, as shown in Figure 5.2, from the resulting context menu.

Figure 5.2

Show Package Contents menu item

Inside the `BasicAppBundle`, you find four files: `Info.plist`, `BasicAppBundle`, `Basic AppBundle.icns`, and `BasicAppBundle.jar`, as shown in Figure 5.3. Java application bundles don't get simpler than this example.

Figure 5.3

Package contents tree fully expanded

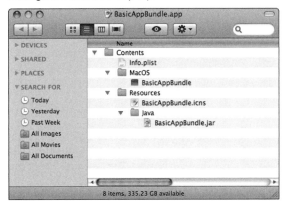

Every application bundle must have an executable targeting your OS. Looking at the contents of the `BasicAppBundle.app`, `BasicAppBundle.jar` sticks out as our executable, but that is not the case. The actual executable is located here:

```
Contents/MacOS/BasicAppBundle
```

The `BasicAppBundle` file is called by OS X when you double-click the `BasicAppBundle. app` package. In turn, the `BasicAppBundle` executable starts the `BasicAppBundle.jar`. The JAR file is considered a Java resource and is located here:

```
Contents/Resources/Java/BasicAppBundle.jar
```

N O T E
Application bundles are capable of hosting executables for multiple operating systems in a single application bundle. For instance, some bundles have an executable in a folder located at `Contents/MacOSClassic` as well as an executable in `Contents/MacOS`. In theory, an application bundle could host Windows, Linux, and OS X applications in the same bundle.

The `BasicAppBundle.app` package contains an `*.icns` file. Icon files in OS X are created from multiple images designed to look good at varying sizes. OS X takes care of the details of blending the images together, creating a continuous range of sizes from 512 pixels to 16 pixels.

The icon file is here:

```
Contents/Resources/BasicAppBundle.icns
```

I explain icon creation and assembly later in this chapter.

Every application bundle has an `Info.plist`. It is located at `Contents/Info.plist`. `Info.plist` is the information property list file. Open the information property list file by double-clicking it. The `Info.plist` opens in the Property List Editor application, as shown in Figure 5.4.

T I P

The Property List Editor is installed with the Xcode development tools. It is located at `/Developer/Applications/Utilities/Property List Editor.app`.

Figure 5.4

Property List Editor with an `Info.plist` displayed

Key	Value
▼ Information Property List	(12 items)
Localization native development reç	English
Executable file	BasicAppBundle
Get Info string	
Icon file	BasicAppBundle.icns
Bundle identifier	com.yourcompany.BasicAppBundle
InfoDictionary version	6.0
Bundle name	BasicAppBundle
Bundle OS Type code	APPL
Bundle versions string, short	0.1
Bundle creator OS Type code	????
Bundle version	0.1
▼ Java	(4 items)
ClassPath	$JAVAROOT/BasicAppBundle.jar
JVMVersion	1.5+
MainClass	BasicAppBundle
▼ Properties	(1 item)
apple.laf.useScreenMenuBar	true

Information property list files are XML files. Writing an `Info.plist` by hand is possible, but extremely unpleasant and error prone. The Property List Editor makes handling `Info.plists` manageable.

Most of the Keys in the `Info.plist` created for the `BasicAppBundle.app` package are reader-friendly, even containing spaces in their names. The human readable key name is another trick of `Info.plist`. To see the actual names of the keys, select View ⇨ Show Raw Keys/Values from the Property List Editor menu. You see that `Executable file` is actually `CFBundleExecutable` and the key `Icon file` is actually `CFBundleIconFile`.

Possibly the most common issue faced when debugging Java applications that you received pre-bundled has to do with the version of Java the application uses. Browse the keys in `Info.plist` until you find the key named `JVMVersion`. If your Java application fails to work because it is using the wrong version of Java, you need to modify the `JVMVersion` value.

TIP

`JVMVersion` in `Info.plist` can specify an exact Java version, the newest version of a specific release, or a minimum release to use. Specify an exact release with a value that is just numbers and dots, such as `1.5.1`. Specify the newest release of a specific version with an asterisk. A value of `1.4*` uses the latest version of 1.4 (1.4.2 on my system). A value of `1.4+` uses the newest Java release available. On my system that is 1.6.0.

Creating Icons

Icons on OS X are beautiful works of art. The first step in creating an icon for your application is to create various sized renderings of the art for your icon with either a raster art program like Photoshop or a vector drawing program such as Illustrator. After you finish your artwork, you assemble an icon using the Icon Composer application.

Until you fail to create your first stunning icon, you do not appreciate the time eye-catching icons take to design and implement. An image that looks great with endless detail at 512 pixels often looks like a blob of color at 32 or even 128 pixels. Designing an icon that looks good at 512 pixels and good at 16 pixels takes an enormous effort. On top of that, the icon must look good when dynamically sized to other odd sizes such as 149 pixels.

Just when you are pleased with a nice square icon that looks good at every imaginable size, your boss comes back and says, "Let's think outside the box." It is time to look at custom image masks that make your icon appear round, shaped like your company logo, or some really odd shape that only upper management truly appreciates.

Such is the life of an icon designer.

As a Java programmer working on OS X applications, you need to know the basics of icon creation. If you work for a large company, your company should find a graphic artist to create the final icons. You, as the programmer, need to understand enough mechanics of icon creation to explain to your graphic artist what she needs to provide for you to construct the icon.

Also, until you have final icon components from the artist, you need to create a temporary icon. From my experience, some folks have a tough time imagining how the application works if you merely say, "Pretend there is an icon that I double-clicked." In the following sections, I explain Apple's guidelines for icon creation, basic features of Photoshop, and basic features of Illustrator. Additionally, I give steps for creation of a quick-and-dirty icon as a placeholder until you have final art.

Understanding Human Interface Guidelines for icons

Apple provides extensive Human Interface Guidelines for the creation of application icons. In this section, I give a brief overview of the guidelines for creating icons that comply with Apple's Human Interface Guidelines.

CROSS-REF

In Chapter 6, I explore more details of Apple's Human Interface Guidelines.

NOTE

Apple's Human Interface Guidelines for icons are located here:

```
http://developer.apple.com/documentation/UserExperience/
Conceptual/AppleHIGuidelines/XHIGIcons/XHIGIcons.html#//
apple_ref/doc/uid/20000967-TP6
```

Beginning with OS X 10.5, Apple again pushed the envelope by demanding that icons look good at 512x512 pixels. A 16x16 hack job by an engineer is not going to cut it in the highly visual world of OS X. An icon that looks good at 512x512 requires an artist's hand.

As a programmer, be aware of the icon requirements for your project. When it comes time to do a little knowledge transfer with the icon designer, you need to let the designer know what art is needed and what is required for your family of icons to conform to Apple's guidelines.

Icons scale from 512x512 pixels to 16x16 pixels for OS X application icons. One icon is typically created from five icons of various sizes. The actual square icons that need supplying during icon creation are 512, 256, 138, 32, and 16. Creating a set of icons that act and appear as one icon requires a base image that works at 16x16 and then more detail for the larger icons.

Most good icons do not appear not square, even though they are. Some transparency makes icons stand out and lose their blocky feel. Transparency works for outlining the icon or adding shadows to the icon. Use a bit mask in your icons design avoiding boxy-looking icons.

Applications and files saved from the application should have icons with a specific perspective. Their icons should appear as though they sit or lay on a desk in front of you. Utility applications should appear to lay flat on the computer screen in front of you. The slight difference helps users determine what type of file or application they see, even when they are unfamiliar with the specific application.

Application icons communicate their function at a glance. Some applications are so abstract that an explanation through pictures is not possible, but most applications should display a picture that relates to the primary function of the product. For instance, chess programs often display a chess piece, and word processors display pen and paper or a typewriter. In some cases, an application-related logo is enough.

If your application is more of a utility with limited scope of use, then the colors of the icon should tend towards grays and feel less vibrant than other icons. Utility icons should look reserved, as if to say, "We mean business."

TIP

Get a good feel for the difference in utility application icons and normal application icons by comparing the icons of application in your `/Applications/Utilities` folder to the icons in your `/Applications` folder. Look especially close at Apple's pre-installed software for good examples.

Many complex applications come with supportive tools. For instance, many games come with level design tools. Supportive applications should have icons that integrate the icon of the main application that they support. Having related icons provides users with a visual clue that the applications are also related.

If your application saves files, the saved files should have icons related to the saving application. Typically, the base for a saved file's icon is a piece of paper with the top-right corner folded over. An image related to the saving application's icon should appear prominently on the paper to allow for quick identification of which application created the document. Also, the file type should be printed at the bottom of the paper icon.

NOTE

Java classes and JARs are treated as documents by OS X. Check the icon associated with both. Hiding the document status of JARs is the reason for bundling them as Java application packages.

Application plug-ins also have icons. In the case of application plug-ins, the icon should look like a cube building block with two sides and the top displayed. The left side should contain the application icon for the application that the plug-in is for. The right side of the block should contain the plug-in specific icon. The top surface should be connectors found on a building block.

TIP

The application, the files the application creates, and utility programs that support the primary application are all related. These related files and applications should share an icon theme that makes it obvious they are related.

Creating icons with Photoshop

Photoshop is an extremely powerful program. It has a huge number of features. Entire books and university classes exist teaching details of Photoshop's use. The few pages I include in this book about Photoshop do not give more than a glimpse of the power of Photoshop in the hands of a graphic artist.

You are likely a Java programmer. You are not expected to know the details of Photoshop's use or to perform the duties of a graphic artist. However, you need to know some basics about Photoshop so you can hold meaningful conversations with the actual artist explaining what is needed. Understanding a few basics of Photoshop facilitates knowledge transfer when it is time to get an artist to create icon images and other project art.

Also, having a temporary icon as a placeholder in your project or build scripts makes automation of builds easier. In this section, I explain important features of Photoshop and basic icon art creation with Photoshop. I explain assembly of the application icon later in this chapter.

Photoshop is a raster art program. Raster art programs create pictures with pixels. Photoshop has many advanced features that belong to the realm of vector art programs, but Photoshop is easiest to understand from the perspective of raster art programs.

NOTE

Vector art programs tend to scale images sizes better than raster art programs, which is why Adobe includes many features, such as type, as vector-based tools.

Create a new Photoshop document by selecting File ➪ New.... The New dialog box appears, as shown in Figure 5.5. Photoshop documents are images. The documents may have different types of channels depending on the color mode selected or multiple layers that display when selected, but Photoshop documents are only images. There is no scratch area off to the side. Everything seen in the document window makes its way to the final image generated by Photoshop.

Figure 5.5

New document creation dialog box

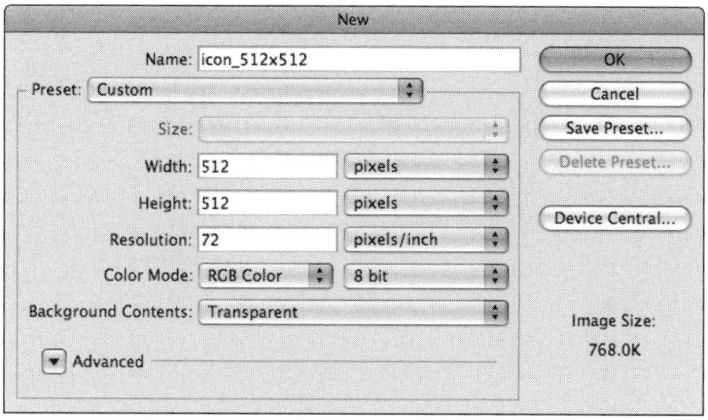

Select a meaningful name for your document. For instance, `icon_512x512` for the largest icon art. Do not append a file type in the New document dialog box. Select the file type of your icon art when you save the Photoshop document.

When creating icon art, set the Preset drop-down to Custom. Set the width and height units of your document to pixels, and then set the width and height to 512, 256, 128, 32, or 16, depending on the image or mask that you are creating.

The color mode drop-down gives the options: Bitmap, Grayscale, RGB Color, CMYK Color, and Lab Color. Select RGB Color 8 bit with Background Contents of Transparent for the creation of your icon images. Bitmap and Grayscale are useful, too, if you are creating custom masks for your icon instead of just using the icon art's default transparency.

CAUTION

Do not use CMYK Color for creation of icon images. CMYK Color is targeted to printing and gives a more restrictive color palette than RGB Color. It is tempting to select CMYK over RGB, because it has more colors describing each pixel, but in this case, more is less.

Notice the floating toolbar, shown in Figure 5.6. Most of your image manipulation starts with this toolbar. At first glance, the floating toolbar contains 20 tools. However, every tool that has a triangle in the lower-right corner is actually part of a tool group. Select a tool, and then click and hold to see the tool's entire tool group, as shown in Figure 5.7.

If you check all the toolbar tool groups, you find a total of 59 separate tools. Most of those tools also have multiple properties that you can adjust. You have lots of options for tool use in Photoshop.

Figure 5.6

Photoshop's
floating
toolbar

Figure 5.7

The lasso tool group

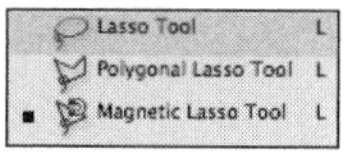

Don't let all those tools scare you. I explain the more useful tools in this section.

Three of Photoshop's tool groups target selection. The Shape Selection tool group, shown in Figure 5.8, selects circles, ovals, rectangles, and single columns or rows of pixels.

Figure 5.8

Shape selections group

TIP

Add to the current selection by holding the Shift key while using a selection tool. Subtract from a current selection by holding the Option key while using a selection tool.

In Adobe Photoshop CS4, the Quick Selection tool and Magic Wand tool, shown in Figure 5.9, comprise another of the selection tool groups. The Quick Selection tool behaves like a combination of paintbrush and a selection tool. The Quick Selection tool is great for selecting swaths of related regions.

The Magic Wand tool selects a single color within a specified tolerance with a single-click. If you toggle contiguous off, then it selects a given color across the entire image instead of limiting the selection to touching pixels that match.

Figure 5.9

The Magic Wand and
Quick Selection tool
group

TIP
Deselect the current selection by typing Command+D.

The most powerful group of selection tools is the lassos tool group, shown in Figure 5.7. There are three lassos: the Lasso tool, the Polygonal Lasso tool, and the Magnetic Lasso tool. All the lasso tools aid in outlining a selection until you close the selection. They are called lassos for that reason.

Use the base Lasso tool by holding down the mouse button and moving the mouse around freehand to select your outline. Releasing the mouse button stops the outline trace and closes the outline.

The Magnetic Lasso gravitates the outline you trace to any close edge. Releasing the mouse button does not close the outline. Instead, releasing the mouse adds a fixed point to the outline you trace. Click and hold the mouse to continue tracing. Double-click the mouse or continue the outline to the opening point of the outline to complete the outline and create your selection.

Create a selection with the Polygonal Lasso tool by single-clicking to create a selection outline. The selections are straight lines, which at first seem limiting. The Polygonal Lasso tool is the most precise of the three lassos. It becomes the most useful selection tool when you zoom in on an image to the point where you see individual pixels. If you need to create highly detailed selections quickly, the Polygonal Lasso tool is your best option. As with the other lassos, double-click at any time or single-click your initial point to close the loop and create your selection.

After you select part of an image, you can move it with the Move tool, shown in Figure 5.10. To drag an image selection with the Move tool, click and hold within the selected area and drag the selection to a new location. If you click and drag outside of the selection area, the entire image moves instead of just the selected area.

Figure 5.10

Move tool

Behavior of the arrow keys differs depending on the tool type you select. If you use a section tool, the arrows move the selection marquee without moving the selected portion of the image. However, if you have selected the Move tool, the arrows move the selected portion of the image with the selection marquee.

TIP
Change to the Move tool quickly by typing v.

Crop your image using either the Crop tool, as shown in Figure 5.11, or the Canvas Size dialog box. The Crop tool is best for situations where the result does not need precise measurements. The Canvas Size dialog box works best when you know the exact width and height of the new image.

Figure 5.11

Crop tool

The Crop tool works like the Rectangular Marquee tool described previously. Select a corner of your desired image, and drag to the opposing corner of your desired image. The resulting selection crops to the new image size when you hit the Return key. If you want to adjust the crop area, select handles on the crop area boundary and drag the crop area boundaries to their new location.

TIP
To deselect a crop area, press the Esc key.

Open the Canvas Size dialog box, shown in Figure 5.12, from the Image ⇨ Canvas Size... menu item. The two key items to remember with the Canvas Size window are the units and the anchors. Make sure you are using pixels. Percent is almost never used in the Canvas Size dialog box, and the measurements such as Inches are more for images designed for printing.

The Canvas Size dialog box's anchors determine where the cropping takes place. Each of the arrows points to the side of the image that the crop is measured from. By default, the center anchor of the Canvas Size dialog box is selected.

TIP
The Canvas Size dialog box allows you to increase the size of the image, as well as crop it. You also can crop the width while increasing the height or crop the height while increasing the width.

A closely related dialog box is the Image Size dialog box, shown in Figure 5.13. Open the Image Size dialog box by selecting Image ⇨ Image Size.... The Image Size dialog box handles resolution changes. It scales images.

Figure 5.12

Canvas Size dialog box

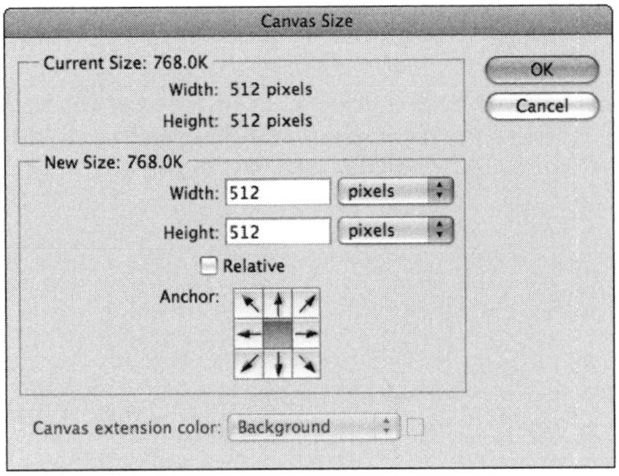

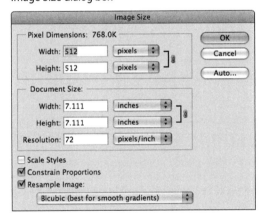

Figure 5.13

Image Size dialog box

Select either pixels or percent for your width and height units in the Pixel Dimensions panel. While the Constrain Proportions check box is selected, the image scales without stretching. If you want to change the width or height independent of the other, just uncheck the Constrain Proportions check box.

Photoshop always stores two active colors: a foreground color and a background color, as shown in Figure 5.14. Click either of the colors to bring up the Color Picker dialog, box as shown in Figure 5.15, which specifies whether it is for choosing the foreground color or the background color with a label in the dialog box's title bar.

Figure 5.14

Foreground
and background
colors

Figure 5.15

Color Picker dialog box

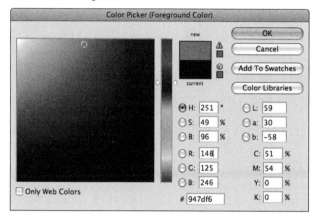

To swap your foreground and background colors, click the double-headed arrow next to the color display on the toolbar. To reset your foreground and background colors to black and white, click the little black-and-white version of the colors on the toolbar.

Another option for selecting colors, other than the Color Picker, is the Eyedropper tool, shown in Figure 5.16. Use the Eyedropper tool to select a color that already exists in your image. The selection becomes the foreground color. However, swapping the foreground and background colors, as described earlier, works for setting your chosen color to the background color.

Figure 5.16

Eyedropper
tool on the
toolbar

Brushes and pencils, as shown in Figure 5.17, are the quickest tools for freehand changes. These tools are especially popular with users of graphics tablets such as Wacom tablets. The most notable difference between a pencil tool and a brush tool is that the pencil has no gradient associated with its stroke, whereas a brush tends to have fuzzy edges.

Figure 5.17

Brush and pencil
tool group

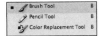

TIP

Brush tools work best for touching up photos where lots of colors bleed together. Pencil tools work best at touching up text and other solid colors.

A common task assigned to application developers is quick fixes to images with stray pixels of the wrong color. Suppose, for instance, that Mr. Baus Mann intercepts you at the door at 6:30 PM on a Friday night and asks you to remove a speck of dust that has found its way into a "vital" image. (Of course, it can't wait for Monday.)

Here's how you make a quick touch up:

1. **Open the image in Photoshop.**

2. **Use the Eyedropper tool to select the color needed for the touchup.**

3. **Zoom in on the speck of dust or other nasty aberration.**

Usually you want to zoom in to the point that you can make out individual pixels. This allows you to avoid changing pixels that have not offended anyone. Zooming in and out is accomplished with the key combinations ⌘+- and ⌘+=, respectively.

4. **Select the Pencil tool, and set the pencil size to 1 pixel.**

5. **Fix the offending pixels.**

Another common task is combining images. Adding images to an existing image is almost just a cut and paste away. Usually an image also needs some resizing. Follow these steps to import images into Photoshop documents at your desired size and place them at your desired location:

1. **Open the image you want to add to your existing Photoshop image with Photoshop.**

   You now have two images open.

2. **Resize the image you want to add to the desired size and resolution. Use the Crop tool, Canvas Size dialog box, and Image Size dialog box to get the image ready for placement.**

3. **Copy the image for placement.**

4. **Paste the copied image into the working Photoshop image.**

   The image appears on a new layer above the existing image. (I explain layers shortly.)

5. **Select the Move tool, and move the pasted image to your desired location.**

Yet another common task is adding words to your image. To add text to a Photoshop document, select either the Horizontal Type tool or the Vertical Type tool, as shown in Figure 5.18. Next, click the image to place the cursor. From that point, adding the text is similar to adding text in Word or TextEdit.

Figure 5.18

Type tool group

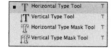

TIP

The active foreground color is the color of the text you type. Change the foreground color while typing to create multi-colored text.

When adding text or pasting images to your Photoshop document, the new text or image drops onto a new layer, as shown in Figure 5.19. Layers separate Photoshop document features so they change when edited without affecting other additions to the image.

Think of layers in terms of overhead projectors. As you overlay transparencies on an overhead projector, the entire image displayed is a combination of all the transparencies on the projector. Layers work the same way.

Figure 5.19

Layers view

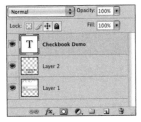

Select an individual layer to make it the active layer. Only the selected layer accepts changes. Combine all layers into one layer by flattening the image with the Layer ➪ Flatten Image menu item.

Assembling a temporary icon for your Java projects is a nice touch while you wait for a real graphic artist to create final icon artwork. Follow these steps to create basic 512x512 icon art, as shown in Figure 5.20:

1. **Open the Grab application in** /Applications/Utilities/**.**

2. **Open your development application.**

   Possibly, the application runs only from inside Xcode or Eclipse at this point, but that is okay.

3. **Using Grab, take a screen capture of a meaningful window in your application.**

   Screen captures are definitely frowned on for icon art, but this is for a temporary development icon.

4. **Save the screen capture, and reopen it in Photoshop.**

5. **Resize the captured image to fit in a 512x512 image. Actually, make the image small enough to place some text under it in a 512x512 image.**

6. **Create a new 512x512 RGB Photoshop document.**

   I use Photoshop CS4 in this example. In other versions of Photoshop, menus and features may have slightly different names, but the process should be similar.

7. **Paste your screen capture into the new document.**

8. **Move the document to the top portion of the document with the Move tool.**

9. **Use the Horizontal Type tool to place the name of the application under the screen capture.**

10. **Export your new image using File ⇨ Save for Web & Devices... menu item.**

The GIF or PNG file format works well if you want to retain transparency when the image is used for creation of the temporary icon.

Figure 5.20

Finished 512x512 icon art of Checkbook Demo

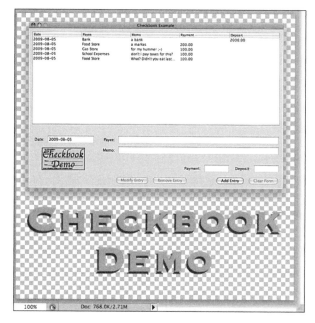

TIP

When using GIF files, icons in OS X are either transparent or not. The masks for icons are black and white only when made from GIFs. Icons made from PNGs have an opacity associated with them. The masks made from PNGs are scaled rather than black-and-white bit masks.

The next section describes using Illustrator. If you want to assemble an icon, just skip to that section. The Illustrator section covers similar material to this section with an Illustrator emphasis.

Creating icons with Illustrator

Like Photoshop, Illustrator is an extremely powerful program. It also has a huge number of features. Entire books and classes exist teaching details of Illustrator use. The few pages I include in this book about Illustrator do not give more than a glimpse of its power in the hands of an artist.

You are a Java programmer. You are not expected to know the details of Illustrator use or to perform the duties of the project graphic artist. However, you need to know some basics about Illustrator so you can hold meaningful conversations with the actual artist, explaining what is needed. Understanding a few basics of Illustrator facilitates knowledge transfer when it is time for an artist to create icon images and other project art.

Also, having a temporary icon as a placeholder in your project or build scripts makes automation of builds easier. In this section, I explain important features of Illustrator and basic icon art creation with Illustrator. I explain assembling the application Icon in the next section.

Illustrator is a vector art program. Vector art programs are good for creation of images that scale in size. Vector art programs, such as Illustrator, describe their art in terms of Bezier curves. No matter how large or small the images get, they stay exactly the same. That is the biggest draw of vector art programs.

TIP

Vector art programs such as Illustrator tend to scale images very well. However, the tremendous scaling involved in OS X icon art requires the project's graphic artist to create multiple pieces of art that work on different scales. If done properly, you may not even notice that the artist is providing multiple pieces of art instead of one piece of resized art.

On the down side, Icon Composer requires raster art such as PNGs or GIFs when constructing icons. Illustrator typically saves files in AI or EPS formats. These formats do not work directly with Icon Composer. Fortunately, Illustrator documents export very nicely to PNG file format.

When creating a new document in Adobe Illustrator, you have the options of Print, Web, Mobil and Devices, Video and Film, Basic CMYK, and Basic RGB document types, as shown in Figure 5.21. Don't let all these options scare you. They are basically all the same type of document. The real difference is in the height, width, unit of measure, and whether you are using RGB or CMYK.

Figure 5.21

Documents drop-down list

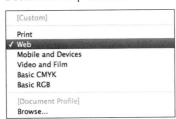

Choose Web for your New Document Profile, as shown in Figure 5.22. Choosing Web sets your color mode to RGB and your units to Pixels. You can just as easily choose Basic RGB. However, you then must change the unit to Pixels. Not a big deal, really.

Figure 5.22

Custom Web document in New Document dialog box

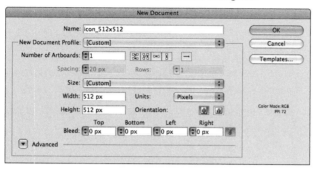

Choose one artboard. One artboard is all you need. Think of artboards as pages of your document. For example, if you design a flyer with a front and back page in Illustrator, you set your artboards to two instead of one.

NOTE

A big difference between Photoshop and Illustrator is that the workspace in illustrator can contain many artboards, but Photoshop documents only contain one image. (I am ignoring channels and layers for simplicity.) Illustrator has a large scratch area around each artboard where items are placed if you do not want them on the artboard. This is very handy when assembling Illustrator artboards.

Set your Width and Height to 512 px when creating icons. Not too surprisingly, that means 512 pixels. If you are making one of the other icon images, adjust the pixel width and height accordingly.

Bleed should be left at zero. Bleed is used for print.

Let me explain bleeds. You have probably seen postcards or flyers where the picture goes all the way to the edge of the paper or card. In large press runs, if ink is printed all the way to the edge of the paper, it bleeds onto rollers. When the ink gets where it isn't supposed to be, it messes up the print job, smearing and duplicating onto parts of the paper it shouldn't be on. So, when printing to the edge of paper, what really happens is that a paper is chosen that is larger than the final size of the printed piece. The paper is then cut down to appear that the printing goes all the way to the edge of the paper. The print that was cut off is called the bleed.

We don't need bleed for icons.

After you have a new document created, you notice a toolbar as in Photoshop. This toolbar is more geared toward vector art than raster art, though.

The foundation of vector tools such as Illustrator is the Pen tool. Use the Pen tool to draw Bezier curves. The initial click with a pen sets a first anchor point. Each additional click sets another anchor point.

Illustrator defaults to straight lines between anchor points. To create a curve between anchors, click and drag out handles from your new anchor point. The position of the handles in relation to the anchors determines the curve touching that anchor.

TIP

Dealing with handles and anchors to generate curves takes some practice. If you remember any calculus, here's a head start. Think of your curves between anchors as functions. Visualize inflection points, minima, and maxima on that function. Place your anchors at those points. Also, your handles must always be tangent to your anchor points.

At the bottom of the toolbar are the Fill and Stroke icons. Fill and stroke have to do with closed polygons. For instance, if you create a square, the stroke is the outline's color. The fill is the interior of the square.

NOTE

Photoshop has background and foreground colors on the toolbar. Illustrator has a fill color and a stroke color. Fill and stroke are both foreground colors. The background color in Illustrator is always transparent.

If you double-click the Fill or Stroke on the toolbar, you open the Color Picker, shown in Figure 5.23. For icons, you should use the RGB settings or enter the RGB hex number directly.

To the upper right of the Fill and Stroke icons is a double-headed arrow pointing at the Fill and Stroke. Clicking this icon swaps the Fill and Stroke colors of the currently selected shape.

To the bottom right of the Fill and Stroke icons is the Default Fill and Stroke icon. It looks like a smaller version of the Fill and Stroke icon. The default colors are black and white.

Figure 5.23

Color Picker

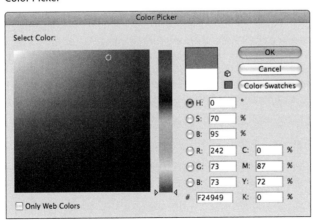

Importing images in Illustrator is called "placing" images. Select File ➪ Place... to bring up the Place dialog box, as shown in Figure 5.24. Make sure Link, Template, and Replace are unchecked. Link is the only one checked by default. Link creates a link to the original image. Link your images if you want changes to the original placed image to automatically appear in the Illustrator document.

After the image is placed on the artboard, make sure you have the Selection tool chosen. The Selection tool is the black arrow. Use the Selection tool to resize the placed image. To resize the placed image while constraining proportions, do the following:

1. **Select the image.**

Selecting the image makes the corner anchors available for dragging.

2. **Hold down the Shift key.**

3. **Drag the corner anchor until the placed image is the desired size.**

As you drag the anchor, the current width and height of the image are displayed to make sizing simpler.

After the image is the desired width and height, use the Selection tool to move the image to your desired location. Notice that Illustrator gives you visual hints when the image is centered on the artboard.

Figure 5.24

Place dialog box

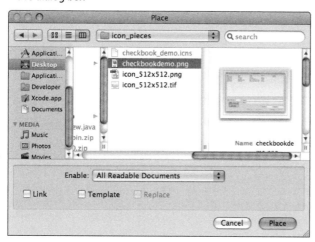

TIP

The default measure shown generally in Illustrator is in points. Points are a common unit used in traditional printing. Change the default measure to pixels by selecting the menu command Illustrator ⇨ Preferences ⇨ Unit & Display Performance.... Then choose Pixels for your General unit.

Handling text in Illustrator is easy. Select the Type tool for placing text. Click on or off the artboard to place your cursor. Finally, use the Selection tool to move the text to your desired location. Editing text in Illustrator is similar to using programs like TextEdit and Word. Look at the bar just under the menu bar for fonts, sizes, alignments, and other text settings, as shown in Figure 5.25.

Figure 5.25

Text bar in Illustrator

While you wait for a graphic artist to make art for your project icon, create some basic art for temporary placement. Follow these steps for creating basic 512x512 icon art using Illustrator:

1. **Open the Grab application in** /Applications/Utilities/**.**

2. **Open your development application.**

   Possibly, the application runs only from inside Xcode or Eclipse at this point, but that is okay.

3. **Using Grab, take a screen capture of a meaningful window in your application.**

   Screen captures are definitely frowned on for icon art. That is okay for a temporary development icon.

4. **Save the screen capture.**

5. **Open Illustrator.**

6. **Create a new document with a 512x512 artboard, and set the units to pixels and the color mode to RGB.**

7. **Place your screen capture in your Illustrator document. Open the Place dialog box by selecting the File ⇨ Place menu item.**

8. **Resize the placed screen capture to fit in on the 512x512 artboard. Actually, make the image small enough to place some text under in a 512x512 image.**

9. **Move the document to the top portion of the artboard with the Selection tool.**

10. **Use the Type tool to place the name of the application under the screen capture on the artboard.**

11. **Export the image as a PNG using File ➪ Export... menu item.**

    The background is transparent by default when exporting Illustrator documents to PNGs.

You now have an icon image, as shown in Figure 5.26. Creating an icon is explained in the next section.

Figure 5.26

Finished 512x512 icon on Illustrator artboard

Assembling the icon

Creating the artwork for icons requires lots of talent. Assembling the finished icon does not. Even mask generation is automated. Create icons on OS X with Icon Composer, as shown in Figure 5.27. Icon Composer is in the directory `/Developer/Applications/Utilities/`.

Images and masks are added to an icon by dragging them to panels inside the Icon Composer. The available sizes are 512, 256, 128, 32, and 16. Usually, masks are pulled directly from the image transparency. Occasionally, you may want to customize the masks.

Figure 5.27

Icon Composer

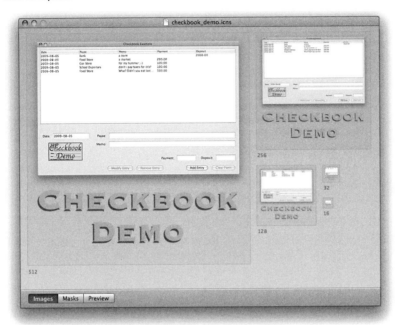

CAUTION

Be careful that any custom masks you create do not indicate opacity in areas where your image is not opaque.

After creating the icon, use the Preview tab at the bottom of Icon Composer to test the icon at a variety of sizes and on a variety of backgrounds. Be sure to test for these problems:

- **Manually resize the icon from largest to smallest size on a neutral background.** Look for jittery transitions between icon sizes. The transform should be so smooth that a normal user does not realize the icon is created from multiple images.

- **View the icon on several backgrounds.** The image should not blend into the background. If the image gets lost in the background, consider adding silhouettes to the icon that make it stand out on similar backgrounds.

- **Resize the icon from largest to smallest.** Details should vanish from the icons, not just become smaller. A general rule is that if a detail becomes too small to be meaningful or understood, the detail should no longer be visible in the icon.

If you already have a 512x512 image, such as a GIF or PNG, to use for your icon, follow these steps to create the icon:

1. **Open Icon Composer from the directory** /Developer/Applications/Utilities/.

2. **Drag the image onto the 512 panel.**

This brings up a Copy dialog box, as shown in Figure 5.28.

Figure 5.28

Icon Composer's Copy dialog box

3. **Select Copy to all smaller sizes.**

4. **Click Import.**

The image is automatically resized to fit all smaller sizes. Also, any transparency in the image is applied to the icon masks.

5. **Use Icon Composer's Preview tab at the bottom of the screen to check your handiwork.**

6. **Save your new icon as an** *.icns **file.**

TIP
Let Icon Composer generate masks automatically from your images. You rarely need to create custom masks.

Creating Packages with Jar Bundler

Jar Bundler turns plain old JAR files into friendly OS X feeling application packages with minimal fuss. Jar Bundler is located in /Developer/Applications/Utilities/Jar Bundler. app. Jar Bundler is installed with your Xcode tools from your system install disk.

Jar Bundler does just that. It creates bundles out of JAR files. The first step in creating a bundle with Jar Bundler is creating a runable JAR file from your project. Add any resource files that make sense to your application JAR. You do not need to make your application JAR double-clickable. Leave libraries as separate JAR files, and add the libraries to your package using Jar Bundler.

TIP

If you want to automate the bundle creation of your application with a tool such as Ant, use Jar Bundler once to create a fully functional OS X application. Then strip it down and reassemble it using your build tool.

Alternatively, create your application with Jar Bundler, and then have your build tool directly modify your working package with new builds.

Understanding Jar Bundler options

Jar Bundler has three tabbed views: the Build Information tab, the Classpath and Files tab, and the Properties tab. The Build Information pane handles `main-class`, application arguments, and Java version settings. With the Classpath and Files pane, you configure the main application JAR and associated library JARs used for the application. Using the Properties pane, set the JVM options, OS X properties, and Java properties that your application uses.

In the Build Information pane, set the main class for the application, arguments to pass the main class, the preferred JVM version, and a custom icon. To set the main class, simply type the fully qualified class name of the main class—in other words, the package name followed by the class name. Here's an example: com.genedavis.CheckbookDemo.

Arguments to main are command-line arguments that your application uses. These are different from the arguments passed to your Java VM. These are the args passed to

```
public static void main(String[] args) {}
```

NOTE

Advanced Java applications often include Apache's Command Line Interface (CLI) library. CLI takes care of parsing command-line arguments in POSIX, GNU, Java, short and long styles. The Web site for the CLI API is

```
http://commons.apache.org/cli/index.html
```

The CLI API is available under an Apache style license.

Choosing a custom icon is pretty straightforward. I covered icon creation with Icon Composer earlier in this chapter. If you change your application icon and recreate the application bundle, the icon change does not always take right away. In cases where the icon does not change quickly, I recommend copying an image file into the application's `Contents/Resource/`

folder and then deleting the image file. That usually refreshes the bundle's icon so the application icon shows up properly in the Finder.

TIP

View the directory structure of an OS X application by Control-clicking (or right-clicking) the application and choosing Show Package Contents from the context menu.

The Build Information pane is shown in Figure 5.29. The JVM version setting in the Build Information pane's Options panel is easy enough, as long as you keep in mind the meanings of * and +. The asterisk means *use the newest version of this JVM release*. For instance, the setting of 1.5* refers to the newest Java 5 release and ignores Java 1.6 versions. The plus means *use the newest JVM, but minimally this VM*. So 1.5+ indicates that Java 6 should run your application, if it is the newest JVM on the computer, but never use Java 4.

Figure 5.29

Jar Bundler's Build Information tab

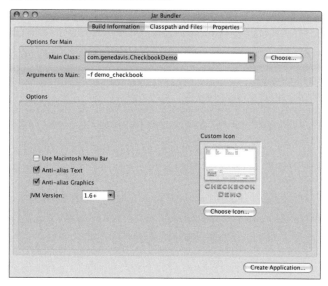

After you create a JAR from your application and see that the associated libraries are also in the JAR, then you are ready for the Classpath and Files tab of the Jar Builder, shown in Figure 5.30. Add your JARs to the Additional Files and Resources panel using the Add... button. The $JAVAROOT path for the JAR files is added automatically to the Additions to Classpath panel.

Figure 5.30

Jar Bundler's Classpath and Files tab

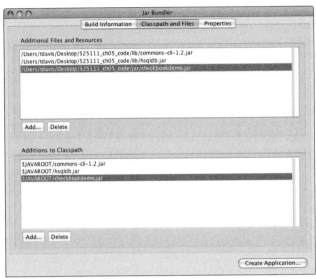

The Properties tab, shown in Figure 5.31, contains the JVM arguments, OS X properties, and Java properties needed by your application. Don't let the number of fields and properties on this pane deter you. Moving the mouse over any of the pane elements gives you context-sensitive help. Also, the default properties on this pane are often enough to get your development apps working.

Table 5.1 describes the properties available on the Properties tab of the Jar Builder.

Table 5.1 Jar Builder Properties Tab	
Property	*Description*
Type	The type indicator specifies this is an application. Keep the default value of `APPL`. Type is the `CFBundlePackageType` property.
Identifier	The fully qualified name of your application's `main-class`. An example is `com.genedavis.CheckbookDemo`. This is an alternative to using the Signature property. Identifiers are not registered with Apple. Identifiers are stored in the `CFBundleIdentifier` properties.
Signature	Java applications usually use Identifiers instead of Signatures. A signature is a unique code registered with Apple. Signatures are unique to single applications. To register your own, see `http://developer.apple.com/datatype/`. Signature is the `CFBundleSignature` property.
Version	Your application version number is in the form of #.#.#. The `CFBundleGetInfoString` property stores this information.

Property	Description
Get-Info String	This is the human readable version displayed by Finder's Get Info command.
Short Version	This is the short human readable version information.
Heap Minimum Size	This is a shortcut for the VM option $-Xms$.
Heap Maximum Size	This is a shortcut for the VM option $-Xmx$.
VM Options	Options are passed directly to Java. VM Options are stored in the `Java/VMOptions` property.
Allow Mixed Localizations	This is exactly as the name implies. You would rarely need to deselect this check box.
Development Region	This denotes the region or language of the application.
Bundle Name	This is the display name of your application in the application menu. The bundle name is used if this property is not set.
Info Dictionary Version	This is the property file format for this bundle. Typically, you should not modify this property.
Set Working Directory...	This toggles the working directory to the Java folder in the bundle—that is `Contents/Resources/Java/`. The property is stored in `Java/Properties/WorkingDirectory/` property.
Additional Properties	This holds additional key-value Java properties stored in `Java/Properties/<key>`.

Figure 5.31

Jar Bundler's Properties tab

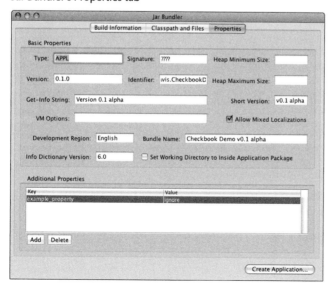

Demonstrating Jar Bundler

Now that you understand Jar Bundler and how to make icons, it is time for you to create an application bundle. For this section, I have created the Checkbook Demo application to give you an idea of how a real application is configured with Jar Bundler. The pieces of the Checkbook Demo and the final application bundle are both on the book's Web site.

NOTE
The Ch05.zip file on the Web site contains the source files, classes, JARs, and the icon and images you need to complete the bundle in this section. Ch05.zip also contains an example of the bundled application.

The Checkbook Demo has the following features:

- Command-line arguments targeting the application
- Libraries contained in external JAR files
- A custom icon
- A target JVM
- Images loaded at runtime
- About and preferences JFrames associated with the proper applications MenuItems
- A Bundle Name property differing from that of the Bundle's name
- An embedded HSQLDB database targeting a ~/<user name>/Documents/ directory

NOTE
HSQLDB is available from `http://hsqldb.org/` under a BSD style license.

Now let's create the Checkbook Demo application bundle. The steps for creating the application icon are detailed earlier in the chapter. Modify the steps to suit your own development project:

1. **Open Jar Bundler.**

Jar Bundler is located in `/Developer/Applications/Utilities/Jar Bundler.app`. You should be in the Build Information tab by default.

2. **Set the Main Class to** com.genedavis.CheckbookDemo**.**

The Main Class is the same as the `main-class` property specified to make a JAR double-clickable.

3. **Set the Arguments to Main to** -f demo_checkbook**.**

These arguments are passed to the application's `main()` method for parsing.

4. **Set the JVM Version to** 1.6+.

Remember that the plus sign means "highest version of Java, but minimally this version."

5. **Choose an icon.**

Icon creation is detailed earlier in this chapter. You should find an actual artist to create the icon's art, but you can easily create temporary art for a placeholder icon.

6. **Select the Classpath and Files tab.**

7. **Add the** common-cli-1.2.jar, **the** hsqldb.jar, **and the** checkbookdemo.jar **to the Additional Files and Resources.**

These files are provided on the book's Web site. The Additions to Classpath is populated automatically as you add the JAR files to Additional Files and Resources.

8. **Select the Properties tab.**

9. **Set the Version to** 0.1.0.

10. **Set the Identifier to** com.genedavis.CheckbookDemo.

11. **Set Get-Info String to** Version 0.1 alpha.

12. **Set Short Version to** v0.1 alpha.

13. **Set Bundle Name to** Checkbook Demo v0.1 alpha.

14. **Click the Create Application button.**

15. **Select a location on your hard drive to save the application bundle.**

You now have a fully functional OS X friendly application bundle. You cannot save the Jar Bundler configuration. However, you can easily update the directories of an application bundle with an Ant build.

CROSS-REF
I discuss details of Ant builds in Chapter 4.

Producing Installations

Presumably, you now have a working OS X application bundle. The simplest approach to distributing your application is to zip it, stick it on a Web site or FTP site, and make the link available to your users. Remember that OS X applications are actually folder trees with many resources. Placing the application bundle in a zip file keeps all the application's resources together during distribution.

To zip the application bundle, from the Finder Control-click (or right-click) the bundle and select Compress <your app name>. Another option is to create the ZIP from the Terminal. Start by using `cd` to change to the bundle's directory, and type `zip -r my_app.zip *` to place the application in a zip file called `my_app.zip`. (If using `*`, make sure the application is alone in the directory, because everything in the directory is added to your zip file.)

If you are looking for a fancier distribution, then read on. This chapter covers several common approaches to distributing and installing OS X applications.

TIP

Get your application some publicity by submitting information about it to `www.apple.com/downloads/macosx/submit/`. The listing will appear on Apple's OS X download page.

Understanding OS X installations

OS X installations fall into two broad categories: simple drag-and-drop installations and installer-based installations.

If your application does not require an installer, keep it simple with a drag-and-drop installation. If you have a basic application in a bundle that is completely self-contained, then there is little need for a custom installer. However, even with simple application bundles, it is convenient for the Applications folder alias to appear immediately next to the bundle your user wants to install.

More complex installations may require startup items added to the computer, user templates for application documents, multiple application bundles with tools supporting the main application, user editable property files, installation of command-line tools, and even system-wide OS changes such as to properties.

Creating DMGs for drag-and-drop installations

Simple installations of the drag-and-drop variety often use DMGs. DMGs are disk images. Double-clicking a DMG results in a virtual disk mounting on your desktop. Your application bundle is in the newly mounted disk (maybe with a `Read Me` file) and is dragged by the end user to the `/Applications` folder.

Apple recommends compressed disk images as the preferred application distribution method. Create disk images with the Disk Utility application. Follow these steps to create a new disk image with Disk Utility:

1. **Double-click Disk Utility, which is located in** /Applications/Utilities/.

2. **Create a new disk image by clicking the New Image icon at the top of Disk Utility, which opens a configuration dialog box, as shown in Figure 5.32, for your new disk image.**

3. **Name your** *.dmg **in the Save As text box.**

Figure 5.32

Disk Utility disk image creation dialog box

Save As:	
Where:	📁 Desktop

Volume Name:	Disk Image
Volume Size:	100 MB
Volume Format:	Mac OS Extended (Journaled)
Encryption:	none
Partitions:	Single partition – Apple Partition Map
Image Format:	read/write disk image

(Cancel) (Create)

4. **Name your mounted volume by placing the mounted volumes name in the Volume Name text field.**

Usually, the volume name and filename are similar, if not the same.

5. **Customize any of the dropdown configurations that fit your project.**

The other configuration options are pretty much self-explanatory. However, make sure the Volume Size is large enough to hold your application. If you require your end user to enter a password to decrypt your image, then add encryption.

6. **Click the Create button.**

You now have an empty mounted disk image on your Desktop.

NOTE
Apple has an excellent resource document on application distribution at this site:

```
http://developer.apple.com/documentation/Porting/
Conceptual/PortingUnix/distributing/distibuting.html
```

TIP
Don't worry about making a disk image that is bigger than your application needs. The DMG file compresses, taking only the disk space actually needed for your installation.

Set up your new disk image with a drag-and-drop installation. The goal is to have your application bundle and an alias to the /Applications directory on the new disk image. The background of the disk image root folder should contain an explanation to the end user that he needs to drag the application to the /Applications alias.

Follow these steps to set up the disk image:

1. **Drag a copy of your application bundle to the new disk image.**

2. **Make an alias of the** /Applications **folder.**

3. **Drag the alias to the new disk image.**

4. **Rename the** Applications alias **folder to** Applications**.**

5. **Add your background image to the disk image.**

   Usually, resources the user is not meant to see are placed off-screen so they become visible only through scrolling.

6. **Control-click (or right-click) the background of the disk image folder.**

7. **Select Show View Options from the context menu.**

8. **Set the background image of the disk image to a drag-and-drop graphic.**

   This is the image you added to the disk in Step 5.

TIP

Programmers often create a background image for the installation DMG that contains a large arrow pointing from the application to the `Applications` folder alias. The arrow usually is accompanied by a terse statement, such as "Drag <app name> to Applications folder."

The final task in creating your distribution DMG is converting it to a read-only volume. Follow these steps:

1. **From Disk Utility, select the mounted DMG.**

2. **Select Convert... from the Images menu.**

3. **Set the Image Format to read-only.**

4. **Save your image.**

That's all there is to creating fancy drag-and-drop installations. In the next sections, I explain general information about PackageMaker installations and izPack installations.

Creating PKG bundles

Though drag-and-drop is the preferred installation method, it is not the only option on OS X. Apple also provides PKG files. PKG stands for Package. Several types of bundles on OS X are called packages (with a lowercase *p*), but only PKG folders are called Packages (with an upper-case *P*). In this book, I call Package bundles PKGs exclusively to avoid confusion with the broader term *package*.

PKG folders bundle all the resources necessary to install an application. The only thing PKG folders don't contain to install an application is the actual installation application. Instead, when you double-click a `*.pkg`, OS X starts the `Installer.app`. Installer understands PKGs and uses the contents to guide your end users through the installation process.

Oddly enough, the Installer application does not create PKGs. That task falls to PackageMaker, shown in Figure 5.33. PackageMaker is found in `/Developer/Applciations/Utilities/`.

Figure 5.33

PackageMaker main window

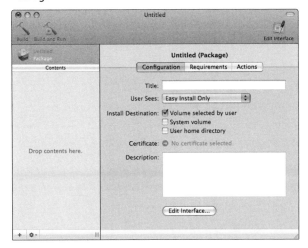

CAUTION

Be careful when creating PKGs. An improperly created PKG can at the very least lead to an unusable application, but at the worst it can cripple the end user's computer. Nothing shuts down a software company quicker than "bricking" a few customers' computers.

NOTE

A wonderful PackageMaker tutorial by Stéphane Sudre is located at

`http://s.sudre.free.fr/Stuff/PackageMaker_Howto.html`

NOTE

The PackageMaker User Guide is found at the Apple Web site at

```
http://developer.apple.com/DOCUMENTATION/DeveloperTools/
Conceptual/PackageMakerUserGuide/Introduction/
Introduction.html
```

Upon opening PackageMaker, you see a dialog box requesting your organization and minimum target OS version. As a Java developer, your organization is your root package name, something like `com.yourcompanydomain`.

PackageMaker is a feature-rich installation creation tool. PackageMaker provides customization of every step of your installation process. When you have finished configuring your installation, click the Build icon at the top of the main PackageMaker window to create your final PKG bundle.

Creating izPack installations

Many Java applications are customized and distributed to platforms besides OS X. If your project is one of these, then izPack is a good choice for your project. izPack is a pure Java cross-platform installer that works well with OS X. It also supports i18n (internationalization) with 10 languages currently supported.

NOTE

izPack is available under an Apache style license from `izpack.org`.

izPack emphasizes scripted builds, especially with Ant or shell scripting. Create builds in izPack as XML description files. After the XML installation description is completed, compile your build with izPack's compile command. Because izPack supports both shell scripting and Ant, integration with Xcode and other popular Java IDEs is possible.

CROSS-REF

Chapter 4 discusses shell scripting, Ant, and XML, which are all useful when creating izPack installations.

As I mentioned earlier, izPack installations are compiled from XML installation description files. Special XML tags in the description file indicate the location of resources associated with the installation. Resources include license agreements, images, and data files.

Two installation types are supported by izPack. The traditional approach is the single file approach. izPack creates a single JAR file as an installer. The JAR file contains all the resources needed to complete the installation. In many cases, this works fine.

The other izPack installation solution distributes the installation between a local JAR installation program and the Internet. The resources in this option exist on the Web. izPack pulls the resources from the Web as needed. Depending on the user's customizations of his installation, this solution results in optimized downloads that waste less bandwidth.

Now you may think to yourself, "A JAR-based installer isn't very Mac-friendly." (If you actually thought that, give yourself a gold star!) Not to worry. Not only can you use Jar Bundler (described earlier in this chapter) to convert izPack installation JARs into user-friendly applications, but izPack comes with a tool specifically made to do the same thing. The name of the utility is izpack2app, which copies your installation JAR into a preexisting application bundle. So whether you use izpack2app or Jar Bundler makes no difference.

Summary

This chapter is about application bundle creation and installations. Bundles are not always packages, but packages are always bundles. Packages, such as application bundles, appear to the user as though they are single files. Application bundles are folders that contain all the resources an application needs to run.

Apple's Human Interface Guidelines for application icon creation are very specific about acceptable styles of application icons. I explain the guidelines and the use of Icon Composer for the assembly of OS X icons. Both Photoshop and Illustrator are common tools of choice when creating icon artwork. You can create a temporary icon for use with nightly builds until you have final artwork from your company's graphic artist.

You assemble Java applications into full-fledged OS X application bundles with Jar Bundler. After bundling, four types of common installations are used to deliver those applications to end users. They are ZIP'ed bundles, drag-and-drop DMGs, PKG installation bundles, and the cross platform installer izPack.

Bringing Guidelines, APIs, and Languages Together

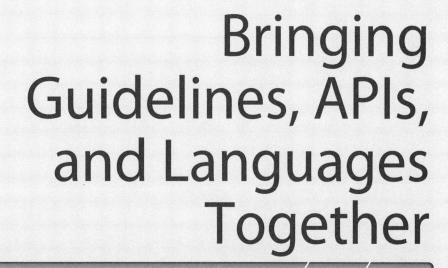

Porting and Designing

M ost computer companies build only one piece of the puzzle. One company makes an OS. Another company assembles hardware into a box. Yet another company creates software to sell. Still other companies create the APIs and widgets to mix it up with all the other companies' offerings.

While Apple, like all large companies, contracts out pieces of their products and assembles important technologies, they also are in control of the entire product. Apple creates computers from the ground up. Hardware, operating system, and applications are all designed, integrated, and sold by Apple.

This end-to-end control of production gives Apple power to design the best personal computers on the planet. Their operating system is probably Apple's greatest strength. OS X is designed with unparalleled modularity.

Recently Apple did the incredible by moving its whole operating system from PowerPC to Intel architecture without an entire rewrite. Such a change is on the scale of moving a sports arena in one piece to a new city without seeing it collapse. The move was successful in large part because of the modular structure of Mac OS X.

In this chapter, I explain the structure of OS X. I introduce the layers of OS X. I explore Darwin with an emphasis on BSD tools and libraries. I also give a quick introduction to Apple's Human Interface Guidelines.

Exploring Mac OS X Structure

Mac OS X is elegant and complex. OS X is an OS on top of an API on top of an OS on top of a kernel. OS X is a beautiful graphic environment and a gritty nuts-and-bolts terminal-controlled interface.

OS X is an incredible mix of powerful and pleasant technologies.

In this section, I introduce the major building blocks of OS X. Sitting on top of Apple's hardware, you find Darwin, the three major developer frameworks, and the ever-pleasing human interface, as shown in Figure 6.1.

In This Chapter

Understanding OS X architecture

Taking advantage of Darwin's utilities

Integrating Java tools with Darwin

Implementing acceptable human interfaces

Creating approved software update dialog boxes

Figure 6.1

Layers of OS X

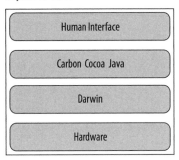

Reviewing the architectural layers

OS X ultimately draws its strength and portability from another operating system, Darwin. Darwin is an OS hiding under the hood of OS X. The reason that OS X successfully moved from PowerPC architectures to Intel-based architectures was because OS X is built on neither architecture. OS X is built on Darwin.

Apple insisted that OS X and its programming frameworks build on Darwin in a hardware agnostic fashion. Hence, when it was time to move OS X to a new architecture, the job was to port Darwin, not OS X. Better yet, Darwin was ported to multiple platforms before OS X was even officially released on Macs.

Darwin sits directly on top of the Mac hardware. Darwin is the foundation under the developer-friendly frameworks that most OS X applications are built on. Darwin also puts the Unix into OS X.

Mac OS X is fully POSIX-compliant. POSIX is an IEEE standard specifying APIs, shell interfaces, and utilities' interfaces. POSIX standardization ensures compatibility between Unix operating systems. Applications created on differing versions of Unix are quickly ported to new operating systems that are POSIX-compliant. OS X enjoys this benefit, too, because hundreds of common Unix tools and applications are available for OS X from volunteer sources.

I return to a discussion of Darwin later in this chapter.

NOTE

POSIX stands for Portable Operating System Interface for Unix. Luckily, the POSIX acronym used the X from Unix instead of the U. Otherwise, we would all be forced to try to pronounce POSIU instead of POSIX.

Most of the applications available to everyday users of OS X are built on three frameworks: Carbon, Cocoa, and my favorite—Java. Apple develops and maintains these three frameworks internally. The base code used for the Java framework comes from Sun's Java, but the actual integration into OS X and the OS X builds are all created by Apple. Apple's involvement in the Java framework development ensures the closest possible compatibility between Java and the native OS.

Carbon is a C-based framework used for porting applications in C and C++ to OS X. Carbon is an excellent choice for porting JNI-based applications to OS X. Java applications that interface with Carbon have access to OS X features ranging from the Quartz 2D graphics library to BSD OS services.

Cocoa is Apple's Objective-C framework. Your first thought may be, "How do you integrate Java and Objective-C?" Objective-C is built on C, so JNI integrates with Objective-C. In fact, the built-in JNI template in Xcode integrates with Cocoa rather than Carbon.

CROSS-REF
Chapter 3 contains instructions for creating a Cocoa-based JNI project in Xcode.

On top of all these frameworks sits the Human Interface. The Apple's Human Interface has led all other Operating Systems since the dawn of personal computing. Apple has a nearly 400-page manual detailing how Human Interfaces on OS X should work. I briefly introduce Apple's Human Interface Guidelines at the end of this chapter.

Benefiting from OS X frameworks

The officially favored approach to wrapping Cocoa and Carbon frameworks for use with Java is JNI. Other approaches such as JNA and JNAerator are also popular. Either way, the library you wrap must contain unique functionality to make the effort worth your time.

Shown in Table 6.1 are descriptions of some important OS X frameworks. Knowing the purposes of OS X frameworks helps you find the libraries you need and avoid spending time with libraries that duplicate features already in Java. I give an overview of Darwin's Unix libraries later in this chapter.

Table 6.1 Important OS X Frameworks

Framework	Description
AppleScriptKit	AppleScript plug-in creation
Carbon	Preferred C-based development layer
Cocoa	Preferred Objective-C development layer
CoreFoundation	Data types and services used by Cocoa and Carbon
CFNetwork	Abstractions of networking protocols
DictionaryServices	Dictionary access
JavaVM	Java
LaunchServices	Open applications and documents
SearchKit	Text searching and indexing
ScreenSaver	Screen saver interfaces

Using Darwin

As I mentioned earlier, Darwin is an operating system. In fact, you can install Darwin on computers with absolutely no other operating system using ISOs provided by Apple. The Source
Browser at http://www.opensource.apple.com/static/iso/, as shown in Figure 6.2, contains links
to Darwin installations.

Figure 6.2

Apple's open-source browser Web site

TIP

If you want to play around with Darwin builds and installs but do not have a spare computer lying around, think of
investing in a product such as VMware Fusion for the Mac. With VMware Fusion, not only can you use Windows from
inside your Mac, but you can install Linux, Darwin, FreeBSD, and other operating systems as though on their own computer. VMware turns your computer into a virtual playground for hacking operating systems without the need for
extra hardware.

Several third-party versions of Darwin have popped up over the years. One currently popular
version is GNU-Darwin, whose home page (www.gnu-darwin.org) is shown in Figure 6.3.

GNU-Darwin combines GNU operating systems and Darwin, providing the typical command line driven OS and GUI capabilities through X11.

Figure 6.3

GNU-Darwin home page

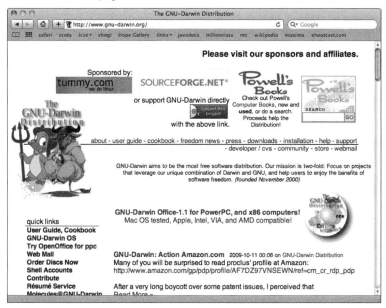

The point is that Darwin is a powerful OS in its own right. OS X sitting on top of Darwin is really just icing on the cake.

Saying Darwin is a customized version of FreeBSD OS is not accurate. Darwin combines Mach 3.0, FreeBSD 5, and other technologies, forming the base on which OS X rests. Mach 3.0 manages protected memory, virtual memory, preemptive multitasking, cooperative threading, and much more. Darwin is much more than a BSD OS distribution. However, for Java programmers, Darwin's integrated BSD OS has special interest.

Examining the BSD foundations of OS X

Integrating Java with Cocoa or Carbon is common when porting applications to OS X. However, if you have an application that demands access from the command line, such as via `ssh`, then you may want to consider integrating your Java application directly with the BSD OS libraries and tools found in Darwin.

TIP

FreeBSD is available from The FreeBSD Foundation. The home page is `http://www.freebsd.org`. Much of the documentation about FreeBSD also applies to Darwin.

Darwin's BSD implementation is fully POSIX-compliant. It contains the POSIX API. Darwin provides the command-line interaction with the operating system. Darwin supports popular scripting languages such as Bash, Perl, Ruby, and Python. Darwin also integrates X11, a Unix windowing system.

Using Darwin tools

Darwin comes with standard Unix tools. These tools range from `chmod` and `ls` to `grep` and `awk`. It may save you time occasionally to use one of the standard Unix tools from inside your Java application rather than recreate the tool in Java code or look all over the Internet for a Java library that already does the job for you.

Use the `Runtime` class to execute command-line tools from inside your Java application. Calling the `exec()` method generates a `Process` object. `Process` contains methods for handling the `InputStreams` and `OutputStream` connected to the executing tool. Communication between your Java application and the Unix tool your program executes is handled by way of these streams.

The following example, `Run.java`, takes a command issued as arguments to the `Run` class and executes the command as though the command were run from the Terminal. Obviously, this class is useful for its illustrative purposes, not as a replacement for Bash.

```
import java.util.Scanner;
import java.io.IOException;
import java.io.InputStream;
import java.io.InputStreamReader;
import java.io.BufferedReader;
public class Run
{
    public static void main(String[] args)
    throws IOException
    {
        StringBuilder sb = new StringBuilder();
        for(String arg : args)
        {
            sb.append(arg + " ");
        }
        String command = sb.toString();
        command = command.trim();
        Runtime rt = Runtime.getRuntime();
        Process proc = rt.exec( command );
        InputStream is = proc.getInputStream();
        InputStreamReader isr = new InputStreamReader( is );
        BufferedReader br = new BufferedReader( isr );
        String in;
```

```
        do
        {
            in = br.readLine();
            if (in != null)
                System.out.println( in );
        }
        while (in != null);
    }
}
```

Once compiled, execute the Run class from the Terminal and pass a command as arguments to Run. For instance,

```
java Run ls -la
```

lists a directory resulting in something similar to the following output.

```
total 48
drwxr-xr-x  8 tdavis   staff    272 Oct 17 17:22 .
drwxr-xr-x  7 tdavis   staff    238 Oct 16 22:53 ..
-rw-r--r--  1 tdavis   staff    586 Oct 16 23:03 Hello.class
-rw-r--r--  1 tdavis   staff    124 Oct 16 23:02 Hello.java
-rw-r--r--  1 tdavis   staff   1319 Oct 17 18:06 Run.class
-rw-r--r--  1 tdavis   staff    842 Oct 17 18:06 Run.java
-rw-r--r--  1 tdavis   staff    805 Oct 16 23:50 greetings.jar
-rwxr-xr-x  1 tdavis   staff     53 Oct 16 23:04 hi
```

The Run class begins by concatenating the args[] array passed to main(). The resulting String is placed in command. Next, the Runtime object is retrieved, and its exec() method is called with command. The result is a Process object containing the running command-line tool. I retrieve the InputStream from the Process object and chain it in typical java.io fashion to obtain a BufferedReader. Finally, I read and print the lines provided to the BufferedReader until the OutputStream is finished as indicated by the null value.

It's really pretty simple.

I list common tools found in Darwin in Table 6.2. The list is not even remotely exhaustive, but it gives you an idea of some of the common tasks already written.

Table 6.2 Common Darwin Commands

at	Sets a time to execute a command
awk	Scans a file and performs instructions on the matching pattern
banner	Creates a huge vertical text banner base of the string passed to the command
basename	Extracts a file or command name from a path and arguments
batch	Executes tasks when system load permits

continued

Table 6.2 Continued

cal	Displays a calendar
calendar	Checks a calendar file for pending appointments or events
cat	Concatenates files
cc	GNU compiler for C, C++ and Objective-C
cd	Changes directory
chgrp	Changes a file's group ownership
chmod	Changes a file's permissions mode
clear	Clears the Terminal
cmp	Byte comparison of files
comm	Compares files
compress	Compresses files
cp	Copies files
date	Prints or changes the date
df	Prints free disk space
diff	Prints file differences
du	Shows size of files or directories in disk blocks
echo	Echo
expand	Expands \t to spaces
file	Displays file's type based on contents rather than extension
find	Searches for files
finger	Snoops information about users
fold	Wraps lines of text
ftp	Executes the file transfer protocol program
grep	Performs a regular expression-based search
groups	Prints groups to which a user belongs
head	Previews first lines of a file
hostname	Prints the computer's current hostname
kill	Terminates a process (Use carefully!)
last	Displays login history
less	Displays the contents of a file
ln	Creates file and directory links
login	Logs users in
lp	Prints a file to the default printer
lpq	Displays a queue of running print jobs

lprm	Removes print jobs
ls	Lists a directory
man	Displays a command line tool's manual
mkdir	Makes a new directory
mv	Moves a file or directory
nice	Modifies the priority of a command
od	Displays a string or file in octal, decimal, hex, or ASCII
passwd	Changes the user's password
ps	Displays a process status
pwd	Prints current path
rcp	Copies remote files
rev	Displays a file with each line reversed
rm	Deletes files or directories
rmdir	Deletes directories
script	Makes a file called `typescript` of an entire terminal session
sleep	Sleeps like `Thread.sleep()` except the increment is in seconds
sort	Sorts a file and prints out the results
split	Splits a file into 1000 line files
strings	Finds readable strings in binary files
sudo	Performs a command as the super user
tail	Displays the end of a file (Watch log files with `tail -f`.)
talk	Chat with another shell user
tar	Archive directories or files
tee	Copies standard in to standard out
telnet	Creates a telnet session
time	Acts as a stopwatch for commands
touch	Changes the modification time of a file to the current time and date; also used to create empty files
tty	Prints the terminal name
ul	Formats underlining
uncompress	Decompresses files
uniq	Outputs a file with duplicate lines removed
units	Converts measures into other units
uptime	Displays the length of time the computer has been running (My OS X boxes usually measure in months.)

continued

Table 6.2 Continued

users	Lists the users currently logged into the computer
unexpand	Restores \t from spaces
w	Displays current activities of users logged in
wc	Displays word count (Use wc -w to count words in * . txt files.)
whatis	Displays a short description of a command
whereis	Displays the directory location of a command
which	Displays the location of a command
who	Lists the users logged in
whoami	Used by the very confused
write	Chat with other users
yes	Repeats y \n
zcat	Prints the contents of compressed files

Exploring the Darwin libraries

Darwin contains the standard Unix C libraries. JNI and JNA are common methods of interfacing with these libraries. I list several of the common libraries in Table 6.3. All standard ANSI C libraries also are available.

Table 6.3 Common Darwin Libraries

Library	Description
assert	Tests the truth of macros
ldap	OpenLDAP API
math	Math functions
memory	Allocates and frees memory
ncurses	A character screens display library; creates windows in the shell
pthread	POSIX threading
regex	Regular expression library

TIP

Explore the header files found at /usr/include/ for a more exhaustive list of POSIX C libraries.

Common Unix APIs are not the only programming libraries found in Darwin. Hidden away in Darwin is the Core Foundation framework. The Core Foundation framework serves as the base for both the Cocoa and the Carbon programming frameworks.

Core Foundation is written in C, but many of the data types work as-is with the Cocoa Foundation interfaces found in the Cocoa Foundation framework. Carbon-based applications often use the data types found in the Core Foundation framework also. The Core Foundation handles data types, strings, URLs, sockets, ports, XML, preferences, collections, dates, and times.

NOTE
Learn more details about the CoreFoundation framework by examining the included headers. All CoreFoundation headers are found here:

```
/System/Library/Frameworks/CoreFoundation.framework
/Headers
```

NOTE
CoreFoundation is actually part of a larger library called CoreServices, which contains AE, CarbonCore, OSServices, CoreFoundation, CFNetwork, LaunchServices, SearchKit, and DictionaryServices.

Scripting Java in the shell

Users directly access Darwin through commands entered in the Terminal or with shell scripts. In Chapter 4, I introduce shell scripting as it applies to compiling Java projects. Earlier in this chapter, I give an example of executing shell commands from inside a Java application. Many other uses exist for combining command-line tools, shell scripting, and Java.

NOTE
Command-line tools are often called utilities in Unix circles.

Most tools used at the command line are based on C or C++. However, you certainly can write your own tools in Java. Of course, you can always `cd` to your Java tool directory and type `java <insert tool name>` every time you want to use your tool, but that is too much work. After all, tools like `cd` and `ls` don't require that kind of exertion. Don't make your Java tools second-class citizens.

The workaround is simple. Wrap your Java file in a shell script. Your Java tool behaves just like C and C++ tools when properly configured. For an example, I use a simple class. It accepts one command-line argument and prints the argument:

```java
public class Hello
{
    public static void main(String[] args)
    {
        System.out.println("Hello " + args[0] + "!");
    }
}
```

The wrapping shell script is even simpler. It simply specifies the shell as `bash` and executes the `java Hello Jon` command. I name the shell script `hi` with no extension and populate it with the following code:

```
#!/bin/bash
# basic Java invocation
java Hello Jon
```

CROSS-REF

Handling arguments passed to shell scripts is explained in Chapter 4. Use your shell script to pass command-line arguments to your Java tool.

The following steps turn this simple code into a full-fledged command-line tool:

1. **Jar your Java Tool.**

   For this example, use the command `jar cvf greetings.jar Hello.class`.

2. **Place the JAR for your Java tool in the** /Library/Java/Extensions/ **directory.**

   This directory is in the system classpath. Placing Java libraries in this directory makes them available to all OS X applications.

3. **Place your shell script in** /usr/local/bin/ **or another** bin **directory that is part of your** PATH.

   Check for acceptable paths by typing `env` in the Terminal and checking the PATH variable. Moving the shell script requires the command `sudo mv hi /usr/local/bin/hi`.

4. **Make the shell script executable by entering** chmod 755 hi **in the Terminal.**

   You must perform this command while in the same directory as your shell script.

TIP

The `sudo` command authorizes administrative commands. Place `sudo` before a command that normally returns `Permission denied`, and `sudo` gives permission. The `sudo` command requires an administrator password.

After completing the preceding steps, enter `hi` in any Terminal window and your Java tool prints `Hello Jon!`, as shown in Figure 6.4.

Figure 6.4

Terminal displaying results of `hi` command

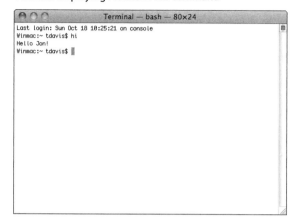

TIP

Passing command-line arguments to your Java tool expands its utility. Apache's Commons CLI library handles parsing command-line arguments nicely. The CLI home page is `http://commons.apache.org/cli/`.

Learning the Human Interface Guidelines

One of the greatest strengths of Mac OS X is the user experience. The consistent positive user experience of OS X owners is the result of Apple's extensive Human Interface Guidelines. The Apple Human Interface Guidelines are contained in a nearly 400-page manual documented here:

```
http://developer.apple.com/mac/library/documentation
    /UserExperience/Conceptual/AppleHIGuidelines
    /XHIGIntro/XHIGIntro.html
```

My goal with this section is not to abridge all 400 pages into a quick read, but to explain some of the more important concepts of the guidelines and to expand on information about the guidelines that I introduced earlier in this book. In this chapter, I explain fundamentals of providing a common experience for OS X users. I explain fundamentals of user interface design and testing. This chapter expands on the software installation instructions in Chapter 5 with information about providing software updates for your users. Finally, I give an overview of OS X technologies that you should consider integrating with your Java applications.

Providing an OS X experience

Experts at Apple specialize in providing users with interfaces that fade into the background. They solved many issues that prevent users from having a good experience with software. You can benefit from their research.

Most OS X users have never read or even browsed the Human Interface Guidelines, but they have internalized the basics. If you are new to OS X, start by exploring some applications that came with your computer.

Take TextEdit, for example. Even before opening the application, notice the icon is simple yet elegant. Even as a free application that ships with every Mac, TextEdit provides an icon that scales well on the Dock when magnification is turned on. The icon is a pen and paper explaining before the user opens the application or reads the name that the purpose of the application is writing.

After you open TextEdit, the menu bar is detached from the document. Application control is separate from the documents created by the application, separating Model and Control for users, not just the programmer.

If the user does not like the current document, he clicks the red close button in the document window and closes the document without closing the application. Remember that the data and application are divorced even from the user's perspective. So, the user now freely opens a new document without needing to restart the application.

On the menu bar, notice a menu named after the application. Every OS X application has an application menu. Three menu items always found in the application menu are Preferences, About, and Quit. Your OS X users expect to find these menu items there and nowhere else.

Designing the greatest and most useful application on the planet is not enough. The first key to success is familiarity. Create software that conforms to user's expectations. If your software behaves the same way other that OS X applications behave, then you don't need to document those features. Users familiar with OS X already know how to use those features.

Familiarity with your design paradigms prevents user disappointment and confusion. You spend less time on supporting the software. Best of all, reviewers focus on reviewing the utility of your software, not on complaining about your non-conformity to UI standards. A couple of bad reviews can seriously harm sales of your prized software. Ignoring the Human Interface Guidelines makes you an easy target for a reviewer in a bad mood.

Designing the user interface

Users know good design. If a user opens your application and intuitively knows what to do, you have a good start on a desirable interface. The only way to know if an interface succeeds is to put it in front of users and get their feedback.

Releasing beta versions of your software to the public, or at the very least a large test group, is essential. Do not let pride of authorship prevent you from changing your interface. If your beta testers overwhelmingly hate something, change it. If your beta users overwhelmingly love a feature, keep it. This advice sounds simple, but it's ignored far too often.

Keep clicks down. By this I mean think about what your users do most often. If their favorite feature can be reached only by browsing through three submenus and then clicking "Advanced Features ..." in a dialog box, you are making them work too hard. Determine what features common users of your software are using and make it easy for them to use those features.

A great technique for uncovering design flaws is to invite beta users to a free training session at your company. Throw in free food and maybe free airfare to making it interesting. Then have the application designers sit down and teach the beta users the software. Go around the room answering questions. Make notes on common or tricky questions.

Hold a design meeting the morning after, and review how the trainees used the software. Could their questions have been prevented with UI changes? Again, do not let pride of authorship get in the way of making a good product. Importantly, make sure someone with enough clout to authorize design changes participates in this process, or it is all a waste of time. The entire process is shown in Figure 6.5.

Figure 6.5

Design, code, test, and analyze

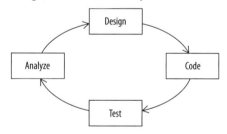

As mentioned in the OS X User Interface Guidelines, your users have a mental model of the tasks they want your software to complete. For instance, music listeners have the concept of music sets internalized, so iTunes realizes this with Playlists. Find out how your users conceptualize their solutions, and emulate this in your software.

Again, get face to face with your users. They are your domain experts. Corner them in a room with a whiteboard. Then map out their mental processes on the white board using UML. This is a wonderful first step to creating your Java-based OS X application.

Another key to a good user interface is "forgiveness." Think "Undo." Users need to feel comfortable exploring and testing features in your application. If they test a feature and cannot undo it, your application is unforgiving. By allowing easy undoes of commands, you encourage your users' exploration of your application and provide a better user experience.

Warn users when they are about to change their data with no possibility of undoing the change. Not warning them results in angry customer-support issues. However, warning users provides for a better user experience.

Remember to include the option in caution dialog boxes to turn off the warning. Experienced users will appreciate it. The example later in this chapter shows how to permanently save option changes in an OS X fashion.

Avoid modal dialog boxes. For instance, the preferences window should not be modal. Let users control the interface. Do not dictate to users what they will do next. Users should always feel in charge of the software, not controlled by the software.

Plan for universal accessibility. Different users have different need and different abilities. Never allow your application to override accessibility features.

Updating software

Provide expected OS X experiences and pleasant user interfaces through following the Apple Human Interface Guidelines. Every part of your application's user experience should provide appropriate non-jarring interaction. As an example in this section, I explain the Human Interface Guidelines on checking for software upgrades.

Make software updates a soothing experience for your users. The trick to a pleasant upgrade experience is good timing. Requests to update software the user is not currently using are unwelcome. Requests to upgrade software when the user is already working with the software are also unwelcome. Bad timing is unsettling to the user and provides for a poor user experience.

OS X users are not accustomed to intrusive dialog boxes while they work. The proper time to tell a user about upgrades is immediately after the software starts. Do not interrupt their productivity with a dialog box sometime after they are already busy.

If you have written software to check the Internet for upgrades, you know it may take some time to complete a check. Reasons include Internet latency or, with complex software, many time-consuming local and remote checks. How do you prevent a long start up for your customer and provide customers with upgrade alerts only at start up of your application?

The OS X way is as follows:

1. **At startup, create a thread to check for upgrades.**
2. **If an upgrade exists, set a persistent local flag.**

3. **Wait for the next launch of the application.**

4. **Upon the second launch of the application, check the local flag for upgrade information.**

5. **If the flag is set, notify the user of the update immediately at launch of the application, before he has a chance to use the application.**

6. **If the flag is not set, repeat from Step 1 by starting a thread to check for upgrades.**

CROSS-REF

In Chapter 5, I discuss OS X software installations and software bundling.

These standard steps avoid startup latency for the users. Also, these steps avoid unwanted interruption of the user's activities in your application. Obviously, happy customers buy software, and unhappy customers don't.

Apple's guidelines require that your program provide a preference panel to optionally deactivating automated update checks and a button to "Check Now" for updates. A complex panel is not needed. Simply add a Software Update tab to your preference window. Include a brief message and check box for deactivating the automated checks. Also include a button with the words "Check Now" that does just that, as shown in Figure 6.6.

TIP

Software Upgrade panes may have frequency choice, instead of a simple check box. Users may want to check weekly or monthly instead of every time the application starts.

Figure 6.6

Preferences window containing Software Update tab

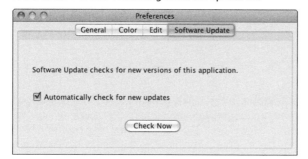

When your flag indicates that a new upgrade exists for an application, show a dialog box giving the user more information. Two versions of update dialog boxes exist. One is for free upgrades, and the other is for commercial (or paid) upgrades.

The upgrade dialog boxes consist of a bold question, an explanation, three option buttons, and a badged caution icon. *Badging* a caution icon means to take a standard OS X caution icon and create a version with your application icon in the bottom-right corner. The standard caution icon is located in the `CoreTypes` bundle here:

```
/System/Library/CoreServices/CoreTypes.bundle
```

Because `CoreTypes` is a bundle, you need to Control-click the bundle and select Show Package Contents to browse inside the bundle. Once inside the bundle, browse to `Contents/Resources/AlertCautionIcons.icns`. Base your badged icon on AlertCautionIcon.icns, and size it to 64x64 pixels. For the example, I use a simple badged caution icon in a PNG.

CROSS-REF
In Chapter 5, I discuss *.icns bundles and Icon Composer.

Free upgrade dialog boxes should give the options to Change Preferences..., Ask Again Later, or Upgrade Now, as shown in Figure 6.7. The Change Preferences... button should open the Software Upgrade tab of the Preferences window. The Ask Again Later button leaves the upgrade flag set and allows the user to continue using the application with no further interruptions. The Upgrade Now button goes ahead with the upgrade of the software.

Figure 6.7

Free update dialog box

A commercial upgrade dialog box, shown in Figure 6.8, contains a very clear message stating that the upgrade costs money. Also, the upgrade never happens from clicking any of the buttons in the alert. The choices provided for users in a paid upgrade dialog box are Change Preferences..., Ask Again Later, and Learn More.... The first two buttons behave just as in the free upgrade dialog box. The Learn More... button opens a Web browser displaying a page with more information about the commercial upgrade.

NOTE

Paid upgrades are never performed from within the software but are downloaded as separate installations after purchase.

Figure 6.8

Commercial update dialog box

NOTE

Examples of the Preference window with Software Upgrade tab, as well as both the paid and free upgrade dialog boxes, are available on the book's Web site.

The following example illustrates doing an automated software update check and paid upgrade dialog box. This example uses a couple of JSPs on a Tomcat Web server. The update check is performed on `localhost` instead of a remote Web server. The project and Web server with JSPs are all on the book's Web site.

NOTE

The Tomcat Web server is a pure Java application available from the Apache Software Foundation at `http://tomcat.apache.org/`. It is available as open-source software under an Apache style license.

Download the `UpgradeApplication` from the book's Web site. Also download the Tomcat server associated with the `UpgradeApplication`. The Tomcat server is self-contained and needs no special installation to run on `localhost`.

NOTE

Localhost is a special address, meaning your local computer. To reach a Web server running on your local computer, use the address `http://localhost/`. In the case of Tomcat, the server runs on port `8080`, so to reach a default installation of Tomcat running on `localhost`, use the address `http://localhost:8080/`.

If you prefer to use a clean Tomcat installation, simply download the Core Binary Distribution from the Tomcat site. I used version 6.0.20, but newer versions likely have the same installation process for new Web pages. Not much has changed there in many years of Tomcat releases.

After downloading and unzipping Tomcat, make sure the `*.sh` files in the `bin` directory are given permission to execute. Also, check Tomcat to make sure it is working properly by following these steps:

1. **Unzip Tomcat to a convenient directory.**

   For this example, a folder on the `Desktop` works.

2. **Using the Terminal application,** cd **to the Tomcat** bin **directory.**

3. **Enter the command** chmod 755 *.sh **to make all Tomcat shell scripts executable.**

4. **Start Tomcat by entering** ./startup.sh **in Terminal.**

   This command assumes you are currently in the Tomcat `bin` directory. You also may start Tomcat from the main Tomcat directory by entering `./bin/startup.sh`.

5. **Open** http://localhost:8080/ **with Safari, and verify that you see the default Tomcat installation page.**

   A line near the top should say something like, "If you're seeing this page via a Web browser, it means you've set up Tomcat successfully. Congratulations!"

CROSS-REF

I explain the inner workings of shell scripts in Chapter 4. If you are curious about how the Tomcat shell scripts work, open them in Xcode and take a look. You won't hurt anything by just looking.

TIP

To start Tomcat, enter `./startup.sh` from the Terminal in Tomcat's bin directory. To stop Tomcat, enter `./shutdown.sh` from the same bin directory.

NOTE

The default Web page displayed by Tomcat is located in the `ROOT` folder of the `webapps` directory. Web pages in Tomcat are organized as Web applications in folders of the Web application's name inside the `webapps` folder. `ROOT` is a special default Web application displayed at the "root" of the Web site's URL.

Now you have verified that Tomcat works correctly. The default Web page is shown in Figure 6.9. The two additional Web pages used in this example are in a subfolder of `webapps` called `upgrade_example`. Check Tomcat to make sure these pages are displayed properly. The addresses are as follows:

```
http://localhost:8080/upgrade_example/about_upgrade.jsp
```

and

```
http://localhost:8080/upgrade_example/get_current_build.jsp
```

The `get_current_build.jsp` displays simply 2010 as its content. The content of `about_upgrade.jsp` is shown in Figure 6.10.

Figure 6.9

Tomcat's default Web page

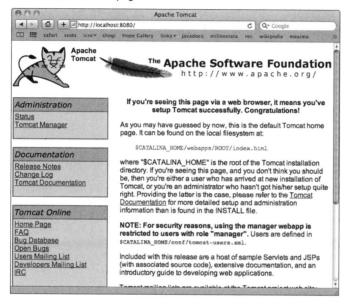

Figure 6.10

The `about_upgrade.jsp` Web page

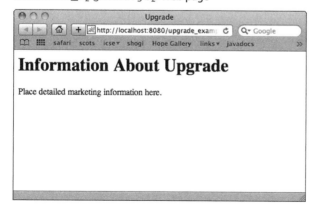

If you open the `get_current_build.jsp` file in Xcode, you find it contains only `2010` without even a carriage return. In the `about_upgrade.jsp` file, you find the following code.

```
<html>
<head>
   <title>Upgrade</title>
</head>
<body>
<h1>Information About Upgrade</h1>
<p>
Place detailed marketing information here.
</p>
</body>
</html>
```

Nothing in either Web page actually requires JSP over HTML at this point, but presumably you will create more dynamic content for an actual production application. However, for a piece of shareware or freeware, your current version page can be as simple as a single build number. At the end of the day, the real object is to get your code working properly and in a user-friendly manner, not to make your program jump through hoops.

CROSS-REF

In Chapter 3, I explain the creation of Java Swing application projects in Xcode.

Now we move on to examining the client application in this example. The application is an Xcode project based on the Java application project template found in older versions of Xcode. The project is just a starting point, and it needs some refactoring to bring it into a nice Model View Controller paradigm. However, for the purpose of showing you a basic software update implementation, it works just fine.

The project consists of five Java classes: `AboutBox`, `FreeUpgradeDialog`, `PaidUpgradeDialog`, `PreferencesJFrame`, and `UpgradeExample`. `UpgradeExample` contains the `main()` method at the bottom of the file. The `main()` method contains much of the controlling implementation of the update algorithm.

Here is the `main()` method from the `UpgradeExample` class:

```
public static void main(String args[])
{
   mainFrame = new UpgradeExample();

   Preferences prefs = PreferencesJFrame.prefs;
   boolean upgradeFound =
      prefs.getBoolean("upgrade_found", false);

   if (upgradeFound)
```

```
        {
            JDialog d1 = new PaidUpgradeDialog(mainFrame);
            d1.setVisible(true);

            // If this was a free upgrade the following would
            // occur instead of the PaidUpgradeDialog

            //JDialog d2 = new FreeUpgradeDialog(mainFrame);
            //d2.setVisible(true);
        }
        else
        {
            Thread upgradeCheckThread = new Thread(new Runnable()
                                                  {
                public void run()
                {
                    Preferences prefs = PreferencesJFrame.prefs;
                    boolean autoCheckPref =
                        prefs.getBoolean ("auto_upgrade_check", true);

                    if ( autoCheckPref &&
                        BUILD_NUMBER < PreferencesJFrame.checkBuild())
                    {
                        prefs.putBoolean ("upgrade_found", true);
                    }
                }
            });
            upgradeCheckThread.start();
        }
    }
```

The `main()` method starts the application simply by constructing the `UpgradeExample` class. The rest of the main method deals with the upgrade algorithm. You might consider moving the algorithm into a separate method in a control class in production-quality code.

First, I get the `Preferences` object. Java's `Preferences` class is found in the `java.util.prefs` package introduced in Java 1.4. It is responsible for persisting OS agnostic preferences between invocations of your application. To obtain a properly configured Preferences object, call `Preferences.userNodeForPackage()` passing in a class representative of your application's main Java package. For instance, I call the following in `PreferencesJFrame`:

```
        Preferences.userNodeForPackage(PreferencesJFrame.class);
```

I use the Preferences object to check the status of two properties. I check the `upgrade_found` property to see if the last check for an upgrade succeeded. Further down, I check whether the `auto_upgrade_check` property allows my application to automatically check for newer versions on the Web.

If I have found an upgrade previously, I open a dialog box to inform the user. This is the appropriate time to inform the user, because the application has just started and the user has not yet begun work with the application. This the least unsettling approach to informing the user of the upgrade.

I provided dialog boxes for both commercial (paid) upgrades and free upgrades with this project. To use the dialog boxes in your own project, replace the attention icon with an attention icon badged with your application icon and modify the dialog box text.

If no upgrade was previously found, I create a Thread to check the Web, or in our case localhost, for the current available build number. In this case, I have hardcoded the build number as a final int. This works for a commercial upgrade, because the upgrade is installed from a downloaded installation file or package. No automated installations happen from within the program as they would with a free upgrade. In a free upgrade, the current version number should persist in the application preferences so you can change the version during an automated upgrade. Finally, I do a check of the Web server with the checkBuild() method described shortly.

As mentioned earlier, I provide custom JDialogs for both paid and free upgrades. If you are familiar with Swing and AWT, nothing too surprising is hidden away in their code. Here are the three action event handlers for PaidUpgradeDialog:

```
private void changePreferencesClicked(ActionEvent e)
{
    UpgradeExample.prefs.setVisible(true);
    this.setVisible(false);
    this.dispose();
}
private void askAgainLaterClicked(ActionEvent e)
{
    this.setVisible(false);
    this.dispose();
}
private void learnMoreClicked(ActionEvent e)
{
    try
    {
        String aboutURL =
            "http://localhost:8080" +
            "/upgrade_example/about_upgrade.jsp";
        URI uri = new URI(aboutURL);
        Desktop dt = Desktop.getDesktop();
        dt.browse(uri);
    }
    catch (IOException ioe)
    {
        ioe.printStackTrace();
    }
```

```
      catch (URISyntaxException use)
      {
         use.printStackTrace();
      }
      finally
      {
         this.setVisible(false);
         this.dispose();
      }
   }
```

The `ChangePreferencesClicked()` method sets the `PreferencesJFrame` visible so the customer can easily modify the Software Update preferences. Ideally, the Software Update preference tab is focused. Minimally, make the `JFrame` and desired tab visible.

The `askAgainLaterClicked()` method only disposes of the dialog box. The customer sees this dialog box again the next time the application starts up. All flags and preferences remain the same.

The action you want is `learnMoreClicked()`. Because this is a paid application, the action opens a Web site with marketing information about the new version of your application. I perform the magic of opening the Web site with the `Desktop` object. Obtain an instance of the `Desktop` with this code:

```
   Desktop.getDesktop();
```

Open your preferred URL with a call to `Desktop`'s `browse()` method, passing in the URL as a `String`.

CAUTION

This UpdateExample application relies on the Tomcat server, mentioned earlier in the chapter. Start the Tomcat server before running the UpdateExample.app, or the example application will find no server on localhost:8080 with which to connect.

Checking the current application version against the currently available application version happens in the `checkBuild()` method. I placed the `checkBuild()` method in the `PreferencesJFrame` class as shown here:

```
   private int checkBuild()
   {
      int retval = -1;
      try
      {
         String address =
             "http://localhost:8080/upgrade_example" +
             "/get_current_build.jsp";

         URL url = new URL(address);
```

```
            URLConnection connection = url.openConnection();
            InputStream is = connection.getInputStream();
            Scanner scanner = new Scanner(is);
            retval = scanner.nextInt();

        }
        catch (MalformedURLException mue)
        {
            mue.printStackTrace();
        }
        catch (IOException ioe)
        {
            ioe.printStackTrace();
        }

        return retval;
    }
```

TIP

When using java.util.prefs.Preferences, the actual preferences are stored in *.plist files in ~/Library/Preferences or /Library/Preferences.

I check the Web site for the current version of the application using a Scanner. I simply call scanner.nextInt() to find the build number represented as an int. Setting up the Scanner is simple too. A Servlet, JSP, or even HTML file returns the build number, so use a URL object created from a String containing the Web site address. Take the URL and instantiate a URLConnection with a call to openConnection(). At this point, get an InputStream from the connection, and construct your Scanner object.

At this point, you simply need to be concerned with a couple of exceptions: MalformedURLException and IOException. I'm sure those exceptions will never be an issue, though. After all, the Internet never fails us. (By the way, if you believe that Internet connections never have issues, I own a bridge you may be interested in purchasing.)

Integrating OS X technologies

The upgrade example in this chapter integrates OS X style menus. As you have undoubtedly noticed by now, on OS X menus appear at the top of the screen rather than at the top of the application JFrame. Top menus contain several special menu items, but do not require you to leave the comfort of a pure Java language environment. In Chapter 7, I explain details of Apple-specific Java libraries provided with OS X.

When you are ready to leave your pure Java comfort zone, OS X provides several built-in technologies to give your users a more Mac-like experience. Much of this book explains how to interface Java applications with common OS X languages such as JavaScript, AppleScript, Objective-C, and C to take full advantage of available Mac libraries, frameworks, and features.

Your Java application can step outside the Java box. Consider creating advanced Screen Savers. What useful Dashboard widgets can increase your productivity? Imagine integrating your application with Address Book, iCal, or iTunes. Even working in the Terminal or via ssh, your command-line applications can bring a great user experience interfacing with ncurses. OS X is a feature-rich operating system. Do not confine yourself or your creative genius.

Summary

I began this chapter by describing the architecture of OS X. The operating system is made up of multiple modular layers. These layers include the human interface, the programming frameworks, Darwin, and the actual Mac hardware. The modularity of OS X lends to its strength as a modern operating system.

Darwin sits on top of the Mac hardware and is the foundation of OS X. Darwin is an operating system in itself. Darwin is open-source software, and several operating systems are based on it. You can integrate Java directly with Darwin through calls to Runtime's `exec()` method, turning Java programs into command-line tools with shell scripts and calling Unix C libraries included in Darwin directly with JNI.

The Human Interface interacts with OS X users. Apple provides an extensive 400-page manual explaining proper creation of user interfaces for OS X. Apple provides several technologies for use in your applications, including AddressBook, iTunes, and iCal. I provided the Xcode project, UpdateExample, as an illustration of implementing the Human Interface Guidelines for software update checks into your Java applications.

Integrating Windows, Menus, and Dialog Boxes

N ot too long ago, Apple deprecated and then removed all the Cocoa Java libraries from OS X. A common perception was that Apple was backing away from support of Java development on OS X. This perception is not accurate. A more correct statement is that Apple has streamlined Java on OS X.

Properly written Java applications are still first-class citizens of OS X. The application menu is fully available to Java applications. System events such as quit events are available. Even the Help Viewer is available to Java applications on OS X.

Using Apple's provided libraries, you can create applications that look and feel just like other OS X applications. You can adhere to Apple's Human Interface Guideline when creating your Java applications. Your users need never realize that your application is Java-based and not written in C or Objective-C.

All this OS X integration is available without JNI. At some point, you may desire to venture into the realm of JNI. JNI is the preferred solution for interfacing Java applications with Cocoa or Carbon frameworks in situations where Cocoa or Carbon integration is completely unavoidable. Most applications do not need to go to this extreme. Most common integration tasks are available from the packages `com.apple.eio` and `com.apple.eawt` without the need for JNI.

Chapter 8 contains an overview of JNI as used with the `com.apple.eawt.CocoaComponent` class. Chapter 9 provides a deeper look at JNI for OS X Cocoa, Carbon, and Darwin integration. This chapter shields you from more complex integration and stays in the realm of (mostly) pure Java calls involving the `com.apple.eio` and `com.apple.eawt` packages. This chapter is a JNI-free zone.

In this chapter, I introduce OS X file system peculiarities, such as file types and creators. I explain Dock menu integration. I provide an example of implementing HTML-based help books with your applications. Also, I explain the three most common application menu items used in Java applications.

NOTE

All the example code in this chapter is available on the book's Web site.

NOTE

I do not discuss either the `com.apple.eawt.ApplicationBeanInfo` or the `com.apple.eawt.CocoaComponent` in this chapter. The `ApplicationBeanInfo` class is not intended for direct use in your applications. The `CocoaComponent` class requires some JNI, so I put off discussion of the class until Chapter 8.

Learning com.apple.eio.FileManager

The `com.apple.eio` package contains only one class. The class is `FileManager`. `FileManager` contains only static methods. So you never construct `FileManager` instances.

OS X disk formats save information not accessible, or at least not immediately available, with standard Java calls. Application bundle locations, bundle resource locations, file types, and file creators are all available through the `com.apple.eio.FileManager` class.

This section explores bundle locations, resource locations, file type codes, and creator codes. I also provide an example of using the `FileManager` in a short program that identifies file type codes and creator codes.

Finding application bundles

OS X developers often need to find the location of the application bundle that started their Java application. The trick to finding the application bundle is calling the following:

```
FileManager.getPathToApplicationBundle()
```

This class returns a Java `String` representing the path to your Java application bundle. As an example, if the `getPathToApplicationBundle()` method is called from inside an application named `My App.app` located on the `Desktop`, the returned `String` looks something like this:

```
/Users/the_user_name/Desktop/My App.app
```

Locating bundle resources

Another common task that proves difficult without Apple's Java APIs is finding application bundle resources. Apple provides three versions of the `FileManager.getResource()` method to make finding resources easy. All three methods return a String specifying the full file path to the requested resource.

These are the signatures of the three `getResource()` methods:

```
public static String getResource(
                    String fileName)
public static String getResource(
                    String fileName,
                    String subDirectory)
public static String getResource(
                    String fileNameWithoutExtension,
                    String subDirectory,
                    String extension)
```

These three methods throw `FileNotFoundExceptions`, as you probably expect. The first two methods take a filename with an extension such as `.txt` or `.png`. The final method expects the root name as the first parameter and the extension as the last parameter.

Getting and setting file types and creators

On OS X, files are identified by file extensions. Also, files are identified by types and creators. A type identifies what type of data is in a file or if a file is executable. A creator identifies what application should open a file. Extensions, types, and creators all serve as clues to the operating system as to what to do with files.

C A U T I O N

A file's creator is not necessarily its actual creator. For instance, your program may export a screen capture to a PNG, but purposely set its creator to Adobe Photoshop, because your application cannot open PNGs.

N O T E

Many files do not set their type or creator. Applications that do not set their type or creator have a default value of 0.

Types and creators are both represented by four bytes. Of course, four bytes conveniently fit into 32bit `int`s. Java has lots of those.

These methods are available for handling types and creators from `FileManager`:

```
public static int getFileType( String fileName )
public static int getFileCreator( String fileName )
public static void setFileType( String fileName, int type )
public static void setFileCreator(String fileName, int creator )
public static void setFileTypeAndCreator(
                    String filename,
                    int type,
                    int creator)
```

Each of these methods throws an `IOException`.

The use of these five `FileManager` methods is straightforward. Use full paths for the first parameter and Java `int`s for the types and creators.

TIP

When "exporting" files rather than saving files from your applications, set the exported file's creator to an application that handles that type of file. For example, if you exported a *.png file from your application, you might set the creator to Photoshop instead of your application.

What is not so straightforward is figuring out what the common types and creators are that you want to use when creating your documents. The `FileManagerExample` application that follows provides you with a quick, easy tool for finding Java `int`s representing types and creators. The `FileManagerExample` also demonstrates the use of the `FileManager` class.

The source and a double-clickable Java application bundle version of this program are both found on the book's Web site.

```java
package com.genedavis;
import java.awt.Container;
import java.awt.event.ActionEvent;
import java.awt.event.ActionListener;
import java.io.File;
import java.io.IOException;
import javax.swing.JButton;
import javax.swing.JFileChooser;
import javax.swing.JFrame;
import javax.swing.JOptionPane;
import javax.swing.JPanel;
import com.apple.eio.FileManager;
public class FileManagerExample
{
    JFrame mainFrame;

    public static void main( String[] args ) throws Exception
    {
        new FileManagerExample();
    }

    public FileManagerExample()
    {
        mainFrame = new JFrame("File Manager Example");
        Container pane = mainFrame.getContentPane();
        pane.setLayout( null );

        JButton button = new JButton("Open Dialog");
        mainFrame.add( button );
        button.setBounds(120, 70, 160, 32);
```

```
      button.addActionListener(new ActionListener()
      {
         public void actionPerformed(ActionEvent ae)
         {
            Thread t = new Thread(new Runnable()
            {
               public void run()
               {
                  openDialog();
               }
            });
            t.start();
         }
      });

      mainFrame.setSize(400, 200);
      mainFrame.setVisible(true);

   }

   private void openDialog()
   {
      try
      {
         JFileChooser jfc = new JFileChooser();
         jfc.showDialog(mainFrame, "Get Type and Creator");

         File file = jfc.getSelectedFile();
         String path = file.getCanonicalPath();

         // Get the creator and type using FileManager
         int creator = FileManager.getFileCreator(path);
         int type = FileManager.getFileType(path);

         JOptionPane.showMessageDialog(
               mainFrame,
               "File: " + path + "\n\n" +
               "Creator: " + creator + "\n" +
               "Type: " + type);
      }
      catch (IOException ioe)
      {
         ioe.printStackTrace();
      }
   }
}
```

The book's Web site contains the source for the `FileManagerExample` class. The source is in the `file_manager_example` project. I created the `file_manager_example` project based on the Xcode Organizer Java Application template. The project is an Ant-based project, so you can integrate it into most popular Java IDEs.

To build the project, open Terminal from the `/Applcations/Utilities/` directory. Change your directory to the project directory root with the `cd` command. Enter the command `ant` in the Terminal. The Ant project creates a Mac OS X application bundle and places it in the `dist/` directory. Navigate to the project `dist/` directory from Finder and double-click your new application to run the example.

CROSS-REF

In Chapter 3, I explain use of Organizer to create Java project templates.

This application opens a `JFrame`. The `JFrame` contains one button. Clicking the button opens a file browser. Select a file with the file dialog box; and if it has a type and creator, they are displayed, as shown in Figure 7.1. Otherwise, `0` is displayed for each value.

Figure 7.1

Message dialog box showing a file path, type, and creator

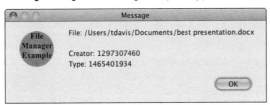

I use the `FileManager` class near the end of the `openDialog()` method. I call both `getFileCreator()` and `getFileType()`. Both static methods return `int` values. I display those two values in the message dialog box.

Investigating com.apple.eawt Classes

Most applications need a Help Viewer, a customized Dock menu, or at least a working preference menu item in the application menu. Intercepting system quit events, implementing an application menu preference item, and providing menu item searching from a Help menu on your screen menu may not "wow" your customers, but your OS X customers will notice if those features are missing. The `com.apple.eawt` package contains the classes for all these tasks.

Manipulating the Dock

One of the most obvious features of OS X is the Dock. When magnification is turned on, beautiful icons seem to burst into view as users mouse over them. Properly bundled Java applications take full advantage of the Dock and Dock menus.

The `com.apple.eawt.Application` class provides several methods for manipulating the OS X Dock. The `Application`'s `setDockIconImage()` method allows you to customize your Dock icon beyond displaying your default application bundle icon. Also, the `Application`'s `setDockIconBadge()` method enables system badging of the Dock icon. (In this context, badges are small images attached to an application's Dock icon that provide visual clues as to the current state of the application.)

The `com.apple.eawtApplication` method most commonly used by Java developers is the `setDockMenu()` method. This method places custom menu items and submenus on the dock.

Follow these steps to customize the Dock menu:

1. **Instantiate your application's** JFrame.

2. **Create a** java.awt.PopupMenu **for use in the Dock.**

3. **Add menu items and submenus to the** PopupMenu.

4. **Add your** PopupMenu **to your** JFrame **with the** add() **method.**

5. **Instantiate a** com.apple.eawt.Application **object.**

6. **Add your** PopupMenu **to your** Application **object using the** setDockMenu() **method.**

TIP

I encourage Java application bundling on OS X. However, if you want to forgo the joys of creating application bundles for your Java applications and still want to have a nice-looking name and icon in the OS X Dock, I have a couple of command line arguments for you.

The `-Xdock:name=<some name>` argument customizes your application name in the Dock, and the `-Xdock:icon=<some path>` argument customizes your Dock icon. For example,

```
java -Xdock:name="My App" -cp ame.jar ¬
    com.genedavis.ApplicationMenuExample
```

sets `com.genedavis.ApplicationMenuExample` to run under the name `My App`.

TIP

When running a bundled application in headless mode, meaning no menu or Dock icon, use a combination of the `java.awt.headless` property set to `true` and `LSUIElement` set to 1. Set both properties in your `Info.plist`.

Some employers may not want a full application bundle created for their cross-platform Java application. Never fear, Dock modifications are available from double-clickable JAR files as well as bundled applications. The following example works well from the command line, a double-clickable JAR, and an application bundle.

The following source is for the `DockExample` class. `DockExample` follows the steps I stated for modifying the Dock menu with a `PopupMenu`. The `DockExample` class illustrates adding custom menus and menu items to the OS X Dock. The final Dock menu for the Dock Example program is shown in Figure 7.2. The source files for Dock Example are on the book's Web site.

Figure 7.2

Modified Dock menu from DockExample class execution

```java
package com.genedavis;
import java.awt.Menu;
import java.awt.MenuItem;
import java.awt.PopupMenu;
import java.awt.event.ActionEvent;
import java.awt.event.ActionListener;
import javax.swing.JFrame;
import javax.swing.JOptionPane;
import com.apple.eawt.Application;
public class DockExample {
    public static void main( String[] args )
    {

        //create the JFrame
        final JFrame mainFrame = new JFrame("Dock Example");


        // Make sure the dock exists before you
        // attempt to modify it.
        Application app = new Application();
        PopupMenu popup = new PopupMenu();
        Menu submenu = new Menu( "Nested Menu" );
```

```java
// create MenuItems (not JMenuItems)

MenuItem firstItem =
    new MenuItem("First Menu Item");
MenuItem secondItem =
    new MenuItem("Second Menu Item");

MenuItem thirdItem =
    new MenuItem("Third Menu Item");


// create action listeners

firstItem.addActionListener(
    new ActionListener () {
        public void actionPerformed ( ActionEvent ae )
        {
            JOptionPane.showMessageDialog(
                mainFrame,
                "First Action");
        }
    });
secondItem.addActionListener(
    new ActionListener () {
        public void actionPerformed ( ActionEvent ae )
        {
            JOptionPane.showMessageDialog(
                mainFrame,
                "Second Action");
        }
    });

thirdItem.addActionListener(
    new ActionListener () {
        public void actionPerformed ( ActionEvent ae )
        {
            JOptionPane.showMessageDialog(
                mainFrame,
                "Third Action");
        }
    });

// make the JFrame visible before adding popup
mainFrame.setSize(400, 200);
mainFrame.setVisible(true);
//adding menus and menu items
popup.add( firstItem );
popup.add( secondItem );
```

```
        submenu.add( thirdItem );
        popup.add( submenu );

        // your popup must be added to your JFrame
        // even though it is used by the Dock
        mainFrame.add( popup );

        // finally you are ready to set the
        // custom Dock menu
        app.setDockMenu( popup );
    }
}
```

The book's Web site contains the source for the `DockExample` class. The source is in the `dock_example` project. I created the `dock_example` project based on the Xcode Organizer Java Application template. The project is an Ant-based project, so you can integrate it into most popular Java IDEs.

To build the project, open Terminal from the `/Applcations/Utilities/` directory. Change your directory to the project directory root with the `cd` command. Enter the command `ant` in the Terminal. The Ant project creates a Mac OS X application bundle and places it in the `dist/` directory. Navigate to the project `dist/` directory from Finder and double-click your new application to run the example.

Opening the Help Viewer

Help Viewer is the Apple help system. Help Viewer displays help books created for application documentation purposes. OS X users are accustomed to the Help Viewer, so again, the Apple-provided technology is the best API to use in your OS X Java applications.

In this section, I explain simple Help Viewer integration into Java applications. This section explains `Info.plist` properties associated with help, help book creation, help book placement, and integration into the menu bar.

Follow three steps to implement Help Viewer integration:

1. **Create Web pages with relative links containing your support pages.**

This is your help book.

2. **Place your help book in a subdirectory of your application bundle's** Resources **folder.**

I chose the name of `help_book` for the directory in this section's example.

3. **Set the** CFBundleHelpBookName **and** CFBundleHelpBookFolder **properties in your application's** Info.plist **file.**

As I mentioned earlier, Help Viewer displays help books. A help book, in its simplest form, is a collection of HTML 4.01 pages. Many applications ported from other platforms already have HTML-based help systems. HTML is a common approach for help implementation.

HTML is the language of Web pages. If you have a set of customer support pages on your Web site, your first step in creating a help book is retrieving a copy of those pages. All image tags and hyperlinks must contain relative links. The Web developer who set up your Web site understands how to create relative links. Be sure to request relative links, or your help book may contain broken links.

Your entry Web page needs the following lines of code in the header somewhere above the title tag:

```
<meta http-equiv="content-type"
          content="text/html;charset=iso-8859-1">
<meta NAME="AppleTitle" CONTENT="<apple title goes here>">
```

Change `<apple title goes here>` to your desired help book title. The title should not have angle brackets.

Browse your help book with a normal Web browser, such as Safari, in order to test that all the resources are linked properly. Move your help book into your application bundle with the following steps:

1. **Name the entry page for your help book** index.html.

   The filename must be `index.html` in order for Help Viewer to recognize it. It is very likely that the entry page is already named `index`, but with a different file extension, such as `php` or `jsp`.

2. **Create a folder for your help book under the** Resources **folder in the application bundle.**

3. **Copy your help book into the new help book folder.**

NOTE
Relative links are links that give an address "relative" to the current file and directory.

Your application bundle contains a file called `Info.plist`. Double-clicking the `Info.plist` file opens it in the Property List Editor. Using the Property List Editor, add the `CFBundleHelpBookName` and the `CFBundleHelpBookFolder` properties. The alternate names for these properties are `Help Book identifier` and `Help Book directory name`.

The CFBundleHelpBookName identifies the help book to the system. Choose a name that you feel is appropriate. The name actually displayed in the Help Viewer is taken from the HTML file's head area.

The CFBundleHelpBookFolder names the directory under Resources in which your help book is stored. This folder is the directory you created in Step 2 of the preceding list.

The last step to implementing a basic help book is creating your Help menu. You can use two tricks to make the implementation easier. First, set your menu preference to screen menus. On OS X, menus can reside in the application window or at the top of the monitor. Most OS X application have their menus set to use screen menus instead of menus attached to windows. Set your preferred menu style with the following line of code:

```
System.setProperty( "apple.laf.useScreenMenuBar", "true" );
```

Second, call openHelpViewer() on your com.apple.eawt.Application object when your help menu item is selected.

Create your menu bar, menus, and menu items using JMenuBar, JMenu, and JMenuItem, just as you do with other Java applications. Also, add your JMenuBar to your JFrame as normal. Create a JMenu titled Help and add a menu item to the Help menu for opening the Help Viewer. The action performed by the help menu item is openHelpViewer().

That's all you need to do to create a basic OS X-compliant help book for your Java application.

When you run your Java application from the application bundle, notice that you get an extra search field under your help menu for free. Probably the coolest feature of this free search is that it searches for menu items matching the search parameters. For instance, if you have a JMenuItem titled "Coolest Feature of All Time" hidden away in 16 layers of submenus, all your user has to do is type "Coolest Feature" into Help ⇨ Search and the built-in help system displays the menu item they desire.

Now an example is in order. The following example is available on the book's Web site. The code consists of a three-file help book, one main class named HelpViewerExample, and an application bundle.

As I just mentioned, the book's Web site contains the source for the HelpViewerExample class and the help files. The source is in the help_viewer_example project. I created the help_viewer_example project based on the Xcode Organizer Java Application template. The project is an Ant-based project, so you can integrate it into most popular Java IDEs.

To build the project, open Terminal from the /Applcations/Utilities/ directory. Change your directory to the project directory root with the cd command. Enter the command ant in the Terminal. The Ant project creates a Mac OS X application bundle and places it in the dist/ directory. Navigate to the project dist/ directory from Finder and double-click your new application to run the example.

The following three basic HTML files are interlinked creating a base help book. The file index. html is the entry point for the help book. Help books, like Web pages, use files named index. html for their default page.

NOTE

The official Apple Help Book Programming Guide is available here:

```
http://developer.apple.com/mac/library/documentation
/Carbon/Conceptual/ProvidingUserAssitAppleHelp
/user_help_intro/user_assistance_intro.html
```

The following source code is for the `index.html` page. This is the entry page for your help book. Notice the two `meta` tags mentioned earlier. The `meta` tag containing the `AppleTitle` attribute should not appear in other help book Web pages.

```html
<html>
    <head>
        <meta http-equiv="content-type"
              content="text/html;charset=iso-8859-1">
        <meta NAME="AppleTitle" CONTENT="Help Viewer Example">
        <title>Help Viewer Example</title>
    </head>
    <body bgcolor="white">
        <h1>Help Book Example</h1>
        <h2>Table of Contents</h2>
        <p>This is the Help Viewer Example.</p>
        <ul>
            <li><a href="topic_1.html">Topic 1</a></li>
            <li><a href="topic_2.html">Topic 2</a></li>
        </ul>
    </body>
</html>
```

The following source code is for the `topic_1.html` page. Notice the relative hyperlinks in anchor tags.

```html
<html>
    <head>
        <title>Help Viewer Example: Topic 1</title>
    </head>
    <body bgcolor="white">
        <h1>Topic 1</h1>
        <p>This is the Help Viewer Example Topic number 1.</p>

        <ul>
            <li><a href="index.html">Table of Contents</a></li>
            <li><a href="topic_2.html">Topic 2</a></li>
        </ul>
    </body>
</html>
```

The following source code is for the `topic_2.html` page, for completeness:

```html
<html>
    <head>
        <title>Help Viewer Example: Topic 2</title>
    </head>
    <body bgcolor="white">
        <h1>Topic 2</h1>
        <p>This is the Help Viewer Example Topic number 2.</p>

        <ul>
            <li><a href="index.html">Table of Contents</a></li>
            <li><a href="topic_1.html">Topic 1</a></li>
        </ul>
    </body>
</html>
```

I placed these three HTML files in the application bundle. Their location is `Contents/Resources/help_book`. I named the help book folder `help_book`.

The `Info.plist` file contains the two help book specific properties, `CFBundleHelpBookName` and `CFBundleHelpBookFolder`, as shown in Figure 7.3. `CFBundleHelpBookName` is set to the value of `Help Viewer Example Help`. `CFBundleHelpBookFolder` is set to `help_book`.

Figure 7.3

Info.plist for Help Viewer Example application

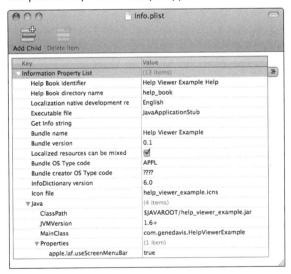

The following code is the source for the `HelpViewerExample` class. `HelpViewerExample` is the only Java class in this example. In `HelpViewerExample`, I instantiate a `com.apple.eawt.Application` object. I configure the menu bar to display as a screen menu rather than in the Java `JFrame`. Next, I set up a `JFrame`, complete with menu bar and `Help` menu, and `Example Help Book` menu item. Finally, I set the `JFrame` to visible.

```
package com.genedavis;
import java.awt.event.ActionEvent;
import java.awt.event.ActionListener;
import javax.swing.JFrame;
import javax.swing.JMenu;
import javax.swing.JMenuBar;
import javax.swing.JMenuItem;
import com.apple.eawt.Application;
public class HelpViewerExample {
    public static void main( String[] args )
    {

        // com.apple.eawt.Application
        final Application app = new Application();

        // setting the look and feel to use apple screen menu
        System.setProperty( "apple.laf.useScreenMenuBar", "true" );

        JFrame mainFrame = new JFrame( "Help Viewer Example" );

        // configuring and adding menubar to mainFrame
        JMenuBar jmb = new JMenuBar();

        JMenu fileMenu = new JMenu( "File" );
        JMenu editMenu = new JMenu( "Edit" );
        JMenu windowMenu = new JMenu( "Window" );
        JMenu helpMenu = new JMenu( "Help" );

        jmb.add( fileMenu );
        jmb.add( editMenu );
        jmb.add( windowMenu );
        jmb.add( helpMenu );

        JMenuItem newItem = new JMenuItem("New" );
        JMenuItem openItem = new JMenuItem( "Open..." );

        JMenuItem cutItem = new JMenuItem( "Cut" );
        JMenuItem copyItem = new JMenuItem( "Copy" );
        JMenuItem pasteItem = new JMenuItem( "Paste" );
```

```
JMenuItem helpExampleItem =
    new JMenuItem("My Example Help Book");
// event that opens the help book is here
helpExampleItem.addActionListener(
    new ActionListener () {
        public void actionPerformed ( ActionEvent ae )
        {
            app.openHelpViewer();
        }
    });

fileMenu.add( newItem );
fileMenu.add( openItem );

editMenu.add( cutItem );
editMenu.add( copyItem );
editMenu.add( pasteItem );

helpMenu.add( helpExampleItem );
mainFrame.setJMenuBar( jmb );

// setting the size of the JFrame
mainFrame.setSize( 400, 200 );

// making the JFrame visible
mainFrame.setVisible( true );

    }
}
```

Once bundled, the example Help menu contains a Search menu item and the Help Book Example menu item as shown in Figure 7.4. When you select Help ⇨ Example Help Book, the Help Viewer displays the `index.html` entry page, as shown in Figure 7.5.

Figure 7.4

Help menu from the Help Viewer Example application

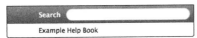

Figure 7.5

Help Viewer display of `index.html` for the Help Viewer
Example application

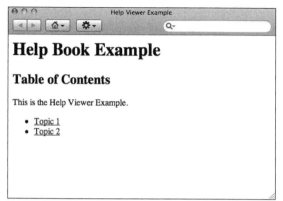

Handling About, Preferences, and Quit

All windowed OS X applications contain an application menu. The application menu is right
next to the apple menu in the top-left corner of the screen. When Java applications are not
packaged in application bundles, the application menu is branded with the fully qualified Java
name of the application's main class. For instance, `com.genedavis.`
`ApplicationMenuExample` is the application menu name of this section's example when
run from a JAR, as show in Figure 7.6.

If an application is properly bundled, the title of the application menu matches the actual application name, as shown in Figure 7.7. Many users are confused by a class name when they are
expecting an application name. Properly bundled applications present more professional-look-
ing user interfaces and confuse fewer users.

When you are ready to bundle your Java application, use the Jar Bundler application installed
with Xcode to create and properly name your application bundle. Bundling your Java application results in a properly branded application menu. The Jar Bundler application is located in
the `/Developer/Utilities/` directory.

CROSS-REF

In Chapter 5, I introduce bundling of Java applications in depth.

Figure 7.6

Application menu branded with fully qualified class name

 com.genedavis.ApplicationMenuExample

Figure 7.7

A bundled application menu branded with the application name

Application Menu Example

TIP

The first step to creating an application bundle is packaging your Java application in a JAR file. Make a JAR file quickly from the Finder by selecting the files and folders you desire to JAR. Next, Control-click (or right-click) the selection. Choose Compress Items from the contextual menu. Finally, change the name of the resulting `Archive.zip` file to `some_name.jar`. After all, JAR files are really just ZIP files.

The application menu contains three menu items of interest to Java application developers. The menu items are the About menu item, the Preferences... menu item, and the Quit menu item, as shown in Figure 7.8. These menu items are not available through the standard Java APIs. However, Apple provides two classes and an interface that provide access to these menu items.

TIP

Versions of the About and Quit menu items are provided by default by OS X. However, the behavior does not satisfy the needs of your advanced programs. For instance, if you do not handle the Quit event, your users' unsaved documents summarily disappear without the chance of recovery when your users accidentally quit without saving.

Figure 7.8

Application menu for Application Menu Example

About Application Menu Example	
Preferences...	⌘,
Services	▶
Hide Application Menu Example	⌘H
Hide Others	⌥⌘H
Show All	
Quit Application Menu Example	⌘Q

With just a few simple steps, the About, Preferences..., and Quit menus integrate with your application. I give a detailed example of the integration steps later in this section, but here's a short version:

1. **Extend** com.apple.eawt.ApplicationAdapter **to create your own** ApplicationAdapter.

2. **Implement the** handleAbout() **method in your** ApplicationAdapter.

3. **Implement the** handlePreferences() **method in your** ApplicationAdapter.

4. **Implement the** handleQuit() **method in your** ApplicationAdapter.

5. **Instantiate a** com.apple.eawt.Application **object.**

6. **Call** setEnableAboutMenu() **on your** Application **object with the argument of** true.

7. **Call** setEnablePreferencesMenu() **on your** Application **object with the argument of** true**.**

8. **Call** addApplicationListener() **on your** Application **object with your** ApplicationAdapter **implementation as the argument.**

TIP

The javadoc for the `Application` class, the `ApplicationAdapter` class, and the `ApplicationListener` interface is found here:

```
http://developer.apple.com/mac/library/documentation
/Java/Reference/JavaSE6_AppleExtensionsRef/api/com
/apple/eawt/Application.html
```

The `Application` class is the key class when integrating with the application menu. The `Application` class provides the About, Preferences..., and Quit events to an `ApplicationListener`. In the case of the preceding steps, the `ApplicationAdapter` is an implementation of the `ApplicationListener` interface. Figure 7.9 is a diagram showing the relationship of these classes with the applicable methods.

Figure 7.9

`Application` class, `ApplicationAdapter` class, and `ApplicationListener` interface

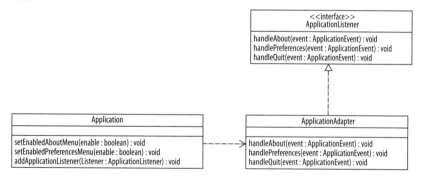

The Application Menu Example application found on the book's Web site demonstrates implementing the three menu items in the application menu. The application consists of four classes. The classes are `ApplicationMenuExample`, `AMEListener`, `AMEAboutBox`, and `AMEListener`. The Application Menu Example is diagrammed in Figure 7.10.

Figure 7.10

Application Menu Example application

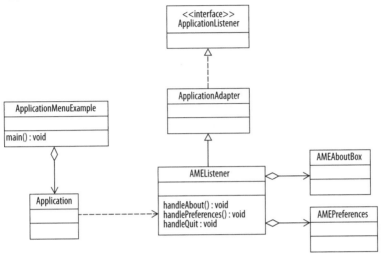

As I mentioned, the book's Web site contains the source for the `ApplicationMenuExample`, `AMEListener`, `AMEAboutBox`, and `AMEListener` classes. The source is in the `application_menu_example` project. I created the `application_menu_example` project based on the Xcode Organizer Java Application template. The project is an Ant-based project, so you can integrate it into most popular Java IDEs.

To build the project, open Terminal from the `/Applcations/Utilities/` directory. Change your directory to the project directory root with the `cd` command. Enter the command `ant` in the Terminal. The Ant project creates a Mac OS X application bundle and places it in the `dist/` directory. Navigate to the project `dist/` directory from Finder and double-click your new application to run the example.

The `ApplicationMenuExample` class contains the `main()` method. In the `main()` method, I instantiate the `Application` object and then set the About and Preferences... menu items to enabled. Next, I instantiate the `AMEListener` and add it to the `Application` object. Finally, I create the application's `JFrame`.

Here is the source for the `ApplicationMenuExample` class:

```
package com.genedavis;
import javax.swing.JFrame;
import com.apple.eawt.Application;
public class ApplicationMenuExample {
    public static void main( String[] args )
    {
```

```
Application app = new Application();

app.setEnabledAboutMenu(true);
app.setEnabledPreferencesMenu(true);

AMEListener listener = new AMEListener();
app.addApplicationListener( listener );

JFrame mainFrame = new JFrame("Application Menu Example");
mainFrame.setSize(400, 200);
mainFrame.setVisible(true);

    }
}
```

The `AMEListener` extends the `ApplicationAdapter`. The `ApplicationAdapter` is an implementation of the `ApplicationListener`. Extending the `ApplicationAdapter` simplifies implementing the `ApplicationListener`, if you do not want the bother of implementing all the `ApplicationListener` methods.

The following source is the source for the `AMEListener` class. Notice that only the `handleAbout()`, `handlePreferences()`, and `handleQuit()` methods are implemented. Both the `AMEAboutBox` and the `AMEPreferences` JDialogs are contained by the `AMEListener`. They are merely set to visible as needed.

Notice that all three methods call `setHandled( true )`. The system does not assume that these three events are handled correctly. You must notify the system when each event is handled.

The `handleQuit()` method deserves a note or two. Quitting from the Dock, from the application menu, and from the Command+Q key combination all require this method implementation. Providing this method implementation gives your users a natural Mac experience. Here's the code:

```
package com.genedavis;
import javax.swing.JOptionPane;
import com.apple.eawt.ApplicationAdapter;
import com.apple.eawt.ApplicationEvent;
public class AMEListener extends ApplicationAdapter
{

    private AMEAboutBox about = new AMEAboutBox();
    private AMEPreferences preferences = new AMEPreferences();

    @Override
    public void handleAbout ( ApplicationEvent e )
    {
        about.setVisible( true );
        e.setHandled(true);
    }
```

```
@Override
public void handlePreferences ( ApplicationEvent e )
{
    preferences.setVisible( true );
    e.setHandled(true);
}

@Override
public void handleQuit( ApplicationEvent e )
{
    JOptionPane.showMessageDialog( null, "Quit handled." );
    e.setHandled(true);
    System.exit(0);
}
}
```

Persisting Preferences

`AMEPreferences` is the preferences dialog box for the Application Menu Example app. As shown by `AMEPreferences`, Java applications on OS X should use the `java.util.prefs.Preferences` class to persist application preferences.

CAUTION

It is very common for applications (Java and non-Java alike) on Unix operating systems to persist user preferences and other configurations in dot directories in users' home directories. Don't let that convention throw you.

The next example is the source for the `AMEPreferences` class. If you run the Application Menu Example app, you see that the preferences dialog box has one working preference, as shown in Figure 7.11. The preference is a simple check box. The preference value is stored in the `sample_preference` preference. It is retrieved with a call to `getBoolean()` on the `Preferences` instance. It is set with a call to `putBoolean()` on the `Preferences` object.

Figure 7.11

The preference dialog box for Application Menu Example

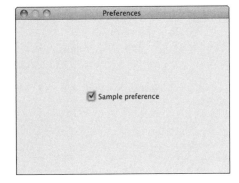

The only tricky part of using the `java.util.prefs.Preferences` class is instantiating it. The storage location is based on the package name of the class that you pass the `Preferences` constructor. I usually use the class that contains my `main()` method when instantiating a `Preferences` constructor.

TIP
If you want to modify your Java preferences by hand, navigate to the `~/Library/Preferences` directory. Then open the `com.apple.java.util.prefs.plist` file in the Property List Editor.

CAUTION
If multiple applications use the same package to store preferences, naming conflicts can occur. When naming conflicts occur with preferences, the applications can overwrite each other's preferences. Choose wisely, and you will never have naming conflicts.

```java
package com.genedavis;
import java.awt.*;
import java.awt.event.*;
import java.util.prefs.Preferences;
import javax.swing.*;
public class AMEPreferences extends JDialog
{
   private Preferences prefs =
      Preferences.userNodeForPackage(
         ApplicationMenuExample.class);
   private JCheckBox sampleCheckBox;

   public AMEPreferences()
   {
      boolean samplePref =
         prefs.getBoolean ("sample_preference", false);
      initComponents();
      sampleCheckBox.setSelected(samplePref);
   }
   private void changePreference(ActionEvent e)
   {
      JCheckBox jcb = (JCheckBox) e.getSource();
      boolean selected = jcb.isSelected();
      prefs.putBoolean ("sample_preference", selected);
   }
   private void initComponents()
   {
      sampleCheckBox = new JCheckBox();
      setTitle("Preferences");
      Container contentPane = getContentPane();
      contentPane.setLayout(new BorderLayout());
      sampleCheckBox.setText("Sample preference");
```

```
    sampleCheckBox.setHorizontalAlignment(SwingConstants.
CENTER);
        sampleCheckBox.addActionListener(new ActionListener() {
            public void actionPerformed(ActionEvent e) {
                changePreference(e);
            }
        });
        contentPane.add(sampleCheckBox, BorderLayout.CENTER);
        setSize(400, 300);
        setLocationRelativeTo(null);
    }
}
```

Creating Human Interface compliant About boxes

Apple's Human Interface Guidelines are very specific about the design of About boxes. About boxes provide branding, versioning, and copyright for your application. About boxes are optional, but most software has them. Users often open the About box looking for contact information.

Your About box should contain a title bar with no title. The title bar should contain the three window control gem icons on the left side with only the red window closing icon active. About boxes are not resizable. About boxes are modeless. Allow users to move their About boxes. About boxes do not appear in application window lists. About boxes remain visible, even when the application is not in focus.

These are typical contents of an About box:

- Graphic branding, such as an application icon
- Application name
- Version info, matching the version displayed by the Finder
- Copyright (optional)
- Contact information (optional)
- Credits (optional)
- A button opening a company Web page (optional)

I provide an example of an About box with the AMEAboutBox class, shown in Figure 7.12. To conform with the Human Interface Guidelines, the AMEAboutBox is not modal. This means that the About box does not block users from working in other windows while the About box is open.

Also, the About box is not resizable or minimizable. The only window control that is active is the red closing icon in the top-left corner of the About box. In Java, this is accomplished with a custom JDialog, rather than with a JWindow or JFrame. JWindows do not have the title bar with the close control. JFrames have no way of disabling the minimize button.

Figure 7.12

The About box for Application Menu Example

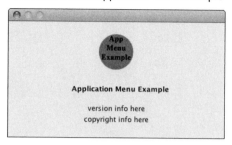

Finding your mouse location

Occasionally, you want to know where your mouse is on the screen. You can use two methods to find your mouse location. Your choice of methods depends on the version of OS X you are coding against.

Prior to the Java 1.5 release for OS X, finding the mouse location on the screen was handled with the `com.apple.eawt.Application` class. The method `getMouseLocationOn-Screen()` was called. The `getMouseLocationOnScreen()` returns an AWT `Point` object containing the mouse pointer's hot spot on the monitor.

Since the release of Java 1.5, Apple deprecated the `getMouseLocationOnScreen()` method. On newer version of OS X, use a combination of the `MouseInfo getPointer-Info()` method and the `PointerInfo`'s `getLocation()` method. The result is the same. The `getLocation()` method returns an AWT `Point` object.

NOTE

Location coordinates on the monitor are arranged the same way as the location in **JFrames**. The upper-left corner is `(0, 0)` and the lower-right corner is `(resolution width - 1, resolution height - 1)`.

CAUTION

Location coordinates can be negative when moving the mouse to a second monitor to the right or above the current monitor.

The following example, `FindTheMouse`, illustrates the old and new methods for finding the location of the mouse on the screen.

```
package com.genedavis;
import java.awt.MouseInfo;
import java.awt.Point;
import java.awt.PointerInfo;
```

```java
import com.apple.eawt.Application;
public class FindTheMouse
{
    public static void main(String[] args)
    {

        Application app = new Application();
        PointerInfo pi;
        Point p1, p2;

        while (true)
        {
            p1 = app.getMouseLocationOnScreen();

            pi = MouseInfo.getPointerInfo();
            p2 = pi.getLocation();

            System.out.println(
                "Old way (" + p1.x + ", " + p1.y + "), \n" +
                "New way (" + p2.x + ", " + p2.y + ")\n\n");

            try
            {
                Thread.sleep(500);
            }
            catch (Exception e)
            {}
        }
    }
}
```

To compile the `com.genedavis.FindTheMouse` class from the Terminal, place the class in a directory structure matching the package structure. Then use the following command:

```
javac com/genedavis/FindTheMouse.java
```

After compiling the `FindTheMouse` class, use the following command to run the application from the Terminal:

```
java com.genedavis.FindTheMouse
```

The `FindTheMouse` class contains only a `main()` method. First, I create the `com.apple.eawt.Application` class, and then I put the application into an infinite while loop. The loop checks the mouse location with the old method,

```
p1 = app.getMouseLocationOnScreen();
```

and then checks the mouse location with the new method,

```
pi = MouseInfo.getPointerInfo();
p2 = pi.getLocation();
```

The code then prints out the locations, as shown in Figure 7.13, and sleeps for half a second. If you see a difference between the mouse location retrieved with the old and new method, the difference is probably because the mouse is moving while the locations are retrieved.

Figure 7.13

Results of executing the `FindTheMouse` class in the Terminal

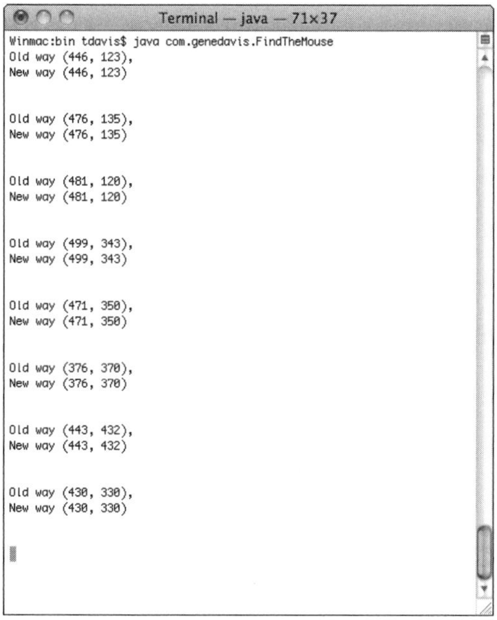

Summary

In this chapter, I discussed the `com.apple.eio` and `com.apple.eawt` packages. OS X has several common features not covered by the pure Java APIs, so it requires additional APIs for Java applications to feel like native applications. These features include application bundle resources, the Help Viewer, the Dock, and the application menu.

The `com.apple.eio.FileManager` contains static methods for handling OS X-specific features related to files. `FileManager` includes methods for finding paths to application bundle resources. It contains a method for finding your application's enclosing bundle. It also contains methods for getting and setting file types and creators.

I discussed two of the classes found in the `com.apple.eawt` package. The classes I explained are the `Application` class and the `ApplicationAdapter` class. These classes contain methods for handling Dock modifications, system events, and help books.

In this chapter, I purposely avoided discussion of the `CocoaComponent` class because of its advanced nature. It requires the use of JNI. I begin discussion of JNI and OS X integration in Chapter 8.

Embedding Cocoa Components

The application menu, the Dock, the Help Viewer, and other features are all available to your Java application. If you want your application to look native, you can make it look and feel like any Cocoa or Carbon application.

You can do more than just make your Java application look and feel like Cocoa and Carbon applications. The com.apple.eawt package contains one class that allows you to embed native GUI widgets and interfaces directly into your JFrames and other Java Containers. This class is the CocoaComponent class.

The CocoaComponent integrates with native Objective-C GUI elements. The elements are Objective-C NSView objects. The native code you write instantiates an NSView and then passes the NSView reference back to the Java CocoaComponent. You place the CocoaComponent in the Java Container of your choice.

Using CocoaComponents requires knowledge of JNI, C, and Objective-C. Also, an understanding of the Cocoa framework is useful. I explain the JNI, C, and Objective-C code used in this and other chapters. I do not attempt to thoroughly teach C or Objective-C. Rather, I attempt to give you a basic understanding of C and Objective-C as it applies to implementing CocoaComponents.

I explain JNI on OS X more thoroughly in Chapter 9. Other chapters also use JNI as the basis of examples, such as screensaver integration and ncurses support. Apple suggests using JNI for Java interaction with native Apple technologies. Learning JNI opens many Apple technologies to your Java application development.

In this chapter, I explain basic JNI for the integration of CocoaComponents with Swing and AWT. I begin by explaining basic Java interaction with Objective-C objects by way of JNI. I explain the creation of C header files with javah.

Of course, some C and Objective-C are involved. When I use C and Objective-C, I explain the details of the code so Java developers can understand it. I give as many details as are relevant to this chapter.

After explaining the basics of JNI and Objective-C integration, I delve into a deeper explanation of CocoaComponent use of JNI.

 In This Chapter

Integrating CocoaComponents

Examining NSViews

Building JNI applications with Ant

Finding method signatures with Javap

Creating JNI headers with Javah

Introducing Objective-C

Events and data traveling to and from Java and Objective-C are rarely compatible. I explain passing events in both directions, while making their data compatible. I also explain how to avoid blocking and locking your applications while passing events around.

Integrating Objective-C and Java

Objective-C and Java are worlds apart. Pointers, defines, and other C holdovers pervade Objective-C. Most Objective-C application developers still handle their own memory management without the benefits of automated garbage collection. Delving into Objective-C will remind you why you chose Java as your preferred language.

On the other hand, Objective-C is an advanced and powerful Object-Oriented language. Many of the design patterns applied to Objective-C application development feel familiar to Java developers. After learning Objective-C, Java developers often find themselves wishing Java had a few of Objective-C's features.

Objective-C is based on ANSI C. Objective-C is an Object-Oriented version of C. More than one developer has pointed to Objective-C and said Objective-C succeeded where C++ failed. If you know a smattering of C and understand Java, learning Objective-C is easy. Expect to be productive in Objective-C in a few hours.

NOTE

Much of your understanding of Object-Oriented Programming (OOP) from Java carries over to Objective-C. Often the Objective-C syntax is very different from Java, or concepts, such as interfaces, have more richness in Objective-C, but after the initial learning curve Objective-C is very friendly to Java programmers.

Because Objective-C is based on C, JNI is a natural fit for integration of Java and Objective-C. The preferred development framework supported by Apple is the Cocoa framework. The Cocoa framework is an Objective-C framework. Full integration of your Java application with most Cocoa libraries is only a few JNI calls and callbacks away.

Follow these steps to create a basic JNI bridge to native code:

1. **Create the native code in C, Objective-C, or C++.**

2. **Create the Java class that will handle JNI communication.**

3. **Label methods that will call native C methods with the** native **keyword.**

4. **Create private methods that your native C functions will use for callbacks to Java.**

5. **Add a static block in the Java class to load your native library.**

6. **Compile your Java class that handles the JNI interaction.**

7. **Execute the** javah **command on the command to create a C header file.**

8. **Execute the** javap **command to find the method signature of your private Java methods.**

These are the methods you use to accept messages from your native code.

9. **Write a C interface hooking up your native C, C++, or Objective-C code to your Java class.**

The C interface `#includes` the header file created with `javah` and implements the callback to Java.

10. **Compile your native source into a dynamic library for loading by your JVM.**

The second example later in this chapter implements these steps. These steps are a little overwhelming the first time, so the first example actually implements only a base subset of these steps. The overall layout of code when hooking Java to Objective-C follows the pattern of Java connected to C by way of JNI, and the C code communicating with Objective-C, as shown in Figure 8.1.

Figure 8.1

Connecting Java to Objective-C by way of JNI and C

Using Native in Java

In this chapter, I present two examples. The first sample program, `NativeLogExample`, demonstrates the creation of a simple JNI application where Java communicates unidirectionally with an Objective-C object. I find it easiest to learn (or explain) new programming paradigms with simple examples, so this first JNI class is stripped of all extras.

The second example, later in this chapter, details full communication from Java to an NSView and from an `NSView` to a Java `CocoaComponent`. The second example is much more complex, so unless you are already familiar with JNI on OS X, don't skip the first example.

The first example follows a shorter list of steps than mentioned previously:

1. **Create the native code in C and Objective-C.**

2. **Create the Java class that will handle JNI communication.**

3. **Label methods that will call native C methods with the** native **keyword.**

4. **Add a static block in the Java class to load your native library.**

5. **Compile your Java class that handles the JNI interaction.**

6. **Execute the** javah **command on the command to create a C header file.**

7. **Write a C interface hooking up your native C and Objective-C.**

   The C interface #includes the header file created with javah.

8. **Compile your native source into a dynamic library for loading by your JVM.**

While the steps don't appear much smaller than the preceding list, this first example requires less complex code. Handling the callbacks is rather tricky. Callbacks require several JNI-specific references and attaching/detaching threads. The first example has no callbacks.

CROSS-REF
I explain JNI is greater detail in Chapter 9.

NOTE
The full source for the `NativeLogExample` and the other example in this chapter are on this book's Web site.

JNI has a steep learning curve. Lots of technologies are involved. If you don't understand some basics of C, JNI is nearly impossible to learn. Familiarity with pointers is a must. Be sure to read the "Overview of C Pointers" sidebar for a brief review of C pointers.

Overview of C Pointers

The most notable feature of C is pointers. Pointers are loved and hated: loved for their power and utility, hated for their obfuscative tendencies.

Pointers are unavoidable in C. You cannot understand even trivial C code without understanding pointers. If you haven't touched C in a while, you might want a quick refresher on pointers. If you have never used C, a quick overview of pointers will make this chapter's examples a little easier to follow.

When passing variables in Java method calls, the variables may pass by value or by reference depending on the variable type. Primitives are passed by value. All objects are passed by reference.

C has a similar concept of passing by value and passing by reference, except the details are not as nicely hidden as they are in Java. In C, every variable is passed by value unless you explicitly pass it by reference.

The C equivalent of the Java reference is the pointer. For the purpose of this discussion, I treat pointers as though they are just a more powerful form of reference. In C, whether a variable is a pointer to a value or an actual value is decided at the time of variable declaration. C introduces special notation to handle pointer declarations and pointer use.

In C, just as in Java, the following statement declares a variable i of type int:

```
int i;
```

In C and Java, this is a value, not a pointer (or a reference). In Java, the int i cannot be passed by reference. (Just pretend Java has no auto boxing of int primitives into Integer objects for now.) In C, you can send a pointer to i instead of the actual value of i.

The notation for creating a pointer to `i` is as follows:

```
&i
```

Placing the `&` before the variable name returns its pointer. If you wanted to send a pointer to `i` as a function argument, the call might look something like this:

```
my_function( &i );
```

I already mentioned that C can declare variables as points rather than values. Declare pointers in C with the `*` symbol. For instance, the following code declares a pointer to an `int` variable called `ip`:

```
int *ip;
```

In Java terminology, you just made a reference to an `int`.

Note that `ip` is not an `int`. The variable `ip` is pointer to an `int`. You cannot store an `int` in `ip`; you must store an `int` pointer in `ip`. For example, in the following code, I create an `int` called `i`, get a pointer to the `int` called `i`, and place that pointer in `ip`:

```
int   i = 3;
int *ip = &i;
```

Obviously, pointers are of no use if you cannot get the information to which the pointer points. In other words, how does C determine the `int` value to which `ip` points?

C obtains the value through another use of the `*` symbol. The act of obtaining the value pointed to by the pointer is called *dereferencing*. Here is an example:

```
int  i = 3;
int *ip = &i;
int anotherInt = *ip;
```

The value stored in `anotherInt` is 3.

If this were all the complexity of pointers, I am sure Java programmers would flock to C. However, C does much more with pointers. Pointers can point to pointers. Pointers can point to functions. You can increment pointers to perform operations on arrays without bothering with indices.

Learning pointers takes time. After you learn pointers, C turns into an elegant and powerful language for you. To do any significant JNI work, you need to learn pointers.

NOTE

Both Ant-based example projects for this chapter are on the book's Web site. The first example project is named `native_log_example`. The second is named `nsbutton_in_jframe`. Because both are Ant-based projects, you can integrate into most popular IDEs. I explain Ant projects in detail in Chapter 4.

The following example is called `native_log_example`. The example project is found on the book's Web site. I provide an Ant `build.xml` file with the project to aid in building the project. Later in this chapter, I go over the `build.xml` file provided for this project.

The following source is the `NativeLogExample` class. As with other Java classes, you should put the `NativeLogExample` class in a file named after the class. In this case, you should name the file `NativeLogExample.java`. Alternatively, you can open the file from the book's Web site.

The `nativeLogExample` class contains static blocks and native methods. Unless you have written JNI applications in the past, you likely have never seen or heard of static blocks or native methods in Java programs. Most Java applications have little use for either. However, JNI uses both static blocks and native methods.

The `NativeLogExample` class demonstrates a static block of Java code and a method with the native label:

```java
package com.genedavis;
import java.io.File;
import java.io.IOException;
public class NativeLogExample {
    // executed during class load
    static
    {
        // Use System.load() to load directly from a non-system
        // path. Be sure to catch an IOException if used
        // File lib = new File("objc_bin/libNativeLogger.jnilib")
        // System.load( lib.getCanonicalPath() );

        //use System.loadLibrary() when loading from a system
        //library path
        System.loadLibrary("NativeLogger");
    }

    /**
     * It all begins here
     */
    public static void main(String[] args)
    {
            NativeLogExample nl = new NativeLogExample();
            nl.log("Hello world! (of course)");
    }

    // native method call
    private native void log(String message);
}
```

Static blocks are code blocks that execute when the `ClassLoaders` loads a class. To use a static block, place the following code outside of all methods, but inside the class definition:

```java
static
{
    // Place initialization code here.
}
```

Place your code between the curly braces. By convention, position static blocks somewhere near the top of the class, so they are easily noticed. Static blocks execute before any other code, meaning that code in static blocks executes before the `main()` method is called.

TIP

To learn about static blocks, try writing some purely procedural programs in Java using a static block instead of a `main()` method. Static blocks do have limitations, and this is a good exercise to learn those limitations.

However, avoid static blocks when writing actual production-quality code.

Static blocks execute in the order that they load. This means that static blocks within a class execute in the order they appear. However, if you have static blocks in multiple classes, the order in which the classes load is undefined. Do not make static blocks in one class depend on static blocks in another class.

Static blocks are not very object oriented, so avoid them. However, occasionally you need to perform some class or object initialization before the main() method executes. JNI library loading and initialization of native libraries are two cases where use of static blocks is justified in Java.

The NativeLogExample class uses a static block to load the native library NativeLogger. (I explain creation of the NativeLogger library later in this chapter.) If you look around the example code for a class named exactly "NativeLogger," you will be disappointed.

JNI uses dynamic libraries. On OS X, the naming convention for dynamic libraries is as follows:

```
lib<library name>.jnilib
```

When loading a dynamic library for use in JNI, load the library by name and ignore the extras. In the case of a library named NativeLogger, the actual filename for the library is this:

```
libNativeLogger.jnilib
```

The call for loading the NativeLogger library is this:

```
System.loadLibrary("NativeLogger");
```

Two common ways of loading dynamic libraries exist. If your library is in the system path or specified a known path to the JVM, System.loadLibrary() works fine. The JVM finds the library and loads it. However, if the program knows the location of the library and the library is not in the system path, use the System.load() method.

The System.load() method takes an absolute path as an argument. Do not worry about the absolute path if you only know the relative path. Create a File object from your relative path, and then call getCanonicalPath() on the new File object. This creates an absolute path from your relative path. The only catch (quite literally) is that the process needs to be enclosed in a try-catch to catch potential IOExceptions.

I place one native method in the NativeLogExample class. The method is as follows:

```
private native void log(String message);
```

Note that it is not implemented. Native methods are implemented in native C (or C or Objective-C) code. The naming conventions for the native implementation are nasty. You can create the methods signatures by hand, but I do not recommend it. Instead use javah.

Creating headers with javah

Before writing the C implementations of your Java class's native methods, run `javah`. The `javah` tool is a command-line tool for creation of C header files from Java classes with `native` methods.

CROSS-REF

In Chapter 4, I discuss many of the common Java command-line tools. Javah is among the tools I discuss.

These are the steps for running `javah`:

1. **Open the Terminal.**
2. **Determine the directories containing your compiled Java classes.**
3. **Determine the directory in which to place your C header file(s).**
4. **Run** javah.

   The common options are `-classpath` for your Java classpath and `-d` for the directory in which you create the new header(s).

For example, creating a C header for the implementation of the Java `NativeLogExample` class might look like the following:

```
javah -classpath java_bin -d objc_src com.genedavis.NativeLogExample
```

If you want all your JNI method declarations in the same header file, use the `-o` option instead of the `-d` option. The `-o` option specifies the path and name of a header file in which to place all C method signatures.

The JNI header file is generated automatically from the `NativeLogExample` using `javah`. I named the file I generated `native_log_example_jni.h`, and its source follows:

```
/* DO NOT EDIT THIS FILE - it is machine generated */
#include <jni.h>
/* Header for class com_genedavis_NativeLogExample */
#ifndef _Included_com_genedavis_NativeLogExample
#define _Included_com_genedavis_NativeLogExample
#ifdef __cplusplus
extern "C" {
#endif
/*
 * Class:      com_genedavis_NativeLogExample
 * Method:     log
 * Signature:  (Ljava/lang/String;)V
 */
```

```
JNIEXPORT void JNICALL Java_com_genedavis_NativeLogExample_log
  (JNIEnv *, jobject, jstring);
#ifdef __cplusplus
}
#endif
#endif
```

This entire header defines only one native method, `log()`. The actual C method declaration is this:

```
JNIEXPORT void JNICALL Java_com_genedavis_NativeLogExample_log
  (JNIEnv *, jobject, jstring);
```

The method name log() in Java becomes this function in C:

```
Java_com_genedavis_NativeLogExample_log()
```

At first glance, this new name seems overly complex, but the complexity prevents naming collisions. Also, because `javah` did all the work naming the function, it is not too painful. The name starts with "Java," followed by the package and class name where the native method is initially declared, and is finished off by the actual Java native method name.

CAUTION

The `javah` generated header file changes every time `javah` is run. Do not place any comments or code into header files generated by `javah`, or the comments/code will vanish with your next full build.

Exploring the C side of JNI

When writing JNI bridges to Objective-C, I prefer buffering the Objective-C classes from the JNI interface. I place the C implementations of the Java native methods in a separate C file. I find this buffer prevents purely procedural code from mixing with Object-Oriented code. Generally, you should avoid mixing the two types of programming in the same file. It makes the code more legible.

In the case of this project, I placed the JNI implementation code inside a `*.m` file. The `.m` extension indicates that Objective-C is found in the file. Objective-C extends ANSI C, so using Objective-C in a file that is mostly ANSI C is convenient. In this case, Objective-C is providing `#import`, instantiation of the Objective-C class `NativeLogExample`, and an object release pool. Usually, C uses `#include`. When headers are defined improperly, `#include` can actually include the same library in your compiled code multiple times. Luckily, Objective-C defines the `#import` that, like the Java `import`, prevents multiple includes of code without any additional work by you the programmer.

The following source is the implementation of the automatically generated JNI header file. Notice the import of the `native_log_example_jni.h`. The `native_log_example_jni.h` header is the header generated from the Java class containing the native `log()`

method. The filename is `nle.m`. As I mentioned earlier, the lowercase `m` in the filename extension signifies an Objective-C file.

```
#import <jni.h>
#import <stdio.h>
#import <Cocoa/Cocoa.h>
#import "native_log_example_jni.h"
#import "NativeLogExample.h"

// This is the entry point from Java to the Objective-C code
JNIEXPORT void JNICALL Java_com_genedavis_NativeLogExample_log
    (JNIEnv * jenv, jobject job, jstring my_jstring)
{
    // Every thread must be wrapped in an NSAutoreleasePool
    // This prevents memory leaks
    NSAutoreleasePool       *pool = [[NSAutoreleasePool alloc] init];

    // converting the jstring to an NSString
    // 1. get a jchar array from the jstring
    // 2. get the length of the jstring
    // 3. instantiate the NSString
    // 4. free the jvm resources (no garbage collector here)
    const jchar *chars = (*jenv)->GetStringChars(jenv, my_jstring, NULL);
    NSUInteger str_len = (*jenv)->GetStringLength(jenv, my_jstring);
    NSString *message = [NSString
                            stringWithCharacters:(UniChar *)chars
                            length:str_len];
    (*jenv)->ReleaseStringChars(jenv, my_jstring, chars);

    // instantiating a NativeLogExample object
    NativeLogExample *nfe = [[NativeLogExample alloc] init];

    // calling the log() method on the NativeLogExample instance
    // passing an NSString to the method log()
    [nfe log: message];

    // destroy instances
    [message release];
    [nfe release];

    // destroying the NSAutoreleasePool
    [pool release];
}
```

I start the `nle.m` file by importing two standard headers. They are `jni.h` and `stdio.h`. These are both C headers, and as you have guessed, `jni.h` is required when implementing JNI native methods. Next, I import the Objective-C framework called Cocoa. Finally, I import the two project header files: `native_log_example_jni.h` and `NativeLogExample.h`. `NativeLogExample.h` defines the Objective-C class used in this example.

NOTE

Including the `stdio.h` header in C is similar to importing the `java.io.*` library in Java. Both contain code necessary for common I/O operations for their respective languages.

Cleaning Up Objective-C

C, and to a lesser extent Objective-C, requires programmers to clean up after themselves in ways that Java programmers usually ignore. Most C and Objective-C programs do not use a garbage collector of any sort. Newer releases of Objective-C come with a garbage collector, but the garbage collection is not built with JNI in mind, so don't use it with JNI or you may see needed Objective-C variables garbage collected at unpleasant times.

CAUTION

Even in Java, garbage collection occasionally happens on classes being used with JNI. Watch out for class instances that the garbage collector doesn't realize are in use. When all Java references from Java to a Java object containing JNI callbacks disappear, the garbage collector may not notice that native code is still using the object instance. Place a reference to the Java object in a safe place, such as a static variable in an active class, to prevent it from being garbage collected.

When Objects are created and then never removed from memory, you get a memory leak. In trivial programs, memory leaks are not much of a problem. However, when dealing with a small memory leak replicated thousands or millions of times, the leak can kill your application.

Objective-C environments without garbage collection handle object removal through reference counting and auto release pools. The concept is straightforward. All Objective-C objects are stored as references, similar to Java. Count the existing references. If the number reaches 0, clean up the memory storing the object. Essentially, this is manual garbage collection.

Follow these steps to perform memory management of Objective-C objects:

1. **Create a reference pool.**

   Normal GUI-based Objective-C applications have their own reference pool. JNI applications usually need their own reference pool created.

2. **Add one to your reference count, when a new reference to your object is created.**

   Typically, this is automatic.

3. **Subtract one from your reference count, when a reference to your object is released.**

   Your reference count is decremented by calling the `release` method.

4. **Clean the object out of memory when the reference count for the object reaches 0.**

The reference pool and the object work together to make this happen behind the scenes. More advanced Objective-C programmers may choose to customize this process.

5. **Remove the auto release pool from memory when it is going out of scope.**

The first step of removing an auto release pool from memory is reducing all its object reference counts to 0, thereby repeating Step 4 with each object still in the pool.

N O T E

Apple maintains extensive documentation on Objective-C memory management issues. This is a good reference to read:

```
http://developer.apple.com/mac/library/documentation
/Cocoa/Conceptual/MemoryMgmt/MemoryMgmt.pdf
```

The call to the native implementation is a new thread as far as Objective-C is concerned. The first thing I do in `nle.m` in the `Java_com_genedavis_NativeLogExample_log()` function is create an instance of `NSAutoreleasePool` to handle reference counting. The last thing I do in the same method is release the `NSAutoreleasePool`.

I use `release` methods to remove objects. The `release` method call does not directly clean up Objective-C objects from memory. Instead, it reduces the reference count of the object by 1. If the reference count reaches 0, then the object knows to clean up after itself. After the reference count reaches 0 and the object cleans up any of its used resources, the object is removed from memory.

Calling Objective-C methods

Objective-C methods look very different from their Java equivalents. Objective-C surrounds method calls with square brackets. Also, each parameter to an Objective-C method gets a description built right into the code. The extra description helps Objective-C self-document.

Using an example from the `nle.m` file, the following method call probably looks a little intimidating:

```
[NSString stringWithCharacters:
    ( UniChar * ) chars
    length: str_len ];
```

`NSString` is a class. `stringWithCharacters` is a method name. `length` is a continuation of the method name, describing the second argument to the method. Both `chars` and `str_len` are variables. `( UniChar * )` is simply a cast, as you expect to see in Java.

The Java equivalent of the above function call, might look like this:

```
String.stringWithCharactersLength ( (char[]) chars, str_len );
```

Converting Java Strings to NSStrings

As it turns out, NSStrings (the Objective-C equivalent to String) are not too different from Java Strings. They share a common unicode base. That is UTF-16. The common base for NSStrings and Java Strings makes conversion relatively simple. Four statements handle the conversion in the native log() implementation.

```
const jchar *chars = (*jenv)->GetStringChars(
                                        jenv,
                                        my_jstring,
                                        NULL);
NSUInteger str_len = (*jenv)->GetStringLength(jenv, my_jstring);
NSString *message = [NSString
                        stringWithCharacters:(UniChar *)chars
                        length:str_len];
(*jenv)->ReleaseStringChars(jenv, my_jstring, chars);
```

Follow these steps:

1. **Obtain the Java** String **as a** jchar*.

   Accomplish this with a call to the GetStringChars() function contained in the JNI environment.

2. **Get the length of the string.**

   The length of the string is obtained with another call to the JNI environment. Strings are essentially character arrays in C. Because C does not track the length of arrays, strings in C contain a value of 0 at the end of the string. (This is referred to as *null terminating*.) You must manually place this value of 0 when creating strings in C. That is why I need the string length.

3. **Create an** NSString **by providing a pointer to the raw unicode characters and the length of the final string.**

4. **Free the JVM resources in the JNI environment.**

   Now that I have my string's value safely copied to a shiny new NSString, it is time to release the JNI environment's string resources. Again, I call a function in the JNIEnv* variable, named jenv, to release the resources.

CROSS-REF

In Chapter 9, I explain more Java string conversions for OS X JNI programming.

CAUTION

Always remember to release the JNI environment resources when you are done with them. They are finite.

Introducing Objective-C objects

Objective-C is an OOP language. So of course, objects play a central role in the language. In this section, I discuss Objective-C classes and creation of instances.

On the Java side, `CocoaComponent` usage consists of a Java class extending `CocoaComponent`. On the Objective-C side, `CocoaComponents` consist of an Objective-C class implementing a protocol called `AWTCocoaComponent`. (Protocols are analogous to Java interfaces.) Because `CocoaComponent` requires Objective-C classes, I introduce a basic Objective-C class in this first example. I hold off implementing the `AWTCocoaComponent` protocol until the second JNI example.

NOTE

Objective-C contains protocols and interfaces. Java interfaces perform the same function as either Objective-C protocols or Objective-C interfaces in the Java language.

Objective-C classes are often placed in one file or split into two files, mostly depending on the style of the programmer and the complexity of the class. Objective-C classes consist of an interface that defines the methods and variables contained by the class and an implementation that implements the interface. When the class is split into two files, the interface is placed in a header file (`*.h`), along with any `#defines` and `#imports` the class needs. The implementation is placed in an Objective-C file (`*.m`), along with a `#import` statement importing the class interface. When the class is placed in only one file, the interface and implementation both go in a file with the `.m` extension.

The Objective-C class I use in the first JNI example exists in two files. The header is in the file `NativeLogExample.h`. The following is the source for the class interface:

```
#import <jni.h>
#import <Cocoa/Cocoa.h>
// defining the NativeLogExample class
@interface NativeLogExample : NSObject {
    // instance variable declarations go here
}
// one method named log takes an NSString object
-( void ) log: (NSString *) message ;
@end
```

The interface starts by importing the `Cocoa.h` header. JNI uses the `jni.h` header, but this class lets the `nle.m` code take care of all the messy JNI. So I do not import `jni.h` in this interface file. In the next example's class header, I do import `jni.h` because the Objective-C class interacts with JNI directly.

TIP

Both standard Java commenting styles are supported by Objective-C. The comment styles `//` and `/* */` have the same use in Objective-C as in Java. Alas, Javadoc comments don't have special meaning in Objective-C.

Interfaces in Objective-C take the following form:

```
@interface ClassName : SomeSuperClass <ProtocolImplemented> {
    variable declaration;
}
method declaration;
@end
```

Interfaces work differently in Objective-C than in Java. In Objective-C a declared *interface* is merely a declaration of one class. Although this use of interfaces exists in Java, it is not common. Objective-C uses what are called *protocols,* in addition to interfaces. Protocols more closely match the Java expectation and use of interfaces. Both Objective-C interfaces and Objective-C protocols together equate to Java interfaces.

Instead of surrounding interface declarations with curly braces as Java does, Objective-C surrounds interfaces with @interface and @end.

Interfaces defined with @interface do not extend other interfaces. (Remember, Objective-C @interfaces are class definitions.) Instead, @interfaces extend classes. In other words, Objective-C class extensions are handled by their class definitions—the interfaces. The colon (:) is used in place of the keyword extends that Java uses.

Class and object scoped methods and variables are defined in @interfaces. Objects and methods of class scope begin with a plus symbol (+). Objective-C's + is the equivalent of Java's static keyword. Methods and variables of object scope begin with a minus symbol (-). In the example code, the NativeLogExample contains one method named log of object scope.

The implementation of the NativeLogExample is in a file called NativeLogExample.m. The implementation for the Objective-C class NativeLogExample follows here:

```
#import "NativeLogExample.h"
// implementing the NativeLogExample class
@implementation NativeLogExample
// in Java this method signature would look like
// public void log (NSString message) { ... }
-( void ) log: (NSString *) message {

    // NSLog sends a log message to standard out
    // the message must be formatted. %@ is the
    // format specifier for objects. 'message' is
    // an object.
    NSLog( @"%@", message );

}
@end
```

The class implementation imports its own interface, and that is it. By convention, the file with the class implementation should import only one header: its interface. The interface takes care of all other imports.

Objective-C class implementations take the following form:

```
#import InterfaceDeclaration
@implementation ClassName
method implementations
@end
```

Notice that implementations start with the @implementation and end with the @end. Some programmers mix C-style functions into class implementations. I avoid this and instead place needed C-style functions into separate files that I then import into the class interface for use in the Objective-C class.

TIP

The commands @interface, @implementation, and @end are actually compiler directives, not keywords. The use of compiler directives is not surprising because Objective-C is built on top of ANSI C.

You can compile the C and Objective-C code using gcc directly if you like. The command for compiling the NativeLogExample and the nle.m file is something similar to the following:

```
gcc
            -bundle
            ./objc_src/nle.m
            ./objc_src/NativeLogExample.m
            -o ./objc_bin/libNativeLogger.jnilib
            -I/System/Library/Frameworks/JavaVM.framework/Headers
            -I ./objc_src/
            -framework JavaVM
            -framework Cocoa
```

The gcc command should be one line, not multiple lines. I formatted the gcc command for legibility.

The sample gcc command assumes that you have the headers and code in a subdirectory called objc_src. The command-line argument to create a dynamic library from the C and Objective-C is -bundle. Sometimes, I see -dynamic instead of -bundle; however, -dynamic can cause problems when loading multiple libraries for use with JNI. You are better off using -bundle to generate your dynamic library.

The argument -o specifies the name of the output file. The OS X convention for naming dynamic libraries in JNI is lib<name>.jnilib. The -I argument specifies directories of headers to search while building. The -framework argument specifies libraries used in the build. In this case, I use the JavaVM framework because the resulting library uses JNI. I also specify the Cocoa framework because I use an NSAutoreleasePool.

If you have followed the explanation of this first example up to this point, you have a fully work-able Java–Objective-C application. It runs with the following command or one modified to match your classpath:

```
java -Djava.library.path=objc_bin -cp java_bin/ ¬
com.genedavis.NativeLogExample
```

The output is not too spectacular, but it is a good first step. Running your new JNI application results in output similar to the following:

```
2009-10-29 20:22:24.683 java[8280:d07] Hello world! (of course)
```

Developing JNI with Ant

Setting up projects to handle `javac`, `javah`, and `gcc` is painful. If you want to move your project to a new IDE or share the project with a programmer using a different IDE, "painful" becomes horribly difficult. Set your build up with Ant or a similar build tool, and your project is more portable. Ant integrates with all Java IDEs. Best of all, Ant on OS X supports `gcc` through the `exec` tag, so even if your IDE does not officially support C or Objective-C, building the native code is no problem.

CROSS-REF
In Chapter 4, I explain Ant build.xml files in detail.

TIP
Xcode fully supports Objective-C syntax coloring and hints, even if your favorite IDE does not. Many IDEs support exter-nal editors for project files. Configure Xcode as your editor for *.m and *.h files. Often setting Xcode to the default application in the Finder is enough. Sometimes your IDE needs an extra preference set in order for it to use Xcode as the editor for *.m and *.h files. For example, in Eclipse, set the File Associations preference for *.m files and *.h files to Xcode.

I set up an Ant build for this example in the project's `build.xml` file. The source for the Ant `build.xml` file follows:

```xml
<?xml version="1.0" encoding="UTF-8"?>
<project
    name="Native Log Example"
    default="run"
    basedir=".">
  <property name="java.source" value="java_src" />
  <property name="objective.c.source" value="objc_src" />
  <property name="java.bin" value="java_bin" />
  <property name="native.bin" value="objc_bin" />

  <target
    name="explain"
```

```
          description="Explains the objective of the build">

          <echo>Building the full Java and Native source.</echo>

    </target>

    <target
       name="clean"
       description="Removes previous build">

          <echo>Cleaning Java and Native bin folders...</echo>

          <delete dir="${java.bin}" />
          <delete dir="${native.bin}" />

    </target>

    <target
       name="java-build"
           depends="clean"
       description="Builds the Java source">

          <echo>Building Java...</echo>

          <mkdir dir="${java.bin}"/>
          <javac srcdir="${java.source}" destdir="${java.bin}" />
    </target>

    <target
       name="native-header-build"
       description="Builds the native headers file">

          <echo>Creating native header file...</echo>

          <mkdir dir="${native.bin}"/>
          <javah
             outputfile="${objective.c.source}/native_log_example_jni.h"
             classpath="${java.bin}">

             <class name="com.genedavis.NativeLogExample" />

          </javah>
    </target>

    <target
       name="native-build"
       description="Builds the native lib*.jnilib">
```

```
        <echo>Creating native lib*.jnilib</echo>

        <exec executable="gcc">

            <arg value="-bundle"/>

            <arg value="./${objective.c.source}/nle.m"/>
            <arg value="./${objective.c.source}/NativeLogExample.m"/>

            <arg line="-o ./${native.bin}/libNativeLogger.jnilib"/>
            <arg
value="-I/System/Library/Frameworks/JavaVM.framework/Headers"/>
            <arg line="-framework JavaVM"/>
            <arg line="-framework Cocoa"/>

        </exec>
    </target>

    <target
        name="build"
        depends="explain, java-build, native-header-build, native-build"
        description="builds full Java and Native byte code.">
        <echo>Build complete</echo>
    </target>

    <target
        name="run"
        depends="build"
        description="cleans, builds, and then runs app">
        <!--
        java
            -Djava.library.path=objc_bin
            -cp java_bin/
            com.genedavis.NativeLogExample
        -->
        <java
            classpath="${java.bin}/"
                classname="com.genedavis.NativeLogExample"
                fork="true">
                <jvmarg value="-Djava.library.path=${native.bin}" />
        </java>
    </target>
</project>
```

I discuss most of the Ant tasks used in this build.xml in Chapter 4. However, the `javah` and `gcc` integrations are new. The `native-header-build` target contains the task for `javah` execution. I chose the `outputfile` attribute instead of the `destdir` attribute. The `outputfile` attribute specifies a file in which to place all JNI headers. The `destdir` specifies a directory, and javah creates multiple header files in that directory. Typically, you use outputfile if you have few native methods to implement. Use destdir if your project has many native methods to implement.

Alternately, if you want better control over naming and destination directories for a project with many native methods, run the javah task several times to produce multiple header files with names and locations of your choice.

I run the gcc command inside of an exec task. Some commands run from inside exec need a full path specified. Because gcc is in the system path, simply executing gcc is enough. I pass the arguments to gcc in with the arg tag. Arguments that require two parameters use the line attribute. Arguments that require only one parameter use the value attribute.

When only building the application, use the command ant build from the Terminal. When building and running the application, use the command ant run from the Terminal. The result of executing ant run appears very similar to this output generated on my Mac:

```
Buildfile: build.xml
explain:
     [echo] Building the full Java and Native source.
clean:
     [echo] Cleaning Java and Native bin folders...
   [delete] Deleting directory /Users/tdavis/Desktop/ch08_code/
   native_log_example/java_bin
   [delete] Deleting directory /Users/tdavis/Desktop/ch08_code/
   native_log_example/objc_bin
java-build:
     [echo] Building Java...
    [mkdir] Created dir: /Users/tdavis/Desktop/ch08_code/native_
   log_example/java_bin
    [javac] Compiling 1 source file to /Users/tdavis/Desktop/
   ch08_code/native_log_example/java_bin
native-header-build:
     [echo] Creating native header file...
    [mkdir] Created dir: /Users/tdavis/Desktop/ch08_code/native_
   log_example/objc_bin
native-build:
     [echo] Creating native lib*.jnilib
build:
     [echo] Build complete
run:
     [java] 2009-10-26 20:42:48.029 java[3652:1303] Hello world!
   (of course)
BUILD SUCCESSFUL
Total time: 2 seconds
```

The line tagged run indicates the following output is the result of running the freshly built application. In this example, the output of run is:

```
[java] 2009-10-26 20:42:48.029 java[3652:1303] Hello world! (of course)
```

The only difference between this output and the output when running the `java` command yourself is that the output is prepended with `[java]`. The prefix `[java]` indicates that the line was generated from the `java` tool.

Coding with the CocoaComponent

Now that you understand basic JNI integration, simple Objective-C programming, and setting up Ant builds for Java/Objective-C hybrid projects, you are ready to examine `CocoaComponent` use. When including `CocoaCompoments` in your project, expect to use at least one Java class with native declarations, at least one interface class in C, and one Objective-C class. Your applications likely need more native integration than one of each, but that is the minimum.

In the remainder of this chapter, I explain details of using the `CocoaComponent`. I provide an additional example as an illustration of my explanations. The example demonstrates embedding an `NSButton` in a `JFrame`. The source is available on the book's Web site. The name of the project is `nsbutton_in_jframe`.

Integration of `CocoaComponent` into a JNI application is a more complex than the example JNI project from earlier in this chapter. The main components in projects that use `CocoaComponents` are the following:

- Java-based `CocoaComponent` child
- JNI-based header for Java-to-C communication definitions
- C implementation
- Objective-C `NSView` child declaration
- Objective-C `NSView` child implementation

The pieces fit together as shown in Figure 8.2.

Figure 8.2

CocoaComponent integration

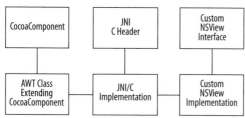

The `CocoaComponent` example I provide consists of the most basic code possible while making the example useful for integration into your projects. The `NSButton` in this project is really just a placeholder. You can substitute any `NSView`-based object needed in your project. You can even substitute your own custom widgets, as long as they descend from `NSView`.

I provide these project files for the next example:

- CustomNSButton.java
- NSButtonExample.java
- nbe.h
- nbe.m
- nsbutton_example_jni.h
- NSButtonExample.h
- NSButtonExample.m

The source associations are shown in Figure 8.3. Essentially, Figure 8.2 and 8.3 are the same. Figure 8.3 shows an actual implementation, so it appears more complex than the more conceptual presentation of Figure 8.2.

Figure 8.3

CocoaComponent example files

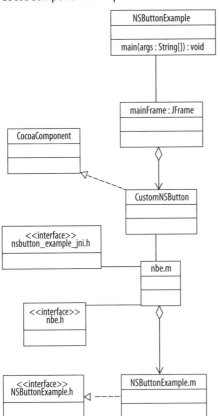

The example application creates and displays an NSButton in a JFrame, as shown in Figure 8.4. The title of the button is set with a call to CocoaComponent's sendMessage(). When the NSButton is clicked, a JOptionPane message dialog box pops up announcing the click, as shown in Figure 8.5. The application demonstrates placement of Cocoa Application Kit GUI elements in Java windows. The application also demonstrates events propagating from Java to Objective-C and events propagating from Objective-C to Java.

Figure 8.4

NSView in a JFrame

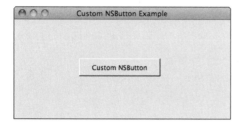

Figure 8.5

NSButton clicked

Understanding CocoaComponent

The CocoaComponent class belongs to the com.apple.eawt package. It is part of the Apple Java Extensions. The CocoaComponent is designed to wrap children of Objective-C's NSView class in such a way that they integrate with AWT. The CocoaComponent class is a child of java.awt.Canvas and behaves like any Canvas class.

To use CocoaComponent, extend it with your own class. Then add it to your own Java Container. In my example, I add it to a JFrame's content pane. Override the size methods to set the minimum, maximum, and preferred size of your CocoaComponent.

Sure, it sounds easy. After you look through the source of the example CocoaComponent child, I discuss the tricky bits.

The following is the source for the CocoaComponent child, CustomNSButton class:

```java
package com.genedavis;
import java.awt.Dimension;
import javax.swing.JOptionPane;
import com.apple.eawt.CocoaComponent;
public class CustomNSButton extends CocoaComponent
{
    // executed during class load
    static
    {
        //used to load from a system library path
        System.loadLibrary("CustomNSButton");
        setupNativeCallbacks();
    }

    /**
     * Supersedes the createNSView() method.
     */
    public native long createNSViewLong();

    /**
     * Performing setup on the Native end.
     */
    public static native long setupNativeCallbacks();
    /**
     * This version of the createNSView() is
     * not used anymore, but you need to implement
     * it until it is removed from the API.
     */
    @Override
    public int createNSView() {
        return 0;
    }
    /**
     * Providing max size of NSButton.
     */
    @Override
    public Dimension getMaximumSize() {
        Dimension dim = new Dimension(150, 32);
        return dim;
    }
    /**
     * Providing minimum size of NSButton.
     */
    @Override
    public Dimension getMinimumSize() {
        Dimension dim = new Dimension(150, 32);
```

```
      return dim;
   }
   /**
    * Providing preferred size of NSButton.
    */
@Override
public Dimension getPreferredSize() {
   Dimension dim = new Dimension(150, 32);
   return dim;
}

public void setCustomTitle(String title)
{
   sendMessage(1, title);// 1 arbitrarily chosen
}

/**
 * Called from C. Do not call locally!
 *
 * Find the signature of this method in the
 * compiled class by calling:
 *
 * javap -private -s CustomNSButton
 *
 * from the command line.
 */
@SuppressWarnings("unused")
private void customButtonClicked()
{
   // Remember that your system will lock up
   // if you don't give back the native thread
   // BEFORE trying to use Java AWT.

   Thread t = new Thread(new Runnable() {
      public void run()
      {
         JOptionPane.showMessageDialog(
               null,
               "You clicked the custom NSButton!");
      }
   });

   t.start();
}
}
```

Four tasks in Java integrate `CustomNSButton` with its native counterpart:

- Implement `sendMessage()` calls for any messages intended to pass to the `NSView`.
- Create `private` Java methods for callbacks from the native code.
- Declare a `native` method, `createNSViewLong()`.
- Provide a `static` block to load the dynamic library and initialize native code.

Implementing sendMessage()

You can send messages to your `CocoaComponent`'s `NSView` with the `sendMessage()` method. You don't need to override the `sendMessage()`; you simply call it. In the `CustomNSButton` class, I call the `sendMessage()` method from the `setCustomTitle()` method.

The `sendMessage()` method takes two parameters: `int` and `Object`. Neither parameter interacts with `CocoaComponent` or the underlying `NSView`. As the software architect or programmer, you choose the values of the parameters and their meanings, and then you write the native code to interpret the `int` and `Object`.

Normally when writing JNI, you declare `native` methods, and all your Java to native code communication happens with those calls. Then, after your JNI functions interpret your calls, you pass the data to your native objects. The `CocoaComponent`'s `sendMessage()` method removes the JNI step from your AWT to NSView communication. As I detail later, calling `sendMessage()` on your `CocoaComponent` results in a method call directly into your `NSView` implementation. Both the `int` and `Object` are passed to the `NSView` for handling.

Use the `int` parameter in `sendMessage()` to pass a message id. The message id represents a native method to which you forward the message. My example uses only one message id. However, with multiple message ids, set up a switch statement in the native code, and pass each message off to an appropriate method for handling.

The `Object` parameter in `sendMessage()` is the data associated with the message id. Because you are passing a `java.lang.Object`, there is no limit to what `Object` you can send to the native code. Just keep in mind that you have to write native code to deal with extracting data from that `Object`, and then you have to interpret that data in a way that makes sense to your native code.

I recommend keeping the message `Object`s simple, if possible. For instance, in the sample code I pass a `String`. Java `String`s are UTF-16 strings, just as `NSString`s are. Passing Java `String`s to Objective-C and interpreting those strings is simple. When you are pressed to meet a deadline, you will appreciate simple.

Creating Java callback methods

When Java methods are called from native code, those calls are called callbacks. At some point, you need asynchronous method calls when using JNI. For instance, if your native code performs a long calculation or does a network call to a busy server, you don't want to wait for the return.

Instead, follow these steps:

1. **Set up a Java callback.**

2. **Spawn a thread in your native environment.**

3. **Have that thread perform a call to Java when a return value is finally available.**

In the case of `CustomNSButton`, I wrap an `NSButton`. When a user clicks the button, an event needs to propagate to the `CustomNSButton` class. The callback I use is the `customButtonClicked()` method.

TIP

Debugging JNI is painful. Do not make it harder by reusing callback methods. Keep them private and unused by the Java code. Call them only from native code.

JNI is not restrained by visibility. This means `private` methods are not hidden from native JNI callbacks. Take advantage of it. Hide your callbacks from your Java code.

The callback method in `CustomNSButton` is the `customButtonClicked()` method. It is `private`. I do not call the `customButtonClicked()` method from the Java code. I added the `@SuppressWarnings("unused")` annotation to prevent the compiler from complaining about an unused method. (The method is used by the native code via JNI.) Keeping the callback method `private` makes debugging callbacks simpler. You know the method is called only from the native code. If the method is called when it shouldn't be called, then you know to look in the native code for your problem.

As soon as the callback method, `customButtonClicked()`, is called, I pass the data to a new thread. I return the thread making the callback. Always return threads coming from callbacks immediately. Otherwise, you may lock up your application or impair performance of the native code.

Declaring createNSViewLong()

The `createNSViewLong()` method in `CocoaComponent` replaces the older (and deprecated) `createNSView()` method. The purpose of the `createNSViewLong()` method is instantiating your native `NSView`. The return value is a pointer to the native `NSView` wrapped by your `CocoaComponent`. The super class, `CocoaComponent`, handles the connection to your native `NSView` using the returned pointer.

The best way to handle the `createNSViewLong()` method is to make it a `native` method. Let your native JNI code perform the instantiation of the `NSView`. After instantiating the `NSView`, get your `NSView`'s pointer and return it to Java as a `long`.

NOTE

The `createNSView()` method returned an `int`. When Mac OS X ran off a 32-bit architecture, the preferred way to pass a pointer to Java from JNI was as an `int`. However, now OS X is a fully 64-bit OS. Pointers from JNI are passed to Java as `long` values. That is why a new `createNSView()` method exists.

Initializing native code

Your Java program needs to initialize your native C and Objective-C code. There is nothing too magical about initializing the native code. From the Java side, include a `static` block in your Java class. In the `static` block, load your code from a dynamic library. After loading the native library, call an initialization method. The initialization method is a `native` method of your choosing.

The only other Java code needed to initialize native code when extending `CustomNSButton` is the `native` declaration of `createNSViewLong()`. The `createNSViewLong()` method is called by the `CocoaComponent` implementation. It obtains a pointer to the underlying Objective-C `NSView`.

Consider the native initialization that occurs in `CustomNSButton`:

```
static
{
    System.loadLibrary("CustomNSButton");
    setupNativeCallbacks();
}
public native long createNSViewLong();
public static native long setupNativeCallbacks();
```

The `System.loadLibrary()` method loads the dynamic library containing the project's native code. The `setupNativeCallbacks()` method is a call to a method I declared as `native`. In other words, `setupNativeCallbacksc()` is implemented in the `CustomNSButton` library. The method `createNSViewLong()` is declared as `native` with additional initialization of the native library happening after the `CocoaComponent` calls the method.

I return to a detailed discussion of initialization of the native library later in this chapter. I discuss initialization further when I discuss the JNI environment.

Introducing NSView

The `CocoaComponents` wrap `NSViews` for use in Java GUI applications. Wrapping `NSView` opens up most, if not all, predefined and custom Cocoa widgets for use in AWT and Swing. To share the significance of the Java `CocoaComponent`, I explain the Objective-C `NSView`.

The Objective-C `NSView` class shares a similar position in the Cocoa framework as the `java.awt.Component` class shares in the Java API. Essentially, all widgets, buttons, tools, and panels in the Application Kit framework descend from `NSView`. `NSView` children include `NSButton`, `NSTabView`, `NSOpenGLView`, and `NSColorWell`. The `NSView` contains the largest tree in Cocoa's Application Kit (with the exception of its parent, `NSResponder`).

`NSView` handles events and basic drawing in Cocoa applications. `NSViews` are placed in `NSWindows` in similar fashion as `Components` are placed in `JFrames` and `Windows` in Java.

NOTE

The Cocoa framework is an umbrella framework. An umbrella framework is a framework that does not contain any libraries, just other frameworks. The Cocoa framework contains the Application Kit framework. The NSView class is part of the Application Kit.

NOTE

The online reference for NSView is located here:

```
http://developer.apple.com/mac/library/documentation
/Cocoa/Reference/ApplicationKit/Classes/NSView_Class
/Reference/NSView.html
```

The online documentation for the Application Kit framework is located here:

```
http://developer.apple.com/mac/library/documentation
/Cocoa/Reference/ApplicationKit/ObjC_classic/Intro
/IntroAppKit.html
```

Embedding NSView in Swing

As I have stated, CocoaComponents are wrappers for native NSViews. Using CocoaComponents, you can embed NSViews in Swing and AWT just like other java.awt. Components. Follow these steps:

1. **Set the layout manager for your container.**

2. **Construct your** CocoaComponent.

3. **Set the size for your** CocoaComponet.

4. **Add your** CocoaComponent **to a container.**

No worries. After your CocoaComponent is written, the process for adding the NSView to Swing or AWT has no unusual steps.

TIP

Common wisdom is that Swing and AWT don't mix. Reality is that they mix fine, if you are careful. The important rule is that you should never draw Swing components over AWT components that do not contain them.

The classic mistake is to place a Swing drop-down menu where it draws over an AWT Component not containing the drop-down menu. In this case, the AWT component always draws over top of the Swing component.

NOTE

If downloaded from the Web site, both projects in this chapter clean, build, and run with a single command, ant. Simply run the Terminal application found in the /Applications/Utilities/ directory. Change the directory to the project directory with the cd command. Finally, enter the ant command to build and run the project.

The following code creates a JFrame and embeds a CocoaComponent in the JFrame:

```java
package com.genedavis;
import java.awt.Container;
import java.awt.event.ActionEvent;
import java.awt.event.ActionListener;
import java.awt.event.MouseAdapter;
import java.awt.event.MouseEvent;
import javax.swing.JButton;
import javax.swing.JFrame;
import javax.swing.JOptionPane;
public class NSButtonExample {
    public static void main(String[] args)
    {
        // true prevents deadlock, but may cause JNI calls
        // to return asynchronously instead of synchronously.
        System.setProperty(
                "com.apple.eawt.CocoaComponent.CompatibilityMode",
                "false");

        new NSButtonExample();
    }

    public NSButtonExample()
    {

        final JFrame mainFrame =
            new JFrame("Custom NSButton Example");
        Container pane = mainFrame.getContentPane();
        pane.setLayout( null );

        CustomNSButton button = new CustomNSButton();
        mainFrame.add( button );

        button.setSize( button.getPreferredSize() );
        button.setLocation(120,70);

        mainFrame.setSize(400, 200);
        mainFrame.setVisible(true);

        // cannot call until the button is visible
        // or a null pointer exception occurs.
        button.setCustomTitle("Custom NSButton");

    }
}
```

These steps allow you to use the custom CocoaComponent in this code example:

1. **Create a** JFrame.

2. **Set the** JFrame**'s content pane layout manager.**

3. **Instantiate the class that extends** CocoaComponent.

4. **Add the** CocoaComponent **instance to the** JFrame**'s content pane.**

5. **Set the size and location of the** CocoaComponent.

CAUTION

Remember that through inheritance, a class is an implementation of its parent. Therefore, I use the name CocoaComponent frequently when referring to children of CocoaComponent.

CAUTION

In the example, I set the NSButton label with a call to an Objective-C method using the CocoaComponent method, sendMessage(). To ensure that the NSView (in this case, NSButton) is constructed, do not sendMessages() until the containing window or frame is set to visible.

Employing the JNI Environment

Execute the javah application against the compiled CustomNSButton class to generate your needed JNI header file. Using javah from inside an Ant project makes lots of sense, too. The Ant target for running javah in this project follows:

```
<target
    name="native-header-build"
    description="Builds the native headers file">

    <echo>Creating native header file...</echo>

    <mkdir dir="${native.bin}"/>
    <javah
        outputfile="${objective.c.source}/nsbutton_example_jni.h"
        classpath="${java.bin}">

        <class name="com.genedavis.CustomNSButton" />

    </javah>
</target>
```

NOTE

Remember that the ${some.variable.name} notation places a variable contained by ${} into the containing string.

The interesting part of the `javah`-generated header file, `nsbutton_example_jni.h`, follows:

```
/*
 * Class:     com_genedavis_CustomNSButton
 * Method:    createNSViewLong
 * Signature: ()J
 */
JNIEXPORT jlong JNICALL Java_com_genedavis_CustomNSButton_
    createNSViewLong
  (JNIEnv *, jobject);
/*
 * Class:     com_genedavis_CustomNSButton
 * Method:    setupNativeCallbacks
 * Signature: ()J
 */
JNIEXPORT jlong JNICALL Java_com_genedavis_CustomNSButton_
    setupNativeCallbacks
  (JNIEnv *, jclass);
```

Notice that the `sendMessage()` method from `CocoaComponent` is not represented. `CocoaComponent` handles connecting the `sendMessage()` method directly to the underlying `NSView`. This saves time for you as a programmer. Obviously, if you want more direct control, you can refuse to use the `sendMessage()` method and implement your own native methods for sending messages to the `NSView`.

The code for the C implementation of the generated header is much more complex than the earlier example's C implementation. It consists of a header file and an Objective-C file. The header, `nbe.h`, is simply this:

```
// function prototype(s) for callbacks to Java
// defining INCLUDED_NBE_H to prevent multiple inclusions
// of this code. Obviously, not a problem with the
// example, but still a good habit with C.
#ifndef INCLUDED_NBE_H
#define INCLUDED_NBE_H
void notifyJavaThatButtonWasClicked( void );
#endif
```

However, the Objective-C file, `nbe.m`, contains the source for the incoming messages, callbacks to Java, and code for obtaining a `JavaVM`, `jobject`, `jmethod`, and the `JNIEnv` references as needed. Here is the full source:

```
#import <jni.h>
#import <AWTCocoaComponent.h>
#import <stdio.h>
#import <Cocoa/Cocoa.h>
#import <nsbutton_example_jni.h>
```

```
#import <NSButtonExample.h>
#include "nbe.h"

// retaining references to jvm and methods
// never retain env references as they change
// NOTE: in C "static" means ...
// "global, but only visible in this file"
static JavaVM *jvm;
static jmethodID buttonClickMethod;
static jobject customNSButtonJavaObject;

// This function tells Java to provide the newest
// version of the JNI library. Otherwise, you do NOT
// have access to any features added after Java 1.1!!!
JNIEXPORT jint JNICALL JNI_OnLoad(JavaVM *vm, void *reserved)
{
   jvm = vm;
   return JNI_VERSION_1_6;
}
// Called from Java to set up the method ids;
// obtaining method callbacks is a potentially slow
// process, so getting them ahead of time is advised
JNIEXPORT jlong JNICALL
Java_com_genedavis_CustomNSButton_setupNativeCallbacks
(JNIEnv *env, jclass jclazz)
{
   buttonClickMethod =
       (*env)->GetMethodID(
                      env,
                      jclazz,
                      "customButtonClicked",
                      "()V");
}


// Remember the createNSViewLong() method in the
// Java class, CustomNSButton? This is the native
// implementation of that method.
JNIEXPORT jlong JNICALL
Java_com_genedavis_CustomNSButton_createNSViewLong
(JNIEnv * env, jobject jobj)
{
   // storing the Java object that called this function.
   // NOTE: The object, not the class is stored
   // NOTE: clean up of a global ref usually entails
   // calling DeleteGlobalRef().
   customNSButtonJavaObject =
     (*env)->NewGlobalRef(env, jobj);
```

```
    // Every thread must be wrapped in an NSAutoreleasePool
    // This prevents memory leaks
    NSAutoreleasePool        *pool = [[NSAutoreleasePool alloc]
    init];

    NSButtonExample *customButton = nil;

    // instantiating Objective-C NSButtonExample object
    customButton = [[NSButtonExample alloc] init];

    // add NSButtonExample customization code here
    // no customization performed in this example

    // destroying the NSAutoreleasePool
    // time to clean up after myself
    [pool release];

    // return reference to native custom NSButton
    return (long)(uintptr_t) customButton;
}

// notifies Java via the callback
void notifyJavaThatButtonWasClicked( void )
{

    JNIEnv *env = NULL;
    jint env_error = JNI_OK;
    BOOL detach = NO;

    // Use the JVM reference to get an up-to-date
    // JNIEnv. JNIEnv variables need constant
    // updates
    env_error = (*jvm)->GetEnv(
                            jvm,
                            (void **)&env,
                            JNI_VERSION_1_6);

    // Making sure that this is not part of a
    // Java thread yet.
    if ( env_error == JNI_EDETACHED)
    {
        // Attaching this thread to a JVM thread
        env_error = (*jvm)->AttachCurrentThread(
                                            jvm,
                                            (void **)env,
                                            NULL);

        // assuming there was no error attaching the
```

```
        // current thread to the JVM, remember to detach
        // the from the JVM when done calling the Java
        // method.
        if (env_error == JNI_OK)
        {
                detach = YES;
        }
}

// This is the actual method call to the method
// reference "buttonClickMethod" on the object
// "customNSButtonJavaObject".
(*env)->CallVoidMethod(
                        env,
                        customNSButtonJavaObject,
                        buttonClickMethod);

// All done. Time to detach the thread.
if (detach)
{
(*jvm)->DetachCurrentThread( jvm );
}

}
```

Caching the needed elements for handling callbacks from the native `NSView`, is a little tricky. This section explains avoiding common pitfalls of performs and scope when arranging callbacks; I cover `JavaVM` pointers, `jobject` pointers, `jmethod` points, and `JNIEnv` pointers.

Obtaining a JavaVM

`JavaVM` pointers represent an entire JVM. `JavaVM` pointers are most commonly used in creating JVMs from native code. In the case of using `CocoaComponent`, I don't create a JVM from native code. Instead, I grab a reference to the JVM for use in handling user-generated events that need callbacks to Java.

The best way to grab a pointer to the JVM in a native library is when the JVM loads the native library. When loading a JNI-based dynamic library, Java calls the `JNI_OnLoad()` function. The first argument to `JNI_OnLoad()` is a JavaVM pointer.

For quick reference, here again is the code for the `JNI_OnLoad()` function in `nbe.m`:

```
JNIEXPORT jint JNICALL JNI_OnLoad(JavaVM *vm, void *reserved)
{
    jvm = vm;
    return JNI_VERSION_1_6;
}
```

The `JavaVM` pointer is good for as long as the `JavaVM` exists. Unless you are creating and destroying JVMs from native code, `JavaVM` points won't go bad. So I grab the pointer during the onload call and keep it in a `static` variable for future use.

NOTE

In C, `static` means something different than in Java. If `static` is used when defining a variable outside a function in C, it restricts visibility of the variable to code in that physical file. When `static` is used while defining a variable inside a function, the variable's value is retained as a local variable between calls to the function.

TIP

When unloading a dynamic native library, Java calls the `JNI_OnUnload()` function. Place your cleanup code for the dynamic library in the `JNI_OnUnload()` function.

Obtaining a jobject

As you probably can guess, `jobject`s represent Java class instances. There are three types of `jobject` pointers: local, global, and weak global references. Local references go out of scope and clean up as soon as a native call returns to the JVM. Both types of global references remain valid after the native method call returns. Both types of global references are candidates for caching.

I choose to cache a global reference in the `nbe.m` example instead of a weak global reference. The difference between weak global and standard global `jobject` references is that weak global references allow for the underlying object to be garbage collected. I have no need for garbage collecting the referenced object. Normally, the choice between weak and standard `jobject` references comes down to whether the Java `Object` is consuming many resources.

I create the `jobject` reference in `nbe.m`, in this function:

```
Java_com_genedavis_CustomNSButton_createNSViewLong()
```

Here is the full source for the native `createNSViewLong()` function:

```
JNIEXPORT jlong JNICALL
Java_com_genedavis_CustomNSButton_createNSViewLong
(JNIEnv * env, jobject jobj)
{
    customNSButtonJavaObject =
      (*env)->NewGlobalRef(env, jobj);

    NSAutoreleasePool  *pool = [[NSAutoreleasePool alloc] init];

    NSButtonExample *customButton = nil;
    customButton = [[NSButtonExample alloc] init];

    [pool release];
```

```
        return (long)(uintptr_t) customButton;
    }
```

The call to `(*env)->NewGlobalRef(env, jobj)` actually created the global `jobject` reference. I store the global reference in the `static` variable `customNSButtonJava Object`.

Obtaining a jmethod

Object references are stored in `jobject` pointers. So it is no surprise that method references are stored in `jmethod` pointers. References to methods stay good between native calls. Caching `jmethod` pointers is perfectly safe if the JVM itself won't go away.

Remember the static block in `CustomNSButton`. In the static block, I call `setupNative-Callbacks()`. In the native implementation of that method, I grab the `jmethod` reference. In fact, that is the only operation performed in the native implementation.

Here again is the source for quick reference:

```
JNIEXPORT jlong JNICALL
Java_com_genedavis_CustomNSButton_setupNativeCallbacks
(JNIEnv *env, jclass jclazz)
{
    buttonClickMethod =
        (*env)->GetMethodID(
                            env,
                            jclazz,
                            "customButtonClicked",
                            "()V");
}
```

The function call `GetMethodID()` retrieves the `jmethod` pointer, `buttonClickMethod`. The `GetMethodID()` function takes the `JNIEnv` pointer, a `jclass` pointer, the name of the method, and a signature for the method. The native method call provides both the `JNIEnv` pointer and the `jclass` pointer. Just use the variables passed in on the method call. The method name, in this case "`customButtonClicked`", is just the name of the Java method.

The method signature needs a little more discussion. Potential method overloading in Java creates the need for distinguishing methods with similar names but different signatures. The format for a method signature is as follows:

```
(<argument><argument><...>)<return>
```

Methods with no arguments contain an empty set of parentheses. Methods with no return value ends with a `V`. In the case of the method `customButtonClicked()`, the signature is "`()V`". Retrieve more complex method signatures with the `javap` tool.

The command for obtaining all the method signatures in `CustomNSButton` is this:

```
javap -s -private CustomNSButton
```

To run `javap` against your own class, just change the name of the class in the `javap` command to the name of your class. Run the `javap` tool against the compiled `CustomNSButton` class, and it returns the following results:

```
public class com.genedavis.CustomNSButton extends com.apple.eawt.
  CocoaComponent{
public com.genedavis.CustomNSButton();
  Signature: ()V
public native long createNSViewLong();
  Signature: ()J
public static native long setupNativeCallbacks();
  Signature: ()J
public int createNSView();
  Signature: ()I
public java.awt.Dimension getMaximumSize();
  Signature: ()Ljava/awt/Dimension;
public java.awt.Dimension getMinimumSize();
  Signature: ()Ljava/awt/Dimension;
public java.awt.Dimension getPreferredSize();
  Signature: ()Ljava/awt/Dimension;
public void setCustomTitle(java.lang.String);
  Signature: (Ljava/lang/String;)V
private void customButtonClicked();
  Signature: ()V
static {};
  Signature: ()V
}
```

Each method signature is clearly stated. Just copy the results to the `GetMethodID` when retrieving `jmethod` references.

CAUTION

Run the `javap` tool against compiled classes, not source files.

TIP

Obtaining `jmethod` and `jfield` (corresponding to Java attributes) pointers is relatively expensive. If you need repeated access to Java methods or fields, cache the pointers for performance improvements.

Obtaining a JNIEnv

JNIEnv references provide the means for calling most of the methods you need when handling JNI native method implementations. You will get very accustomed to typing the following:

```
(*env)->SomeMethodNames();
```

The pointers I discussed so far are valid between native calls. JNIEnv is not valid across threads. Never cache JNIEnv pointers.

JNIEnv pointers are the first argument to all methods in JNI, so getting a new one that is valid on your current thread is usually not difficult when the thread is provided by the JVM. However, when you handle threads generated by user events on an NSView, you need to get your own JNIEnv pointer.

The notifyJavaThatButtonWasClicked(void) function in nbe.m provides an example of obtaining a JNIEnv pointer from a JavaVM pointer. For convenience, the source for notifyJavaThatButtonWasClicked(void) follows:

```
void notifyJavaThatButtonWasClicked( void )
{

    JNIEnv *env = NULL;
    jint env_error = JNI_OK;
    BOOL detach = NO;

    env_error = (*jvm)->GetEnv(
                            jvm,
                            (void **)&env,
                            JNI_VERSION_1_6);

    if ( env_error == JNI_EDETACHED)
    {
        // Attaching this thread to a JVM thread
        env_error = (*jvm)->AttachCurrentThread(
                                            jvm,
                                            (void **)env,
                                            NULL);

        if (env_error == JNI_OK)
        {
                detach = YES;
        }
    }

    (*env)->CallVoidMethod(
                            env,
                            customNSButtonJavaObject,
                            buttonClickMethod);
```

```
      if (detach)
      {
      (*jvm)->DetachCurrentThread( jvm );
      }
   }
```

Follow these steps to obtain a JNIEnv pointer:

1. Cache a JavaVM pointer cached.

Typically, caching a JavaVM pointer when your dynamic library loads is easy. Cache the JavaVM pointer when JNI_OnLoad() is called.

2. Declare a JNIEnv pointer.

The declaration looks like this:

```
JNIEnv *env = NULL;
```

3. Retrieve the correct JNIEnv pointer from the JavaVM.

This is the call:

```
(*jvm)->GetEnv(
            jvm,
            (void **)&env,
            JNI_VERSION_1_6);
```

The function GetEnv() takes a JavaVM pointer as the first argument. The GetEnv() function takes a JNI version as the last parameter. The JNIEnv pointer is filled with the proper value by the GetEnv() function in a similar manner because Java methods often set the value of Java objects passed into the methods as arguments.

4. Attach the current thread to the JVM.

The JNIEnv pointer does no good, if your current thread is not attached to the JVM. The error code returned by GetEnv() indicates the attached status of the current thread.

Check the return value against JNI_EDETACHED. If the current thread is not attached, call the following to attach the thread:

```
(*jvm)->AttachCurrentThread(
                        jvm,
                        (void **)env,
                        NULL);
```

Finally, all this work getting a valid JNIEnv allows you to perform a callback using the CallMethod(). The actual call in nbe.m follows:

```
(*env)->CallVoidMethod(
                        env,
                        customNSButtonJavaObject,
                        buttonClickMethod);
```

The word "void" in the `CallVoidMethod()` function indicates that the return value of the method you are calling is void. If there are arguments to the method, pass the appropriate JNI variables in to the function call as additional argument to the function call.

TIP
There are several version of the `Call*Method()` function. For a complete list of provided call method functions, see the `jni.h` file. A simple search by filename in the Finder provides the location of `jni.h`.

Handling Events

This section explains events in the context of `CocoaComponent` implementations. Most `NSViews` require user interaction and interaction from the Java code. Events are the last piece of the `CocoaComponent` puzzle that you need to understand.

The source for the Objective-C object, `NSButtonExample`, is found in the files `NSButtonExample.h` and `NSButtonEample.m`. As always, glancing at the Objective-C interface gives a quick overview of the Objective-C class. The following source is found in the `NSButtonExample.h` file on the Web site:

```
#import <jni.h>
#import <AWTCocoaComponent.h>
#import <Cocoa/Cocoa.h>
#include "nbe.h"

@interface NSButtonExample : NSButton <AWTCocoaComponent> {
}
-( id ) init;
- (void)mouseDown:(NSEvent *)theEvent;
-( void ) awtMessage: ( jint ) awtMessageID
           message: ( jobject ) messageObject
               env: ( JNIEnv * ) jni_env;
@end
```

From this interface, you can see the `NSButtonExample` class extends `NSButton`. `NSButton` is an `NSView`. Not too surprisingly, `NSButtons` generate click events.

The `NSButtonExample` interface declares no variables.

The `NSButtonExample` declares the `init:` method, the `mouseDown:` method, and the `awtMessage:` method. The `init:` method is the class constructor. The `mouseDown:` method captures clicks on the `NSButtonExample`. The `awtMessage:` method receives method calls from the Java `CocoaComponent`'s `sendMessage()` method.

The implementation source from `NSButtonExample.m` follows:

```
#import "NSButtonExample.h"
@implementation NSButtonExample
```

```
-( id ) init
{
   return [super init];
}
- (void)mouseDown:(NSEvent *)theEvent
{
   notifyJavaThatButtonWasClicked();
}
// receives sendMessage() calls
// from Java CocoaComponent
-( void ) awtMessage: ( jint ) awtMessageID
            message: ( jobject ) messageObject
               env: ( JNIEnv * ) jni_env
{
   // Normally I would check the id to see which
   // message this was, but I only have one
   // implemented, so no need for a switch
   // statement this time.

   // converting the jstring to an NSString
   // 1. get a jchar array from the jstring
   // 2. get the length of the jstring
   // 3. instantiate the NSString
   // 4. free the jvm resources (no garbage collector here)
   const jchar *chars = (*jni_env)->GetStringChars(jni_env,
   messageObject, NULL);
   NSUInteger str_len = (*jni_env)->GetStringLength(jni_env,
   messageObject);
   NSString *message = [NSString
                         stringWithCharacters:(UniChar *)chars
                         length:str_len];
   (*jni_env)->ReleaseStringChars(jni_env, messageObject, chars);
   // setting the title of this button
   [self setTitle: message];
}
@end
```

When you implement an NSView, follow this pattern:

- Implement an `init:` method to handle configuration and initialization of the NSView.
- Implement user event handler(s).
- Implement `awtMessage:` to handle `sendMessage()` from the Java CocoaComponent.

The `NSButtonExample` implementation handles mouse-down events by passing the event to the `notifyJavaThatButtonWasClicked()` function found in the `nbe.m` file. Once in the `notifyJavaThatButtonWasClicked()` function, retrieve a valid `JNIEnv` pointer, attach the current thread to the JVM, and issue a callback to the `private` `customButtonClicked()` method in the `CustomNSButton` class.

After I have the Application Kit's thread in Java, create a new `Thread` to handle the event, while returning the `Application Kit`'s thread. Never allow an AWT thread to call an Application Kit's method in a way that may block the thread, and never allow an Application Kit's thread to call an AWT method in a way that may block the Application Kit's thread. The `JOptionPane` used in this example definitely blocks, so I call it on a separate thread.

Always play nice with threads that aren't yours. It sounds like some sort of rule of etiquette, but it actually prevents deadlocks and perceived performance issues.

The `awtMessage:` method in the `NSButtonExample` implementation handles incoming `sendMessage()` calls. (Note that the `JNIEnv` pointer is actually the last parameter, not the first as you might expect with JNI related functions.) The `jint` is the `int` representing the message id. The `jobject` represents the message data.

In the case of this example, the `jobject` is a Java String. These are conversion steps for the `jobject` to an `NSString`:

1. **Obtain the Java** String **as a** jchar*.

   You accomplish this with a call to the `GetStringChars()` function contained in the JNI environment.

2. **Get the length of the string.**

   The length of the string is obtained with another call to the JNI environment. Strings are essentially character arrays in C. Because C does not track the length of arrays, strings in C contain a value of 0 at the end of the string. (This is referred to as *null terminating*.) You must manually place this value of 0 when creating strings in C. That is why I need the string length.

3. **Create an** NSString **by providing a pointer to the raw unicode characters and the length of the final string.**

4. **Free the JVM resources in the JNI environment.**

   Now that I have my string's value safely copied to a shiny new `NSString`, it is time to release the JNI environment's string resources. Again, I call a function in the `JNIEnv*` variable, named `jenv`, to release the resources.

Other `jobject` types actually require more steps to translate, so for simple messages I stick with sending strings from Java to Objective-C.

Summary

This chapter is about using the CocoaComponent from the Apple Java Extensions' com. apple.eawt package. When delving into the complexities of using the CocoaComponent, understanding the basics of JNI is helpful. Even trivial implementations of the CocoaComponent require basic JNI skills.

Java classes that handle JNI, usually contain native Java methods and static code blocks. The command-line tool, javah, creates JNI header files for use with C. The javah tool does this by investigating a compiled class's methods and then creates the C headers based on those Java methods tagged with the native key word.

CocoaCompoments wrap Objective-C classes that extend NSView. Implement your CocoaComponent on the Java side by extending CocoaComponent and implementing the createNSViewLong() method as a native method. CocoaComponent is an AWT Canvas, so add it to any appropriate AWT or Swing hierarchy.

Communication between Objective-C NSView implementations and Java CocoaComponent requires the sendMessage() method and native callbacks to Java. Use the sendMessage() method to send messages to your native NSView implementation. Use callbacks to message Java from your NSView when users trigger events on the NSView.

When implementing NSView objects for use in the CocoaComponent, implement the AWTCocoaComponent protocol. The AWTCocoaComponent protocol provides the receiving method for messages sent from the CocoaComponent's sendMessage() method. The awtMessage: method provides your NSView implementation with a message id, a message object, and a copy of the current JNI environment.

As an Objective-C class, your NSView needs to define a class implementation and a class interface. A *.h file contains the interface. A *.m file contains the class implementation. Though discouraged, both Objective-C object interface and Objective-C object implementation may exist in a single file. If so, place them in an *.m file.

Architecting Alternative Applications

Understanding JNI

Apple ships Java on every Mac. Java is an important part of OS X. Many applications for OS X are Java-based. Apple has a very strong commitment to providing a stable OS X-integrated Java experience to its users.

However, Java is just a small part of OS X. I describe in earlier chapters the Cocoa frameworks, Carbon frameworks, and Unix libraries. Many of these libraries are written for C or C-based languages.

Thankfully, Java is not a C-based language. Normally, you don't have to worry about pointers, cleaning up memory, allocating memory, and a host of other nasty little details that C-based languages deal with all the time.

Still, access to Cocoa, Carbon, and POSIX libraries is useful sometimes. The standard approach on OS X to access Cocoa, Carbon, and Unix libraries from Java is Java Native Interfaces (JNI). JNI provides access to all Cocoa frameworks, Carbon frameworks, and POSIX libraries from Java.

JNI tends to frighten beginning and advanced Java programmers. Visions of pointers to pointers and function callbacks passed around with esoteric #define statements cause dread, and even hardened Java programmers cringe when the acronym "JNI" is spoken.

Remember, the famous words of Douglas Adams. "DON'T PANIC. JNI really isn't any more difficult than creating Java GUI layouts by hand. JNI just takes practice." (OK, he didn't say that last bit, or the center part either.)

In Chapter 8, I explain using `CocoaComponents`. `Cocoa Components` require JNI, so I gave a quick introduction to C and Objective-C integration with Java in the context of `CocoaComponents`.

In this chapter, I explain the basics of JNI. I introduce several opaque structures provided by JNI. I explain in detail the use of JNI in communicating from Java to C. I also explain communicating from C to Java.

In This Chapter

Creating JNI applications

Integrating JNI with projects

Using Objective-C with JNI

Understanding OS X JNI threading

Passing strings

In this chapter, I explain use of the Invocation API. The invocation API allows C-based programs to create Java Virtual Machines dynamically. The full importance of the invocation API becomes apparent in Chapter 10, when I demonstrate wrapping the Cocoa Screen Saver Framework in Java. Using the invocation framework, you can create custom Java launchers for your OS X application bundles. You can even use the techniques in this chapter (and in Chapter 10) to wrap Interface Builder-created views for use as your front end in otherwise pure Java applications.

Reviewing JNI

Java Native Interfaces (JNI) give Java access to native C-based programs. Consider the ubiquitous nature of C. Every modern programming language with any sizable user base can interface with C. By extension, any modern language of any import also can interact with Java, because Java can speak C.

The key, of course, is JNI. Java programmers don't generally like C, so JNI isn't discussed much. It is basically the embarrassing relative no one talks about. However, the bad reputation is mostly unjustified.

In less than 50 lines of code, you can produce a fully functional JNI program. Admittedly, it won't do much, but you have to start somewhere. The most basic JNI program, diagrammed in Figure 9.1, contains a Java `native` method, a `javah`-generated C header, and a short C library.

Figure 9.1

Basic JNI-based program

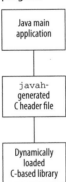

When your Java program needs to call native libraries, follow these steps:

1. **Declare your native methods in Java.**

This is the easiest of the steps and requires merely that you use the `native` keyword when declaring unimplemented Java methods.

2. **Generate any needed C header files.**

Perform this step with a call to `javah`. The `javah` command-line tool examines a Java class looking for methods declared as `native`. All native method signatures are translated into C for use in the C implementations.

3. **Implement the C header files.**

The C JNI libraries have several defined types that mirror Java's primitives and objects. Implementing the native end of Java methods requires some knowledge of the Java types available in C.

JNI requires native methods and static blocks. Native methods and static blocks don't typically get used in Java, except when creating JNI-based calls. If this is your first experience with JNI, you may never have heard of static blocks or the native keyword.

On the Java side, JNI uses an unimplemented `native` method to indicate methods implemented in the C code as functions. This little bit of magic sounds too good to be true, but that is pretty much all there is to creating a JNI method signature in Java. (Obviously, the C implementation is a little more complex, but not much.)

A native method is declared like this:

```
public native void someName();
```

The return type and the parameters passed to the method can be anything found in other methods. Native methods can be declared as `static` or as regular instance methods. Access to the method can be `private`, `protected`, `public`, or the implicit package-private. For all practical purposes, the method signature is similar to an abstract method signature, except that native code contains the implementation, instead of a subclass written in Java.

The other common task on the Java end is loading native libraries that contain the implementations of `native` Java methods. Loading libraries for use in JNI usually happens before the program starts. Loading the native libraries occurs in static blocks of code.

A static block of code looks like a normal static method stripped down to the curly braces. Usually static blocks of code are placed near the top of a method declaration, to make them stand out. A static block of code looks like this:

```
static
{
    // expressions go here ...
}
```

NOTE

Sometimes JNI uses no native methods or static blocks of code. For instance, in the first invocation example in this chapter, C starts the JVM and calls a Java method. No static block or native methods are in the first invocation example.

The two approaches most often taken when loading native libraries are calling the `System` class method named `loadLibrary()` and calling the `System` method `load()`. The `load Library()` method is used when your library is in a predefined location specified during JVM start up. The `load()` method is used when you load a library from a file system location defined while your Java program is running.

The first approach to loading native libraries looks something like this:

```
System.loadLibrary("SomeLibrary");
```

The second common approach is a little more complex and looks like this:

```
try
{
    File lib = new File("objc_bin/libSomeLibrary.jnilib");
    String path = lib.getCanonicalPath();
    System.load( path );
}
catch (IOException ioe)
{
    ioe.printStackTrace();
}
```

CAUTION

Remember to get the native library name correct when loading it. The filenames of dynamic JNI libraries take the form `lib<name>.jnilib`. However, when using the `System` class method `loadLibrary()`, refer to the library name, not the filename.

C programs often start a JVM and call Java methods. Starting JVMs from C is rather involved, so I save that discussion for later in the chapter. Starting a JVM and supplying that JVM with statically linked native method implementations is the realm of the Invocation API. For now, I stick to explaining how Java programs load and call native libraries, not how C programs load and call Java libraries.

After declaring your native methods, compile your Java class. You must now create your native C header files. For the examples in this book, one header is all you create. Even in real-world setting, programs commonly have only one class that defines native methods and only one header file generated from that class.

Generate your C header file using `javah`. The `javah` command takes classes as arguments. Remember to use fully qualified class names with `javah`. For instance:

```
javah com.mycompany.MyClass
```

C implementations of native Java methods must `#include` the C header generated by `javah`. Also, the implementing C file must `#include` the `jni.h` header, but this is usually done indirectly by the `javah`-generated header. The C code itself need not be complex.

Calling native code

Explaining JNI doesn't teach you JNI. You need to see and try some code examples. The following example is found on the book's Web site. The project uses Ant, but you can build and run just as easily from the command line or any Java-aware build tool of your choice.

The first example is the `hello_darwin` project. The project is split into three source files: `HelloDarwinExample.java`, `native_greeting_jni.h`, and `darwin.c`. The project implements the basic JNI example diagrammed in Figure 9.1.

The following source is the code for the `HelloDarwinExample` class.

```
package com.genedavis;
public class HelloDarwinExample {
    // executed during class load
    static
    {
        // used to load from a system library path
        System.loadLibrary("NativeGreeter");
    }

    public static void main(String[] args)
    {
            HelloDarwinExample hde = new HelloDarwinExample();
            hde.hi();
    }

    // native method call
    private native void hi();
}
```

The `HelloDarwinExample` class contains the following:

- a `static` block
- a `main()` method
- a `native` method

I load the native library using the static block. I chose to use the shorter method of loading the library, mostly because short code is easier to read. Some programmers demand that you use the longer version. Both methods work fine.

The native method is private but does not need to be private. I could have given it any visibility. I made this native method simple. It does not contain arguments or a return value. However, there are no restrictions on the arguments and return values defined by native methods.

Creating a C header file from the `HelloDarwinExample` class is a simple call of `javah`. From the Terminal, `cd` to your compiled Java class directory and use the following command:

```
javah com.genedavis.HelloDarwinExample
```

In the case of the chapter's sample code from the book's Web site, run the command from the `hello_darwin/java_bin/` directory.

If you want to specify a name for your header file, use the −o option. Your command might look like this:

```
javah -o my_jni_header.h com.genedavis.HelloDarwinExample
```

NOTE

The `javah` command does not create a native declaration of the `main()` method, only the `hi()` method. That is because the `hi()` method is declared as `native`.

In the example's project, I force the header file to the name of `native_greeting_jni.h`. The following source is for the `native_greeting_jni.h` file. The `native_greeting_jni.h` file is generated using the `javah` tool from the `HelloDarwinExample` class.

```
/* DO NOT EDIT THIS FILE - it is machine generated */
#include <jni.h>
/* Header for class com_genedavis_HelloDarwinExample */
#ifndef _Included_com_genedavis_HelloDarwinExample
#define _Included_com_genedavis_HelloDarwinExample
#ifdef __cplusplus
extern "C" {
#endif
/*
 * Class:      com_genedavis_HelloDarwinExample
 * Method:     hi
 * Signature: ()V
 */
JNIEXPORT void JNICALL Java_com_genedavis_HelloDarwinExample_hi
  (JNIEnv *, jobject);
#ifdef __cplusplus
}
#endif
#endif
```

Looking at the `javah`-generated header, you may notice that the header is designed to work with C++ as well as C. This is convenient for diehard OOP programmers that want to avoid procedural programming all together. C makes tutorials easier to follow than C++, so I avoid C++ in this book.

Notice that the file starts with this line:

```
/* DO NOT EDIT THIS FILE - it is machine generated */
```

You can ignore this line. Yes, the file is automatically generated. However, if you know you won't be rewriting the header or modifying method signatures, there is nothing mystical about the header file. In fact, you can easily copy the relevant C header source to a new header file and use it instead. The new header might look like this:

```
#include <jni.h>
#ifndef _Included_com_genedavis_HelloDarwinExample
#define _Included_com_genedavis_HelloDarwinExample
/*
 * Class:      com_genedavis_HelloDarwinExample
 * Method:     hi
 * Signature: ()V
 */
JNIEXPORT void JNICALL Java_com_genedavis_HelloDarwinExample_hi
  (JNIEnv *, jobject);
#endif
```

Do whatever makes sense for your project.

CAUTION

If you modify the `javah`-generated header, be careful not to destroy your changes by running `javah` to generate a new version of the same file you modified. Move your changes to a new file that won't disappear if you accidentally (or intentionally) run `javah` again.

In case your C is rusty or you are learning C as you read this chapter, I provide a blow-by-blow explanation of the header file. You can start off by thinking of C header files as similar to Java interfaces. (I just made lots of C programmers very angry by making that statement.) As your C improves, you will find header files to be far more interesting than Java's interfaces.

NOTE

C header files are filled with preprocessor directives and not much C. These directives are typically handled before the C program compiles. Preprocessor directives modify the C in your native application, preparing it for compilation. Many C books (and classes) ignore preprocessor directives, but no one writes useful C programs without a large number of directives.

All the lines that look like Java comments are exactly that. They are C comments. Even if the compiler complains a bit, most C compilers support both `//` and `/* */` style comments. C does not have an equivalent to Javadoc comments. Sorry.

This is the first line that influences the program:

```
#include <jni.h>
```

The `#include` (pronounced "pound include") acts like `import` does in Java. Commonly, angle brackets surround names of system library headers and quotation marks surround library headers you created.

This is the next important line:

```
#ifndef _Included_com_genedavis_HelloDarwinExample
```

In Java, you import classes, enums, interfaces, and packages without any concern that duplicate import statements might cause duplicate code to actually appear multiple times in the final running program. Java takes care of preventing duplicate imports from resulting in actual duplicate code loading into the JVM.

C has no such guarantee. If you #include a header twice, the library can end up in memory twice. C programmers use preprocessor directives to check for multiple #includes and eliminate the duplicates.

In pseudo code, the preprocessor check looks like this:

```
Does the variable named after this header file exist?
No?
Define the variable and name it after this file.
Define the methods and do other stuff
Yes?
Return without doing anything.
```

You probably notice it is an if statement and has similarities to a synchronized block in Java. The behavior is very similar, though no multithreading is involved. These statements are of note:

```
#ifndef _Included_com_genedavis_HelloDarwinExample
#define _Included_com_genedavis_HelloDarwinExample
/* header source goes here. */
#endif
```

The most important bit of the header is the function signature. It looks like this:

```
JNIEXPORT void JNICALL
Java_com_genedavis_HelloDarwinExample_hi
(JNIEnv *, jobject);
```

This function represents the Java method hi() in the HelloDarwinExample class. The return type is void. The function name is as follows:

```
Java_com_genedavis_HelloDarwinExample_hi
```

The two arguments to the function are a JNIEnv pointer and a jobject. JNIEXPORT and JNICALL are defined in jni.h, but you can almost always ignore them. (Ignore them, but don't delete them.)

You are already familiar with most of the common return types and arguments to JNI functions, as shown in Table 9.1. The one argument that is probably new to you is the JNIEnv *. JNIEnv is literally the JNI environment. It is an opaque type containing functions relating to the JNI environment. Supposing the JNIEnv * variable is named env, the syntax for calling JNIEnv functions usually looks like this:

```
(*env)->SomeFunction();
```

Table 9.1 Common JNI Method Arguments and Return Types

JNI C Type	Java Equivalent
jclass	java.lang.Class
jobject	java.lang.Object
jmethod	java.lang.reflect.Method
jstring	java.lang.String
jdouble	primitive double
jfloat	primitive float
jlong	primitive long
jint	primitive int
jshort	primitive short
jbyte	primitive byte
jchar	primitive char
jboolean	primitive Boolean

The actual implementation of your native Java method is contained in the darwin.c file. The following source is for the darwin.c file. The darwin.c file implements the function definition found in the javah-generated header.

```
#include <stdio.h>
#include "native_greeting_jni.h"

JNIEXPORT void JNICALL Java_com_genedavis_HelloDarwinExample_hi
   (JNIEnv * a, jobject b)
{
   printf("\n\nHello Darwin!!!\n\n");
   return;
}
```

I have described the use of the JNIEnv *, but not the purpose of the jobject. Whenever a native Java method is implemented in C as a function, the first two arguments represent the caller of the function. JNIEnv is the JNI environment that called the function. The second argument is the Java object or class to which the native method belongs.

In other words, if the `native` method was `static`, a reference to the containing `class` is passed to the native implementation as a `jclass`. If the `native` method was in an instance (an object, not a class), then the second argument to the native implementation is a `jobject`. The `jobject` is a reference to the actual object that contained the `native` Java method.

Compiling the mixed Java-C applications by hand is a good way to get familiar with how all the pieces fit together. It doesn't take long to get old, though. All the JNI examples in the chapter come with Ant projects to take care of the details for you. I describe using Ant to build JNI projects later in this chapter.

CROSS-REF
I describe Ant builds in detail in Chapter 4.

After building the `HelloDarwinExample` application, run it from the command line with the following command:

```
java -Djava.library.path=objc_bin -cp java_bin/ ¬
com.genedavis.HelloDarwinExample
```

The results are shown in Figure 9.2.

Figure 9.2

The output of running the `HelloDarwinExample` class

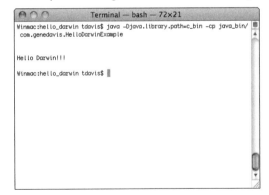

Returning native variables to Java

JNI involves more work than pure Java. Writing JNI is worth your time only if it saves you time or if it adds features to your program not available in Java. Believe it or not, some tasks are impossible from Java, so they require JNI or similar technologies.

One example of an impossible task is single character input from the Terminal. The Terminal (like consoles in other operating systems) enters a line of text to the running program with the user presses Return or Enter. You cannot retrieve characters as they are typed in the Terminal from a pure Java program.

A simple JNI program provides single character reading from the Terminal. The next JNI example is the `SingleCharReader` application. The `SingleCharReader` provides Java with the capability to instantly read keystrokes as the user types them in the Terminal. This is useful for command-line utilities, Terminal User Interfaces, text-based games, and any application that is not GUI-based. (Yes, they still exist.)

Looking at the source, you see that this application is not much more complex than the first example in this chapter. Yet, this application extends the Java API in a useful way. JNI has that kind of power. Sometimes, just a few lines of JNI can save you tons of work, or even save a project from failure.

The `SingleCharReader` project consists of one Java class, one C header file, and one C source file, as shown in Figure 9.3. As you have already guessed, the Java class is named `SingleCharReader`. The `javah`-generated C header is called `native_getch_jni.h`. The C source file is called `char_reader.c`.

Figure 9.3

The organization of the `SingleCharReader` project

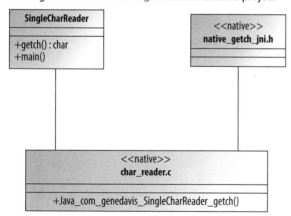

The following source is for the `SingleCharReader` class:

```
package com.genedavis;
public class SingleCharReader {
    // executed during class load
    static
```

```
{
    // used to load from a system library path
    System.loadLibrary("CharGrabber");
}

public static void main(String[] args)
{
        SingleCharReader scr = new SingleCharReader();

        System.out.println(
            "Enter characters (type 'q' to quit)\n");


        char myChar = ' ';

        while (myChar != 'q')
        {
            // use native call
            myChar = scr.getch();

            System.out.println(
                "-->" +
                myChar +
                "<--\n");
        }
}

    // native method call
    private native char getch();
}
```

The `SingleCharReader` class starts with a static block. The static block loads the dynamic library named `CharGrabber` using the `System.loadLibrary()` method. As I mentioned earlier, static blocks execute before the main method in a program, so the library is already loaded before the application's `main()` method executes.

N O T E
Because the library `CharGrabber` is a dynamic library, the actual filename is `libCharGrabber.jnilib`.

C A U T I O N
Remember to include the native libraries when running your Java applications. For instance, you can add an argument to the `java` command, such as `-Djava.library.path=<path to lib>`.

The `SingleCharReader` contains one native method. The native method is `getch()`. The method signature is as follows:

```
private native char getch();
```

Notice the `getch()` method has a return value of `char`. The native code returns a `char` to the Java code. This is the `char` representing the user's most recent keystroke.

The `SingleCharReader` also contains the application's `main()` method. The `main()` method instantiates an instance of the `SingleCharReader`. Then loops read characters from the user's keystrokes until the user types q.

NOTE

The `SingleCharReader`'s native method could easily be a static method, instead of an instance method. Making an instance method is more a matter of style, and it's up to the individual programmer.

I generate the C header with the `javah` tool. As I mention earlier, there is nothing magical about this header or any header generated by `javah`. In fact, after you are used to the headers generated by `javah`, you may choose to save yourself a step and write your own JNI headers by hand.

The following source is for the `native_getch_jni.h` header file generated with `javah` from the `SingleCharReader` class.

```
/* DO NOT EDIT THIS FILE - it is machine generated */
#include <jni.h>
/* Header for class com_genedavis_SingleCharReader */
#ifndef _Included_com_genedavis_SingleCharReader
#define _Included_com_genedavis_SingleCharReader
#ifdef __cplusplus
extern "C" {
#endif
/*
 * Class:      com_genedavis_SingleCharReader
 * Method:     getch
 * Signature: ()C
 */
JNIEXPORT jchar JNICALL
Java_com_genedavis_SingleCharReader_getch
(JNIEnv *, jobject);
#ifdef __cplusplus
}
#endif
#endif
```

The header file is very similar to the preceding header file. It has a check for C++ and a check for prior #includes. The header #includes jni.h, and the header defines the project's sole native method implementation, getch().

The function name is as follows:

```
Java_com_genedavis_SingleCharReader_getch
```

The name is certainly long. Glancing at it, you can see the parts easily enough. "Java" means this is a Java native method implementation. "com_genedavis" means the implemented method is from the com.genedavis package. "SingleCharReader" is the name of the class containing native method definition. Finally, "getch" is the name of the actual native method implemented.

TIP
You do not have to use long function names for native implementations of JNI methods. With a little extra code, you can associate custom names with your native Java methods. I explain registering native methods later in this chapter when I discuss Java callbacks to C applications.

The following source is for the char_reader.c file. The char_reader.c file implements the getch() method from the SingleCharReader class.

```c
#include <stdio.h>
#include <termios.h>
#include <unistd.h>
#include "native_getch_jni.h"
JNIEXPORT jchar JNICALL
Java_com_genedavis_SingleCharReader_getch
(JNIEnv * my_jenv, jobject my_jobj)
{
    jchar ch;
    struct termios old_term, new_term;
    //storing the old settings
    tcgetattr ( STDIN_FILENO, &old_term );
    // making a copy of the old settings
    // to modify
    new_term = old_term;
    // modifying the copy of the terminal settings
    // so there is no echoing and no buffering
    // just flipping bits here
    new_term.c_lflag &= ~( ICANON | ECHO );
    // setting the modified terminal settings
    // to be active
    tcsetattr ( STDIN_FILENO, TCSANOW, &new_term );
    // getting the character
    ch = getchar();
    // resetting the terminal settings to the old settings
    tcsetattr ( STDIN_FILENO, TCSANOW, &old_term );

    return ch;
}
```

The `Java_com_genedavis_SingleCharReader_getch()` function starts by defining a `jchar` and two `termios` structs. The `jchar` type is the JNI version of a Java `char` primitive. Structs of type `termios` represent the behavioral configuration of the terminal I/O. (That's terminal with a lowercase "t".) Think of `termios` as the developers' terminal I/O preferences.

The `tcgetattr()` function populates a provided `termios` struct with the current internal `termios` structure. I use the `tcgetattr()` function to save the current state of the terminal settings before modifying them. Changing the terminal I/O behavior in a program and not resetting it after the program is finished is generally frowned upon.

I set the `new_term` struct to the same values as the `old_term`, making a clone of the current terminal I/O settings. I modify the new `termios` structure so that echo is no longer set and buffering is turned off; then I make the `new_term` settings active.

Now, I can call `getchar()` and receive characters as the user types them. After I have a character from the user, I reset the terminal I/O settings with the original settings I stored in `old_term`.

CROSS-REF

I flesh out the **SingleCharReader** application in Chapter 11 for use in an example Terminal User Interface application.

If you are working from the project from the book's Web site, use the following command to run the `SingleCharReader` application:

```
java -Djava.library.path=c_bin -cp java_bin/ ¬
com.genedavis.SingleCharReader
```

Execute the `java` command from the `char_reader` directory. The output looks similar to Figure 9.4.

Figure 9.4

The Terminal output when running the `SingleCharReader` application

```
Winmac:char_reader tdavis$ java -Djava.library.path=c_bin -cp java_bin/ com.genedavis.SingleCharReader
Enter characters (type 'q' to quit)

-->c<--

-->h<--

-->a<--

-->r<--

--> <--

-->q<--

Winmac:char_reader tdavis$
```

Invoking Java from native code

Native code takes the form of fully modern Cocoa applications, pure C-based command-line tools, or legacy code, just to name a few. Sometimes you want to run Java code from inside native applications. Sometimes, you want to incrementally port C applications to Java. Creating Java Virtual Machines (JVMs) from inside native applications involves JNI's Invocation API.

The first two examples in this chapter deal with calling native code from an existing JVM. Both of those examples assume that you are running a Java application. If you want to execute Java from a native application, those examples don't solve your problem. When you write a program in C and execute it, no pre-existing JVM is available to execute Java byte code. In order to call Java from native code, you need a JVM.

But where do new JVMs come from? (Admit it. You've always wanted to ask.)

New JVMs come from calls to the `JNI_CreateJavaVM()` function. When JVMs get old, you get rid of them with calls to `DestroyJavaVM()`. There are more details, of course, but knowing those two functions is a good start.

CAUTION

You can create only one JVM for any process. If your program or another programmer's plug-in might need to reuse a JVM created with the Invocation API, do not destroy it with the `(*jvm)->DestroyJavaVM(jvm);` call.

TIP

The Jar Bundler discussed earlier in this book uses a small native application to launch the JVM and execute the bundled JAR file. Using the Invocation API, you can write your own custom Java application launcher. A bonus of creating your own launcher is that you can choose a custom entry method or methods other than the traditional `main()` method. Many languages besides Java run on JVMs. (For a short list, see `http://en.wikipedia.org/wiki/List_of_JVM_languages`.) If you run a language other than Java on a JVM, creating a custom application launcher may make sense for your language.

Another use of custom Java application launchers is simple obfuscation of code. Starting your application from a method other than `main()` gives hackers one more hurdle to overcome when cracking your software security.

Follow these steps for calling Java byte code from inside native applications:

1. **Create** JavaVMInitArgs.

Minimally, `JavaVMInitArgs` contain the version of JNI (1.6) and the `JavaVMOption` array.

2. **Create a** JavaVMOption **array.**

These options are commonly passed to the `java` command in the Terminal, so you probably already know them. At the very least, you should pass in the location of your Java classes using the `-Djava.class.path=some/path/` argument. Add these options to the `JavaVMInitArgs` in preparation for creating the JVM.

3. Call `JNI_CreateJavaVM()`.

Calling `JNI_CreateJavaVM()` creates a JVM. Your new JVM just sits there doing nothing useful until you actually call a method on it. When you execute the `java` command from the Terminal, it creates a JVM with this function call and then finds the specified class with a `static main()` method to call. However, you are under no obligation to call a `main()` method.

4. Find the class containing the method you want to call.

Use the environment generated with the creation of the Java VM to call `FindClass()`. When calling `FindClass()`, the naming convention for Java classes is to name the classes as you do in Java, except that the periods are replaced with forward slashes.

5. Get the ID of the method you want to call.

Methods in Java are often overloaded. That means multiple methods exist in the same class with the same name, but different method signatures. When getting methods, you must specify both the method name and the method signature.

6. Call your Java method from your native program.

Call your static method from one of the many `CallStaticMethod()` functions. Pass the `JNIEnv*`, the `jclass` reference, and the `jmethodID`, followed by the actual arguments to the Java method.

7. Destroy your JVM.

Destroy your JVM only if you know for sure it is not needed again. Programs can create JVMs only once. If your application or another developer's plug-in requires the JVM after you destroy it, that's too bad. It's not coming back.

Creating a JVM from native code requires lots of steps. Here is an example. The project is called `first_invocation`, and of course it is found on the book's Web site.

The `first_invocation` project consists of a C application and a single Java class with one short static method, as shown in Figure 9.5. The C application calls the Java method with two `ints` as parameters and receives an `int` as a return value.

Figure 9.5

The `first_invocation` project

NOTE

When examining the `first_invocation` project, notice that the project has no header files. When creating a JVM and calling a Java method, you likely won't need to run `javah`.

The following code is the source for `simple_jvm_invoker.c`. This application is a native application that starts a JVM, so the `main()` function is found in this C source file:

```c
#include <jni.h>
#include <stdio.h>
int main(void)
{
    // declaring the JVM and environment
    // variables
    JavaVM *jvm;
    JNIEnv *env;
    // setting up arguments to JVM
    JavaVMInitArgs jvm_args;
    // Always declare the newest version of
    // JNI you want to use. JNI_VERSION_1_6
    // corresponds to Java 6.
    jvm_args.version = JNI_VERSION_1_6;
    // JavaVMOptions are the options
    // you are already familiar with
    // from the command line
    JavaVMOption options[1];
    // in this project the Java classes are
    // all contained in the java_bin directory
    options[0].optionString = "-Djava.class.path=java_bin/";
    // The option array length MUST be declared.
    // remember this is C, and array lengths
    // are not known unless your program explicitly
    // stores them.
    jvm_args.nOptions = 1;
    // setting the options
    jvm_args.options = options;
    jvm_args.ignoreUnrecognized = JNI_FALSE;

    // creating the JVM
    JNI_CreateJavaVM(
                    &jvm,
                    (void**)&env,
                    &jvm_args);
    // obtaining the Java class com.genedavis.FirstInvocation
    jclass fiClass = (*env)->FindClass(
                                    env,
                                    "com/genedavis/
    FirstInvocation");
```

```
// obtaining a reference to
// com.genedavis.FirstInvocation.advancedMath()
jmethodID mid = (*env)->GetStaticMethodID(
                                          env,
                                          fiClass,
                                          "advancedMath",
                                          "(II)I");

// calling com.genedavis.FirstInvocation.advancedMath()
int result = (*env)->CallStaticIntMethod(
                                         env,
                                         fiClass,
                                         mid,
                                         1,
                                         1);

// printing the result returned from Java call
printf("\n1+1=%d\n\n", result);

// shutting down the JVM
(*jvm)->DestroyJavaVM(jvm);
}
```

Creating JVMs

You create the JVM with a call to `JNI_CreateJavaVM()`. The source looks like this:

```
JNI_CreateJavaVM(
                &jvm,
                (void**)&env,
                &jvm_args);
```

The three arguments are `jvm`, `env`, and `jvm_args`. They are references to a `JavaVM`, a `JNIEnv`, and a `JavaVMInitArgs`. The `jvm` and `env` variables are populated by the call to `JNI_CreateJavaVM()`. The `jvm_args` variable helps initialize the `JavaVM`.

After you have a JavaVM and a JNIEnv, you can find any class loaded by the JVM. Use the FindClass() function. As I mentioned earlier, the first argument is the JNIEnv*. The second argument is the fully qualified Java class name as a string. Use forward slashes instead of periods in the fully qualified class name.

Calling Java methods from C

JNI identifies Java methods by their containing class, their method name, and their type signature. Overloaded methods share class name and method name. The only distinguishing trait for overloaded methods is their type signature.

Type signatures combine the return type and the arguments to a method in one symbolic string. The type signature string contains a whole bunch of symbols that are a bit tricky to decipher. For instance, this method

```
void myMethod() { ... }
```

has a type signature of

```
()V
```

The parentheses surround the arguments, and the V is the void return type.

In this example

```
public int myMethod(
    java.lang.Object,
    byte bt,
    char c,
    boolean bn) { ... }
```

has a type signature of

```
(Ljava/lang/Object;BCZ)I
```

You may be worried about how to come up with type signatures on your own. Beginners usually use the javap tool with the -s and -private arguments. This tool displays a list of all type signatures in the requested class.

CAUTION
Dealing with voids in type signatures is tricky. If a return type is void, use a capital V. If the argument list is empty, use empty parentheses, not (V). The type signature ()V is valid. The type signature (V)V is never valid.

TIP
Run javap -s <fully qualified class name> to find the type signatures of the class's methods.

Coming up with type signatures on your own is not hard. Keep these points in mind:

- Type signatures end with a return type (like UML), rather than begin with a return type as standard Java does.
- Type signatures contain no spaces or commas.
- Type signatures with no parameters contain a set of empty parentheses.
- Type signatures with a void return type end in V.
- Use Table 9.2 to look up symbols you don't know.

Table 9.2 Method Type Signature Symbols

JNI Method Call Symbol	Java type
Ljava/lang/Object;	java.lang.Object
Ljava/lang/String;	java.lang.String
Lcom/genedavis/Example;	com.genedavis.Example
D	double
J	long
I	int
S	short
B	byte
C	char
Z	Boolean

I call the Java method in the `simple_jvm_invoker.c` file with the following C code:

```
int result = (*env)->CallStaticIntMethod(
                                          env,
                                          fiClass,
                                          mid,
                                          1,
                                          1);
```

The function name is `CallStaticIntMethod()`. The word "Static" in the function name indicates that the Java method called is a `static` method. The word "Int" indicates the return type of the function. Table 10.3 shows the JNI types used as return types to all the CallStatic*Method() functions provided by JNI.

The `CallStaticIntMethod()` function is one of many `Call*Method()` functions. Call method functions come in four varieties. One variety eliminates the word "Static" from the function name. Those functions are for calling instance methods. Two other versions of call method functions end in V and A. These accept Java method arguments differently than the method I show. Table 9.3 contains a list of all the common `CallStatic*Method()` functions conforming to this section's example code.

NOTE
Functions are associated with procedural programming, and methods are associated with OOP programming. Therefore, C has functions and Java has methods—never the other way around.

Table 9.3 JNI Call Static Methods

Call Method	JNI Return Type
CallStaticVoidMethod (JNIEnv *env, jclass clazz, jmethodID methodID, ...)	void
CallStaticObjectMethod (JNIEnv *env, jclass clazz, jmethodID methodID, ...)	jobject
CallStaticDoubleMethod (JNIEnv *env, jclass clazz, jmethodID methodID, ...)	jdouble
CallStaticFloatMethod (JNIEnv *env, jclass clazz, jmethodID methodID, ...)	jfloat
CallStaticLongMethod (JNIEnv *env, jclass clazz, jmethodID methodID, ...)	jlong
CallStaticIntMethod (JNIEnv *env, jclass clazz, jmethodID methodID, ...)	jint
CallStaticShortMethod (JNIEnv *env, jclass clazz, jmethodID methodID, ...)	jshort
CallStaticCharMethod (JNIEnv *env, jclass clazz, jmethodID methodID, ...)	jchar
CallStaticByteMethod (JNIEnv *env, jclass clazz, jmethodID methodID, ...)	jbyte
CallStaticBooleanMethod (JNIEnv *env, jclass clazz, jmethodID methodID, ...)	jboolean

Implementing Java calls from native code

As mentioned earlier, implementing Java methods for calls from native code is the same as writing normal Java. From the Java side, it is no different than writing normal Java code.

The following is the source code for the FirstInvocation class. The FirstInvocation class contains no static blocks and no native methods. You use static blocks to load native implementations of native methods. There are no Java callbacks to the native code, so there are no native methods and no static blocks of code.

```
package com.genedavis;
public class FirstInvocation {

    public static int advancedMath(int a, int b)
    {
        return a+b;
    }
}
```

TIP

In this chapter's invocation examples, I call static Java methods from native C code. I recommend sticking with static methods when calling Java code from native applications because it is simpler. If you have a compelling reason for calling an instance method instead, you can instantiate jobjects from jclasses and call the methods on the jobjects instead.

If you use a Java method for calls from C, don't use that same method for calls from Java code. Eventually, you will find bugs in your JNI. You do not want to complicate debugging by sharing Java methods with C and Java.

TIP

When creating Java methods for native code to call, I usually declare the methods as `private` to discourage calls to the same method from inside my Java code. This may make it harder for the JIT compiler to optimize the JNI, but it's worth it in adding clarity to the code.

TIP

Always javadoc comment your Java methods that accept calls from native code. Make it as obvious as possible that the Java method is accepting native calls.

When you run the `simple_jvm_invoker` from the Terminal, the output is similar to that shown in Figure 9.6.

Figure 9.6

The `simple_jvm_invocation` output

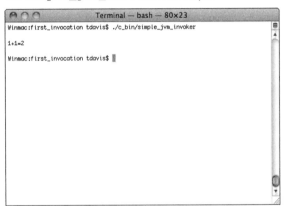

Returning Java calls to native code

If you build a custom Java launcher, then you might get away with only C calls to Java. However, if you want to wrap an Interface Builder project, or as in Chapter 13, a Screen Saver Framework project, then you need to know how to make Java call callbacks to native code.

The next example is in the `callback_from_java` project on the book's Web site. The `callback_from_java` project is set up as a Model View Controller (MVC), as shown in Figure 9.7. The example project actually contains no view code, but that is irrelevant for the example. Use a file such as app_starter.c to wrap your favorite C-based view. Your view can be anything from a Cocoa Interface Builder project, a Screen Saver Framework project (demonstrated in Chapter 13), or a cross-platform Qt project.

Figure 9.7

The `callback_from_java` source diagram

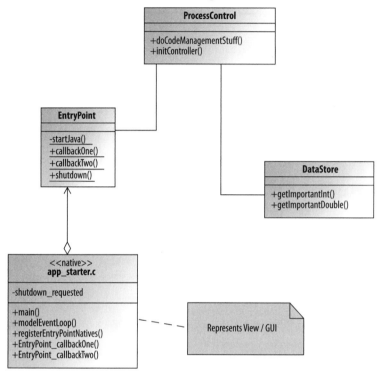

The key to the `callback_from_java` project is that the view is written in a C-based language and completely separate from the model and controller. Only events and view updates exchange between the controller and the view. All communication takes place through a simple `EntryPoint` class that acts as a wrapper around the view.

In the `callback_from_java` project, the application starts in the view, but very quickly passes control to `ProcessControl` that acts as the MVC model's controller. Starting the application from the view allows the view to act as a wrapper to a host of C++, C, and Objective-C centric frameworks. Don't bother figuring out a way to launch your project differently from the original C-based technology; just wrap the technology and pass control quickly to the application's Java controller.

NOTE

By wrapping a C-based GUI and starting the GUI from C, you are turning your view into an extended Java application launcher.

The following source is for the `app_starter.c` file. In the `callback_from_java` project, this file acts as the Java launcher and wraps the view in the `EntryPoint` class:

```c
#include <jni.h>
#include <stdio.h>
#include <unistd.h>
// shutdown flag
jboolean shutdown_requested = JNI_FALSE;

// loops waiting for the controller to
// finish and request shutdown
void modelEventLoop(void)
{
    int secs = 0;
    // check for exit request
    while (! shutdown_requested)
    {
    // sleeps for 1/10 second
        usleep(100000);
        printf("woke...\n", (secs/10));
    }
}
// Java "native" callbacks from JNI
// header file

//Class:     com.genedavis.EntryPoint
//Method:    void callbackOne(int)
void
JNICALL EntryPoint_callbackOne
(JNIEnv * env, jclass jc, jint data)
{
    printf("important int from data store: %d\n", data);
}
//Class:     com.genedavis.EntryPoint
//Method:    void callbackTwo (float)
void JNICALL EntryPoint_callbackTwo
(JNIEnv * env, jclass jc, jdouble data)
{
    printf("important double from data store: %f\n", data);
}
//Class:     com.genedavis.EntryPoint
//Method:    void shutdown (int)
void JNICALL EntryPoint_shutdown
(JNIEnv * env, jclass jc, jint data)
{
    // ignoring the data, but in a real
    // application, the data variable
    // represents an exit value
```

```c
        shutdown_requested = JNI_TRUE;
}
void registerEntryPointNatives
(JNIEnv * env, jclass jc)
{
    // fill with Java's native names,
    // followed by javp style signature
    // and the C version of the method
    // names
    JNINativeMethod natives[] =
    {
        {
            "callbackOne",
          " (I)V",
            &EntryPoint_callbackOne
        },

        {
            "callbackTwo",
          " (D)V",
            &EntryPoint_callbackTwo
        },

        {
            "shutdown",
          " (I)V",
            &EntryPoint_shutdown
        }
    };

    // adding the methods from the C
    // side instead of the Java side
    (*env)->RegisterNatives(env, jc, natives, 3);
}

int main(void)
{
    // declaring the JVM and environment
    // variables
    JavaVM *jvm;
    JNIEnv *env;

    // setting up arguments to JVM
    JavaVMInitArgs jvm_args;

    // Always declare the newest version of
    // JNI you want to use. JNI_VERSION_1_6
    // corresponds to Java 6.
    jvm_args.version = JNI_VERSION_1_6;
```

```
    // JavaVMOptions are the options
    // you are already familiar with
    // from the command line
    JavaVMOption options[1];

    // in this project the Java classes are
    // all contained in the java_bin directory
    options[0].optionString = "-Djava.class.path=java_bin/";

    // The option array length MUST be declared.
    // remember this is C, and array lengths
    // are not known unless your program explicitly
    // stores them.
    jvm_args.nOptions = 1;

    // setting the options
    jvm_args.options = options;
    jvm_args.ignoreUnrecognized = JNI_FALSE;

    // creating the JVM
    JNI_CreateJavaVM(&jvm, (void**)&env, &jvm_args);

    // obtaining the Java class com.genedavis.EntryPoint
    jclass entryPointClass =
        (*env)->FindClass(env, "com/genedavis/EntryPoint");

    // registering the statically linked native methods
    // for com.genedavis.EntryPoint
    registerEntryPointNatives(env, entryPointClass);

    // obtaining a reference to
    // com.genedavis.EntryPoint.startJava()
    jmethodID mid =
        (*env)->GetStaticMethodID(env, entryPointClass,
    "startJava", " ()V");

    // starting controller with a call to
    // com.genedavis.EntryPoint.startJava()
    (*env)->CallStaticVoidMethod(env, entryPointClass, mid);

    // announcing success
    printf("\n\nStarted Conroller\n");

    // Model's event loop
    modelEventLoop();
    // shutting down the JVM
    (*jvm)->DestroyJavaVM(jvm);

}
```

In the last section, I described most of the code found in the `app_starter.c` file. The important addition is the `registerEntryPointNatives()` function. In this function, I do away with both dynamic loading and long function names for native implementations of `native` Java methods. The `registerEntryPointNatives()` function sets up the Java callbacks to C.

I use these steps for creating Java callbacks to C:

1. **Create function stubs for the native C implementations of your Java callbacks.**

Note that you can create short function names. The naming convention is up to you.

2. **Create and populate a** JNINativeMethod **array.**

The `JNINativeMethod` array is a list of methods you want to register. Each `JNINativeMethod` contains the name of the Java `native` method you are implementing, the method type signature, and a function pointer to the local C implementation of the method.

3. **Call** RegisterNatives().

`RegisterNatives()` takes arguments of `JNIEnv*`, `jclass`, `JNINativeMethod[]`, and your array length.

N O T E
The valid values of a `jboolean` are `JNI_FALSE` and `JNI_TRUE`.

N O T E
This example statically links the native methods called by Java, so no dynamic libraries are called. No static blocks of code are needed in the Java source, because of the static linking of the native method implementations.

The `RegisterNatives()` function allows you to statically link your C implementations of Java callbacks. That is why the `EntryPoint` class has no static block, as the first two examples in this chapter contained. No rule says you have to statically link this type of project; I merely want to demonstrate that you can statically link libraries in JNI projects.

The following source is for the `EntryPoint` class:

```
package com.genedavis;
/**
 * This class is a link between the Java
 * based controller and C (or Objective-C)
 * startup code. The C-based code could
 * also be a full-fledged View built in
 * Interface Builder or another C-accessible
```

```java
 * tool.
 *
 * @author T. Gene Davis
 */
public class EntryPoint
{
    /**
     * Simply starts the Java-based
     * controller of this application.
     *
     * In more advanced applications, this
     * could represent events from a GUI
     * or from a C library.
     */
    @SuppressWarnings("unused")
    private static void startJava()
    {
        ProcessControl pc = new ProcessControl();
        pc.doCodeManagementStuff();
    }

    /**
     * View update. This call is non-blocking.
     * However, in cases that the thread
     * potentially blocks, make Model updates on
     * a separate thread!
     *
     * @param i just an int
     */
    public static native void callbackOne(int i);


    /**
     * View update. This call is non-blocking.
     * However, in cases that the thread
     * potentially blocks, make Model updates on
     * a separate thread!
     *
     * @param d just an double
     */
    public static native void callbackTwo(double d);

    /**
     * Exiting the entire application.
     */
    public static native void shutdown(int exitValue);
}
```

The `EntryPoint` class acts as a wrapper for the C code. The C code in this example equates to a view in similar projects. This starts the ProcessControl in the startJava() method. From that point on, the control of the application passes to the ProcessControl, and the C code returns to its primary function as GUI.

The `startJava()` method is called from the C code. It is the only method called from the C code in this project. In a real project, you might have many events from the GUI calling several Java methods, or you might describe all your events in such a way that they are funneled through one Java method to the controller for handling.

The `callbackOne()` method, `callbackTwo()` method, and `shutdown()` method are all `native` methods. Each method has a C implementation set up by the `RegisterNatives()` function call in the `app_starter.c` file.

The following source is for the `ProcessControl` class. The `ProcessControl` class represents the controller in a complex Java project:

```java
package com.genedavis;
/**
 * This class represents the controller in
 * a traditional Model View Control design.
 * Obviously, in a real application, the
 * elements of the Model View Control are
 * more complex, but this simplified model
 * serves to illustrate the concept.
 *
 * @author T. Gene Davis
 */
public class ProcessControl
{
    /**
     * If the C-based code is a GUI, give
     * it back its thread!
     */
    public void doCodeManagementStuff()
    {
        // creating a separate thread for
        // the controller to use
        Thread controlThread =
            new Thread(new Runnable(){
                public void run()
                {
                    initController();
                }
            });

        // starting the new controller thread
        // the native code's thread is then
```

```
        // returned.
        controlThread.start();
    }

    /**
     * If there is a control loop, it
     * goes here.
     */
    public void initController()
    {
        // initializing data store
        DataStore ds = new DataStore();

        // represents data retrieval
        int intData = ds.getImportantInt();
        double doubleData = ds.getImportantDouble();

        // Updating View ... Could be a GUI
        // in some cases. If there is a potential
        // for blocking, make GUI updates on a
        // separate thread.

        EntryPoint.callbackOne(intData);
        EntryPoint.callbackTwo(doubleData);

        // All done. Let C code know it's
        // time to shut down the JVM.
        EntryPoint.shutdown(0);
    }
}
```

When starting a Java application from a C GUI, the GUI almost always contains some sort of application event thread. Never hold onto event threads. Whether from Cocoa applications or Swing projects, quickly create a new thread to handle your code and return the event thread to its proper owner. Failing to do so often results in blocking code, and at the very least it makes the application appear unresponsive to the user.

The first call to `ProcessControl` is to the `doCodeManagementStuff()` method. I create and start a new Java `Thread` immediately. Then I return the native thread to its owner. Meanwhile, my new Java Thread calls `initController()`. In a real application, the `initController()` method is where controller setup begins and any controller application loops start.

The following source is for the `DataStore` class. This class represents the model in this MVC-based project. It contains two methods that return important numbers. Had this been a real application, it would have hooked into a database, flat file, directory service, or other common data store.

```java
package com.genedavis;
/**
 * This class represents the data store in
 * a traditional Model View Control design.
 *
 * @author T. Gene Davis
 */
public class DataStore
{

    /**
     * Returns int 42.
     */
    public int getImportantInt()
    {
        return 42;
    }

    /**
     * Returns double PI.
     */
    public double getImportantDouble()
    {
        return Math.PI;
    }
}
```

The output from the callback_from_java project is shown in Figure 9.8.

Figure 9.8

The `callback_from_java` output

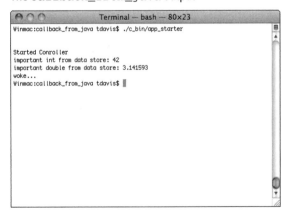

Building JNI Applications from Ant

Building JNI projects baffles many popular IDEs, so I use Ant build projects to handle the complex details. Ant projects integrate into all common IDEs. By using an Ant build, the developers on your project are not constrained to use a particular IDE, thus improving their productivity.

The following source is the `build.xml` file for building the `HelloDarwinExample` from the beginning of this chapter:

```xml
<?xml version="1.0" encoding="UTF-8"?>
<project name="Hello World" default="run" basedir=".">
    <property name="java.source" value="java_src" />
    <property name="c.source" value="c_src" />
    <property name="java.bin" value="java_bin" />
    <property name="native.bin" value="c_bin" />

    <target
        name="explain"
        description="Explains the objective of the build">

        <echo>Building the full Java and Native source.</echo>

    </target>

    <target
        name="clean"
        description="Removes previous build">

        <echo>Cleaning Java and Native bin folders...</echo>

        <delete dir="${java.bin}" />
        <delete dir="${native.bin}" />

    </target>

    <target
        name="java-build"
    depends="clean"
        description="Builds the Java source">

        <echo>Building Java...</echo>

        <mkdir dir="${java.bin}"/>
        <javac srcdir="${java.source}" destdir="${java.bin}" />
    </target>

    <target
        name="native-header-build"
```

```
            description="Builds the native headers file">

            <echo>Creating native header file...</echo>

            <mkdir dir="${native.bin}"/>
            <javah
                outputfile="${c.source}/native_greeting_jni.h"
                classpath="${java.bin}">

                <class name="com.genedavis.HelloDarwinExample" />

            </javah>
        </target>

        <target
            name="native-build"
            description="Builds the native lib*.jnilib">

            <echo>Creating native lib*.jnilib</echo>

            <!--
            gcc
                -bundle
                ./c_src/darwin.c
                -o ./c_bin/libNativeGreeter.jnilib
                -I/System/Library/Frameworks/JavaVM.framework/Headers
                -I ./objc_src/
                -framework JavaVM
            -->
            <exec executable="gcc">

                <arg value="-bundle"/>
                <arg value="./${c.source}/darwin.c"/>
                <arg line="-o ./${native.bin}/libNativeGreeter.jnilib"/>
                <arg value=
"-I/System/Library/Frameworks/JavaVM.framework/Headers"/>
                <arg line="-framework JavaVM"/>

            </exec>
        </target>

        <target
            name="build"
            depends=
            "explain, java-build, native-header-build, native-build"
            description="builds full Java and Native byte code.">

            <echo>Build complete</echo>
```

```
        </target>

        <target
            name="run"
            depends="build"
            description="cleans, builds, and then runs app">
            <!--
            java
                -Djava.library.path=objc_bin
                -cp java_bin/
                com.genedavis.HelloDarwinExample
            -->
            <java
                classpath="${java.bin}/"
                    classname="com.genedavis.HelloDarwinExample"
                    fork="true">
                    <jvmarg value="-Djava.library.path=${native.bin}" />
            </java>
        </target>
    </project>
```

This Ant `build.xml` file contains examples of all the `targets` necessary to build any of the JNI projects described in this chapter. The native-header-build target handles the `javah` commands. The native-build target handles the `gcc` commands. The java-build target handles the `javac` commands.

In a JNI project, I usually handle running the application outside the actual Ant project. Don't feel constrained to do this. With a little messaging, you can run your compiled project from within your IDE or Ant project, if you wish.

CROSS-REF
In Chapter 4, I give details of Ant project creation and use.

Integrating with Objective-C

Apple encourages Objective-C as a primary language for OS X development. Many of the frameworks provided by OS X are written for Objective-C programs. These frameworks have no Java equivalent.

After reading this chapter and picking up some basic Objective-C, wrapping Objective-C frameworks in Java using JNI should not be a problem. None of the Objective-C frameworks that OS X offers are a barrier to Java development.

When wrapping Objective-C (and C-based libraries), don't worry about wrapping every feature. Wrap only the objects and functions that you actually plan to use. Otherwise, you'll get bogged down in endless details that don't pertain to your project.

I recommend avoiding direct calls to Objective-C classes from Java. Instead use a C-based buffer file (or files), as shown in Figure 9.9. Placing the JNI code in a C file keeps the code simple to understand and promotes easy maintenance of your JNI.

Figure 9.9

Objective-C / Java integration

Learning Thread Safety

The first rule of thread safety in JNI is not to hang onto threads. This is especially the case with AWT and Cocoa application threads. Pass your data through JNI, and then spawn a new thread to process the data. Failing to do so may result in a deadlocked application.

A thorough quality assurance cycle to your development process is likely to catch any threading issues you didn't think of. However, consider the rules in this section while writing your JNI code. Most have to do with the life of JNI references and IDs.

Reusing JavaVMs references

JavaVM references created with JNI go bad only if you destroy the JVM. Destroy a JVM if only the application definitely doesn't need to use it again. OS X processes can create a JVM only once. (This limitation prevents potentially horrible memory leaks.)

Be aware that if you are working with an application that uses plug-ins, another developer may provide a plug-in that uses Java, too. The other module may have already created a JVM before your code loads. It also is possible that the other developer's module may need the JVM after you are completely done with the JVM.

The proper way to create a JVM in Java is to first check for the existence of a JVM. Then, if a previously created JVM doesn't exist, create your own. Here is a code snippet that accomplishes just that:

```
JavaVM *jvm;
// checking for existing JVM
// This is a must! Multiple JVMs cannot be created
// in one process
jsize jvmCount = 0;
```

```
int foundJVM = JNI_GetCreatedJavaVMs(&jvm, 1, &jvmCount);
if (foundJVM == 0 && jvmCount > 0)
{
    // succeeded in getting an existing JVM
    // attaching this thread
    (*jvm)->AttachCurrentThread(jvm, (void**) &env, NULL);
}
else
{
    // no JVM found, ... creating the JVM
    // this thread is automatically attached
    JNI_CreateJavaVM(&jvm, (void**)&env, &jvm_args);
}
```

Threading with JNIEnv

JNIEnv references are thread-specific. Never store or reuse a JNIEnv. Some attributes of JNIEnv are thread-specific, so always use the provided JNIEnv.

In some cases, you may need a new JNIEnv, because none was provided or it was not passed on to your implemented method. Don't despair. You can always get the current JNIEnv from the JNI JavaVM. The following code snippet grabs the current JNIEnv from the JavaVM:

```
JNIEnv *env = NULL;
jint env_error = JNI_OK;

// Use the JVM reference to get an up-to-date
// JNIEnv. JNIEnv variables need constant
// updates
env_error = (*jvm)->GetEnv(
                            jvm,
                            (void **)&env,
                            JNI_VERSION_1_6);
```

Globalizing jclasses and jobjects

Both jclass and jobject are local references. These references cannot be reused in other threads. However, both jclass and jobject local references may be changed into global references. Global references work across threads just fine.

Two types of global references exist: strong and weak. Strong global references refer to classes and objects that are not unloaded by the JVM until destroyed with a call to JNI's DeleteGlobalRef() function. Weak global references may be loaded or unloaded by the JVM, but the reference is still valid throughout the process. Weak global references are cleaned up with a call to DeleteWeakGlobalRef().

The following code snippet is an example of creating a weak global reference from a local jclass reference:

```
jclass localJavaWrapperClass =
    (*env)->FindClass(env, "com/genedavis/OSXScreenSaverWrapper");
// make reference global (multi-thread accessible)
jclass javaWrapperClass =
    (*env)->NewWeakGlobalRef(env, localJavaWrapperClass);
// don't need local reference anymore
(*env)->DeleteLocalRef(env, localJavaWrapperClass);
```

Follow these steps to create a global `jclass` or `jobject`:

1. Obtain a local reference.

2. Make a global reference from the local reference.

3. Delete the local reference.

Saving jmethodIDs

Java methods in JNI are referred to by ID, not reference. The code for obtaining method IDs is discussed earlier in this chapter. It usually looks something like this:

```
jmethodID mid =
    (*env)->GetStaticMethodID(env, someClassRef, "myMethod", " ()V");
```

JNI method IDs do not change or expire. Also, JNI calls to obtain method IDs are relatively expensive. Always save your method IDs to reuse in other threads.

Converting Strings

JNI uses `jstrings`. Cocoa uses `NSStrings`. Carbon uses `CFStrings`. Sometimes it seems that every C-based framework and language has different conventions for handling strings. The problem for you as a programmer is that you need to transfer string variables between these different conventions.

On the bright side, Java and OS X character conventions both use UTF-16. If you run into conversion examples using UTF-8 standards, be aware that the examples are outdated.

The best source for string conversion info is Technical Note TN2147 located on Apple's developer site. The current address is:

```
http://developer.apple.com/mac/library/technotes/tn2005/tn2147.html#TNTAG6
```

Here is an example of converting a JNI jstring to an NSString, based off Technical Note TN2147.

Follow these steps for this example:

1. **Obtain the Java** String **as a** jchar*.

   Accomplish this with a call to the GetStringChars() function contained in the JNI environment.

2. **Get the length of the string.**

   The length of the string is obtained with another call to the JNI environment. Strings are essentially character arrays in C. Because C does not track the length of arrays, strings in C contain a value of 0 at the end of the string. (This is referred to as *null terminating*.) You must manually place this value of 0 when creating strings in C. That is why I need the string length.

3. **Create an** NSString **by providing a pointer to the raw unicode characters and the length of the final string.**

4. **Free the JVM resources in the JNI environment.**

   Now that I have the string's value safely copied to a shiny new NSString, it is time to release the JNI environment's string resources. Again, I call a function in the JNIEnv* variable, named jenv, to release the resources.

Here is the source for the preceding steps:

```
const jchar *chars = (*jenv)->GetStringChars(
                                        jenv,
                                        my_jstring,
                                        NULL);
NSUInteger str_len = (*jenv)->GetStringLength(jenv, my_jstring);
NSString *message = [NSString
                        stringWithCharacters:(UniChar *)chars
                        length:str_len];
(*jenv)->ReleaseStringChars(jenv, my_jstring, chars);
```

Finding More JNI Details

JNI is a rich and complex subject. Using the information found in this and other chapters in this book, you can create many useful OS X integrated applications. Even so, you may find the need for even more information. Several Web sites give additional details about JNI. I mention three specifically in this section.

Apple provides technical notes on many Java-related topics, including JNI. Look for Technical Note TN2147, shown in Figure 9.10. Its title is JNI Development on Mac OS X. This technical note gives additional information on string conversions, graphics, thread safety, and invoking JVMs from Carbon-based and Cocoa-based applications.

Here is the current link for Technical Note TN2147:

```
http://developer.apple.com/mac/library/technotes/tn2005/tn2147.html
```

Figure 9.10

The JNI Development on Mac OS X Web site at developer.apple.com

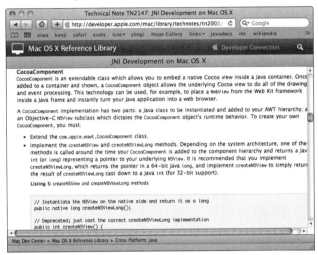

Sun provided a Java Native Interfaces book with the release of Java 1.2, shown in Figure 9.11. It has wonderful detail, and explanations cover most of the JNI specification. I especially recommend reading Chapter 10: Traps and Pitfalls. Because it's written for Java 1.2, the book is a little out of date, but still very useful.

This is the current link for the HTML version of the book found on the Web:

```
http://java.sun.com/docs/books/jni/html/jniTOC.html
```

No list of JNI resources is complete without the site for the Java 1.6 JNI Specification, shown in Figure 9.12. The code examples in the specification tend to be C++ oriented. The main difference between using C and C++ versions of JNI is that when calling the C versions of the JNI functions, the first parameter is usually JNIEnv * env. The JNIEnv* is not present in the C++ versions of the same JNI function calls.

The current link to the Java 1.6 JNI specification is here:

```
http://java.sun.com/javase/6/docs/technotes/guides/jni/spec/jniTOC.html
```

Figure 9.11

The Java Native Interface book site at java.sun.com

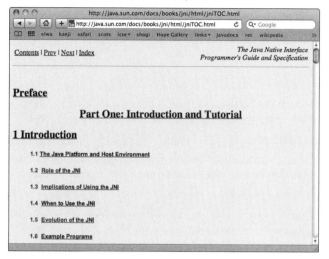

Figure 9.12

The Java Native Interface Specification documentation Web site at java.sun.com

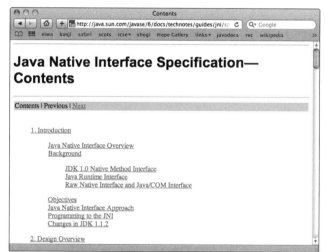

Finally, browse the `jni.h` header file. All the JNI C functions are in there. Locate a copy of `jni.h` by using the Finder to search for it. Not all `jni.h` files are the same, though. Find the one supplied with the Java 1.6 implementation. Open the `jni.h` header in Xcode for syntax coloring.

Summary

Java applications interface with native code using JNI. C is the typical native language with which Java interfaces. However, Java may use JNI to interface with Objective-C and C++.

JNI applications use static blocks to load dynamically linked libraries. Dynamic libraries load using the `System.loadLibrary()` method. The filename of dynamic libraries takes the form of `lib<name>.jnilib`. Dynamic libraries contain the native implementation of `native` Java methods.

C-based applications create Java Virtual Machines using JNI's Invocation API. When creating a `JavaVM` for use in native applications, create the `JavaVMOptions` and place them in the `JavaVMInitArgs`. Create the `JavaVM` with a call to the `JNI_CreateJavaVM()` function.

Understanding how javah and javap work helps the development process. Building JNI applications from the command line is a good learning experience, but it's slow. Use a build tool such as Ant to automate the process.

All but the simplest JNI applications need to anticipate threading issues. Avoid blocking OS X application threads and Java AWT threads. When in doubt, spawn a thread to return AWT and native application threads.

Creating Screen Savers

Berkeley Systems released the famous "Flying Toasters" screen saver in 1989. It was part of the After Dark package for Apple's Macintosh computers.

Flying toasters!

Wow!

It was stunning. Companies lost lots of productivity to employees staring at their screen savers. Screen savers brought a lighthearted element to the cold world of electronics.

Later, businesses realized that screen savers were a great place to leave branding. Company logos floating around screens became common. Also, marketing and sales information appeared scrolling across the screens of unused computers in retail outlets.

Eventually someone realized that with the power of the Internet, screen savers could extend the number-crunching capabilities of financially limited research institutions. Projects such as SETI@home and Climateprediction.net turn hordes of unused computers into massive distributed supercomputers with screen saver applications. IBM's involvement in the World Community Grid uses a similar approach for medical research, creating a grid with more power than many supercomputers.

When a computer is not in use, the screen saver activates. In most cases, your computer is not using its CPU to crunch numbers when in screen saver mode. In even a small organization, that is lots of idle time wasted, unless, of course, you write or install your own screen saver to make use of that idle time.

Screen savers range from whimsical diversions to marketing applications to number-crunching research devices. Watching screen savers is fun. Writing screen savers is even more fun.

At the time of this writing, no Java libraries are specifically made for writing screen savers on OS X. This does not mean you cannot write screen savers for Java. In fact, using the techniques I discuss in this book, writing a simple wrapper around OS X's Cocoa Screen Saver Framework is easy.

After you have a short JNI wrapper around an Objective-C screen saver class, the entire world of Java opens up to writing screen savers for OS X.

In This Chapter

Understanding
screen savers

Invoking the JVM from
Objective-C

Drawing to NSViews
from Java

Exploring the screen
saver framework

Constructing SAVER
bundles

In this chapter, I explain the basics of the Screen Saver Framework. I explain the internals of SAVER packages. I also (most important) explain how to use Java to write your own screen savers.

Do not think for a moment that because you write Java, you cannot write OS X screen savers. Java and OS X screen savers are a great combination. Whether you want to explore visually entrancing screens or number-crunching applications, I explain how to get started with your Java screen saver dream project.

Understanding Screen Savers

Before implementing a Java screen saver for OS X, you need to understand the basics of implementing native Objective-C screen savers for OS X. The Screen Saver Framework for OS X is small. It takes only a couple of minutes to understand the framework itself.

You can find Apple's Screen Saver Framework Reference Web site, shown in Figure 10.1, here:

```
http://developer.apple.com/mac/library/documentation
/UserExperience/Reference/ScreenSaver/ObjC_classic/
```

Figure 10.1

Screen Saver Framework Reference Web site

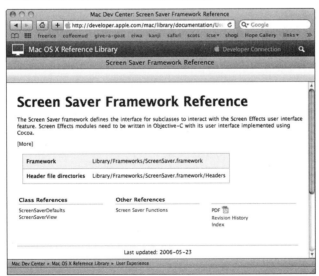

All OS X screen savers extend the Objective-C `ScreenSaverView` class, shown in Figure 10.2. The `ScreenSaverView` class extends `NSView`. `NSView` allows drawing on `ScreenSaver View` instances.

Figure 10.2

Objective-C
`ScreenSaverView`
class

ScreenSaverView
initWithFrame:isPreview:
startAnimation
stopAnimation
isPreview
animateOneFrame
drawRect:
performGammaFade

CROSS-REF

You may remember `NSView` classes from Chapter 8. The `CocoaComponent` class enables the embedding of `NSView` objects in Java GUIs. However, I do not use the `CocoaComponent` in this chapter.

When a screen saver starts up, the `initWithFrame:isPreview:` method initializes the screen saver. The second `BOOL` parameter indicates whether the computer is actually idle or just running the screen saver in preview mode. If your screen saver does number crunching or data processing, you only want to draw pretty pictures (without crunching numbers) in preview mode. System Preferences starts screen savers in preview mode when users set the screen saver preferences and set the active screen saver.

After initialization, OS X calls the screen saver's `startAnimation` method. Depending on how your screen saver works, there may be overlap between the purpose of the `start Animation` and `initWithFrame:isPreview:` methods.

Each time the screen saver view refreshes, the `animateOneFrame` method is called. The `animateOneFrame` method equates to the AWT `paint()` method. The main difference between `animateOneFrame` and the `paint()` method is that the `animateOneFrame` method is called at regular intervals, such as 30 times per second, whereas the `paint()` method waits for a `repaint()` request to redraw.

Implementing the `drawRect:` method also refreshes the screen saver view. The `drawRect:` method is useful for graphics-intensive situations where you need only part of the screen refreshed. The `drawRect:` method requires the `animateOneFrame` method to invalidate the current screen with a call to `setNeedsDisplay:`. Implementing the `drawRect:` method is much more involved than implementing just the `animateOneFrame` method.

The `stopAnimation` method indicates that the screen saver is shutting down. For number-crunching screen savers, make sure your numbers get saved quickly after OS X calls this method. If the `stopAnimation` method does not return quickly, expect OS X to shut down your screen saver for you.

CAUTION

Screen saver development changed with the release of Snow Leopard (OS X 10.6). Screen savers built for previous versions of OS X do not run on Snow Leopard. Screen savers built for Snow Leopard do not run on older versions of OS X.

Implementing screen savers

Xcode has a screen saver project template for Objective-C-based screen savers, as shown in Figure 10.3. Whether implementing an Objective-C screen saver or a Java screen saver, this project template is a good starting point.

Figure 10.3

Choosing a Screen Saver project template in Xcode

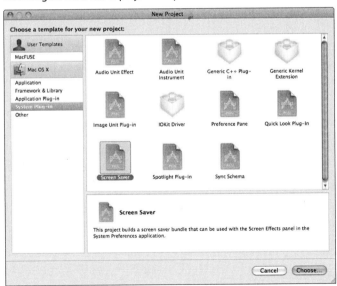

Create an Objective-C screen saver project by following these steps:

1. **Open Xcode.**

2. **Select File ➪ New Project....**

3. **Select System Plug-in from the left navigation panel.**

4. **Select Screen Saver as shown in Figure 10.3.**

5. **Click the Choose... button in the bottom corner of the dialog box.**

6. **Name your project, as shown in Figure 10.4.**

Figure 10.4

Name your screen saver project.

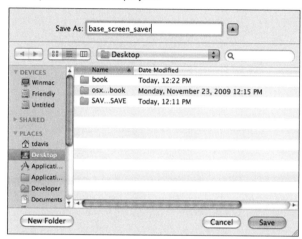

After creating a screen saver project, Xcode's project window opens. If you do not use Xcode as your standard IDE, the Groups & Files tree on the left side of the Xcode project window may look a little intimidating. It looks scarier than it is. The only folder that concerns you is the Classes folder.

In the Groups & Files tree, find the Classes folder and expand it. You should see two files in the folder: a *.m file and a *.h file. The *.m file is the screen saver class implementation. Select the screen saver class implementation, and your Xcode project window should look similar to Figure 10.5.

NOTE

In Objective-C, the classes have separate declarations and implementations. The declaration is called an @interface and placed in a *.h file. The implementation is called a @implementation and placed in a *.m file.

Figure 10.5

Screen saver implementation displayed in Xcode

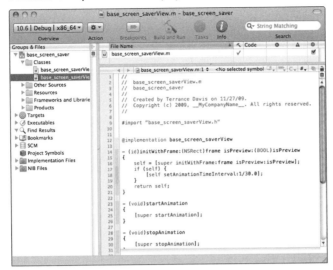

The screen saver implementation your project starts with is a fully functional screen saver. It draws only a black screen, so it's not very exciting, but it still makes a good starting point. Try the following steps to test your screen saver:

1. **Select Build ⇨ Build to create a screen saver from your project.**

2. **Navigate to your newly built screen saver in the Finder.**

   The new screen saver is most likely in your project at `build/Debug/<project name>.saver`, as shown in Figure 10.6.

3. **Copy the screen saver to your** ~/Library/Screen Savers/ **directory.**

4. **Open System Preferences, and select the Desktop & Screen Saver preferences.**

5. **Select your screen saver.**

   Your new screen saver is under the Other node near the bottom of the list, as shown in Figure 10.7. Your screen saver should produce a perfectly unexciting solid black screen.

Figure 10.6

Screen saver build in Debug folder

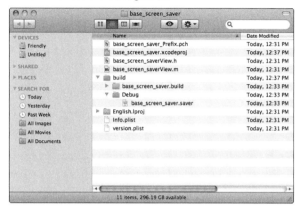

Figure 10.7

Screen saver preferences with base_screen_saver selected

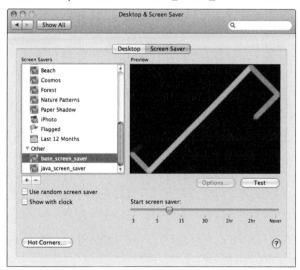

In this chapter, I make the assumption that you are a Java programmer and not necessarily familiar with Objective-C. The next few sections explain the Objective-C source for the screen saver project you created and tested. Objective-C, like Java, is an Object-Oriented Programming language (OOP). Many concepts you already know from Java apply to Objective-C.

NOTE
The source for the projects in this chapter is on the book's Web site.

Initializing

You can use two methods for initializing screen savers. They are the `initWithFrame:` method and the `initWithFrame:isPreview:` method. I use the `initWithFrame:isPreview:` method for the examples, because it is used for previews as well as non-preview initialization. The default source in the Xcode project template for `initWithFrame:isPreview:` is as follows:

```
- (id)initWithFrame:(NSRect)frame isPreview:(BOOL)isPreview
{
    self = [super initWithFrame:frame isPreview:isPreview];
    if (self) {
        [self setAnimationTimeInterval:1/30.0];
    }
    return self;
}
```

Objective-C does not always translate directly to Java, but the equivalent code using Java syntax might look like this:

```
public Object initWithFrameAndIsPreview(NSRect frame, boolean
    isPreview)
{
    ScreenSaverView ssv = super.initWithFrameAndIsPreview (
                                    frame,
                                    isPreview );
    if (ssv != null)
    {
        ssv.setAnimationTimeInterval( 1/30.0 );
    }
    return ssv;
}
```

Methods in Java are called using a dot notation, such as this:

```
someObject.myInstanceMethod();
```

In Objective-C, the same call looks like this:

```
[someObject myInstanceMethod];
```

The dot is replaced with a space, and the whole expression is surrounded with square brackets. This part of Objective-C is easy enough for Java programmers.

Methods that begin with `init` in Objective-C are closely related to class constructors in Java. Objective-C class instantiation typically looks like the following:

```
MyClass *mcObject = [[MyClass alloc] init];
```

The same code in Java looks like this:

```
MyClass mcObject = new MyClass();
```

The class init method is responsible for calling other appropriate init methods. This eventually leads to the calling of your `initWithFrame:isPreview:` method.

In Java, `this` refers to the current class instance executing. The Objective-C equivalent is `self`. In the default Xcode template, self is used to call the following:

```
[self setAnimationTimeInterval:1/30.0];
```

This code calls the `setAnimationTimeInterval:` method and sets the time interval for calls to `animateOneFrame`. The argument is in parts of a second. The default setting updates the screen 30 times per second. Thirty redraws per second should be plenty for most screen savers.

N O T E

Colons in Objective-C method signatures indicate an argument to the function. Objective-C method names actually split into parts describing each parameter the method takes. Objective-C methods that don't have colons in their names don't take any arguments.

Starting and stopping animation

Before `animateOneFrame` is called, `startAnimation` is called. The `stopAnimation` method indicates the screen saver is stopping. The default template source for both methods follows.

```
- (void)startAnimation
{
    [super startAnimation];
}
- (void)stopAnimation
{
    [super stopAnimation];
}
```

The equivalent code using Java syntax looks like this:

```
public void startAnimation()
{
    super.startAnimation();
}
public void stopAnimation()
{
    super.stopAnimation();
}
```

Objective-C methods begin with either a minus sign or a plus sign. The minus sign indicates the method is an instance method. The plus sign indicates the method is a class method. The Java equivalent to the Objective-C class method is the `static` method. The Java equivalent to the minus sign starting Objective-C methods is a non-`static` method.

Drawing an animateOneFrame

The Objective-C `animateOneFrame` method is called in time intervals you specify. The default set by the Xcode template is 30 times per second. Here is the default Xcode screen saver template code for the `animateOneFrame` method:

```
- (void)animateOneFrame
{
    return;
}
```

The equivalent code using Java syntax looks like this:

```
public void animateOneFrame() { }
```

TIP

Many graphics techniques are available for drawing screen savers. The Objective-C `animateOneFrame` method is a great place to test drawing code. Then after you are sure the drawing code works, wrap your drawing methods with JNI and make them available to your Java screen savers.

Creating simple screen savers

This chapter contains two example screen saver projects. The first is a basic screen saver that draws a woven pattern on the screen with one line. The project is called `base_screen_saver`.

I use the `base_screen_saver` to illustrate simple Objective-C screen saver implementation. Later in the chapter, I wrap the first project in Java code and move the drawing logic (the control logic) to the Java code. Understanding the `base_screen_saver` is important, because the Java screen saver expands on this first example. After you understand the two screen saver examples in this chapter, the types of Java screen savers you can create are limitless.

The following source is the @interface for the Objective-C base_screen_saverView class found in the base_screen_saverView.h file. The Java equivalent of the Objective-C @interface is the Java interface. However, @interfaces are meant for use with one and only one class.

TIP

The features of the Java interface are encompassed in Objective-C by a combination of the @interface and the @protocol.

```
#import <ScreenSaver/ScreenSaver.h>

@interface base_screen_saverView : ScreenSaverView
{
    double x1;
    double y1;

    BOOL nw;
    BOOL ne;
    BOOL sw;
    BOOL se;

    CGFloat redChoice;
    CGFloat greenChoice;
    CGFloat blueChoice;

    NSSize screenSize;
}
- (void) drawScreen;
- (void) pickColor;
- (void) drawRectangleX: (CGFloat) x
                     y: (CGFloat) y
                 width: (CGFloat) width
                height: (CGFloat) height;
- (void) setColorRed: (CGFloat) red
               green: (CGFloat) green
                blue: (CGFloat) blue
               alpha: (CGFloat) alpha;
@end
```

In Objective-C, *.h files contain #imports, variable declarations, and method declarations. The #import in Objective-C is very similar to Java's import. The main difference between C's #include and Objective-C's #import is that #import takes care of duplicate #imports automagically.

Understanding the base_screen_saverView.h file is a bit easier if you understand the format of Objective-C header files. The typical structure of Objective-C *.h files is as follows:

```
#import <Some/Libraries.h>
@interface MyClassDeclaration : MySuperClass
{
    // variable declarations go here
}
// method declarations go here
@end
```

If you create a header without an @interface definition, then you may choose to ignore most of this format and stick to a more traditional C-style header format. Remember, if you stick to using #import instead of #include, you do not need to worry about duplicate #includes.

In the base_screen_saverView source, only the methods and variable unique to the base_screen_saverView class are defined. Other methods and variables that exist in the ScreenSaverView and NSView super classes are not redefined even if they are overridden in the child.

The following source is the implementation of the base_screen_saverView class found in base_screen_saverView.m. The full source is a bit long, so I break it up with explanations to make it more readable.

```
#import "base_screen_saverView.h"
```

Notice that the file includes only one import statement. The only import that should exist in an Objective-C implementation file is the import of the interfaces file for the class. All the other imports should appear in the *.h file.

```
@implementation base_screen_saverView
- (id)initWithFrame:(NSRect)frame isPreview:(BOOL)isPreview
{
    self = [super initWithFrame:frame isPreview:isPreview];
    if (self) {
        [self setAnimationTimeInterval:1/30.0];
    }
    return self;
}
```

The initWithFrame:isPreview: method is untouched from the Xcode screen saver project template. I place all the initialization code for the screen saver in the startAnimation method.

```
- (void)startAnimation
{
    [super startAnimation];
    NSLog( @"started animation" );
```

```
    screenSize = [self bounds].size;
    x1 = SSRandomFloatBetween( 0.0, screenSize.width - 10.0 );
    y1 =  SSRandomFloatBetween( 0.0, screenSize.height - 10.0 );

    int direction = SSRandomIntBetween(1, 4);
    switch ( direction )
    {
        case 1:
            nw = YES;
            break;
        case 2:
            ne = YES;
            break;
        case 3:
            sw = YES;
            break;
        default:
            se = YES;
            break;
    }

    [self pickColor];
}
```

In the `startAnimation` method, I obtain the size of the display area using the call to `[self bounds].size`. Then I generate the starting point of the weave from the width and height of the display. After obtaining the display size, I randomly generate the initial direction of the weave. I finish off by calling the `pickColor` method that randomly sets the current drawing color.

The functions `SSRandomFloatBetween()` and `SSRandomIntBetween()` are provided by the Screen Saver Framework as utility calls. Random-number generation is so common in screen savers that the creators of the Screen Saver Framework included both methods to make life easier on screen saver developers.

```
    - (void)stopAnimation
    {
        [super stopAnimation];
        NSLog( @"stopped animation" );
    }
```

The `stopAnimation` method does not require any extra code in this example. In the next example, the `stopAnimation` calls the Java wrapper to handle screen saver cleanup.

The `NSLog()` function is useful for debugging the Objective-C side of screen savers. Open the Console application found at `/Applications/Utilities/Console.app`, and any output from `NSLog()` is displayed.

```objc
- (void)drawRect:(NSRect)rect
{
    [super drawRect:rect];
}
- (void)animateOneFrame
{
    [self drawScreen];

    return;
}
```

In the `animateOneFrame` method, I call the `drawScreen` method to take care of painting. Doing the drawing in a separate method is just one step closer to the Java screen saver wrapper. In the next example, the screen saver drawing method is moved to the Java code.

```objc
- (BOOL)hasConfigureSheet
{
    return NO;
}
- (NSWindow*)configureSheet
{
    return nil;
}
```

Configure sheets provide users the ability to change the screen saver options. Neither of the examples in this chapter uses configure sheets. When not providing a configure sheet, return NO from `hasConfigureSheet` and return `nil` from the `configureSheet` method.

```objc
- (void) drawScreen
{

    // set current color

    [self setColorRed: redChoice
              green: greenChoice
               blue: blueChoice
              alpha: 0.5];

    // draw current position

    [self drawRectangleX: x1
                    y: y1
                width: 10
               height: 10];

    // move square

    if (nw)
    {
```

```
      x1--;
      y1++;
   }
   else if (ne)
   {
      x1++;
      y1++;
   }
   else if (sw)
   {
      x1--;
      y1--;
   }
   else if (se)
   {
      x1++;
      y1--;
   }


   // bounce off walls

   if (y1 < 1)
   {
      if (se)
      {
         se = NO;
         ne = YES;
         [self pickColor];
      }
      else if (sw)
      {
         sw = NO;
         nw = YES;
         [self pickColor];
      }
   }

   if (y1 > screenSize.height - 11.0)
   {
      if (ne)
      {
         ne = NO;
         se = YES;
         [self pickColor];
      }
      else if (nw)
      {
```

```
        nw = NO;
        sw = YES;
        [self pickColor];
    }
}

if (x1 < 1)
{
    if (sw)
    {
        sw = NO;
        se = YES;
        [self pickColor];
    }
    else if (nw)
    {
        nw = NO;
        ne = YES;
        [self pickColor];
    }
}

if (x1 > screenSize.width - 11.0)
{
    if (se)
    {
        se = NO;
        sw = YES;
        [self pickColor];
    }
    else if (ne)
    {
        ne = NO;
        nw = YES;
        [self pickColor];
    }
}

}
```

The `drawScreen` method sets the current fill color and then draws a rectangle at the currently selected location. After taking care of drawing, the method goes on to set the next location and of the rectangle, and if necessary, select the next fill color.

Notice the use of `YES` and `NO` where in Java you see `true` and `false`. `YES` and `NO` are the Objective-C equivalent of Java's `true` and `false`.

```
- (void) pickColor
{
   redChoice = SSRandomFloatBetween( 0.0, 1.0 );
   greenChoice = SSRandomFloatBetween( 0.0, 1.0 );
   blueChoice = SSRandomFloatBetween( 0.0, 1.0 );
}

- (void) drawRectangleX: (CGFloat) x
                     y: (CGFloat) y
                 width: (CGFloat) width
                height: (CGFloat) height
{
   NSRect rectToDraw;
   rectToDraw = NSMakeRect (x, y, width, height);
   [NSBezierPath fillRect: rectToDraw];

}
```

Using `NSBezierPath` is only one of the methods for drawing your screen saver. Both example screen savers in this chapter use `NSBezierPath`'s fillRect: method to draw. I explain other options `NSBezierPath` provides, near the end of this chapter.

```
- (void) setColorRed: (CGFloat) red
               green: (CGFloat) green
                blue: (CGFloat) blue
               alpha: (CGFloat) alpha;
{
   NSColor *colorToSet;
   colorToSet = [NSColor colorWithCalibratedRed: red
                                          green: green
                                           blue: blue
                                          alpha: alpha];
   [colorToSet set];

}
@end
```

The two files in this chapter contain the source necessary to create the first screen saver example. In order to explore Objective-C screen saver creation, I recommend that you modify the behavior of this example and test it as your system screen saver. Modifying code teaches you more about OS X screen saver creation than any amount of documentation.

Integrating Java Controllers

Now that you have seen an Objective-C screen saver, you are ready to explore Java-based screen savers. Java screen savers on OS X wrap the Objective-C Screen Saver Framework. Java screen savers wrap the framework by creating a child of `ScreenSaverView` that exposes desired drawing methods, and then using JNI's Invocation API, Java takes control of the screen saver's `startAnimation`, `animateOneFrame`, and `stopAnimation` methods.

CROSS-REF

In Chapter 9, I explain and demonstrate the JNI Invocation API. The Invocation API is required for creation of Java screen savers on OS X. If you do not already understand the Invocation API, read Chapter 9 before attempting to understand the `java_screen_saver` project. The `java_screen_saver` project builds on information found only in Chapter 9.

In this section, I explain Java screen saver creation using the `java_screen_saver` project found on the book's Web site. I describe all the code necessary to set up a Java screen saver. After the initial wrapping of the Objective-C screen saver is complete, any additional Java code is just standard Java. The tricky bit is setting up your JNI to wrap the functionality of the Objective-C screen saver that is invoked by your system.

Wrapping Objective-C with Java

The components of the `java_screen_saver` project are shown in Figure 10.8.

In the `java_screen_saver` project, I create a child of the Objective-C `ScreenSaverView` class and name it `ScreenSaverChild`. I then integrate the `ScreenSaverChild` class with the code in `SSWrapper.m`.

`SSWrapper` uses some Objective-C syntax, but it's written more in C fashion. `SSWrapper` is not a class; it is a collection of functions. I take care of the JNI Invocation code in `SSWrapper`.

`SSWrapper` starts or obtains a JVM and obtains a global reference to the Java `OSXScreenSaverWrapper` class. The `OSXScreenSaverWrapper` class is responsible for handling calls from the underlying Objective-C and for making callbacks to the native code from Java. Because of the brevity of this example, the `OSXScreenSaverWrapper` class also creates the `WeaveSS` objects. In a more flushed out program, the JNI wrapper should hand off this responsibility to a controller class of some sort.

The Java `WeaveSS` class draws the actual woven patterns on the screen. Each `WeaveSS` instance draws one path. The more instances of `WeaveSS` that `OSXScreenSaverWrapper` creates, the more lines of color the screen saver has weaving at the same time.

Figure 10.8

The Java screen saver wrapping an
Objective-C `ScreenSaverView`

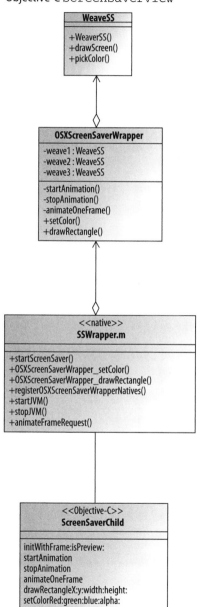

Creating an Objective-C base of a Java screen saver

OS X needs a screen saver configuration it recognizes, so the first step of creating a screen saver is creating the OS X interface. In this case, the interface is an Objective-C object extending the `ScreenSaverView` class. The name of my `ScreenSaverView` child is `ScreenSaver Child`. (It is an easy name to remember, anyway.)

NOTE

Remember that Objective-C classes are often split into two files, an `@interface` file and an `@implementation` file. The interface is a `*.h` file and the implementation is a `*.m` file. For example, the `ScreenSaverChild` interface is contained in a file named `ScreenSaverChild.h`. The `ScreenSaverChild` implementation is contained in a file named `ScreenSaverChild.m`.

The following source is for the Objective-C `ScreenSaverChild` interface:

```
#import <ScreenSaver/ScreenSaver.h>
#include "SSWrapper.h"
@interface ScreenSaverChild : ScreenSaverView
{
}
- (void) drawRectangleX: (CGFloat) x
                    y: (CGFloat) y
                width: (CGFloat) width
               height: (CGFloat) height;
- (void) setColorRed: (CGFloat) red
               green: (CGFloat) green
                blue: (CGFloat) blue
               alpha: (CGFloat) alpha;
@end
```

As you can see from the `ScreenSaverChild` `@interface`, I expose methods allowing the drawing of rectangles and the setting of colors. Both the `drawRectangleX:y:width:height:` method and the `setColorRed:green:blue:alpha:` method are used by callbacks from the Java code.

The following source is for the Objective-C `ScreenSaverChild` implementation. This example is very similar to the `base_screen_saverView` class in the first example. The main difference is that the logic from the `drawScreen` method in `base_screen_saverView` is now in the Java `WeaveSS` class.

```
#import "ScreenSaverChild.h"

@implementation ScreenSaverChild
- (id)initWithFrame:(NSRect)frame isPreview:(BOOL)isPreview
{
    self = [super initWithFrame:frame isPreview:isPreview];
    if (self) {
        [self setAnimationTimeInterval:1/30.0];
```

```objc
   }
   return self;
}
- (void)startAnimation
{
   [super startAnimation];

   NSSize screenSize = [self bounds].size;
   int x1 = screenSize.width;
   int y1 = screenSize.height;

   setScreenSaver(self, x1, y1);
   startJVM();

}
- (void)stopAnimation
{
   [super stopAnimation];

   stopJVM();
}
- (void)drawRect:(NSRect)rect
{
   [super drawRect:rect];
}
- (void)animateOneFrame
{
   animateFrameRequest();
}
- (BOOL)hasConfigureSheet
{
   return NO;
}
- (NSWindow*)configureSheet
{
   return nil;
}
- (void) drawRectangleX: (CGFloat) x
                     y: (CGFloat) y
                 width: (CGFloat) width
                height: (CGFloat) height
{
   NSRect rectToDraw;
   rectToDraw = NSMakeRect (x, y, width, height);
   [NSBezierPath fillRect: rectToDraw];

}
- (void) setColorRed: (CGFloat) red
```

```
                    green: (CGFloat) green
                     blue: (CGFloat) blue
                    alpha: (CGFloat) alpha;
   {
      NSColor *colorToSet;
      colorToSet = [NSColor colorWithCalibratedRed: red
                                            green: green
                                             blue: blue
                                            alpha: alpha];

      [colorToSet set];

   }
   @end
```

Invoking a JVM for a Java screen saver

The next step in the process of creating a Java screen saver is creating a JVM. Also, you need to hook up the Java and Objective-C methods. I divided this task into two files named SSWrapper.m and SSWrapper.h. The SSWrapper.m file is a little complex, so I break up the source with annotations explaining the code.

The following source is for the SSWrapper.h header file. The SSWrapper.h file contains all the #includes and #imports for the SSWrapper.m file. The SSWrapper header does not contain an interface definition because I did not define SSWrapper as an Objective-C class. Nothing prevents you from making SSWrapper into a class in your Java screen savers. Above all else, clarity in the code is most important. Make your decision based on code maintainability.

```
#import <Cocoa/Cocoa.h>
#include <jni.h>
#include <stdio.h>
#include <unistd.h>
#import "ScreenSaverChild.h"
```

I used #include instead of #import for jni.h, stdio.h, and unistd.h, because they are all written to handle multiple includes. However, #import works in these cases too. Using #include is just a stylistic choice here.

The following source is for the SSWrapper.m file. The SSWrapper.m file is extremely important to the process of creating a Java screen saver. SSWrapper.m obtains the JVM reference and the jmethodIDs, and it registers the names and function implementations of Java's native callbacks.

```
#include "SSWrapper.h"
// shutdown flag
jboolean shutdown_requested = JNI_FALSE;

// reused JNI variables
JavaVM *jvm;
```

```
jmethodID midAnimate;// an ID not a reference!
jclass javaWrapperClass;// a global, not local, reference
// Screen Saver variables
ScreenSaverChild *myScreenSaver;
jint ssWidth;
jint ssHeight;

void setScreenSaver(ScreenSaverChild *ss, int w, int h)
{
    myScreenSaver = ss;
    ssWidth = w;
    ssHeight = h;
}
```

The jvm variable is literally the variable that holds a reference to the JVM. The midAnimate
jmethodID holds an ID to the Java method for animating the screen saver. The javaWrap-
perClass reference holds a global reference to the OSXScreenSaverWrapper class. The
setScreenSaver() function stores a reference to the ScreenSaverChild instance,
along with the width and height of the screen.

```
// Java "native" callbacks from JNI
// header file

//Class:     com.genedavis.OSXScreenSaverWrapper
//Method:    void setColor(double,double,double,double)
JNIEXPORT void
JNICALL OSXScreenSaverWrapper_setColor
(JNIEnv * env, jclass jc, jdouble red, jdouble green, jdouble
    blue, jdouble alpha)
{
    [myScreenSaver setColorRed: red
            green: green
             blue: blue
            alpha: alpha];

}
//Class:     com.genedavis.OSXScreenSaverWrapper
//Method:    void drawRectangle (double,double,double,double)
JNIEXPORT void JNICALL OSXScreenSaverWrapper_drawRectangle
(JNIEnv * env, jclass jc, jdouble x, jdouble y, jdouble width,
    jdouble height)
{
    [myScreenSaver drawRectangleX: x
                                y: y
                            width: width
                           height: height];
}
```

The `SSWrapper` file creates two native implementations for Java callbacks:

```
OSXScreenSaverWrapper_setColor
OSXScreenSaverWrapper_drawRectangle
```

Looking at the names of both functions, it is obvious that `javah` did not create these method names. The function names are far too simple to be `javah`-generated. Both methods are registered native methods set up by this function:

```
registerOSXScreenSaverWrapperNatives
```

Conveniently, that is the next function in the code.

```
JNIEXPORT void registerOSXScreenSaverWrapperNatives
(JNIEnv * env, jclass jc)
{
    // fill with Java's native names,
    // followed by javp style signature
    // and the C version of the method
    // names
    JNINativeMethod natives[] =
    {
        {
            "setColor",
            " (DDDD)V",
            &OSXScreenSaverWrapper_setColor
        },

        {
            "drawRectangle",
            " (DDDD)V",
            &OSXScreenSaverWrapper_drawRectangle
        }
    };

    // adding the methods from the C
    // side instead of the Java side
    (*env)->RegisterNatives(env, jc, natives, 2);
}
```

The `registerOSXScreenSaverWrapperNatives` function creates a JNINativeMethod array containing the two native methods defined by the Java `OSXScreenSaverWrapper` class. The two methods are then registered by the `RegisterNatives()` function. These two function implementations are statically linked instead of dynamically linked.

```
void startJVM(void)
{
```

```
        NSLog( @"Called startJVM()" );


        // declaring the JVM and environment
        // variables
        JNIEnv *env;

        // setting up arguments to JVM
        JavaVMInitArgs jvm_args;

        // Always declare the newest version of
        // JNI you want to use. JNI_VERSION_1_6
        // corresponds to Java 6.
        jvm_args.version = JNI_VERSION_1_6;

        // JavaVMOptions are the properties
        // you are already familiar with
        // from the command line
        JavaVMOption options[1];

        // The Java JAR file is placed in the Resources
        // directory of the *.saver bundle. This code
        // locates the JAR file in the bundle and then sets
        // the -Djava.class.path= option so that the
        // JVM knows where to find the Java classes.
        NSString * javaOption = @"-Djava.class.path=";
        NSBundle* myBundle =
            [NSBundle bundleForClass:[myScreenSaver class]];
        NSString* myJar =
        [myBundle pathForResource:@"weaver_screen_saver" ofType:@"jar"];
        javaOption = [javaOption stringByAppendingString:myJar];
        options[0].optionString = (char*) [javaOption UTF8String];

        // The option array length MUST be declared.
        // Remember this is C, and array lengths
        // are not known unless your program explicitly
        // stores them.
        jvm_args.nOptions = 1;

        // setting the options
        jvm_args.options = options;
        jvm_args.ignoreUnrecognized = JNI_FALSE;
```

At this point, you are ready to create a JVM. However, screen savers are modules in a larger process, which implies that a JVM may already exist. Never assume you are the only one creating JVMs. Only one JVM can be created per process, so if a JVM already exists, you cannot create a second one. Also, if a JVM was created and destroyed, you are still barred from creating another JVM. If you are running in preview mode, because the user is using System Preferences to choose a screen saver, and the user clicks the Test button to test your screen saver, your test needs to grab the existing JVM from the preview screen saver instance.

In short, look for existing JVMs before creating JVMs. When finished with a JVM, remember not to destroy it unless you are certain it is not still needed. In the case of screen savers, don't destroy your JVMs.

```
// checking for existing JVM
// This is a must! Multiple JVMs cannot be created
// in one process
jsize jvmCount = 0;
int foundJVM = JNI_GetCreatedJavaVMs(&jvm, 1, &jvmCount);
if (foundJVM == 0 && jvmCount > 0)
{
    // succeeded in getting an existing JVM
    // attaching this thread
    (*jvm)->AttachCurrentThread(jvm, (void**) &env, NULL);
}
else
{
    // no JVM found, ... creating the JVM
    // this thread is automatically attached
    JNI_CreateJavaVM(&jvm, (void**)&env, &jvm_args);
}
```

Now, you have a JVM with a reference in your `jvm` variable. All that remains in this function is to obtain a global reference to the `OSXScreenSaverWrapper` class and use the reference to obtain method IDs for the `startAnimation()` and the `animateOneFrame()` methods.

```
// obtaining the Java class com.genedavis.
OSXScreenSaverWrapper
jclass localJavaWrapperClass =
    (*env)->FindClass(env, "com/genedavis/
OSXScreenSaverWrapper");
javaWrapperClass = (*env)->NewWeakGlobalRef(env,
localJavaWrapperClass);// make reference permanent
// don't need reference anymore
(*env)->DeleteLocalRef(env, localJavaWrapperClass);

// registering the statically linked native methods
// for com.genedavis.OSXScreenSaverWrapper
registerOSXScreenSaverWrapperNatives(env, javaWrapperClass);

jmethodID mid =
(*env)->GetStaticMethodID(env, javaWrapperClass,
"startAnimation", " ()V");
```

```
    (*env)->CallStaticVoidMethod(env, javaWrapperClass, mid);

    midAnimate =
        (*env)->GetStaticMethodID(env, javaWrapperClass,
    "animateOneFrame", " (IIZ)V");
}
```

The previous function handled starting the screen saver. This includes calling the `startAni-mation()` method in the Java code. The code in the next two functions calls the Java methods for animating the screen saver and stopping the screen saver.

```
    void stopJVM(void)
    {

        NSLog( @"Called stopJVM()" );


        JNIEnv *env = NULL;
        jint env_error = JNI_OK;

        // Use the JVM reference to get an up-to-date
        // JNIEnv. JNIEnv variables need constant
        // updates
        env_error = (*jvm)->GetEnv(
                                    jvm,
                                    (void **)&env,
                                    JNI_VERSION_1_6);

        jmethodID mid =
        (*env)->GetStaticMethodID(env, javaWrapperClass,
        "stopAnimation", " ()V");
        (*env)->CallStaticVoidMethod(env, javaWrapperClass, mid);
        // cleaning up the JVM. Do NOT destroy the JVM!
        (*env)->DeleteWeakGlobalRef(env, javaWrapperClass);
    }
    void animateFrameRequest(void)
    {
        JNIEnv *env = NULL;
        jint env_error = JNI_OK;

        // Use the JVM reference to get an up-to-date
        // JNIEnv. JNIEnv variables need constant
        // updates
        env_error = (*jvm)->GetEnv(
                                    jvm,
                                    (void **)&env,
                                    JNI_VERSION_1_6);
```

```
if ([myScreenSaver isPreview])
{
    (*env)->CallStaticVoidMethod(env, javaWrapperClass,
midAnimate, ssWidth, ssHeight, JNI_TRUE);
}
else
{
    (*env)->CallStaticVoidMethod(env, javaWrapperClass,
midAnimate, ssWidth, ssHeight, JNI_FALSE);
}
}
```

That completes the native code and JNI necessary for the Java screen saver. When you make your own Java screen savers, you need to create additional native methods to register with the `RegisterNatives()` functions. Make sure you understand how the Java callbacks to the native screen saver code work, and you will do fine.

T I P

If this is your first experience with the Invocation API, it may seem a bit confusing. Again, review Chapter 9, and keep at it. The Invocation API and JNI are not very difficult. Learning JNI and the Invocation API is mostly a matter of patience.

Interfacing with a screen saver wrapper

In the `java_screen_saver` project, the Java code is about the same length as the native code. In more complex screen savers, the Java code grows much larger than the native code. Most of your variations from this example project will exist in the Java code and the implementation of `OSXScreenSaverWrapper`'s native methods.

All the Java communication from and to Objective-C goes through the `OSXScreenSaverWrapper` class. The `OSXScreenSaverWrapper` class acts as the wrapper for all the native code in the screen saver. The following source is for the Java `OSXScreenSaverWrapper` class:

```
package com.genedavis;
public class OSXScreenSaverWrapper
{
    private static WeaveSS weave1;
    private static WeaveSS weave2;
    private static WeaveSS weave3;

    @SuppressWarnings("unused")
    private static void startAnimation()
    {
        // creating objects that control the drawing
        weave1 = new WeaveSS();
        weave2 = new WeaveSS();
        weave3 = new WeaveSS();
```

```
    }

    @SuppressWarnings("unused")
    private static void stopAnimation()
    {
        // cleaning up
        weave1 = null;
        weave2 = null;
        weave3 = null;
    }

    @SuppressWarnings("unused")
    private static void animateOneFrame(
            int width,
            int height,
            boolean isPreview)
    {
        weave1.drawScreen();
        weave2.drawScreen();
        weave3.drawScreen();

    }

    public static native void setColor(
            double red,
            double green,
            double blue,
            double alpha);

    public static native void drawRectangle(
            double x,
            double y,
            double width,
            double height);
}
```

The first three methods, `startAnimation()`, `stopAnimation()`, and `animateOne-Frame()`, are called from the native code. They correspond to similarly named methods in the Objective-C `ScreenSaverChild` class. I set these three methods as `private` to discourage their use in the Java code. They are meant to be called only from the native code.

The last two methods, `setColor()` and `drawRectangle()`, are declared as `native` methods. These are the callbacks from Java to the native `ScreenSaverChild`. This example screen saver requires only two Java `native` methods. `NSViews` accept many drawing-related commands, so the potential list of useful native methods is very long. I give additional ideas related specifically to `NSBezierPaths`, later in this chapter.

Finishing implementation of a Java screen saver

All that's left is the code for drawing the screen saver animation. WeaveSS instances handle drawing the screen. The following source is for the Java WeaveSS class. I break up the code with explanations of what is occurring.

```java
package com.genedavis;
public class WeaveSS {
    private double x1;
    private double y1;

    private boolean nw;
    private boolean ne;
    private boolean sw;
    private boolean se;

    private double redChoice;
    private double greenChoice;
    private double blueChoice;

    private int screenWidth;
    private int screenHeight;


    public WeaveSS()
    {
        int direction = (int)(Math.random()*4+1);
        switch ( direction )
        {
            case 1:
                nw = true;
                break;
            case 2:
                ne = true;
                break;
            case 3:
                sw = true;
                break;
            default:
                se = true;
                break;
        }

        pickColor();

        x1 = Math.random()*(screenWidth-12)+1;
        y1 = Math.random()*(screenWidth-12)+1;
    }
```

Each WeaveSS object represents one woven line on the screen. The WeaveSS constructor chooses a random movement direction for this instance. WeaveSS chooses a random starting color for itself by calling the pickColor() method. Finally, WeaveSS chooses a starting location for itself.

```
public void drawScreen()
{
    // set current color

    OSXScreenSaverWrapper.setColor(
        redChoice,
        greenChoice,
        blueChoice,
        0.5);

    // draw current position

    OSXScreenSaverWrapper.drawRectangle(
        x1,
        y1,
        10,
        10);

    // move square

    if (nw)
    {
        x1--;
        y1++;
    }
    else if (ne)
    {
        x1++;
        y1++;
    }
    else if (sw)
    {
        x1--;
        y1--;
    }
    else if (se)
    {
        x1++;
        y1--;
    }


    // bounce off walls
```

```
if (y1 < 1)
{
   if (se)
   {
      se = false;
      ne = true;
      pickColor();
   }
   else if (sw)
   {
      sw = false;
      nw = true;
      pickColor();
   }
}

if (y1 > screenHeight - 11.0)
{
   if (ne)
   {
      ne = false;
      se = true;
      pickColor();
   }
   else if (nw)
   {
      nw = false;
      sw = true;
      pickColor();
   }
}

if (x1 < 1)
{
   if (sw)
   {
      sw = false;
      se = true;
      pickColor();
   }
   else if (nw)
   {
      nw = false;
      ne = true;
      pickColor();
   }
}
```

```
if (x1 > screenWidth - 11.0)
{
    if (se)
    {
        se = false;
        sw = true;
        pickColor();
    }
    else if (ne)
    {
        ne = false;
        nw = true;
        pickColor();
    }
}

}
```

The `drawScreen()` method sets the screen saver's drawing color and draws a rectangle in the current drawing location. After taking care of drawing based on the current color and location, the `drawScreen()` method moves the drawing location one point. The `drawScreen()` method finishes by determining whether the motion direction and color should change.

```
public void pickColor()
{
    redChoice = Math.random();
    greenChoice = Math.random();
    blueChoice = Math.random();
}
}
```

The `pickColor()` method randomly chooses a new color for the current `WeaveSS` instance. New colors are chosen when the `WeaveSS` object is constructed and when it reaches the edge of the screen and changes direction.

NOTE

Drawing to `NSViews` (such as a `ScreenSaverView`) is completely resolution-independent. All monitors on OS X are considered to have 72 dots per inch (DPI), no matter what the actual screen resolution is. This means that your drawing does not get bigger or smaller based on the resolution of the screen.

That is all the code necessary to make your own screen saver. Only one task remains. You must package screen savers on OS X in `*.saver` bundles. Creating custom SAVER bundles is the topic of the next couple of sections.

Assembling screen savers manually

Use any common build tool to assemble an OS X screen saver. Before setting up Ant or Xcode to assemble your screen saver, you should know the manual steps for assembling SAVER bundles.

Assembling savers by hand is so simple that you may not get around to automating it for a while.

For a quick screen saver prototype, follow these steps:

1. Create and build your native screen saver code.

Build your native code in Xcode using the Screen Saver project template that I discussed earlier in this chapter.

2. Build your Java code separately in your favorite Java IDE.

3. Jar your Java code.

4. Move the *.saver **file from Xcode project to a safe directory.**

Every time you rebuild your Xcode screen saver project, your `*.saver` bundle is overwritten. Until you are prepared to integrate your Java and Objective-C builds, be careful not to overwrite your fully assembled Java screen saver.

5. Place your JAR in the Resources **directory of the** *.saver **bundle, as shown in Figure 10.9.**

Your Xcode-generated SAVER bundle probably contains a language-specific resource directory, such as `English.lproj`. I removed the `English.lproj` directory for the `java_screen_saver` example, but you may choose to use it, depending on your project.

Figure 10.9

Typical SAVER bundle contents viewed from the Finder

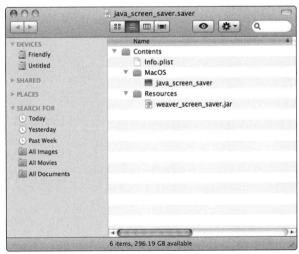

6. **Update the SAVER's** Info.plist.

This step is explained in the next section.

TIP

If you reuse a previously assembled build of your Java screen saver project, you only have to modify the Info.plist the first time you assemble the bundle. On subsequent builds, just copy the new JAR into the Resources folder.

TIP

Control-click a *.saver file to see the Finder context menu. Select Show Package Contents to see the directory structure of the SAVER bundle.

CAUTION

When creating your own Java screen savers, remember to update the name and search location of the project JAR in the invocation of the JVM. In the java_screen_saver project, this code is in the SSWrapper.m file.

Configuring SAVER Info.plist

When setting up a SAVER bundle, you need a properly configured Info.plist, as shown in Figure 10.10. The Info.plist contains key information, such as the name of the Objective-C ScreenSaverView implementation. A SAVER bundle without a properly configured Info. plist does not work.

Figure 10.10

SAVER Info.plist

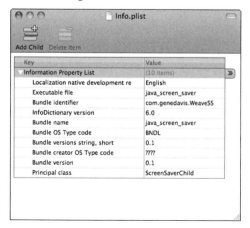

At a minimum, set the following properties in the `Info.plist`:

- Executable file
- Bundle identifier
- Bundle name
- Principal class

The `Executable file` is the name of the file containing the native screen saver and JVM invocation. The `Bundle identifier` is a unique name for OS X to internally identify your screen saver. I suggest using the fully qualified name of the main Java class in the Java screen saver. The `Bundle name` is the name of the bundle as displayed by the System Preferences. The `Principal class` is the name of the Objective-C class that extends the `ScreenSaverView` class.

After you set up your SAVER bundle and properly configure your `Info.plist`, copy your screen saver bundle to the `~/<username>/Library/Screen Savers` directory. You can now set your screen saver to your default screen saver. For instance, opening your screen saver preferences after placing the `java_screen_saver.saver` file in the `Screen Savers` directory gives you the option of selecting a screen saver named `java_screen_saver`, as shown in Figure 10.11.

Figure 10.11

Selecting the `java_screen_saver` in the System Preferences

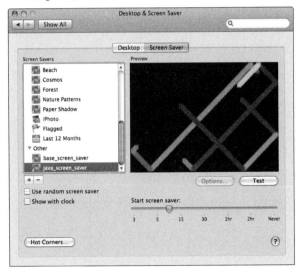

Wrapping NSBezierPath Commands

Screen savers on OS X are NSViews. Because they are NSViews, all the drawing techniques available to NSView (and there are many) are available to your Java-based screen savers. The only catch is that you need to write wrappers for the native drawing code. Most of the hard work is already taken care of for you in the java_screen_saver sample project. Just add to actual wrappers to make the native drawing methods available in your Java code.

Drawing in NSView classes is detailed in Apple's Cocoa Drawing Guide, shown in Figure 10.12. This is the address for Apple's Cocoa Drawing Guide Web site:

```
http://developer.apple.com/mac/library/documentation/Cocoa
/Conceptual/CocoaDrawingGuide/Introduction/Introduction.html
```

Figure 10.12

Cocoa Drawing Guide Web site

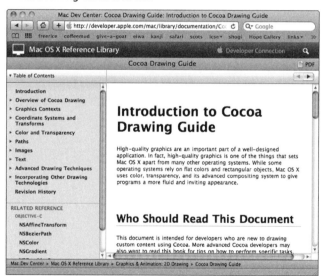

In the java_screen_saver project, I use a sindle NSBezier command to draw the screen saver. The command is found in the Objective-C ScreenSaverChild class and looks like this:

```
[NSBezierPath fillRect: rectToDraw];
```

The NSBezierPath class is capable of much more than drawing filled rectangles. Three of NSBezierPath's class methods for drawing are fillRect:, strokeRect:, and strokeLine FromPoint:toPoint:. The strokeRect: method creates an open rectangle without a fill. The strokeLineFromPoint:toPoint: creates a line.

NSBezierPath also supports full resolution-independent vector drawing. Vector drawing consists of creating curved and straight lines in the same way that Adobe Illustrator does with its pen tool.

For more information on the advanced features of NSBezierPath, see Apple's Cocoa Drawing guide, and check the class reference for the NSBezierPath on Apple's Web site. Find Apple's NSBezierPath Class Reference Web site, as shown in Figure 10.13, here:

```
http://developer.apple.com/mac/library/documentation/Cocoa
/Reference/ApplicationKit/Classes/NSBezierPath_Class/Reference
/Reference.html
```

Figure 10.13

NSBezierPath Class Reference Web site

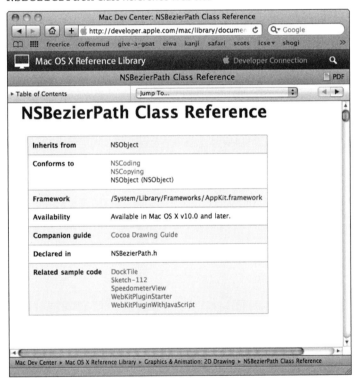

Summary

Screen savers must extend the Objective-C `ScreenSaverView` class. This does not prevent you from writing Java-based screen savers. It just adds an additional step. By using the JNI Invocation API, you can interface a Java controller with a normally Objective-C framework.

I began this chapter with a simple Objective-C-based screen saver example. The example demonstrated stopping and starting screen saver animation. The first example also demonstrated animating frames of the screen saver.

The second example in this chapter expanded upon the first example. The second example is a fully functional Java screen saver. The Objective-C screen saver is stripped of all control code and wrapped by a second set of native code that invokes a JVM. All of the drawing logic is moved to the Java code.

Screen savers must be bundled in SAVER bundles. The Saver bundles have the naming convention of `*.saver`. The SAVER bundles are set up similarly to other application bundles, except that the class that starts the screen saver is a child of the `ScreenSaverView` class. Screen saver bundles must have a properly configured `Info.plist` file in order to be used as a system screen saver.

Creating Terminal Applications

A dvanced programmers take the Terminal seriously. Working from the command line is not suited to every programmer's taste. I know several excellent programmers who avoid the command line whenever they can. However, dismissing the Terminal environment entirely removes an important tool from your repertoire.

Games, editors, utilities, and just about every type of application imaginable are available for the Terminal. Many programmers and system administrators refuse to code outside of the command-line editor's emacs and vi. For quick edits from the Terminal, nano, shown in Figure 11.1, makes a great tool. The point is that Terminal applications' use and development are popular on OS X and in the Unix world.

If you spend much time working in the Terminal, you quickly find Terminal applications performing tricks you never dreamed of trying with `System.out.println()`. Advanced Terminal applications regularly hide passwords as they are entered, change the foreground and background colors of text, manipulate the positions of cursors, and clear the Terminal of unwanted text. Truly impressive Terminal applications even provide menu systems and pop-up dialog boxes within the Terminal window.

Usually, introductory Java books and classes skip past complex Terminal application programming, sticking mostly with basic `System.out.println()` calls. When using ANSI escape sequences, `System.out.print()` and `System.out.println()` become powerful tools. Even the basic `System.out.print()` method can produce colored and stylized Terminal output.

When you are ready to create dialog boxes and menus, a little JNI makes them available through the `ncurses` library. The most advanced user interfaces for the Terminal are created using `ncurses`.

 In This Chapter

Understanding CSI

Exploring ANSI color

Manipulating Terminal views

Using Ncurses with Java

NOTE

Many programmers refer to Terminal applications as "console" applications. On OS X, the Console is an application used to capture logged errors and other output. If you find yourself in a crowd of non-OS X Unix geeks, realize that their "console" is usually synonymous with your "Terminal" and you'll fit in just fine.

Figure 11.1

Nano editor running in OS X Terminal

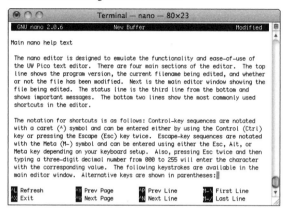

Before continuing, keep in mind that the Terminal is not meant as a rich GUI development environment. If you put too many bells and whistles into your Terminal applications, shell geeks will be turned off to your application. Terminal applications should be clear and clean. Do not treat your terminal applications as remedial GUI applications. Design your terminal applications as no-nonsense interfaces.

Learning ANSI Escape Sequences

ANSI Escape Sequences are the basis of good command-line utility interfaces. ANSI Escape Sequences provide commands for moving the position of the cursor on the Terminal, as well as changing the foreground and background colors of text. ANSI Escape Sequences even provide a code for the dreaded blinking text.

Figure 11.2 shows a simple `System.out.println()` printing to a custom Terminal location and in multiple colors. I bet no one told you `System.out.println()` could do that!

NOTE
All the source code for the examples in this chapter is available on the book's Web site.

The application is called AnsiDemo, and it gives a hint at what you can accomplish with a simple `System.out.println()`. Don't worry too much about the details at this point. I explain how escape sequences work in detail later in the chapter.

Figure 11.2

AnsiDemo in Terminal

This is the source from `AnsiDemo.java`:

```
public class AnsiDemo {
    public static void main(String[] args)
    {
        char esc = 27;
        String clearScreen = esc + "[2J";
        String position1 = esc + "[5;29H";
        String position2 = esc + "[10;1H";
        String color1 = esc + "[30;0m";
        String color2 = esc + "[31;1m";
        String color3 = esc + "[32;1m";
        String color4 = esc + "[34;1m";
        String color5 = esc + "[35;1m";
        String color6 = esc + "[36;1m";
        String reset = esc + " [0m";

        System.out.println(
            clearScreen +
            position1 +
            color1 +
            "Hello " +
            color2 +
            "C" +
            color3 +
            "O" +
            color4 +
            "L" +
            color5 +
```

```
                    "O" +
                    color6 +
                    "R" +
                    reset +
                    position2);
        }
   }
```

No special libraries are needed for displaying the colors above. Also, no special libraries are needed for repositioning text or clearing the screen. The Terminal is configured to understand the set of ANSI Escape Sequences that I use in this application.

Configuring Terminal emulation

Before moving on to diehard ANSI Escape Sequence usage, review the Terminal preferences. Behaviors set in the Terminal Preferences window can make or break the usefulness of many command-line utilities.

Command-line environments use different configurations. Typically, when programming specifically for OS X, you get a standard default Terminal configuration. Having one standard Terminal makes writing native OS X Terminal applications much easier than programming for unknown command lines offered by other vendors. If you program Terminal applications for DOS or Linux, the set of ANSI Escape Sequences varies. In fact, the entire `ncurses` library was written to transparently handle the differences between terminals on different operating systems.

I return to a discussion of `ncurses` later in this chapter.

Occasionally, you may use a Terminal application remotely that does not map exactly to the behavior of your local machine. The Terminal provides a rich set of preferences for supporting customizations to the Terminal. You can customize the look and feel, behavior, and even the encodings supported by the Terminal on your Mac.

Open the Terminal's Preference window by selecting Terminal ⇨ Preferences. Select the Startup tab if it is not visible. The Startup tab, shown in Figure 11.3, displays preferences for the window's color scheme settings and your preferred shell.

Choose the Settings tab, shown in Figure 11.4. The Settings tab displays the preset color schemes for the Terminal. You'll find some very attractive color schemes here. However, if you choose to create your own, just click the add button (+) at the bottom of the window.

Select the Text tab if it is not already selected, as shown in Figure 11.4. The Text tab of the Settings window contains font preferences, text coloring preferences, and cursor preferences. You can even change the color of your cursor.

Figure 11.3

Terminal startup preferences

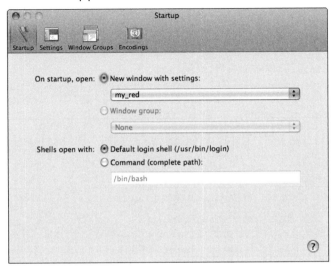

Figure 11.4

Terminal text settings

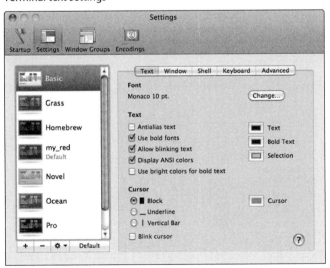

Choose the window tab of Settings, as shown in Figure 11.5. This panel configures the default window size, places useful information in the Terminal title bar, and configures the scrollback. Having unlimited scrollback is useful when debugging scripts and long builds.

CAUTION

The standard Column count expected by command-line tools is 80. Changing the default size of the Terminal window may make some older command-line utilities display improperly.

Figure 11.5

Terminal window settings

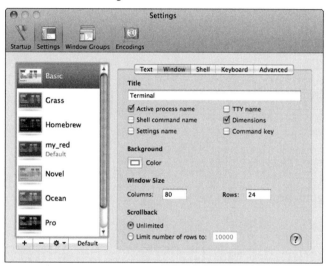

Choose the Shell tab of the Settings preferences, as shown in Figure 11.6. This window allows you to set the closing prompts. Even more interesting is the option of running a command on Terminal startup.

Choose the Keyboard tab of the Settings tab, as shown in Figure 11.7. This panel allows you to modify the default actions of common keyboard keys. For instance, if you use a Terminal application at work that maps F1 differently, modify the action of that key here by double-clicking the row. The dialog box for modifying individual keys is shown in Figure 11.8.

Figure 11.6

Terminal shell settings

Figure 11.7

Terminal keyboard settings

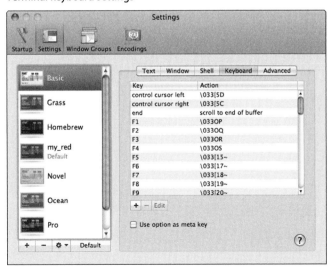

Figure 11.8

Modifying individual keys in the
Terminal keyboard settings

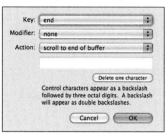

Perhaps the most useful feature on this page is the check box that sets the Option key to work as your meta key. Several Terminal applications, such as emacs, require the use of a meta key combination, which is similar to a Command- or Control-key combo. Normally on OS X you need to use the Escape key as your meta key. The Escape key is far from the normal reach of your pinky, so using the Escape key as a meta key is very distracting. It disrupts your workflow when using command-line utilities.

The fix is simply to click the "Use option as meta key" check box in the Terminal Preferences' keyboard preferences.

Choose the Advanced tab in the Settings preferences, as shown in Figure 11.9. The Advanced tab is at the heart of making the Terminal behave correctly with remote command-line applications. The Emulation section contains a drop-down list allowing you to select how your terminal is declared. You have these choices:

- ansi
- dtterm
- rxvt
- vt52
- vt100
- vt102
- xterm
- xterm-color

Figure 11.9

Terminal advanced settings

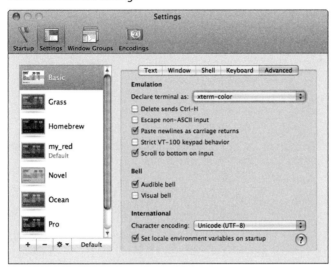

This set of preferences also allows you to set the keypad behavior and the beep (also officially called the "bell") behavior. Also, changing the international character encoding is available with many quick choices including these:

- Unicode (UTF-8)
- Western (Mac OS Roman)
- Western (ISO Latin 1)
- Western (ISO Latin 9)
- Western (Windows Latin 1)
- Western (ASCII)
- Western (NextStep)
- Japanese (Mac OS)
- Japanese (ISO 2022-JP)
- Japanese (EUC)
- Japanese (Shift JIS)

- Traditional Chinese (Big 5 HKSCS)
- Korean (EUC)
- Cyrillic (ISO 8859-5)
- Russian (DOS)
- Cyrillic (Windows)
- Cyrillic (KOI8-R)
- Simplified Chinese (GB 2312)
- Central European (ISO Latin 2)

By clicking the Customize Encodings List at the bottom of the drop-down, you open the Encodings tab of the preferences, as shown in Figure 11.10.

Figure 11.10

Terminal encodings

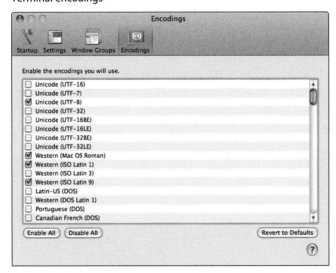

TIP

If you are working in a session of emacs, vi, or nano, either locally or remotely, and the Delete key is not working properly, try toggling the "Delete sends Ctrl-H" check box in the Advanced tab of the Settings area of Terminal Preferences. Sometimes this simple click saves you lots of hassle.

Printing in ANSI color

Now that you have reviewed the Terminal preferences affecting console applications and ANSI escape sequences, you are ready for a better explanation of the sequences.

ANSI escape sequences affect color and position of text in terminals. The escape sequence typically takes the form ESC+[followed by one or more numbers and ended by a letter. For example, the following code produces a green color:

```
ESC[32m
```

Placing the escape character in a string is a bit problematic. Java does not have an escape sequence to represent the escape character. Luckily, escape is easily represented as a char. The char value of escape is decimal value 27. Instead of adding the escape character directly into a String, you can set a char to the value of the escape value and then add the char to the String.

NOTE

Escape in hex is 0x1b. In octal, the escape character is 033.

Using the escape sequence for green text that I mentioned earlier (ESC[32m), here is the code for creating the escape sequence as a Java String:

```
char ESC = 27;
String CSI = ESC + "[";
String green = CSI + "32m";
```

Notice that I named the variable containing ESC+"[" CSI. CSI is the formal name for the beginning of the escape sequence. CSI stands for Control Sequence Introducer. It is called a Control Sequence Introducer because the character combination of ESC+[flags the character set as a control sequence.

NOTE

Sometimes ASCII code 155 is used as a CSI instead of the ESC+[characters used in this chapter. Code 155 is not as widely supported, so I avoid its use.

When setting a color for text in the Terminal, the setting is usually needed only for a word or phrase. After the word or phrase prints, you want the color to change back to the original default the user prefers seeing. This code is used for resetting the color of text printing:

```
ESC[39m
```

In Java code, this escape sequence reverts to default printing:

```
char ESC = 27
String CSI = ESC + "[";
String resetColor = CSI + "39m";
```

Call the reset on colors before changing to a new color. In pseudo code, setting colored text with `System.out.print()` might look something like this:

```
set ansi color
print text
reset ansi color
set another ansi color
print text
reset ansi color
```

In case any of the escape sequence description is confusing, I include a sample program called `BasicColor`. `BasicColor` prints the phrase "Basic Color" in green and then resets the text color to the default user color, as shown in Figure 11.11.

The following source is the code for `BasicColor.java`:

```java
package com.genedavis;
/**
 * Run this class from the Terminal in OS X
 * to see "Hello Color!" in green
 *
 * @author T. Gene Davis
 */
public class BasicColor {
    public static void main(String[] args)
    {
        // ASCII ESC+"[" is known as a
        // Control Sequence Introducer (CSI)

        final char ESC = 27; // in unicode ... \u001B
        final String CSI = ESC + "[";

        // Changes the Terminal color to green
        String green = CSI + "32m";

        // Resets the Terminal color to default
        String reset = CSI + "39m";

        // 1. set foreground color to green
        // 2. print Hello Color!
        // 3. reset the foreground color
        System.out.println(
                green +
```

```
                    "Basic Color" +
                    reset);
        }
    }
```

Figure 11.11

Results of running BasicColor in Terminal

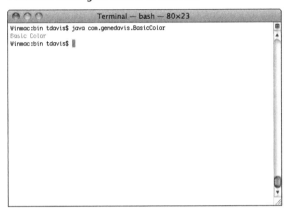

CAUTION

Don't forget to reset the text colors to the user's default color scheme. Forgetting to reset the Terminal colors will annoy your users.

Choosing color brightness

The base colors for ANSI-compliant terminals are limited to black, red, green, yellow, blue, magenta, cyan, and white. The values for the colors are 30-37. These colors have normal and bright versions, doubling the total colors available.

Explicitly choose the color brightness of a color by appending ;0m or ;1m instead of just m to the color escape sequence. The ;0m extension explicitly sets colors to their normal version. The ;1m extension explicitly sets colors to their bright version.

For instance, this code sets the Terminal color to normal red:

```
ESC+[31;0m
```

This sequence of code sets the Terminal color to bright red:

```
ESC+[31;1m
```

In Java, the two versions of red look like this:

```
char ESC = 27;
String CSI = ESC + "[";
String normalRedColor = CSI + "31;0m";
System.out.print( normalRedColor );
```

and

```
char ESC = 27;
String CSI = ESC + "[";
String brightRedColor = CSI + "31;1m";
System.out.print( brightRedColor );
```

When using bright colors, resetting the color with `CSI+"39m"` does not completely reset the color of text to its original color. Instead, you get a bright version of the user's color. To work around this, use the code `CSI+"39;0m"`, which resets the user's text color and sets the color to the normal brightness.

TIP

ANSI escape sequences define bright, normal, and faint versions of colors. OS X's Terminal does not support faint versions of color escape sequences. Most operating systems do not support the faint-colored escapes.

TIP

Another way to reset the text color is the ANSI escape sequence `ESC+[0m`. The `ESC+[0m` sequence resets all modified attributes, not just color.

Setting background colors

Text colors come in two varieties: foreground and background. Foreground colors change the color of the text itself. Background colors change the color surrounding the text. This is similar to the behavior of foreground and background colors in the AWT, except that background colors are localized to the text drawn with them. In AWT code, background colors usually affect an entire panel instead of a localized region.

Normal intensity background colors are specified with `ESC+[40m` thru `ESC+[47m`. Bright background colors are specified with `ESC+[100m` thru `ESC+[107m`.

For example, the following code sets the background to bright green:

```
char ESC = 27;
String CSI = ESC + "[";
String brightGreenBackgroundColor = CSI + "102m";
System.out.print( brightGreenBackgroundColor );
```

Completing the color sequences

In this section, I present tables showing Java code for the ANSI escape sequences I have discussed to this point. Remembering the codes for all the foreground and background colors is a bit intimidating until you have the pattern memorized. I provide tables listing the colors and related sequences to make your life easier.

Table 11.1 contains the Java code necessary to use the normal ANSI color escape sequences. Earlier in the chapter, I provided a code snippet similar to this:

```java
char ESC = 27;
String CSI = ESC + "[";
String yourColor = CSI + "31;0m";
System.out.print( yourColor );
```

The variable `yourColor` contains the control sequence for setting the Terminal text color. Replace `CSI+"31;0m"` from this example with the following sequences, setting the `yourColor` variable to your preferred sequence.

Table 11.1 Normal Foreground ANSI Colors for Terminal Text	
Sequence	Description
CSI+"30;0m"	Normal black foreground
CSI+"31;0m"	Normal red foreground
CSI+"32;0m"	Normal green foreground
CSI+"33;0m"	Normal yellow foreground
CSI+"34;0m"	Normal blue foreground
CSI+"35;0m"	Normal magenta foreground
CSI+"36;0m"	Normal cyan foreground
CSI+"37;0m"	Normal white foreground

Table 11.2 details the Java code necessary to set your escape sequences to bright colors. Again, replace the code for setting `yourColor` with the sequence from the table to produce the desired text attributes.

Table 11.2 Bright Foreground ANSI Colors for Terminal Text	
Sequence	Description
CSI+"30;1m"	Bright black foreground
CSI+"31;1m"	Bright red foreground
CSI+"32;1m"	Bright green foreground

continued

Table 11.2 Continued

Sequence	Description
CSI+"33;1m"	Bright yellow foreground
CSI+"34;1m"	Bright blue foreground
CSI+"35;1m"	Bright magenta foreground
CSI+"36;1m"	Bright cyan foreground
CSI+"37;1m"	Bright white foreground

Table 11.3 details the Java code necessary to set your escape sequences for background colors. Replace the code for setting `yourColor` from earlier in this section with the sequence from the table to produce the desired escape sequence.

Table 11.3 Normal Background ANSI Colors for Terminal Text

Sequence	Description
CSI+"40m"	Normal black background
CSI+"41m"	Normal red background
CSI+"42m"	Normal green background
CSI+"43m"	Normal yellow background
CSI+"44m"	Normal blue background
CSI+"45m"	Normal magenta background
CSI+"46m"	Normal cyan background
CSI+"47m"	Normal white background

Table 11.4 details the Java code necessary to set your escape sequences for bright background colors. Replace the code for setting `yourColor` from earlier in this section with the sequence from the table to produce the desired escape sequence.

Table 11.4 Bright Background ANSI Colors for Terminal Text

Sequence	Description
CSI+"100m"	Bright black background
CSI+"101m"	Bright red background
CSI+"102m"	Bright green background
CSI+"103m"	Bright yellow background

Sequence	Description
CSI+"104m"	Bright blue background
CSI+"105m"	Bright magenta background
CSI+"106m"	Bright cyan background
CSI+"107m"	Bright white background

Table 11.5 details Java code necessary to set additional escape sequences for text manipulation. Again, replace the code for setting `yourColor` from earlier in this section with the sequence from the table to produce the desired escape sequence. Also, because these are not actually colors, you might want to change the variable name. Use the sequence CSI+"0m" to universally reset all modified attributes.

Table 11.5 Additional ANSI settings for Terminal Text

Sequence	Description
CSI+"0m"	Resets all attributes to user's default
CSI+"39m"	Resets foreground without resetting brightness
CSI+"39;0m"	Resets foreground and sets brightness to normal
CSI+"1m"	Sets font intensity to bright (bold text)
CSI+"4m"	Underlines text
CSI+"5m"	Blinks
CSI+"7m"	Turns negative on (visually pleasing highlight)
CSI+"8m"	Turns conceal on
CSI+"22m"	Sets font intensity to normal
CSI+"25m"	Blinks off (Make it stop!)
CSI+"27m"	Turns negative off
CSI+"28m"	Turns conceal off

Concealing passwords

Entering passwords is a common task. Users do not appreciate having passwords visibly echoed. Many work, school, and public environments allow people to see what is typed on a screen, so most programs hide typed passwords.

Terminal applications are no different. Terminal applications prevent onlookers from reading passwords off the screen as users type them. One method for obscuring passwords is to set the foreground and background colors to the same value. This way, when the user types her password, bystanders cannot read the value off the screen.

As it turns out, the Terminal already supports a shortcut for concealing the display of text, including passwords. In Table 11.5, I introduced the "conceal on" (ESC+[8m) and "conceal off" (ESC+[28m) escape sequences. Conceal on sets the current Terminal background color to the same color as the current foreground color, thus rendering the text unreadable by onlookers.

I provide a short application called Conceal demonstrating the use of conceal on and conceal off. The following code is the source for the file Conceal.java.

```
package com.genedavis;
/**
 * Conceal hides text from view. Cutting and pasting
 * the text into TextEdit reveals the hidden text.
 *
 * @author T. Gene Davis
 */
public class Conceal {
    public static void main(String[] args) {
        // ASCII ESC+"[" is known as a
        // Control Sequence Introducer (CSI)

        final char ESC = 27; // in unicode ... \u001B
        final String CSI = ESC + "[";

        // Hides printed text
        String conceal = CSI + "8m";

        // reveals printed text
        String reveal = CSI + "28m";

        // 1. set conceal
        // 2. print Hidden text
        // 3. set reveal
        System.out.println(
                "-->" + conceal +
                "Hidden text" +
                reveal + "<--");
    }
}
```

Figure 11.12 shows the output of Conceal.java. Visually, the Conceal class prints the following:

```
-->              <--
```

If you cut and paste the entire line into a text editor such as TextEdit, you quickly see that the hidden text is still printed. The System.out.println() text is still echoed to the Terminal, but it is invisible to onlookers.

Figure 11.12

Results of running Conceal in Terminal

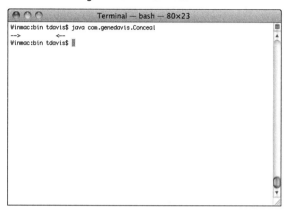

Printing invisible text has purpose. When a terminal ANSI escape sequence for conceal is entered, it not only affects printing, but it also affects anything typed by a user. This includes passwords.

Here is another Java example using the conceal escape sequence. This class is named `PasswordEntry` and actually conceals the text typed by the user. The text is presumably a password that needs obscuring:

```java
package com.genedavis;
import java.util.Scanner;
public class PasswordEntry {
    public static void main(String[] args) {
        // ASCII ESC+"[" is known as a
        // Control Sequence Introducer (CSI)

        final char ESC = 27; // in unicode ... \u001B
        final String CSI = ESC + "[";

        // Hides printed text
        String conceal = CSI + "8m";

        // reveals printed text
        String reveal = CSI + "28m";

        // prepare to read the password
        Scanner scan = new Scanner( System.in );
        String password;
```

```
// request the password and conceal the system in
System.out.print(
        "Enter your password: " +
        conceal );
password = scan.nextLine();

// reveal Terminal type again and share
// the password with the world
System.out.println(
        reveal +
        "Your password is ... " +
        password );
    }
}
```

In the `PasswordEntry` program, I set `CSI` with `ESC+[`. I create `Strings` representing conceal on and conceal off with `CSI`. Next, I print a request for a password, after which I print the conceal escape sequence. While the Terminal is concealing text, I capture the typed password. When the password is entered, I print the code for turning conceal off in the Terminal. All this results in a Terminal looking something like Figure 11.13.

Figure 11.13

Results of running PasswordEntry in Terminal, when your entered password is "ultra secret password"

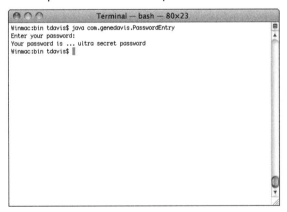

CAUTION

Don't forget to turn conceal off with code `ESC+[28m` or `ESC+[0m`. Failing to do so will irritate your users, as they will not be able to see anything they type or anything your program prints.

Another common approach to entering passwords in Terminal applications is using the `Console` class. The `Console` class contains two methods specifically for collecting passwords from users:

```
public char[] readPassword()
public char[] readPassword(String fmt, Object... args)
```

Both methods turn off echoing, so they are more secure than using the conceal escape sequences. The `Console` class was introduced in Java 1.6.

Introducing Terminal UIs

ANSI escape sequences do much more than make colored text and hide passwords. Properly used, entire Terminal User Interfaces can be designed using ANSI escape sequences. You still need to learn the art of clearing the Terminal, hiding the cursor, and moving the insertion point around the view area. After you have these tasks down, I explain the creation of Terminal User Interfaces from scratch. Near the end of the chapter, I discuss creation of UIs using Charva and ncurses.

Clearing the Terminal

Soon I explain moving the insertion point to any visible portion of the Terminal window. If text is there already, you want the text erased before printing new strings. Depending on your task, you may want to clear entire rows of text, partial rows of text, entire screens, or partial screens. Table 11.6 shows the complete selection of clear codes for the Terminal on OS X.

The pattern for using these codes is similar to the pattern I discussed earlier in the book:

1. **Create an** ESC char.

The ASCII code is 27. Simply assigning the decimal number 27 to a `char` turns out to be a clean and simple way to create this `char`.

2. **Combine the** ESC char **with [to create the CSI.**

CSIs are Control Sequence Introducers. ESC+[is the most common ANSI escape sequence initiator.

3. **Create the sequence, and store it in a** String **for printing.**

Variable names tend to make more sense than escape sequences when reading through code.

This code snippet creates the escape sequence for clearing the Terminal window. After creating the escape sequence, it prints the sequence and clears the Terminal:

```
char ESC = 27;
String CSI = ESC + "[";
String clearTerminal = CSI + "2J";
System.out.print( clearTerminal );
```

Until this point, all the escape sequences ended in m. Most escape sequences do not end in m, so don't forget to check what letter the sequence you use actually should end with.

CAUTION

Remember to use `System.out.print()` rather than `System.out.println()` when printing ANSI escape sequences, or you end up with extra unwanted new lines in your display.

CAUTION

Clearing the Terminal does not remove the text in the Terminal. Instead, it normally scrolls the text off the screen. Never assume that clearing the screen removes sensitive information. Closing the Terminal is the only way to ensure that sensitive information is removed.

Table 11.6 Line and Screen Clearing Sequences

Sequence	Description
CSI+"0J"	Clears from current cursor position to the end of the Terminal view
CSI+"1J"	Clears from current cursor position to the beginning of the Terminal view
CSI+"2J"	Clears the entire Terminal view
CSI+"0K"	Clears from current cursor position to the end of the same line
CSI+"1K"	Clears the current line of text before the cursor from the Terminal view
CSI+"2K"	Clears the entire line of text from the Terminal

When clearing the screen for a Terminal UI, you create the illusion that your user has in fact left the command line even though he is still in the Terminal. Nothing destroys the illusion of having a Terminal UI quicker than a cursor blinking away on the screen.

Luckily, ANSI escape sequences allow you to hide and show cursors at will. The codes for hiding and showing cursors are ESC+[?25l and ESC+[?25h, respectively. The code snippet for hiding the cursor looks like this:

```
char ESC = 27;
String CSI = ESC + "[";
String clearTerminal = CSI + "25l";
System.out.print( clearTerminal );
```

This is the code snippet for showing a previously hidden cursor:

```
char ESC = 27;
String CSI = ESC + "[";
String clearTerminal = CSI + "25h";
System.out.print( clearTerminal );
```

CAUTION

Remember to show your cursor when exiting your application, if you hid it in the application. Otherwise, your user no longer has a cursor at the command line.

CAUTION

The sequence for hiding a cursor ends in a lower case L, not a 1 or uppercase I. Confusing these characters is easy depending on the font in which you read them.

Moving the cursor

The last ANSI escape sequence you need before embarking on your journey into the world of Terminal UIs is the code for moving the cursor. You can use several codes for moving the cursor, but you likely need only two. The following sequence sets the position of the cursor in the Terminal window:

```
ESC+[<row>;<column>H
```

The abbreviated form places the cursor at the top-left corner of the screen:

```
ESC+[H
```

CAUTION

The x and y coordinates in the cursor moving sequence are reversed from where you expect. Row (y) comes first, not second.

The rows and columns in the Terminal are 1 based, instead of 0 based. The default size of the Terminal is 80 columns by 24 rows, as shown in Figure 11.14. I explain how to verify the row and column count later in this chapter. Currently, Java does not contain any built-in methods for verifying the row count or column count in a terminal window.

Figure 11.14

Terminal coordinates

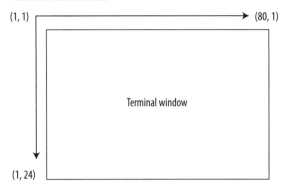

(1, 1) → (80, 1)

Terminal window

(1, 24)

The code for setting the cursor position to row 5 and column 30 looks like this:

```
char ESC = 27;
int x = 30;
int y = 5;
String CSI = ESC + "[";
String moveCursor = CSI + y + ";" + x + "H";
System.out.print( moveCursor );
```

The following code places the cursor at the top-left corner of the Terminal window.

```
char ESC = 27;
String CSI = ESC + "[";
String moveCursor = CSI + "H";
System.out.print( moveCursor );
```

Interacting with the Terminal

At the heart of interacting with Terminal applications is the need to capture keystrokes in real time. Some Terminal applications accept mouse events, but most users of Terminal applications prefer to keep their hands on the keyboard. Using a mouse slows them down. Therefore, mouse-driven Terminal UIs are not acceptable.

As I mentioned in Chapter 9, Java has no built-in method for retrieving characters from the Terminal, before the Enter key is pressed. It turns out Java also has no build-in methods for checking the current view size in the Terminal. In order to make an interactive Terminal application, you must know the viewable size of the Terminal and the latest key press.

Capturing the latest Terminal key press, the viewable columns, and the viewable rows is fairly straightforward with C. In this section, I provide a Terminal User Interface utility written with JNI for capturing these three pieces of data.

NOTE

The lack of a console/terminal character reader in Java has been in various bug fix requests for more than 13 years. The current bug request is bug number 6351276. The current version of the bug report is:

```
http://bugs.sun.com/bugdatabase
/view_bug.do?bug_id=6351276
```

CROSS-REF

I detail JNI usage on OS X in Chapter 9.

The Java portion of the Terminal UI utility is named `TuiUtil.java`. This is the source for the Java class `TuiUtil`:

```
package com.genedavis;
/**
 * Native methods for Terminal UI.
 *
 * @author T. Gene Davis
 */
public class TuiUtil {
    // executed during class load
    static
    {
        // used to load from a system library path
        System.loadLibrary("TUI");
    }

    // native method call
    public native char getch();

    // native method call (tput cols)
    public native int getTerminalColumns();

    // native method call (tput lines)
    public native int getTerminalRows();
}
```

The `TuiUtil` class starts with a static block. The `static` block loads a dynamic library called `TUI`. The actual filename is `libTUI.jnilib`.

The `TuiUtil` class contains three `native` methods: `getch()`, `getTerminalColumns()`, and `getTerminalRows()`. I use an Ant script for generating the native C header file. You may prefer to generate the C header with a direct call to `javah`.

The following code is the source for the JNI header file associated with the `TuiUtil` class. In the project Ant project, the JNI header file is named `native_TuiUtil_jni.h`:

```
/* DO NOT EDIT THIS FILE - it is machine generated */
#include <jni.h>
/* Header for class com_genedavis_TuiUtil */
#ifndef _Included_com_genedavis_TuiUtil
#define _Included_com_genedavis_TuiUtil
#ifdef __cplusplus
extern "C" {
#endif
/*
 * Class:     com_genedavis_TuiUtil
 * Method:    getch
 * Signature: ()C
 */
JNIEXPORT jchar JNICALL Java_com_genedavis_TuiUtil_getch
  (JNIEnv *, jobject);
/*
 * Class:     com_genedavis_TuiUtil
 * Method:    getTerminalColumns
 * Signature: ()I
 */
JNIEXPORT jint JNICALL Java_com_genedavis_TuiUtil_
    getTerminalColumns
  (JNIEnv *, jobject);
/*
 * Class:     com_genedavis_TuiUtil
 * Method:    getTerminalRows
 * Signature: ()I
 */
JNIEXPORT jint JNICALL Java_com_genedavis_TuiUtil_getTerminalRows
  (JNIEnv *, jobject);
#ifdef __cplusplus
}
#endif
#endif
```

The three native method definitions define their return values as `jchars` and `jints`. For simplicity, I do no implicit conversion from the underlying C code to the JNI types. I just use `jchar` and `jint`.

The native implementation of the TuiUtil class is found in a C file called `TuiUtilImpl.c`. Here's the source for the native implementation of the `TuiUtil` class:

```
#include <stdio.h>
#include <sys/ioctl.h>
#include <termios.h>
#include <unistd.h>
#include "native_TuiUtil_jni.h"
// This Terminal Utility works
```

```
// on Mac OS X and likely works on
// other *NIX operating systems
// after recompiling.
// getch()
JNIEXPORT jchar JNICALL
Java_com_genedavis_TuiUtil_getch
(JNIEnv * my_jenv, jobject my_jobj)
{
    jchar ch;
    struct termios old_term, new_term;
    //storing the old settings
    tcgetattr ( STDIN_FILENO, &old_term );
    // making a copy of the old settings
    // to modify
    new_term = old_term;
    // modifying the copy of the terminal settings
    // so there is no echoing and no buffering,
    // just flipping bits here
    new_term.c_lflag &= ~( ICANON | ECHO );
    // setting the modified terminal settings
    // to be active
    tcsetattr ( STDIN_FILENO, TCSANOW, &new_term );
    // getting the character
    ch = getchar();
    // resetting the terminal settings to the old settings
    tcsetattr ( STDIN_FILENO, TCSANOW, &old_term );

    return ch;
}

// getTerminalColumns()
JNIEXPORT jint JNICALL
Java_com_genedavis_TuiUtil_getTerminalColumns
(JNIEnv * my_jenv, jobject my_jobj)
{
    //defining a terminal size struct
    struct ttysize terminal_size;

    //populating the struct
    ioctl(0, TIOCGSIZE, &terminal_size);

    //returning the viewable columns
    return terminal_size.ts_cols;
}

// getTerminalRows()
JNIEXPORT jint JNICALL
Java_com_genedavis_TuiUtil_getTerminalRows
```

```
(JNIEnv * my_jenv, jobject my_jobj)
{
    //defining a terminal size struct
    struct ttysize terminal_size;

    //populating the struct
    ioctl(0, TIOCGSIZE, &terminal_size);

    //returning the viewable lines
    return terminal_size.ts_lines;
}
```

The `TuiUtilImpl.c` file implements the three native methods defined in the `TuiUtil` class. The implementations are simple, so they need no supporting methods. All three implementations are fairly generic Unix solutions, so they should work on other Unix-based operating systems besides Mac OS X.

I implement the `getch()` method as the `Java_com_genedavis_TuiUtil_getch()` function. It defines a `jchar` and two `termios` structs. The `termios` structs store a configuration for the Terminal. In this case, one `struct` stores a Terminal configuration for echoing keystrokes and blocking input to the program until the Return key is pressed. These setting are stored in the `old_term` struct while the modifications for the utility are created in a clone called `new_term`. The customized settings are activated in the Terminal using the `tcsetattr()` function. The `getchar()` function takes care of retrieving the return value for the function, and then I reset the Terminal settings with the `old_term` struct and a call to the `tcsetattr()` function.

If you want to include the `getch()` method in your own code, I recommend moving the code for setting the Terminal echo and blocking to a setup function and a cleanup function, and simply perform the `getchar()` call during your event loop. Either way, for the purpose of explaining the process of getting characters from the Terminal as they are typed, this code works.

Finding the viewable columns and rows of the Terminal is actually easier than getting the latest keystroke. The `getTerminalColumns()` implementation and the `getTerminalRows()` implementation simply populate a `ttysize` struct with the row and column counts by passing the struct to the `ioctl()` function. The column count is stored in the `ts_cols` member. The row count is stored in the `ts_lines` member of the `ttysize` struct.

NOTE

Another solution for finding the viewable rows and columns in the Terminal is passing environment variables on startup of your command-line utility that represent the row and column counts. The downside of this approach is that if the Terminal view is resized after the Java application starts, the application cannot know of the change.

This JNI approach relates the current status of rows and columns even if the Terminal window changes size after the applications starts.

Making dialog boxes and menus

On the book's Web site, I have a project that contains the `TuiUtil` and a simple Terminal application implementation. Included in that project are a simple dialog box class and a simple menu class. These classes are not production quality. My intention is to give you an idea of what JNI methods and ANSI escape sequences need to go into creating even a small Terminal User Interface.

The following source is for the `TuiMessageDialog` class. The `TuiMessageDialog` implements a basic Terminal-based message dialog box. The dialog box functions similar to `JOptionPane`'s `showMessageDialog()` method, only with much less polish. Later in this chapter, I present an example of a more refined ncurses approach that uses the Charva API.

```java
package com.genedavis;
/**
 * Simple message dialog box for Terminal apps.
 *
 * @author T. Gene Davis
 */
public class TuiMessageDialog {

    // setting up the CSI
    private static char ESC = 27;
    private static String CSI = ESC + "[";

    // preset escape sequences
    private static String blackFore = CSI + "30m";

    private static String redBack = CSI + "101m";
    private static String greenBack = CSI + "102m";
    private static String blueBack = CSI + "104m";

    private final static String reset = CSI + "0m";

    /**
     * Handles coloring, centering, and printing of
     * message dialog box.
     *
     * @param message Message for dialog to display
     * @param bkColor
     */
    private static void showMessage(
        String message,
        String bkColor)
    {
        // finding the proper location of the dialog box
        int cols = TuiWindow.tuiUtil.getTerminalColumns();
```

```java
        int rows = TuiWindow.tuiUtil.getTerminalRows();

        int x = (cols - message.length()) / 2 - 1;
        int y = rows / 2 - 2;

        // setting the background color of the dialog box
        System.out.print(
                bkColor +
                blackFore );

        // setting the position of the dialog box
        // and printing the dialog box line by line
        System.out.print( CSI + y + ";" + x + "H" );
        for (int i=0; i< (message.length()+2) ; i++)
            System.out.print(" ");

        System.out.print( CSI + (y+1) + ";" + x + "H" );

        System.out.print(
                " " +
                message +
                " ");

        System.out.print( CSI + (y+2) + ";" + x + "H" );
        for (int i=0; i< (message.length()+2) ; i++)
            System.out.print(" ");

        System.out.print( CSI + (y+3) + ";" + x + "H" );
        for (int i=0; i< (message.length()-4) ; i++)
            System.out.print(" ");
        System.out.print("[OK]   ");

        // resetting the colors to user's preferences
        System.out.print(reset);

        // waiting for user acknowledgement of the
        // dialog box before continuing
        TuiWindow.tuiUtil.getch();
    }

    /**
     * Displays a message in a red dialog box.
     *
     * @param message message to print in the dialog box
     */
    public static void showRedMessage(String message)
    {
        showMessage(message, redBack);
```

```
    }

    /**
     * Displays a message in a green dialog box.
     *
     * @param message message to print in the dialog box
     */
    public static void showGreenMessage(String message)
    {
        showMessage(message, greenBack);
    }

    /**
     * Displays a message in a blue dialog box.
     *
     * @param message message to print in the dialog box
     */
    public static void showBlueMessage(String message)
    {
        showMessage(message, blueBack);
    }

}
```

The `TuiMessageDialog` class contains three public static methods for displaying message dialog boxes in green, blue, and red. The methods could just as easily indicate information, caution, and alert. Each message method passes custom drawing information (in this case, merely color) to the private `showMessage()` method. The private `showMessage()` method does all the real work of drawing the dialog box.

The `showMessage()` method uses the `TuiUtil` class, previously explained, to find the dimensions of the Terminal's viewable area. The message box is then placed in the center of the Terminal. The dialog box is modal and waits until the `TuiUtil`'s `getch()` method finds a key typed before continuing with execution. The `TuiMessageDialog` class does not undraw itself, but rather allows the `TuiWindow` (discussed later) to repaint the Terminal view.

Again, the `TuiMessageDialog` is not for production code. It does not even handle messages that need wrapping. It is simply a demonstration that, using the techniques I discuss earlier in this chapter, you can create a usable dialog box system for your Terminal-based applications.

Using a combination of the ANSI escape sequences and the `TuiUtil` class that I explain earlier in the chapter, you also can create menu bars and menus for your Terminal-based applications. In the following code, I create a basic menu bar for the Terminal. The following code is for the `TuiMenu` class. It is simply a menu bar with hard-coded menu items embedded, but it shows what you can accomplish with techniques I showed earlier in this chapter. It is easy to imagine a fully navigable menu system using similar techniques. However, an example that complex would not fit into a single chapter of a book.

```java
package com.genedavis;
/**
 * Simple menu bar for Terminal apps.
 *
 * @author T. Gene Davis
 */
public class TuiMenu {

    // setting up the CSI
    char ESC = 27;
    String CSI = ESC + "[";
    // preset escape sequences
    String initPosition = CSI + "H";
    String whiteFore = CSI + "37m";
    String grayBack = CSI + "100m";
    String reset = CSI + "0m";
    String underline = CSI + "4m";
    String noUnderline = CSI + "24m";
    /**
     * Paints the menu bar
     */
    public void paint()
    {
        int cols = TuiWindow.tuiUtil.getTerminalColumns();

        System.out.print( initPosition );
        System.out.print(
            whiteFore +
            grayBack );

        for (int i=1; i<= cols; i++)
            System.out.print(" ");

        System.out.print( initPosition );
        System.out.print(
            " " +
            underline +
            "G" +
            noUnderline +
            "reen");

        System.out.print("   " +
            underline +
                "B" +
            noUnderline +
                "lue");
```

```
        System.out.print("   " +
                underline +
                "R" +
                noUnderline +
                "ed");

        System.out.print("   " +
                underline +
                "Q" +
                noUnderline +
                "uit");

        System.out.print( reset );

    }
}
```

The `TuiMenu` simply provides four menu items. Three menu items activate the three versions of the `TuiMessageDialog`. The fourth menu item exits the application. The mnemonic codes are underlined in the menu items using the `ESC+[4m` sequence and underlining is stopped using the `ESC+[24m` sequence.

The menu bar is drawn by placing the cursor at the top-left corner of the screen, using the `ESC+[H` cursor moving sequence, and then printing it with a bright black background. Bright black looks gray, in case you wondered what exactly "bright" black looks like. The proper width of the menu bar is determined with a call to the `TuiUtil` to find the current viewable width of the Terminal window.

NOTE

If nothing else, the demonstration of creating a Terminal-based dialog box and a Terminal-based menu should impress you with the importance of methods for getting single character input from command-line-based applications and also obtaining the viewable dimensions of the window running the command-line application.

Currently, Java's Console application supports neither of these basic features. I hope methods for obtaining this information works its way into the Java specification in the near future.

Creating a Terminal UI

For completeness, I include the `TuiWindow` class. The `main()` method is in the `TuiWindow` class. The `TuiWindow` class combines the `TuiUtil`, the `TuiMenu`, and the `TuiMessage Dialog` in one application. The `TuiWindow` is not meant as a template for creating a Java-based Terminal application. The `TuiWindow`, shown in Figure 11.15, serves as a demo of how to combine the techniques from this chapter when creating a Terminal application.

Figure 11.15

TuiWindow running in Terminal

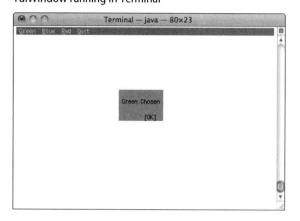

The following source is the `TuiWindow` class:

```java
package com.genedavis;
/**
 * This is a basic windowed terminal application.
 *
 * @author T. Gene Davis
 */
public class TuiWindow {
   public static TuiUtil tuiUtil = new TuiUtil();

   // setting up the CSI
   char ESC = 27;
   String CSI = ESC + "[";

   // preset escape sequences
   String hideCursor = CSI + "?25l";
   String showCursor = CSI + "?25h";
   String reset = CSI + "0m";
   String clear = CSI+"2J";

   TuiMenu menubar;
   /**
    * Create window and start application loop
    */
   public static void main(String[] args) {
      TuiWindow tw = new TuiWindow();
      tw.appLoop();
   }
```

```
/**
 * Initialize window, and display welcome
 * message in a TuiMessageDialog
 */
public TuiWindow()
{
   menubar = new TuiMenu();
   hideCursor();

   paint();

   TuiMessageDialog.showGreenMessage(
         "Terminal Display Demo");

   paint();
}

/**
 * Application loop responsible for clearing
 * the terminal, painting the terminal, and
 * handling events for the keyboard.
 */
private void appLoop()
{

   char myChar = ' ';

   while (myChar != 'q' && myChar != 'Q')
   {
      clearTerm();
      paint();

      // use native call
      myChar = tuiUtil.getch();
      handleEvent(myChar);

   }

   clearTerm();
   resetColors();
   showCursor();

}

/**
 * Handle keys typed
 */
private void handleEvent(char myChar) {
```

```java
        if (myChar == 'r' && myChar != 'R')
        {
            TuiMessageDialog.showRedMessage(
                "Red Chosen");
        }
        else if (myChar == 'g' && myChar != 'G')
        {
            TuiMessageDialog.showGreenMessage(
                "Green Chosen");
        }
        else if (myChar == 'b' && myChar != 'B')
        {
            TuiMessageDialog.showBlueMessage(
                "Blue Chosen");
        }
    }
    /**
     * Reset the graphics to user's preferences.
     */
    private void resetColors()
    {
        //Clear the entire visible display
        System.out.println( reset );
    }

    /**
     * Clear the entire visible display
     */
    private void clearTerm()
    {
        System.out.println( clear );
    }

    /**
     * Paint the Terminal window
     */
    private void paint()
    {
        clearTerm();
        menubar.paint();
    }

    /**
     * Hide Terminal's cursor
     */
    public void hideCursor()
    {
        System.out.println( hideCursor );
```

```
    }

    /**
     * Show Terminal's cursor
     */
    public void showCursor()
    {
        System.out.println( showCursor );
    }
}
```

The `TuiWindow` creates an instance of the `TuiUtil` and stores it in a static variable for use in the application. The `TuiWindow` also takes care of the application loop and cleans up after the application loop receives a request to quit.

NOTE

If you use the `terminal_ui` project from the book's Web site, the project comes with a shell script named `run` to run the built project. The shell script contains only one command:

```
java -Djava.library.path=c_bin -cp java_bin/ com.
    genedavis.TuiWindow
```

You can run the project from the command line in a Terminal window using this command.

Improving Terminal UIs

Graphical User Interfaces (GUIs) provide users with pretty pictures and pleasing graphic navigation. Terminal User Interfaces (which are never called TUIs, but they should be) provide the equivalent user experience for Terminal-based interfaces. Dialog boxes, windows, panels, and menus are all available from inside Terminal UIs, just as they are in available in GUIs. Terminal UIs exist mostly in server, embedded, and headless application environments where administrators care for their applications by way of Terminal interfaces.

In this section, I introduce `ncurses` wrapped with Charva. Charva is a Java-based Terminal User Interface API. The `ncurses` library is C based, so you must wrap it with a JNI library in order to use it in Java. The remainder of this chapter covers an overview of `ncurses`, building Charva for wrapping `ncurses`, testing Charva, and creating a Terminal UI using standard Java development tools.

Introducing ncurses

The ANSI escape sequences detailed earlier in this chapter are supported on most operating systems, but usually with slight variations. Even on OS X, there is no guarantee that a new release of Terminal will not break an application that depends on those specific codes.

For some applications and utilities, variations in ANSI escape sequences do not matter. You may be the only one who uses the tool, or your team may be the only ones who use the tool. Not all useful programs are intended for mass distribution.

In other cases, you want your application to work on as many versions of OS X as possible. (Oh, and maybe to work on those other operating systems, too.) For these cases, the Unix world came up with a solution many years ago. It is a library called `ncurses`.

Ncurses is a C library for creating complex Terminal-based User Interfaces. The ncurses library handles keyboard input, mouse events, cursor placement, colorizing text, and screen updating. Using ncurses, you can manage text-based windows, menus, and panels in a platform-agnostic manner.

The ncurses libraries ship with OS X, so they are readily available. However, using them in Java applications presents problems. Ncurses behaves differently than AWT and Swing. Also, wrapping the libraries in JNI is far too difficult a task for most entry-level programmers.

Wrapping ncurses with Charva

With JNI and the `ncurses` library, you can create a custom API for handling Terminal User Interfaces. However, if your goal is merely creating a Terminal application, then several free libraries can do the wrapping for you. Charva is an excellent choice for creating Terminal-based applications.

N O T E

Another popular Terminal User Interface API is the Java Curses Library. Java Curses Library is a SourceForge project. The Java Curses Library, like Charva, is available under the LGPL license. See the project site here:

```
http://sourceforge.net/projects/javacurses/
```

Charva creates User Interfaces in the same way that AWT and Swing create UIs. Charva clones the AWT and Swing APIs where possible. Sometimes, you can take a working Swing or AWT application, change the package names of the components to `charva.awt` and `charvax.swing` from `java.awt` and `javax.swing`, and find yourself with a working Terminal application. The result is a Terminal-based interface instead of a graphical interface.

Charva is licensed under the GNU Lesser General Public License. The GNU Lesser General Public License is a business-friendly version of the GNU Public License. It allows linking against Charva without restricting licensing of code that uses Charva. APIs that extend rather than just link against Charva have some additional restrictions. For complete details, have your corporate lawyer examine the license that comes with Charva.

Charva is distributed in a standard `*.zip` file. Building Charva for OS X is fairly painless, because it comes with an Ant project to handle all the nasty details. Once built, make sure the JARs and native library are available to your Java project and that you are all set to make your own Terminal applications using Charva.

N O T E

The home page for Charva is located here:

```
http://www.pitman.co.za/projects/charva/index.html.
```

CROSS-REF
I discuss using and modifying Ant scripts in Chapter 4.

To download and build Charva on OS X, follow these steps:

1. **Download Charva.**

Charva source code is hosted on the SourceForge site here:

```
http://sourceforge.net/projects/charva
```

2. **Uncompress Charva either by double-clicking the Charva download in Finder or using the** unzip **tool from Terminal.**

A Finder window showing the extracted contents of the Charva download is shown in Figure 11.16.

Figure 11.16

Charva unzipped

3. **Open Terminal, and** cd **to the uncompressed** Charva **folder.**

The Charva documentation refers to this folder as $CHARVA_HOME.

4. **Set the environment variable for** JAVA_HOME **in your current Terminal window.**

Find the correct location of JAVA_HOME by issuing the /usr/libexec/java_home command in your Terminal window. Set the JAVA_HOME environment variable for the current Terminal window using the command export JAVA_HOME=<home> where <home> is the location given by the command /usr/libexec/java_home.

5. **From the Charva folder, issue the command** ant compile.

Because Charva uses JNI to access ncurses, it must use native files built specifically for OS X. All this work is automated with Ant.

6. **From the Charva folder, issue the command** ant javah.

The javah task prepares the project for building against the native libraries.

7. **Issue the command** ant compile-test **from the Charva folder.**

This task creates the Charva test. I explain the test shortly.

8. **Create the JNI library with the command** ant makeDLL. **Enter** mac_osx **when the build script requests your operating system.**

After you successfully complete these steps, the Charva library is nearly ready to use. The build process created an OS X-specific dynamic library called libTerminal.jnilib. For testing and development, place this library in /Library/Java/Extensions so Java can find and load it when using Charva.

CROSS-REF

I discuss finding JAVA_HOME and other important Java directories correctly on OS X in Chapter 2.

CAUTION

When testing Charva linked application installations, remove the libTerminal.jnilib dynamic library from the /Library/Java/Extensions directory. Your application may find this library instead of the copy in your installation giving you a false positive on your user installation tests.

Verify that the Charva library built properly by running the test application from the Charva folder.

1. **Make the** test.sh **script executable by entering the following command from the Charva directory:**

```
chmod 755 ./test.sh
```

2. **Run the test. Execute** ./test.sh **from the Charva directory.**

3. **Experiment with the test.**

In the Charva test, there are examples of menus, the `JFileChooser` as shown in Figure 11.17a, assorted layouts, the `JTabbedPane` as shown in Figure 11.18a, buttons, and a `JProgressBar` as shown in Figure 11.19a. All of these are implemented for pure Terminal-based applications.

The test application comes with a traditional Java Swing version for comparison purposes. Run the Java Swing version of the Charva test using the command `./test swing`, from the Charva directory. Figures 11.17b, 11.18b, and 11.19b are the Swing GUI versions of Figures 11.17a, 11.18a, and 11.19a.

Figure 11.17

Charva JFileChooser (a); Java Swing version of the Charva JFileChooser (b)

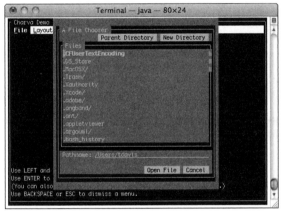

a

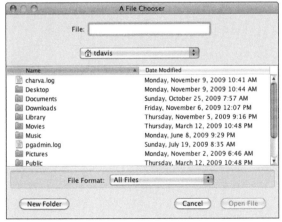

b

TIP
If the Delete key does not work properly in Charva applications (or other Terminal applications), try setting the Delete key to send Ctrl+H in the Terminal preferences. That should clear up the issue.

Figure 11.18

Charva JTabbedPane (a); Java Swing version of the Charva JTabbedPane (b)

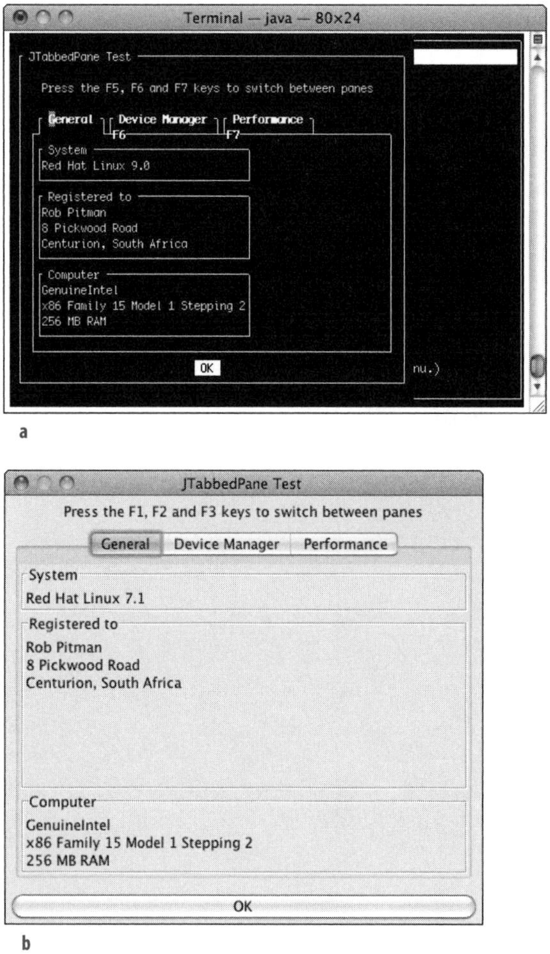

a

b

Figure 11.19

Charva JProgressBar (a); Java Swing version of the Charva
JProgressBar (b)

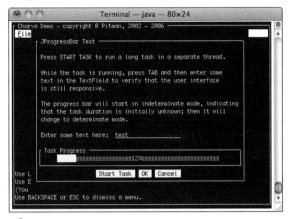

a

b

Creating an advanced Terminal User Interface

Charva allows you to create an advanced Terminal-based User Interface with minimal effort. I
provide an example on the book's Web site in a folder called `charva_test`. For the example, I
create a UI using JFormDesigner. JFromDesigner is a Java UI creator. You easily can use another
UI design tool.

After creating the UI for your application, follow these steps:

1. **Open the generated source code in your favorite IDE.**

2. **Modify AWT and Swing package** imports **to begin with** charva **and** charvax **instead
   of** java **and** javax.

3. **Change any sizes in pixels to sizes in columns and rows.**

4. **Comment out Swing and AWT method calls that do not apply to Terminal-based applications.**

I usually end up removing methods `setDefaultCloseOperation()` that do not apply to Terminal-based applications.

5. **Compile and run from the Terminal.**

I do not know of any IDEs that properly run Terminal-based applications, so you must run the applications directly from the command line instead of clicking the "Run" button in your IDE. Compiling from an Ant script also is easier than configuring the build from an IDE.

The `charva_test` project included on the Web site, shown in Figure 11.20, contains the necessary Ant build script and shell script to create and run a Charva-based Terminal application.

Figure 11.20

The `charva_test` project's directory viewed in Finder

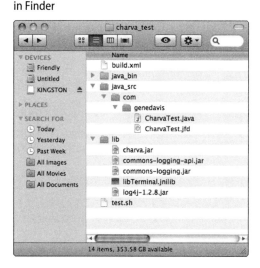

The following source is the Ant script (`build.xml`) I created to build `charva_test`. You easily can modify it to build your Charva-based projects:

```xml
<?xml version="1.0" encoding="UTF-8"?>
<project name="charva_test" default="java-build" basedir=".">
    <property name="java.source" value="java_src" />
    <property name="java.bin" value="java_bin" />
```

```
<target
    name="clean"
    description="Removes previous build">

    <echo>Cleaning Java and Native bin folders...</echo>

    <delete dir="${java.bin}" />
    <delete dir="${native.bin}" />

</target>

<target
    name="java-build"
depends="clean"
    description="Builds the Java source">

    <echo>Building Java...</echo>

    <mkdir dir="${java.bin}"/>
    <javac
        srcdir="${java.source}"
        destdir="${java.bin}"
        classpath="lib/charva.jar" />
</target>
</project>
```

The build script contains two targets, `clean` and `java-build`. The `java-build` target is the default target. The `java-build` target calls clean, creates the necessary `java_bin` directory, and finally calls `javac` to build the Terminal application.

Java-based Terminal utilities and other Java-based Terminal applications usually start from a shell script. The shell script simply wraps the Java application. It provides necessary system setup for the application before launching it. The shell script also provides any necessary cleanup for the application when it exits.

The following is the source for the `charva_test` project's shell script. The script is contained in a file called `test.sh`:

```
#!/bin/bash
/usr/bin/java \
-Djava.library.path=lib \
-cp ".:java_bin/:lib/charva.jar:lib/commons-logging.jar:lib/
    log4j-1.2.8.jar" \
com.genedavis.CharvaTest 2> $HOME/charva.log
# returning the screen to a usable state
stty sane
```

The script defines itself as a `bash` script. It starts the Java application. All exceptions are redirected to $HOME/charva.log (charva.log in your home directory). When the Java application exits, `stty sane` is called to make sure the application's Terminal preferences are removed. However, if you break from the application with Control+C, then `stty sane` is never called.

Earlier, I explained how to place your dynamic library, `libTerminal.jnilib`, in the Java extensions folder for global access. This script does not require that placement. Instead, place your `libTerminal.jnilib` in the project `lib` director, and the application finds it just fine.

TIP

Open a second Terminal window and execute `tail -f charva.log` to watch for exceptions in your Charva-based application.

TIP

When creating a shell script to wrap a Java application, use `*.sh` during development. The extension makes it more obvious that the file is shell script.

When moving the script into a production environment, remove the `.sh` extension, so its name blends in better with other command-line tools like `emacs`, `grep`, `ant`, and so on. In this case, the `test.sh` script becomes simply `test`.

TIP

Charva applications require exception logging in order to run. The default location for logging must reside in the script for starting the Terminal application.

The CharvaTest class contains the UI setup and also the main method for this example. When run, as shown in Figure 11.21, the application displays a menu bar, a label, and several check boxes in the Terminal window. Navigate the application using mnemonics, tabs, arrows, escape, and return.

Figure 11.21

CharvaTest application run in Terminal

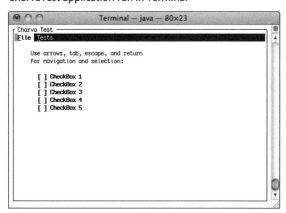

The raw source generated by JFormDesigner follows. The following code contains the modifications I made in order to get the application to run in Terminal with the Charva API. The modifications were minor.

```
package com.genedavis;
import charva.awt.*;
import charva.awt.event.*;
import charvax.swing.*;
/**
 * @author T. Gene Davis
 */
public class CharvaTest extends JFrame {

    public static void main(String[] args)
    {
        CharvaTest ct = new CharvaTest();
        ct.setVisible(true);
    }

    public CharvaTest() {
        initComponents();
    }
    private void quitMIActionPerformed(ActionEvent e) {
        System.exit(0);
    }
    private void simpleMessageMIActionPerformed(ActionEvent e) {
        JOptionPane.showMessageDialog(null, "Just a message dialog.");
    }
    private void initComponents() {
        // JFormDesigner - Component initialization - DO NOT MODIFY
        //GEN-BEGIN:initComponents
        menuBar1 = new JMenuBar();
        fileMenu = new JMenu();
        quitMI = new JMenuItem();
        testsMenu = new JMenu();
        simpleMessageMI = new JMenuItem();
        panel1 = new JPanel();
        panel2 = new JPanel();
        label3 = new JLabel();
        checkBox1 = new JCheckBox();
        checkBox2 = new JCheckBox();
        checkBox3 = new JCheckBox();
        checkBox4 = new JCheckBox();
        checkBox5 = new JCheckBox();
        textarea1 = new JTextArea();
        label2 = new JLabel();
        //======== this ========
        setTitle("Charva Test");
// intentionally commented out ...
// setDefaultCloseOperation(WindowConstants.DO_NOTHING_ON_CLOSE);
```

```
setEnabled(false);
Container contentPane = getContentPane();
contentPane.setLayout(new BoxLayout(contentPane, BoxLayout.Y_AXIS));
//======== menuBar1 ========
{
   //======== fileMenu ========
   {
      fileMenu.setText("File");
      fileMenu.setMnemonic('F');
      //---- quitMI ----
      quitMI.setText("Quit");
      quitMI.setMnemonic('Q');
      quitMI.addActionListener(new ActionListener() {
         public void actionPerformed(ActionEvent e) {
            quitMIActionPerformed(e);
         }
      });
      fileMenu.add(quitMI);
   }
   menuBar1.add(fileMenu);
   //======== testsMenu ========
   {
      testsMenu.setText("Tests");
      testsMenu.setMnemonic('T');
      //---- simpleMessageMI ----
      simpleMessageMI.setText("Simple Message");
      simpleMessageMI.setMnemonic('S');
      simpleMessageMI.addActionListener(
      new ActionListener() {
         public void actionPerformed(ActionEvent e) {
            simpleMessageMIActionPerformed(e);
         }
      });
      testsMenu.add(simpleMessageMI);
   }
   menuBar1.add(testsMenu);
}
setJMenuBar(menuBar1);
//======== panel1 ========
{
   panel1.setLayout(new BorderLayout());
   //======== panel2 ========
   {
      panel2.setLayout(new BoxLayout(panel2, BoxLayout.Y_AXIS));
      //---- label3 ----
      label3.setText("          ");
      panel2.add(label3);
      //---- checkBox1 ----
```

```java
                checkBox1.setText("CheckBox 1");
                panel2.add(checkBox1);
                //---- checkBox2 ----
                checkBox2.setText("CheckBox 2");
                panel2.add(checkBox2);
                //---- checkBox3 ----
                checkBox3.setText("CheckBox 3");
                panel2.add(checkBox3);
                //---- checkBox4 ----
                checkBox4.setText("CheckBox 4");
                panel2.add(checkBox4);
                //---- checkBox5 ----
                checkBox5.setText("CheckBox 5");
                panel2.add(checkBox5);
            }
            panel1.add(panel2, BorderLayout.CENTER);
            //---- textarea1 ----
            textarea1.setText(
                "\nUse arrows, tab, escape, and return\n"+
                "for navigation and selection:");
            textarea1.setEditable(false);
            textarea1.setRows(3);
            textarea1.setEnabled(false);
            panel1.add(textarea1, BorderLayout.NORTH);
            //---- label2 ----
            label2.setText("        ");
            panel1.add(label2, BorderLayout.WEST);
        }
        contentPane.add(panel1);
        setSize(80, 23);
        // JFormDesigner - End of component initialization
        //GEN-END:initComponents
}
// JFormDesigner - Variables declaration - DO NOT MODIFY
//GEN-BEGIN:variables
private JMenuBar menuBar1;
private JMenu fileMenu;
private JMenuItem quitMI;
private JMenu testsMenu;
private JMenuItem simpleMessageMI;
private JPanel panel1;
private JPanel panel2;
private JLabel label3;
private JCheckBox checkBox1;
private JCheckBox checkBox2;
private JCheckBox checkBox3;
private JCheckBox checkBox4;
private JCheckBox checkBox5;
```

```
        private JTextArea textarea1;
        private JLabel label2;
        // JFormDesigner - End of variables declaration  //GEN-END:variables
    }
```

As I mentioned earlier, the CharvaTest class is generated using a GUI design tool called JFormDesigner. The import statements originally read as follows:

```
import java.awt.*;
import java.awt.event.*;
import javax.swing.*;
```

To make them work with Charva, I simply changed the imports to read as follows:

```
import charva.awt.*;
import charva.awt.event.*;
import charvax.swing.*;
```

As part of the conversion to Charva, I commented out one line of code:

```
setDefaultCloseOperation(WindowConstants.DO_NOTHING_ON_CLOSE);
```

If you think about it, Terminal applications do not have close buttons on their title bars, so removing this line of code makes complete sense.

The last change I make to convert this GUI to a Terminal UI is to change the size of the JFrame to a columns-and-rows-based size rather than the pixel-measured size generated by JFormDesigner. The new line of code reads as follows and matches the default size of the Terminal window when opened.

```
setSize(80, 23);
```

Obviously, more complex layouts require more modifications to work with Charva, but as this demonstration shows, Charva does most of the work for you when creating a Terminal User Interface.

Summary

Advanced Terminal applications, also called Console applications, have ASCII-based User Interfaces. These interfaces use ANSI escape sequences for coloring text, clearing screens, and changing the cursor position within the visible Terminal window.

ANSI escape sequences provide lots of variety to text applications, including password hiding. However, basic keystroke capture is missing from Java applications run as command-line utilities. Also, Java does not contain methods for tracking the viewable display of Terminal-based

Java applications. Instead, you must make calls to native C-based libraries when these features are needed. I provide the necessary JNI in this chapter for tracking Terminal view dimensions and keystroke capture.

Using the JNI code I provided in this chapter, I created a basic Terminal User Interface. This sample program serves to show the importance of knowing row and column counts in Terminal-based applications and also the importance of individual `char` capture when running a Terminal interface. Sun provides neither functionality in Java, but I hope they will in the future, because developers continue to express interest in these features.

Charva, Java Curses Library, and other third-party APIs fill the need for Terminal-based User Interface APIs. Most Terminal-based UI APIs link to the `ncurses` library. Ncurses is the native library that handles ANSI escape sequence differences between operating systems.

In this chapter, explain installation and use of Charva. Charva is built as a drop-in replacement for Swing and AWT in Terminal-based environments. Substitute `charva.awt` and `charvax.swing` package names for `java.awt` and `javax.swing` packages to get regular Java Swing and AWT UIs to run from Terminal. Minor modifications are sometimes required, but not many. Most Java GUI development utilities create Charva-based UIs with little extra work from you, the developer.

Appendixes

More Development Tools

I discuss Xcode and several other development tools in this book. Most of the applications reviewed are free (as in food). Some are open source. In this book, I definitely shy away from commercial development tools.

Some commercial tools for Java development are worth a special mention. I have chosen the following tools for mention because of their utility and popularity.

Oh, and they work great on OS X, too!

Exploring Design Tools

Two types of people create computer programs: programmers and developers.

Programmers sit down at a computer and pound out code until something is finished. Programs written this way usually work but are filled with spaghetti code and poor or no modularity. Often, adding desired features to the resulting programs gets harder and harder until finally the code base is thrown away and the process starts over from scratch.

Developers design first and then write clean modular code. It takes longer at the beginning to design and write good code. The plus side is that with proper planning and refactoring, the code base lasts without complete rewrites. Also, adding features to well-designed programs is much easier. In the long run, developers cost less than programmers.

Many developers use the Unified Modeling Language (UML) for designing applications. UML is a design language that expresses itself as diagrams. Diagram types include class diagrams, sequence diagrams, use case diagrams, activity diagrams, and many more.

While full round-trip design and development is possible with many UML tools, most developers use UML only to visualize difficult tasks or complex concepts. You can create UML diagrams as detailed or sparse as needed.

In This Appendix

Investigating UML
design tools

Introducing
JFormDesigner

Examining another
Java IDE

There are several UML design tools for Java code. Two favorites that run well on OS X are MagicDraw and Poseidon for UML. I discuss both in this appendix.

Examining MagicDraw

MagicDraw, shown in Figure A.1, is a UML-based software architecture modeling tool. As is inherently the case with UML tools, it works for business process modeling and general process modeling also. MagicDraw is owned by No Magic, Inc. No Magic's Web site is:

```
http://www.magicdraw.com
```

Figure A.1

MagicDraw

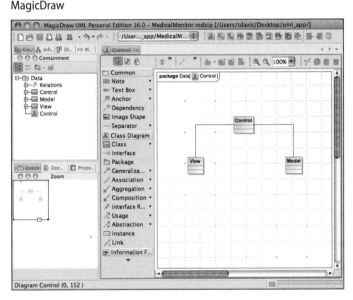

MagicDraw is well organized with icons for all commonly used diagram types across the top of the main window. Common components of diagrams are arranged just to the left of the main diagram window. All diagrams, classes, and packages arranged in a project tree also are visible during design.

Further detailed properties are available for manipulation simply by double-clicking elements in the main diagram display. The properties dialog box, shown in Figure A.2, allows access to a great number of settings by means of a navigation tree. Attributes, operations, relations, documentation, and much more are available for each diagram element through the properties dialog box.

Figure A.2

MagicDraw properties dialog box for a class named Control

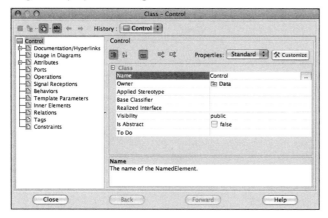

MagicDraw comes in several editions targeting everyone from open-source and student developers with the community edition to high-end professional software architects. MagicDraw Reader is a nice addition, allowing free reading and previewing of MagicDraw diagrams (for instance, by your clients).

Investigating Poseidon for UML

MagicDraw is not the only software modeling tool available on OS X. Poseidon for UML by Gentleware AG, shown in Figure A.3, is another wonderful UML diagramming tool for OS X. Their Web site is:

```
http://www.gentleware.com
```

Poseidon for UML features include Java code generation and reverse engineering for full round-trip design and development. It supports UML documentation creation, as shown in Figure A.4, in HTML or Word. Also, Poseidon for UML allows class diagrams to be automatically arranged onscreen.

Figure A.3

Poseidon for UML

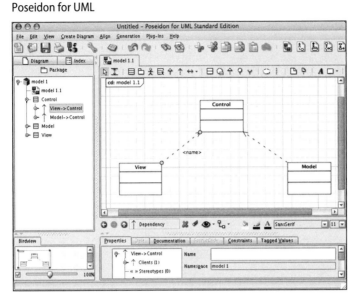

Figure A.4

UMLdoc generation dialog box

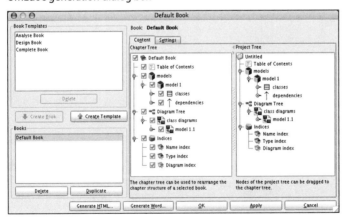

Poseidon for UML comes in several editions, including Community Edition, Standard Edition, and Professional Edition.

Exploring Additional Java Tools

I want to mention two additional tools for Java development: JFormDesigner and IntelliJ IDEA. JFormDesigner is a user interface design tool targeting Swing interfaces. IntelliJ IDEA is a commercial IDE that is very popular among Java developers. Of course, both applications work well on OS X.

Reviewing JFormDesigner

I briefly mentioned JFormDesigner in Chapter 1. JFormDesigner, shown in Figure A.5, is a favorite in the world of Java GUI development. JFormDesigner is maintained by FormDev Software GmbH. Their Web site is:

```
http://www.jformdesigner.com
```

Figure A.5

JFormDesigner

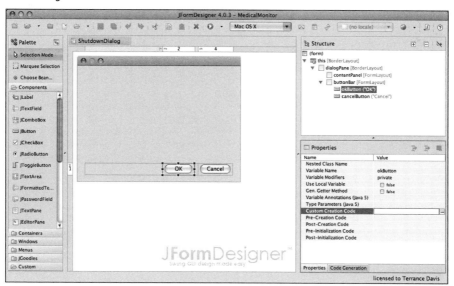

JFormDesigner integrates nicely with OS X, using the top menu bar and command keys as you would expect them. It is so easy to use that you probably won't need to look at the documentation before creating your first layout. Don't be fooled by the excellent interface; JFormDesigner has lots of advanced GUI design features hidden inside.

Design GUIs with JFormDesigner by dragging and dropping widgets from a component palette. The component palette supports customization, even the addition of new beans, shown in Figure A.6. Anytime during design of a GUI, you can test it with the convenient play icon at the top of the window.

Figure A.6

Add bean dialog box

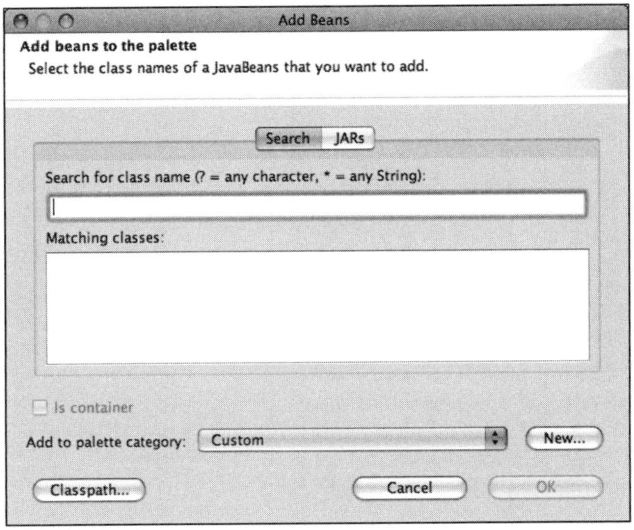

JFormDesigner handles creation and management of events for GUI components. Properties of selected component are in panel to the right of the design panel, for easy access. Assign widget custom code generation for creation or initialization by accessing one of the custom code dialog boxes, as shown in Figure A.7.

JFormDesigner is an extremely powerful Swing layout tool that still manages ease of use.

Figure A.7

Custom widget code creation dialog box

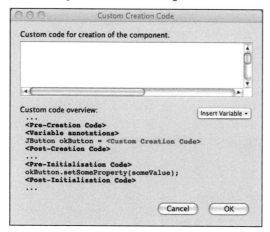

Examining IntelliJ IDEA

IntelliJ IDEA is a popular alternative to the common free Java-friendly IDEs. IntelliJ IDEA, shown in Figure A.8, is maintained by JetBrains s.r.o. Their Web address is:

```
http://www.jetbrains.com
```

Figure A.8

Display of IntelliJ Project XML data in the Project view of IntelliJ IDEA

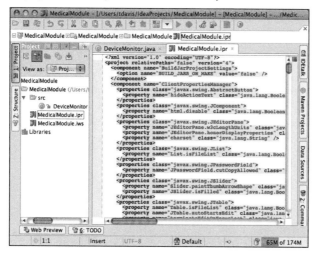

IntelliJ IDEA provides quick code generation. This includes getter and setter creation and generation of override methods. Other shortcuts built into IntelliJ IDEA include code block enclosing for try/catch and if/else blocks.

IntelliJ IDEA contains a GUI design tool, shown in Figure A.9. The GUI tool supports Java layouts, JGoodies Forms, and IntelliJ GridLayoutManager. IntelliJ IDEA migrates hand-coded GUIs and GUIs built with other design tools to IntelliJ IDEA.

Figure A.9

GUI Designer

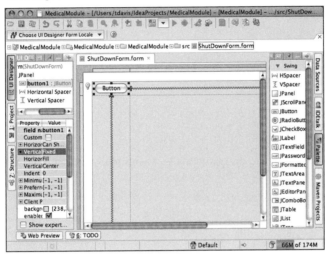

IntelliJ IDEA supports UML class diagramming, shown in Figure A.10. IntelliJ can create class diagrams automatically from existing Java code. As mentioned above, UML is a popular tool for examining object-oriented programs written in languages such as Java.

IntelliJ IDEA has tough competition from several good free IDEs. It remains popular because it has a good set of features. Overall, IntelliJ IDEA is a solid tool for serious developers.

Figure A.10

UML class diagram

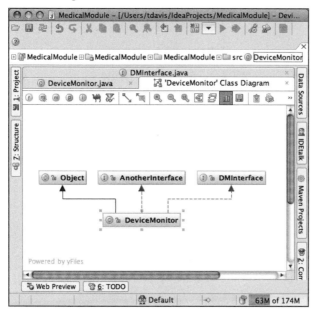

Summary

In this appendix, I discuss four additional commercial tools for Java development on OS X. They are MagicDraw, Poeidon for UML, JFormDesigner, and IntelliJ IDEA.

MagicDraw and Poseidon for UML both come in several editions. As with many commercial products, Poseidon for UML is available as a 30-day evaluation copy. (Inquire with MagicDraw's sales department for any comparable offers.) Both companies offer limited Community editions not only to help out open-source projects, but also to get you interested in buying their other editions. Whether you simply want a good design tool for visualization of difficult chunks of code or you want full round-trip design and development, both products supply targeted editions for you.

JFormDesigner is a GUI design tool targeting Swing development. Simply drag and drop GUI components onto a WYSIWYG layout window to create intricate graphic user interfaces. JFormDesigner integrates as a plug-in with several popular Java IDEs, such as NetBeans, Eclipse, and IntelliJ IDEA.

IntelliJ IDEA is a popular commercial alternative to the various free Java IDEs. It currently comes with a 30-day free trial so you can take it for a test drive. IntelliJ IDEA supports JEE and standard Java development. IntelliJ IDEA comes with a GUI design tool, as well as class diagramming capabilities.

JUnit on OS X

JUnit is a Java test-driven development (TDD) framework. Traditional software development starts with some sort of requirement documents, followed by massive amounts of programming, and finishes off with some sort of manual or automated testing. Test-driven development starts with requirements, followed by the writing of automated tests, and concludes with the creation of the computer program that allows the previously written tests to pass.

The mental reordering that test-driven development requires can make you dizzy at first. It is not for every company. However, test-driven development leads to well-thought-out programs that are easier to maintain than the spaghetti that result from no planning.

JUnit also works for regression testing and more casual testing efforts. Create regression tests by finding bugs in your code. Next, create a test that fails because of the bug. Finally, fix the program, and the test passes. Leave the tests in place, and run these tests frequently to ensure that the bugs do not reappear.

Regression testing is great for projects with lots of developers working on the same code. If the project is managed without clear definitions as to who owns and makes changes to specific code, a programmer may fix a bug that creates other bugs. When another programmer comes along and fixes those other bugs, the programmer may introduce the original bug while fixing the new bug(s). This cycle goes around and around, frustrating developers and their management.

Write a regression test before fixing a test. If you have introduced a new bug inadvertently, the programmer who fixes it will not fix it by reintroducing the old bug. The key is to run these tests as part of every bug fix and to consider the bug still open if the fix does not pass the regression tests.

JUnit is nearly synonymous with testing Java code. In this appendix, I give an introductory example of JUnit's use and explain how to integrate testing with JUnit into Xcode.

In This Appendix

Exploring testing types

Understanding the JUnit

Integrating JUnit
with Xcode

Writing Tests with JUnit

The JUnit team realized that programmers are always busy. A deadline is always looming. They knew that if JUnit wasn't easy to use, JUnit wouldn't be used. As a result, implementing JUnit tests requires little new knowledge. By learning one annotation and one method call, you can successfully write complex test suites. You just can't get much easier than that.

NOTE

JUnit is open-source software. JUnit is licensed under Common Public License - v 1.0. The current JUnit license is located at `http://junit.sourceforge.net/cpl-v10.html`.

NOTE

The JUnit home is located at `http://www.junit.org/`.

To implement a JUnit test, follow these steps:

1. **Choose a class with methods you want to test.**

2. **Create a class to do the testing.**

   I call this the test class.

3. **Create methods to perform tests.**

4. **Use the annotation** @Test **for test methods.**

   Do not put the `@Test` on support methods that do not assert anything.

5. **Use assertion methods to perform the tests.**

Run JUnit using the java command. The target main class is `org.junit.runner.JUnitCore`. `JUnitCore` is followed by a space-separated list of test classes. Running tests from the command line takes the following form:

```
java -cp <tests and JUnit> org.junit.runner.JUnitCore <test classes>
```

I give a working example of using JUnit from the Terminal later in this appendix.

NOTE

The Terminal application is located in `/Applications/Utilities/`.

Testing from Xcode with JUnit

JUnit integrates with most build environments. Integrating JUnit with Xcode does not get as much attention as integrating with Eclipse or NetBeans, so few (if any) tutorials explain Xcode/JUnit integration. This section fills the gap by explaining how to integrate JUnit with Xcode. I use JUnit 4.6 and Xcode 3.2 for the following example.

NOTE

The Xcode project for this example is on the book's Web site. Download the Xcode project for this appendix to avoid creating the XcodeAndJUnit project manually.

Begin by creating a Java Tool project in Xcode for this integration example:

1. **Select File ⇨ New Project from the Xcode menu bar.**

2. **Select Empty Project from the Other templates group on the left, as shown in Figure B.1.**

Figure B.1

Empty Project selected in New Project window

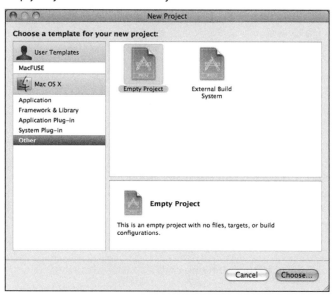

3. **Name the new project** XcodeAndJUnit**.**

4. **Open your new project folder in the Finder.**

5. **Create** src, resources**, and** lib **folders in your project folder.**

Adding the new folders to your project is a little tricky.

6. **Select your** XcodeAndJUnit **project in the Groups & Files tree, Control-click Add ⇨ Existing Files... from the context menu, select the new folders, and add them. When the dialog box appears asking for information on how to add the folders, add them using Create Folder References for any added folders, as shown in Figure B.2.**

Figure B.2

How to add folders in Xcode

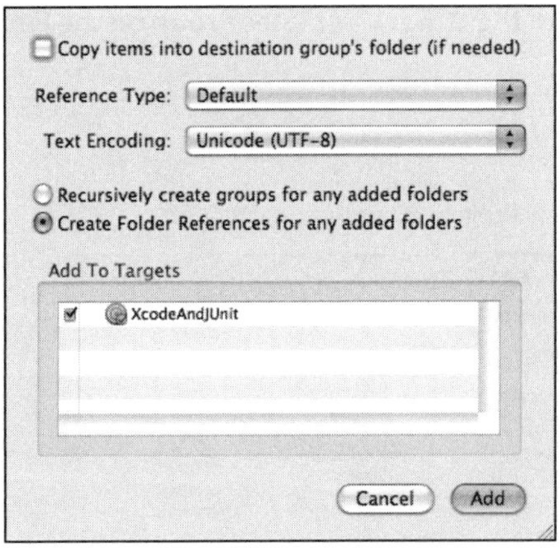

7. **Create a file called** build.xml **at the root of your project in the** XcodeAndJUnit **directory. Create the XML file from within Xcode by selecting** XcodeAndJUnit **and Control-clicking. Select Add ⇨ New File... from the context-sensitive menu. Choose Empty File from the Other template catalog and create the** build.xml **file as part of the** XcodeAndJUnit **project.**

This is your Ant build file. With this setup, Xcode uses Ant when building your project.

8. **Fill** build.xml **with the following code.**

This Ant build is based loosely on the Xcode 3.1 Java tool template, but should work with the latest version Xcode.

CROSS-REF

I explain additional details of Xcode project creation in Chapter 3.

```xml
<?xml version="1.0" encoding="UTF-8"?>
<!--
Based off Xcode 3.1 Java Console Application Project
This is standard Ant, and will work in Xcode 3.2 also.
-->
<project
      name="XcodeAndJUnit"
      default="install"
      basedir=".">
   <property name="src" location="src"/>
   <property name="bin" location="bin"/>
   <property name="jars" location="jars"/>
   <property name="lib" location="lib"/>
   <property name="dist" location="dist"/>
   <property name="resources" location="resources"/>
   <property name="resources_macosx"
             location="resources_macosx"/>
   <property name="compile.debug" value="true"/>
   <!-- lib directory should contain any pre-built jar files
   needed to build the project -->
   <fileset id="lib.jars" dir="${lib}">
      <include name="**/*.jar"/>
   </fileset>
   <path id="lib.path">
      <fileset refid="lib.jars"/>
   </path>
   <!-- Initialization target, for any prelimary setup needed
   to build -->
   <target name="init" description="Preparation">
      <mkdir dir="${src}"/>
      <mkdir dir="${lib}"/>
   </target>
   <target
        name="compile"
        depends="init"
        description="Compile code">
      <mkdir dir="${bin}"/>
      <javac
              deprecation="on"
              srcdir="${src}"
              destdir="${bin}"
              source="1.6" target="1.6"
```

```
                    includeAntRuntime="no"
                    classpathref="lib.path"
                    debug="${compile.debug}">
        </javac>
    </target>
    <target
        name="jar"
        depends="compile"
        description="Build jar">
        <mkdir dir="${jars}"/>
        <jar
        jarfile="${jars}/${ant.project.name}.jar"
        basedir="${bin}"
        manifest="${resources}/Manifest">
            <!-- Inject resources -->
            <fileset
                dir="${resources}/"
                excludes="${resources}/Manifest"/>
        <!-- Merge library jars into final jar file -->
        <zipgroupfileset refid="lib.jars"/>
        </jar>
    </target>
    <target
        name="install"
        depends="jar"
        description=
"Put all the pieces together in the dist directory">
        <mkdir dir="${dist}"/>
        <!-- Copy jars -->
        <copy toDir="${dist}">
            <fileset dir="${jars}">
                <include name="*.jar"/>
            </fileset>
        </copy>
    </target>

    <target
        name="run"
        depends="install"
        description="Run the tool">
        <java
        classname="${ant.project.name}"
        classpath="${bin}"
        fork="true">
        </java>
    </target>
    <target
        name="clean"
        description="Remove build and dist directories">
        <delete dir="${bin}"/>
```

```
        <delete dir="${jars}"/>
        <delete dir="${dist}"/>
    </target>
</project>
```

9. **Create** XcodeAndJUnit.java **in your** src **directory. Create the Java file from within Xcode by selecting** src **and Control-clicking. Select Add ⇨ New File... from the context-sensitive menu. Choose Empty File from the Other template catalog as shown in Figure B.3 and create it in the** src **directory. If there is an extra reference to the file in the Groups & Files tree, remove the reference.**

Figure B.3

Empty File selection

10. **Add the following source to the** XcodeAndJUnit.java **file.**

```java
import java.util.*;
import com.genedavis.*;
public class XcodeAndJUnit
{
    public static void main (String args[])
    {
        BillOfMaterials bom = new BillOfMaterials();

        bom.addGlass(6);
        bom.addSteel(10);
        bom.addOil(1);

        bom.printBill();
    }
}
```

11. Add a Manifest **file to the** resources **directory. Create the** Manifest **file from within Xcode by selecting** resources **directory and Control-clicking. Select Add ⇨ New File… from the context-sensitive menu. Choose Empty File from the Other template catalog and create the** Manifest **file as part of the** ConsoleApp **project in the** resources **directory. If there is an extra reference to the file in the Groups & Files tree, remove the reference.**

The source for the Manifest is simply this:

```
Main-Class: XcodeAndJUnit
```

Your project is not quite ready to use. There are still a few steps to complete. You need an Executable and a Target.

These steps give you a properly configured Target:

1. Control-click the Targets node of the Groups & Files tree.

2. Select Add ⇨ New Target…

3. Select External Target from the Other group, as shown in Figure B.4. Name your new target XcodeAndJUnit, **and add it to your** XcodeAndJUnit **project.**

Figure B.4

External Target selected

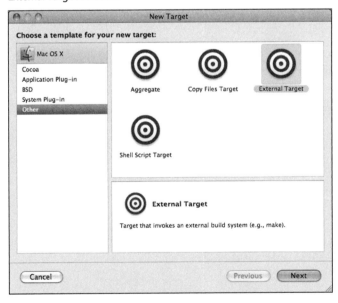

4. **Double-click your new XcodeAndJUnit Target.**

This brings up the Target: XcodeAndJUnit dialog box.

5. **Set the Build Tool to** /usr/bin/ant**.**

6. **Set the Arguments to** -emacs $(ACTION)**, as shown in Figure B.5.**

Figure B.5

Configured target dialog box

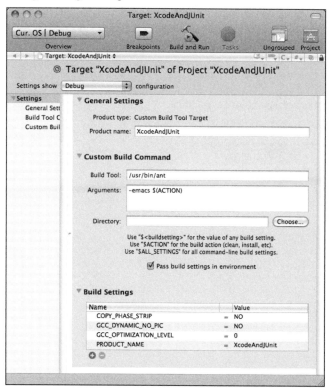

Your Target is ready to use. This allows building and cleaning of the project. Before the next step, temporarily comment out the code in your XcodeAndJUnit class `main()` method and the `import` statements, and then click Build ⇨ Build. This builds an executable JAR for setting up your Executable to run. You should be building a class that only has a `main()` method. (Remember to uncomment the code after the Executable is set up.)

Next, from inside Xcode, create the Executable by taking these steps:

1. **From the Executables context menu, select Add ⇨ New Custom Executable....**

2. **Name your executable** java.

3. **Select the path to your** java **command.**

That is /usr/bin/java.

4. **Add the new Executable to your project.**

5. **Open your new** java **executable by double-clicking it.**

6. **Select the General tab, shown in Figure B.6, and set Custom directory to your project's** dist **directory.**

Figure B.6

General tab in Executable configuration

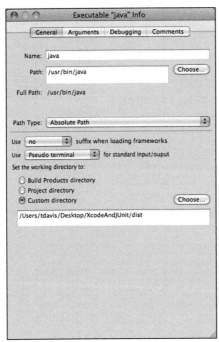

7. **Select the Arguments tab shown in Figure B.7, and add the argument** -cp XcodeAndJUnit.jar XcodeAndJUnit**.**

Figure B.7

Arguments tab in Executable configuration

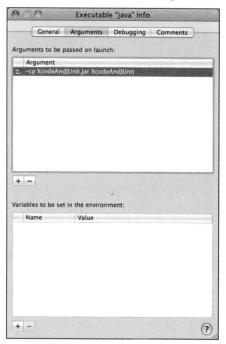

8. **Select the Debugging tab shown in Figure B.8. Set the Java Debugger to the default debugger. Select Wait for next launch/push notification. Deselect all other check boxes.**

Figure B.8

Debugging tab in Executable configuration

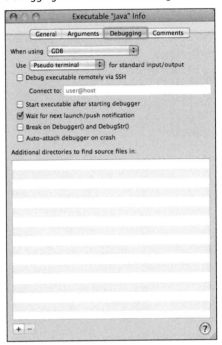

Your project is almost ready to use. In fact, if you select Run ⇨ Console, you can select Build and Run from the Console window to run the application. You won't see anything interesting, though. You have all the code in your `main()` method commented out.

Next, I explain adding JUnit to your project.

JUnit is conveniently packaged as a single JAR. The `junit.jar` is available from `http://www.junit.org/`. The `junit.jar` is named `junit-<version number>.jar`. I refer to it as the `junit.jar` for simplicity.

If you are working from a previously built Xcode project, your project contains a `jar` directory. When including the `junit.jar` in an Xcode project, placing the `junit.jar` in the project's `jars/` directory may be your first impulse. Xcode's `build.xml` contains a `clean` target that deletes the `jars/` directory. If you place the `junit.jar` in the `jars/` directory, every time you clean your project, you also have to add JUnit back to the project.

A closer look at `build.xml` shows the comment "lib directory should contain any pre-built jar files needed to build the project." Place the `junit.jar` in the `lib/` directory. Any JAR'ed libraries used to build the project should be placed in the `lib/` directory.

All JAR'ed libraries placed in the `lib/` directory end up repackaged in the project JAR. In our case, that is the `XcodeAndJUnit.jar`. Bundling `junit.jar` is fine during development, but it should be avoided for release builds. Also, remove test classes from release builds.

For this section's example, I jar `junit.jar` and the test classes in the build. If you want to prevent `junit.jar` and test classes from being built, you can place them in separate test directories, and then create and name the directories something like `test_lib` and `test_src` so they are easily identifiable. Then create a new external target and modify the `build.xml` file so that Ant builds and bundles the tests only when the new target is used.

CROSS-REF

I discuss Ant and build.xml files at length in Chapter 4.

The example code in this section requires Java 1.6. The Java target in Xcode uses Ant. On some OS X distributions, Ant—when run from Xcode—defaults to an older version of Java that cannot build this example's source. A quick fix is to include the `JAVA_HOME` property in the Target's Build Settings, as shown in Figure B.9, with the value being the path to `/System/Library/Frameworks/JavaVM.framework/Versions/1.6.0/Home` or a similar Java `Home` directory.

Figure B.9

Target with `JAVA_HOME` property

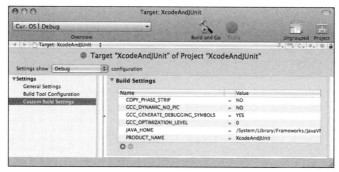

CROSS-REF
Java home paths are discussed in detail in Chapter 2.

In this book, I harp on never hard coding JAVA_HOME. However, development environments are usually personalized to individual projects, computers, and developers. It is very likely that you do not want the target's version of Java in your project to change when you change the Java Preferences. This is one of those rare cases where hard coding JAVA_HOME makes sense.

The code example for this appendix consists of three classes and an enum. This Xcode project represents a rudimentary bill of materials generator. The code is contained in XcodeAndJUnit.java, Pricing.java, BillOfMaterials.java, and BillOfMaterialsTest.java.

NOTE
If you have not yet uncommented the code in the **XcodeAndJUnit** class, do so now.

The XcodeAndJUnit class creates and prints a bill of materials. This class contains the main() method. XcodeAndJUnit is not used during the JUnit test. Deleting this class has absolutely no affect on running the test. This class demonstrates the use of the BillOfMaterials class that is the object of the example test.

Once again, here is the code for XcodeAndJUnit:

```
import java.util.*;
import com.genedavis.*;
public class XcodeAndJUnit
{
    public static void main (String args[])
    {
        BillOfMaterials bom = new BillOfMaterials();

        bom.addGlass(6);
        bom.addSteel(10);
        bom.addOil(1);

        bom.printBill();
    }
}
```

The Pricing enum contains three materials (STEEL, OIL, and GLASS) that are initialized to a unit price in cents. In a real accounting program, I might use BigDecimal, but ints representing cents work in this limited example. The single method, getPricePerUnit(), is provided.

Here is the code for `Pricing`:

```java
package com.genedavis;
public enum Pricing
{
    STEEL (5000),
    OIL   (100),
    GLASS (1500);
    private final int pricePerUnit;

    private Pricing(int ppu)
    {
        this.pricePerUnit = ppu;
    }
    public int getPricePerUnit()
    {
        return pricePerUnit;
    }
}
```

The class I will test with JUnit is `BillOfMaterials`. `BillOfMaterials` offers methods for adding units of glass, oil, and steel to the current bill of materials. The added items are stored in the `lineItems HashMap<String, Integer>`. The `printBill()` method calls the `getTotalCost()` method and the `getBillBody()` methods and then prints the results.

Here is the source for `BillOfMaterials`:

```java
package com.genedavis;
import java.util.*;
import static com.genedavis.Pricing.*;
public class BillOfMaterials
{
    HashMap<String, Integer> lineItems =
        new HashMap<String, Integer>();

    public BillOfMaterials() {}

    public void addGlass(int quantity)
    {
        int ppu = GLASS.getPricePerUnit();
        int price = ppu*quantity;
        lineItems.put("Glass", price);
    }

    public void addSteel(int quantity)
    {
        int ppu = STEEL.getPricePerUnit();
        int price = ppu*quantity;
```

```
        lineItems.put("Steel", price);
    }

    public void addOil(int quantity)
    {
        int ppu = OIL.getPricePerUnit();
        int price = ppu*quantity;
        lineItems.put("Oil", price);
    }

    public int getTotalCost()
    {
        int total = 0;

        for(Map.Entry<String,Integer> entry : lineItems.entrySet())
        {
            int value = entry.getValue();
            total += value;
        }

        return total;
    }

    public String getBillBody()
    {
        String billBody = "";

        for(Map.Entry<String,Integer> entry : lineItems.entrySet())
        {
            int value = entry.getValue();

            int dollars = value / 100;
            String cents = Integer.toString(value);
            cents = cents.substring(cents.length() - 2);

            String product = entry.getKey();

            billBody += product+"        $"+dollars+"."+cents+"\n";

        }

        return billBody;
    }
```

```
public void printBill()
{
    int total = getTotalCost();
    String billBody = getBillBody();

    int dollars = total / 100;
    int cents =  total % 100;

    System.out.print(billBody);

    System.out.println("\n\n   total: $"+dollars+"."+cents);
}
}
```

Finally, I can show you the actual test class, `BillOfMaterialsTest`. Comparing the test method of `BillOfMaterialsTest` with the `main()` method of `XcodeAndJUnit`, you see a strong correspondence. Both create and set up a `BillOfMaterials`. However, `BillOfMaterialsTest` attempts to assert the value of the `BillOfMaterials` `getTotalCost()` method.

The `@Test` annotation and the `assertTrue()` method make this test work. The packages imported are `org.junit.*` and `org.junit.Assert.*`. Once imported, the `assert True()` method and the `@Text` annotation are available. The `@Test` annotation marks a method as being a JUnit test. The `assertTrue()` method is the actual test. Using only one annotation and one method, you can build very powerful unit tests for your projects.

TIP

Many other assert methods are available. See the JUnit documentation available on the JUnit Web site for more information about available assert methods and combining JUnit tests.

Here is the source code for the JUnit test class, `BillOfMaterialsTest`:

```
package com.genedavis;
import org.junit.*;
import static org.junit.Assert.*;
public class BillOfMaterialsTest
{
    @Test
    public void testBillOfMaterials()
    {
        BillOfMaterials testBom = new BillOfMaterials();
```

```
        testBom.addGlass(6);
        testBom.addSteel(10);
        testBom.addOil(1);

        int testTotal = testBom.getTotalCost();
        assertTrue(testTotal == 59100);
    }
}
```

If you have not yet done so, add these three new classes () to the src/com/genedavis directory of your project. You need to create the com and genedavis directories. After you add these classes to your `src/` directory, shown on the far left of Figure B.10, click Build and Run from the Xcode Console. This verifies that the project is working properly. After running your project, you are ready to test.

Figure B.10

Xcode project window with all Java source files in the directory tree on the left

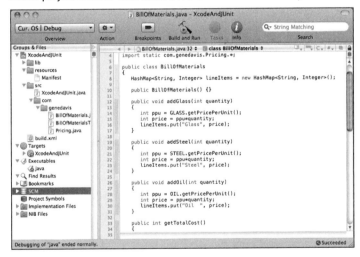

If you want to run JUnit only from the command line at this point, these instructions will take care of running the `BillOfMaterialsTest`:

1. **Open the Terminal.**

2. **Change your directory, using** cd, **to the** bin/ **directory in your Xcode** XcodeAndJUnit **project.**

3. **Use the command** java -cp .:../lib/junit-4.6.jar org.junit.runner.JUnitCore com.genedavis.BillOfMaterialsTest

You should see a result similar to Figure B.11.

Figure B.11

JUnit test results shown in the Terminal

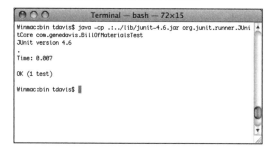

Running the test from inside of Xcode is not much different, and it may be even easier after it has been configured. The following instructions configure and run the JUnit test from Xcode:

1. **Double-click the Executables java leaf of the Group & Files tree on the left side of your Xcode project window.**

This brings up the Executable "java" Info dialog box.

2. **Click the Arguments tab.**

The Arguments tab is shown in Figure B.12.

3. **Add another** -cp **argument that reads as follows:**

```
-cp XcodeAndJUnit.jar org.junit.runner.JUnitCore com.genedavis.
    BillOfMaterialsTest
```

4. **Select the new** -cp **argument, and unselect the original** -cp **argument.**

Do not delete the old argument, because you will want to use it when rebuilding the project. Only one of these -cp arguments may be selected at a time.

Figure B.12

Executable arguments dialog box tab with new -cp

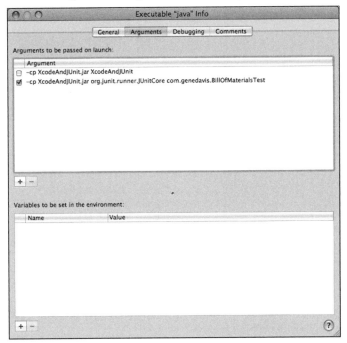

Clicking Build and Run in the Xcode Console should result in output similar to Figure B.13.

Figure B.13

Xcode Console test result

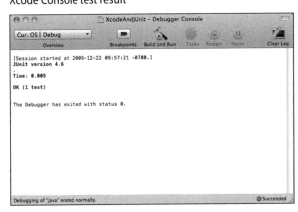

Summary

In this appendix, I explained the uses of JUnit. JUnit is written with test-driven development in mind. JUnit works well for regression testing and more casual testing strategies also.

JUnit is designed for simplicity of use. By learning as little as one annotation and one assertion method, you can create complex test suites. The annotation is `@Test`, and the assertion method is `assertTrue()`.

Integrate JUnit with Xcode by placing the `junit.jar` in the build path. Create one or more JUnit test classes. The last step is to add a new `-cp XcodeAndJUnit.jar org.junit.runner.JUnitCore <tests list>` argument to the Java executable and run the tests

Glossary

About Box A window designed to display the application name, copyright holder, software version number, and a link to the creator's Web site. On OS X, the About Box is accessed from the Application Menu.

Address Book An OS X application designed to track contact information for friends, family, and business associates. Applications that need access to contact information or need to retain contact information on OS X should always interface with this application.

admin (administrator) A user who is all-powerful on a particular computer. The administrator has all permissions to do anything on the computer.

Adobe Systems, Inc. Adobe Systems is known for their graphics and Web design software. Adobe owns Photoshop, Illustrator, Flash, Acrobat, and Dreamweaver. Find Adobe at www.adobe.com.

alpha channel Indicates the transparency of a given image.

alpha release A software release for testing purposes. Alpha releases typically do not have a stable feature set, meaning features may be added or removed before the software application reaches beta.

Ant Target-based build tool. Ant builds consist of one or more files organized into a project containing targets and targets containing individual tasks.

Apache The Apache Software Foundation responsible for organizing many popular open-source, business-friendly projects. Apache also refers to their most popular project, an HTTP server.

API (Application Programming Interface) A collection of libraries for use in software development.

app Short for software application.

Apple Menu The menu at the top left hand corner of an OS X Desktop. The Apple Menu contains System-related menu items and is visible from all applications. The Apple Menu takes its name from the prominent apple-shaped icon on the menu bar.

AppleScript Natural-language-based scripting language for cross-process scripting on OS X. AppleScript allows properly written applications (including Java applications) to act together for common task resolution.

Applet Bundled AppleScript applications or Java Applications embedded in Web pages. These two meanings have nothing to do with each other and can lead to confusion in certain discussions.

Applet Launcher GUI application for testing Java Applets without a Web browser.

appletviewer A command-line application provided for quick display of Java Applets without the need of a Web browser.

Application Menu Found just right of the Apple Menu. The Application Menu contains an application's About, Preferences..., and Quit menu items.

architecture The hardware of a computer. OS X tends to be mostly architecture agnostic.

Archive.zip The default name of a Finder compressed ZIP file. Change this name to prevent name collisions.

arguments Parameters passed to a program on startup or passed to a function/method while running.

ASCII (American Standard Code for Information Interchange) Pronounced "as key." This is a text-based format limited in utility to Roman-based languages. Superseded by Unicode-8.

asynchronous Happening independently. For instance, methods are asynchronous when their return value is sent by a different thread, often after the original method has returned.

AWT (Abstract Window Toolkit) Also jokingly referred to as Another Window Toolkit. This is the original Java windowing toolkit, later expanded by Swing.

badging Placing a small version of an application icon on an alert or information icon. A badge appears in the lower-right corner of an alert or information icon in a dialog box. Badging acts as a visual queue to users, indicating the application to which a dialog box belongs.

base directory The directory that holds an application's folders, data, and executable files. The base directory of OS X also is called the root directory.

Bash The default Unix shell used in Terminal on OS X.

batch A script that processes data, repeating the same changes to multiple pieces of data.

BBEdit Bare Bones Software's text editor. The Bare Bones Software Web site is located at `www.barebones.com`.

beta Feature-complete test release of software. The beta release comes after an alpha release and before a Golden Master release. Beta releases should contain a fixed set of features that will not change before final release of the software. Beta releases often contain features that do not yet work. Beta releases give developers a chance to test software for bugs with real users before declaring the software finished.

Bezier curve A curved path defined by two points and two control points. These curves may be chained to define complex curving paths.

Bezier path See Bezier curve.

binary Base 2 number system.

bitmap A file format defining images.

bleed An area of printed material designed to be cut off, producing the illusion that printing went to the edge of the paper. Using bleeds instead of actually printing to the edge of paper prevents ink build up on press rollers and reduces the likelihood of ghost images appearing on printed material.

block A chunk of code surrounded by curly braces. Also, a mechanism for stopping a threads execution until some event occurs.

bookmark A quick link to section of code in Xcode. Also, bookmarks are used in Web browsers, such as Safari, providing quick access to Web pages.

boot Starting of an application, especially the starting of OS X.

bootstrap A situation involving two events depending on the other event happening first. The prototypical example of a bootstrap problem is, "which came first, the chicken or the egg?" In programming, this kind of problem usually occurs when a program (or OS) cannot be built until it has first been run (indicating it was already built).

breakpoint A point in code where execution is paused for debugging.

bridge Mechanism allowing two disparate technologies to communicate. For example, a bridge allows Java and Objective-C to communicate and act as one program.

BSD (Berkeley Software Distribution) Berkeley Unix. This is a Unix, but not a Linux.

build.xml Default project file for Ant builds.

bundle A folder containing a collection of related files on OS X.

callbacks Allows a function to call back to the executing code. Usually associated with passing of function pointers.

Carbon Along with Java and Cocoa, represents one of the main programming frameworks available on OS X.

cc An alias for gcc on OS X.

Charva Terminal-based User Interface framework. Charva is designed to work as a replacement for Swing and AWT in environments that demand a text-based interface. This is common with terminal- and server-based applications.

clean Refers to the process of deleting compiled classes and assembled products in preparation for building from scratch.

CLI (Command Line Interface) Text-based interfaces such as Terminal for controlling Operating Systems. Many Unix programmers prefer CLIs for their simplicity and speed.

CMYK Four-color process common in printing. C is cyan. M is magenta. Y is Yellow. K is black.

Cocoa Along with Java and Carbon, represents one of the main programming frameworks available on OS X.

Console On OS X, Console is an application for tracking System logs. Often, Unix gurus refer to applications such as Terminal as a console (with a lowercase "c").

Controller Manages the View and Model in a Model-View-Controller environment. Controllers are the brains of applications.

CORBA (Common Object Request Broker Architecture) A cross-language, cross-platform standard for inter-process communication.

cron job A task that repeats at specified intervals, such as nightly or weekly. The `cron` daemon is responsible for the execution of the tasks.

CSI (Control Sequence Introducer) Indicates the beginning of ASCII-based control sequences for changing the display preferences of text output in Terminal windows.

curses Common Unix library for controlling terminal output.

CVS (Concurrent Versioning System) GNU GPL software for versioning software. Similar to SVN in capabilities.

Darwin OS X is built on top of Darwin. Darwin is a POSIX-compliant operating system. Several operating systems are derived from Darwin.

data store Any mechanism for data storage, including databases, flat files, and directory services.

DMG Disk image file format used for distribution of applications for OS X.

DPI (Dots Per Inch) OS X monitors in Cocoa and Carbon are represented programmatically as 72 dots per inch, but likely have more actual pixels per inch. Carbon and Cocoa drawing is resolution-independent.

Eclipse A popular free open-source IDE for development of Java, C, PHP, and other languages. Eclipse is written in Java and is very popular for Java development on OS X.

emacs Popular Terminal-based text editor for OS X.

enterprise Applications that run companies. If an application is multi-tiered, networked, database-driven, capable of scaling, and integral to a business's success, it is often referred to as an enterprise application.

EPS (Encapsulated PostScript) File format designed for storing vector-based graphics.

Finder GUI application responsible for user interaction with the OS. Similar in function to the text-based Terminal application.

flatten Process of composing one image raster image from multiple layers of images. This is a common task in Photoshop and other image-processing programs.

folding Collapsing the view of code or comments in an IDE. Eclipse, Xcode, and other common IDEs provide folding to make program source code more legible.

fork Creating a duplicate process to run the same program. Similar in function to spawning threads, but much more resource intensive.

framework Code libraries that are related and possibly bundled together.

FreeBSD A variant of BSD. See BSD.

freeware Software that is provided for use free of charge. Freeware is often open-source, but not always open-source.

FTP (File Transfer Protocol) Protocol for transferring files over network connections.

gcc (GNU Compiler Collection) GNU's command-line compiler used for compiling Objective-C, C, and C++ on OS X. Xcode uses `gcc` for compiling many project templates.

Gentleware AG Creator of Poseidon for UML, a round-trip UML architecting tool for Java.

GIF (Graphics Interchange Format) A raster art image format popular on the Web. Very useful for storing images with a limited number of colors.

GM See Golden Master.

GNU (GNU's Not Unix) Free open-source POSIX operating system. Not to be confused with BSD.

GNU-Darwin A variant of BSD based on Darwin. See BSD.

Gold Master A production-quality release. This is usually the final build of a software product before it is sold to customers.

GUI (Graphical User Interface) A mouse and picture driven interface for users. Contrasts sharply with TUIs that are normally text and keyboard driven.

Help Viewer Displays application-specific help files. Help Viewer is available to all properly constructed GUI programs on OS X, including Java applications.

home See home directory.

home directory Location of user's personal files and directories, including Desktop and Library. Usually, this directory is located at `/Users/<username>`.

HSQLDB Free, open-source, business friendly embeddable database with an extremely small footprint. HSQLDB is also a pure Java application.

HTML (HyperText Markup Language) The language in which Web pages are written. In syntax, HTML is very similar to XML.

Human Interface Guidelines Apple's recommendations for creating user-friendly applications that fit the look and feel of standard OS X applications.

ICNS File format for OS X icons.

Illustrator Vector art program produced by Adobe.

Info.plist XML file found in application bundles describing the bundle, resource locations, and the other properties of the bundle. Opens with Property List Editor for convenient editing.

Intellij IDEA A popular commercial IDE for Java development. It is sold by JetBrains at `www.jetbrains.com`.

IzPack Java-based packaging and deployment software. IzPack is open-source software and distributed under a business-friendly Apache License. It is found at izpack.org (without "www".)

Java Never heard of it.

JAVA_HOME The home directory of the Java installation currently in use. Java home is available by issuing the command /usr/libexec/java_home from the Terminal.

javah Command-line tool for generating C header files. Used when implementing native Java methods.

javap Class disassembler for Java. Useful when looking for method signatures needed in native C-based JNI code.

JetBrains Creators of Intellij IDEA. Their Web site is www.jetbrains.com.

JGoodies Producers of Java UI libraries and tools.

JNA A wrapper intended to make writing JNI simpler.

JNAerator A GUI-based JNA automation tool.

JNI (Java Native Interface) Provides Java integration with C and C++. Apple provides JNI support as the main integration technique between Java, C, and Objective-C frameworks on OS X.

JSP (JavaServer Pages) Java Web site design language. JSP compiles to Servlets that extend the server they run on.

JUnit The most popular Java-based testing framework.

kernel The software responsible for direct communication between the OS and the hardware. OS X uses the Mach microkernel.

ksh (KornShell) Command-line shell used in Terminal.

legacy Any OS, framework, application, or utility that was replaced with newer software.

Leopard OS X version 1.5 released in October 2007.

LGPL (Lesser GNU Public License) Less-restrictive GNU license designed to allow linking to commercial software.

lifecycle The cycle of creation, maintenance, and decommissioning of software. Usually extended through good design and maintenance practices.

localhost The local computer. Also known as Internet Protocol address 127.0.0.1.

Mach The microkernel used by Darwin. See also kernel.

MagicDraw UML design tool by No Magic, Inc.

make A GNU build tool. Make was the inspiration for Ant.

man Command-line tool for displaying of utility manuals in Terminal.

Maven An alternative Java-based build tool. Maven is roughly equivalent to Ant using Ivy.

Metrowerks The original developer of the CodeWarrior development tools popular on Macs before the release of OS X.

mnemonic Keyboard commands that trigger GUI events such as the selection of a Java MenuItem.

modal Blocking. For instance, modal dialog boxes block the application from accepting input until the dialog box is dismissed.

MPW (Macintosh Programmer's Workshop) Development environment for Macintosh computers predating OS X.

MRJ (Mac OS Runtime for Java) The Java runtime for Mac systems predating OS X.

MVC (Model-View-Controller) A design paradigm that separates data, display, and management into modules call the Model, the View, and the Controller, respectively.

Nano Command-line text editor. Replaces Pico.

ncurses Builds on the curses library.

NetBeans A popular Java IDE sponsored by Sun Microsystems. NetBeans works well on OS X.

NS (NextStep) The predecessor to OS X. OS X is derived from NextStep. The tag of NS is still found on many of the classes and methods used in developing OS X applications.

Objective-C Apple's answer to C++. Objective-C advocates say Objective-C is the Object-Oriented Programming language that C++ was meant to become but failed at becoming.

Objective-C++ Objective-C-based language integrated to work with C++.

OpenStep An API specification released to the public by Next and Sun Microsystems. Closely related to NextStep.

Operating System The application in charge of hiding low-level activities of the computer, such as booting and starting user applications.

package A bundle that behaves as though it is one file rather than a folder. Applications on OS X are bundles that are packages.

Perl (Practical Extraction and Report Language) Also known jokingly as the Pathologically Eclectic Rubbish Lister. Perl is the most-influential scripting language in the history of computers and the Internet. Larry Wall developed Perl in the late 1980s.

Photoshop Raster art creation program sold by Adobe Systems, Inc.

PHP A Web application development scripting language occupying a similar feature space as JSP.

pixel One colored dot displayed on a monitor.

PKG Application distribution format used by the Installer application.

plug-in A module used to extend an application or service.

PNG (Portable Network Graphics) A raster-based graphics file format.

Poseidon for UML A round trip UML design and development tool for Java. It is developed by Gentleware AG, located at `www.gentleware.com`.

POSIX (Portable Operating System Interface for Unix) IEEE Unix Operating System definition.

PowerPC PC architecture used by Macs before the transition to Intel-based architectures.

pthread The underlying thread system on OS X. All threads on OS X at some level are pthreads.

Python A popular open-source dynamic language.

Quartz The underlying image processor for OS X.

RAID (Redundant Array of Inexpensive Disks) Configures multiple disks to operate one large disk or multiple disks to act as backups for each other.

raster Representation of images as bitmaps.

refactor The process of fixing and updating code in small chunks while adding new features, thus extending the overall life expectancy of the software.

regex (regular expressions) Pattern-matching languages for matching text patterns. Most modern regular expression syntaxes (including Java's) are based on Larry Wall's Perl regular expression syntax.

RGB (Red Green Blue) Three-color representation of images for display on computer monitors.

root Refers to root access and sometimes the root directory.

root access Complete administrative access. See admin.

root directory The base directory of the operating system. Usually indicated by '/'.

Round Trip Design and Development Many UML design tools offer the feature of creating diagrams from code and generating code from diagrams. Using this feature is Round Trip Design and Development.

RSS (Really Simple Syndication) Formats for frequently updating information over the Web.

Ruby An interpreted open-source programming language.

SAVER Bundle format used for OS X screen savers.

scp Command-line tools for copying files over ssh.

seed Prerelease software intended to help developers prepare for upcoming software releases.

Servlet Java classes designed as extensions to Java servers. One of the most common Java servers using Servlets is Tomcat.

shareware Software released for distribution in an attempt to increase sales. Most shareware lacks features available to the purchasers of the same product. Most shareware is not open-source or completely free.

shell A text-based environment designed to run in applications like Terminal. Shells provide text-based interfaces with Operating Systems.

Snow Leopard OS X Version 10.6. Released in September 2009.

ssh Text-based remote login client. Frequently used to admin remote servers.

Sun Microsystems, Inc. Creators and maintainers of Java.

svn Command-line utility for running Subversion client. Subversion is a software version control system.

synchronous Synchronous methods return normally in the same thread that called them. This differs from their multi-threaded asynchronous counterparts.

tcsh A shell for use in Terminal.

Terminal Text-based application responsible for user interaction with the OS. Similar in function to the GUI-based Finder application.

terminate Exit a program or shell script. Accomplished in Java with System.exit(0);.

TextEdit Apple's basic text editor shipped with OS X.

thread Similar to a fork, but remains in a single process; not as resource intensive. Threads execute code from the same program simultaneously.

toggle The act of selecting or deselecting a check box.

Tomcat A popular Java-based Web server produced by the creators of Apache. The Web site is `tomcat.apache.org`.

TUI In this book, refers to Terminal User Interfaces, but more commonly refers to Text User Interfaces.

UI (User Interface) A description including both GUIs and TUIs. User Interfaces define application users' interaction with applications. UIs include buttons, windows, text fields, menus, and so on.

UML (Unified Modeling Language) Diagram-based software description language. UML is useful for quick overviews of software architecture, but is also used for full round-trip design and development.

vi Popular Terminal-based text editor. The vi application is available on most Unix Operating Systems, and some non-Unix Operating Systems.

VirtualBox A virtual machine designed to run Windows, Linux, BSD, and other operating systems on OS X computers.

VM (Virtual Machine) Software that allows running of virtual computers on your computer. Java runs on a Virtual Machine called the JVM. Other popular VMs for OS X often run entire operating systems, such as VirtualBox and VMware Fusion.

VMware Fusion A virtual machine designed to run and integrate windows on OS X computers.

wrapper A class or library designed to hide implementation details of another class or library.

WWDC (Worldwide Developer Conference) Apple's annual developer conference featuring Apple technologies.

WYSIWYG (What You See Is What You Get) Computer monitor display that exactly resembles the final printed output. Apple developed a strong relationship with the printing industry based on this popular feature.

X X Window System for local and remote access to computers. X is another option in addition to the Finder and Terminal for controlling your OS. X ships with OS X, Linux, and various Unix-like operating systems.

X11 See X.

Xcode The Objective-C-based development IDE that ships with OS X. This IDE works with many languages including Java.

XML (Extensible Markup Language) Language used for defining other markup languages. XML is used to define views, property files, Ant build projects, and a host of other applications.

ZIP Compression application and format. OS X ships with a command-line zip utility.

zsh The Z shell. Used in Terminal for executing scripts and control of the command line.

Index

Everything You Need to Craft
Killer Code for Apple Applications

Whether you are a seasoned developer or just getting into the Apple platform, Wiley's Developer Reference series is perfect for you. Focusing on topics that Apple developers love best, these well-designed books guide you through the most advanced and very latest Apple tools, technologies, and programming techniques. With in-depth coverage and expert guidance from skilled authors who are proven authorities in their fields, the Developer Reference series will quickly become your indispensable Apple development resource.

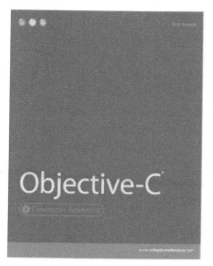

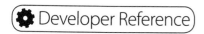

Developer Reference

Now

Take the Book with You, Everywhere

Want tips for developing and working on Apple platforms on your iPhone? Wiley's Developer Reference app puts you in touch with the new Developer Reference series. Through the free app you can purchase any title in the series and then read, highlight, search, and bookmark the text and code you need. To get you started, Wiley's Developer Reference app includes Chapter 21 from *Cocoa Touch for iPhone OS 3*, which offers fantastic tips for developing for the iPhone and iPod touch platforms. If you buy a Wiley Developer Reference book through the app, you'll get all the text of that book including a searchable index and live table of contents linked to each chapter and section of the book.

How to purchase

Go to www.wileydevreference.com and follow the link to the iTunes store.

Wiley's Developer Reference app is free and includes Chapter 21, "Using the Game Kit API" from *Cocoa Touch for iPhone OS 3*. When you're ready for a full Developer Reference book, you can purchase any in the series directly in the app for $19.99.

Here's what you can do

- Jump to the section or chapter you need by tapping a link in the Table of Contents
- Click on a keyword in the Index to go directly to a particular section in the book
- Highlight text as you read so that you can mark what's most important to you
- Copy and paste, or email code samples, out of the book so you can use them where and when needed
- Keep track of additional ideas or end results by selecting passages of text and then creating annotations for them
- Save your place effortlessly with automatic bookmarking, which holds your place if you exit or receive a phone call
- Zoom into paragraphs with a "pinch" gesture

Cocoa Touch and iPhone are trademarks or registered trademarks of Apple, Inc.